National Teachers' Salaries and Pensions 1831–2000 – A historical chronology and review of the role of the INTO

Michael Moroney

IPA
INSTITUTE OF PUBLIC
ADMINISTRATION
50 Years
CELEBRATING PUBLIC SERVICE
1957 - 2007

First published in 2007 by
Institute of Public Administration
57–61 Lansdowne Road
Dublin 4, Ireland
in association with the
Irish National Teachers' Organisation (INTO)
Parnell Square
Dublin 1

ISBN-13: 978-1-904541-42-4
ISBN-10: 1-904541-42-9

British Library Cataloguing-in-Publication Data
A catalogue record for this book is available from the British Library.

Cover design by M & J Graphics, Dublin
Cover image by Padraig Lynch
Typeset by Carole Lynch, Sligo
Printed in Ireland by Future Print, Dublin

Preface

This book, the product of years of scholarly research and more than half a lifetime spent working directly in the area of primary teachers' remuneration and superannuation, is an outstanding contribution to Irish educational literature. It provides a comprehensive record of developments in the area from the beginning of the national school system in 1831 to the present day. Much of the information contained in this book has thus far been undocumented. This new knowledge, interwoven with existing knowledge, much of it from primary sources, is skilfully combined to provide an authoritative and detailed account of the subject.

Teachers' salaries and related pension entitlements at any particular time are significant indicators of how society values and respects the professional contribution of teachers to national development, both economic and social. In this sense, this volume is a study of the evolution of teaching in Ireland as a respected and valued profession. However, improvements in these areas are never the result of a grateful exchequer but stem from powerful and focused advocacy on behalf of teachers. This has been provided by the Irish National Teachers' Organisation since its inception in 1868 and this book provides a study of the evolution of primary teachers as an organised profession. The efforts of the INTO on behalf of primary teachers are fully and fairly documented in this regard.

Covering as it does the greater part of two centuries, it is to be expected that along with significant gains there would be serious setbacks to attempts to secure improvements to remuneration and superannuation. Significant advances for teachers, such as ensuring that the exchequer assumed full responsibility for teachers' salaries in 1892 and the concession of pension entitlements for teachers in 1879, are outlined and evaluated, as are failures at various times to secure salary increases in line with the cost of living and at other times to prevent imposed salary cuts such as occurred on no less than six occasions between 1922 and 1945. Neither is this book concerned only with major issues, but documents and records lesser-known salary issues such as the abolition in 1876 of commission on book sales that was paid to teachers at the time.

Issues such as these, which had long- and short-term consequences for teachers and their families and have long since passed into the realm of history, are as accurately documented and fairly interpreted as more recent issues such as the relatively new changes affecting teachers, the Commission on Pensions and the introduction of the Benchmarking process. This is no mean achievement, given the closeness of the author to more recent issues during his working life. Such balanced commentary is a testimony to the scholarship that is clearly evident in this book.

Just as changes to salary and pensions cannot be considered in a social vacuum, neither can they be accurately assessed without a careful consideration of industrial relations issues. At all times such issues are influenced by the complex interplay that exists between what are now termed the educational partners. Changing relations between teachers' representatives and the state, the churches and the Department of Education over many years are all examined in detail in this book and provide a context for key events in relation to developments in the area of salary and pensions for primary teachers. The skill with which this is done will ensure that this book will appeal not only to the reader with an interest in the specific area of remuneration and superannuation but will also attract the general reader with wider interests and perspectives.

This is a timely and useful publication for, notwithstanding that salary and pension are workers' greatest assets, surprisingly little has been documented in relation to the struggle over decades to seek improvements. As a result, many workers are uninformed about key historical and structural details that even today impact on the payment of salary and pension entitlements. Primary teachers are no exception. Why, for example, do primary teachers make contributions towards their pensions while civil servants do not? When and why were these contribution rates fixed? Who determined the criteria for qualification for a pension and on what basis were these criteria established? Answers to these and other questions are provided in this book in an accessible and very readable manner.

Michael Moroney is superbly qualified to author this volume and his expertise is evident on every page. Having served as Principal teacher for 12 years in his native Waterford he was appointed to the position of Executive Officer in the INTO Head Office. In 1978 he was elected General Treasurer/Deputy General Secretary of the organisation. In that pivotal position at the heart of the union's leadership he had particular responsibility for the negotiation of conditions of service issues, including salary and pensions. His membership of the union's Benefit Funds Committee gave him direct experience of salary and pension hotspots. This, coupled with his personal energy and determination to secure needed improvements in both areas, saw benefits accruing to many teachers.

As the person elected to replace Michael Moroney as General Treasurer of the INTO when he retired in 1997 and as a friend and colleague of long standing, I can personally and professionally testify to his professional ability and efforts on behalf of members. It is both a pleasure and a privilege to be asked to write a preface for this book.

John Carr MA Ed
General Secretary
Irish National Teachers' Organisation
January 2007

Acknowledgements

My involvement in the field of industrial relations, dealing with teachers' salaries, pensions and conditions of service during my entire working life, is a useful indicator of where my primary interests lay. Upon my retirement as General Treasurer INTO, I sought to collate and analyse, in one volume, key developments relating to teachers' pay and conditions that might be of interest to students, human resource practitioners and INTO members. I registered at NUI Maynooth and was very fortunate that Professor John Coolahan agreed to act as my supervisor in completing a PhD thesis on the evolution and development of the remuneration of national teachers in Ireland. To him I owe my deep gratitude. The regular reviews and discussions with this acknowledged expert on every phase of the Irish education system, coupled with his advice and guidance, made the study a most enjoyable and reflective experience.

The documents, many of which were accumulated over the years, were of considerable assistance in my vocational role; but analysing their value and significance would have been immeasurably more difficult had I not enjoyed the experience and pleasure of working with INTO colleagues, officers, officials and staff over a 30-year period. It was a pleasure to serve with them. A special word of thanks to Paul Brennan – a friend since teacher training college, an INTO activist, an NCCA officer – for his valued expertise and his benevolent criticisms.

While every effort has been made to source directly all available relevant reports, particularly those concerning civil servants and teachers, the field of enquiry was such a vast one, spanning almost two centuries, that not all primary references could be successfully located. However, a majority of them were sourced and this was due in no small measure to the unfailing efficiency and collaboration of the personnel in the National Library, Trinity College Library, the National Archives and the Department of Education and Science. I thank all of them for their kindness and indulgence.

To the many officers and friends in the other teacher unions, the officials of the Departments of Education and Finance, the representatives of the Management and Parent Bodies, with whom it was my privilege to serve on councils, tribunals, review bodies and commissions, a sincere thank you.

I wish to acknowledge my appreciation to Declan McDonagh, Executive Director, Institute of Public Administration, who considered the book to be of considerable value as a reference resource and who, together with Eileen Kelly of the IPA, later brought the text through the final production process. IPA Associate Editor, Julie O'Shea, was my designated liaison editor – a wonderful person with incisive editorial and linguistic skills, who could reduce pages of flowery, colourful language to a decisive half page! I am indebted to her.

I wish also to thank my good friend, Padraig Lynch, who even in those far-off days in St Patrick's Teacher Training College, Dublin, was showing his considerable artistic talent. He very kindly produced the inspired cover jacket for the book.

Finally, my very special thanks is due to the INTO. The members and leadership of this major national organisation gave me the opportunity to work within its structures and to become involved in the historical and ongoing changes of the organisation. To John Carr, INTO General Secretary, who generously wrote the preface; to the President and the Central Executive Committee, who agreed to sponsor the editing and production of this work; and to the innumerable members; I trust that they will, on reading the book, adjudge that their support was worthwhile. Coupled with this tribute to the INTO, I thank the EBS Building Society – which has had a life-long association with the INTO – for providing added financial support that enables the book to be distributed more widely than might otherwise be the case.

My late wife Fedelma would have been so proud that I had persevered and managed to complete the book. To our family Kevin, David and Aisling, who played no small part with their continuing interest, and to my partner Maureen, who indulged me in my occasional moans and complaints while bringing this project to fruition, I offer my very sincere gratitude and acknowledgement.

Dublin
January 2007

In memory of Fedelma

Contents

Abbreviations

ASTI	Association of Secondary Teachers Ireland
C&A	Conciliation and Arbitration
CEC	Central Executive Committee
CHA	Catholic Headmasters' Association
CPI	Consumer Price Index
CPSMA	Catholic Primary School Managers Association
CS	Civil Service
CSO	Central Statistics Office
CSORP	Chief Secretary's Official Registered Papers
DEPD	Dáil Éireann Parliamentary Debates
DES	Department of Education and Science
DPS	Department of the Public Service
GNP	Gross National Product
GSO	Government Stationery Office
Hansard	Hansard's Parliamentary Debates
HC	House of Commons
HL	House of Lords
HMSO	Her Majesty's Stationery Office
ICTU	Irish Congress of Trade Unions
IFFTU	International Federation of Free Trade Unions
INTO	Irish National Teachers' Organisation
JMB	Joint Managerial Body (for secondary schools)
MCNEI	Minutes of the Commissioners of National Education of Ireland
MP	Member of Parliament
NPC	National Parents Council
NUET	National Union of Elementary Teachers
NUT	National Union of Teachers
OECD	Organisation for Economic Co-operation and Development
PAYE	Pay-As-You-Earn
PAYG	Pay-As-You-Go
PCW	Programme for Competitiveness and Work
PDs	Progressive Democrats
PERB	Primary Education Review Body
PESP	Programme for Economic and Social Progress
PNR	Programme for National Recovery
PRSI	Pay Related Social Insurance

SPO	State Paper Office
TD	Teachta Dála (member of Dáil)
TUI	Teachers' Union of Ireland
UCD	University College Dublin
VEC	Vocational Education Committee
VTA	Vocational Teachers' Association
WCOTP	World Conference of Teaching Professions

Introduction

This book presents an interpretative record of the development of the remuneration and superannuation schemes for national teachers in Ireland during the period 1831–2000. It is an endeavour to fill a gap in existing knowledge and provide a framework within which future study of this topic can be compared.

History has shown that advances made by civil servants are used as a platform by other public sector employees to achieve similar improvements and, consequently, comparisons are drawn between the provision made for civil servants and that made for teachers during the same relevant periods and with references to the ideas, policies and political events that influenced every movement and change.

The book is divided into two stages. The first stage extends from 1831 to 1922 under the control of the Commissioners of National Education; the second stage begins in 1922 with independence and the control of an Irish Minister for Education.

Stage 1: 1831–1922

Teachers' remuneration passed through a number of very distinct phases, and within these phases there were particular developments. The main relevant events affecting teachers' remuneration and conditions of service during the period 1831–1922 were:

- the payment of a gratuity based on capitation
- the payment of a gratuity from central funds (a salary)
- the introduction of the 'payment-by-results' system
- a pension scheme for national teachers
- the end of the 'payment-by-results' system
- the payment of teachers' total remuneration from central funds
- a revised pension scheme for national teachers
- the Killanin Report and revised salary structures
- the failure to get a pension scheme similar to the civil service scheme.

One of the difficulties experienced by teachers was that the Treasury and the government consistently maintained that teachers were not civil or public servants. As far as the Treasury was concerned, teachers were employees of school managers and the government was just a facilitator distributing gratuities to teachers on behalf of management.

As the school system expanded, more money was required to keep it operational. The Treasury considered that the most effective way of curtailing the amount of money required was to pay Irish teachers very low salaries. Because of their low salaries and the manner in which they were treated by the Education Office and its officers, teachers remained in the lower order of society's social structure. Female teachers were treated even more poorly than male teachers; in all cases they were paid at a lower rate than men and were denied opportunities for promotion.[1]

Teachers' dissatisfaction and discontent with their remuneration was not peculiar to any decade; it was continuous and acrimonious and led to the foundation in 1868 of the Irish National Teachers' Organisation.[2] The organisation had two main objectives: (1) to secure for its members an adequate remuneration, and (2) to secure a pension scheme similar to the one enjoyed by civil servants.

Within a relatively short time, just over ten years after its foundation, the INTO achieved one of its objectives: in 1879 the Westminster parliament was persuaded to grant national teachers a pension scheme with effect from 1 January 1880.[3] The teachers' scheme had elements of the scheme that applied to civil servants, but it was fundamentally different in its main provisions: it was a contributory scheme, and benefit was not necessarily related to service actually given. Nevertheless, it was a watershed in teachers' conditions of employment and was claimed as a major victory by the INTO.[4]

The first real effort to structure teachers' remuneration in a satisfactory manner was implemented in 1892, but, even then, result fees, which were a feature of the 'payment-by-results' system, remained part of the overall package.

Since its inception the INTO had opposed the 'payments-by-results' scheme, and in the 1890s it received strong public support for its opposition from many influential quarters. Eventually, in response to numerous requests, the

---

1   Initially, male teachers outnumbered female teachers in a ratio of two-to-one. By 1900, 5,854 (44.8%) of the 13,074 teachers being paid by the commissioners were male and 7,220 were female (55.2%). Of the 5,854 males, 4,461 (76.2%) were principal teachers, and of the 7,220 females, only 3,618 (50%) were principal teachers.

2   Throughout this study the Irish National Teachers' Organisation will be referred to as the INTO.

3   National School Teachers (Ireland) Act, 1879

4   Historically it was an event of major importance. The national teachers in Ireland were the first group of public employees in Great Britain, outside of the civil service, who were successful in getting a statutory pension scheme. Teachers in Great Britain did not get a pension scheme until 1898.

government was obliged to establish the Belmore Commission in 1897 to review the education system in Ireland. Its principal recommendations resulted in the abandonment of the 'payment-by-results' scheme, the introduction of a new method for the computation of teachers' remuneration and the assumption by the State of total responsibility for a central pay structure.

The Killanin Committee of 1918 was mandated to review the whole system of teachers' remuneration in national schools. It recommended a considerable salary increase for all teachers, and it also recommended a completely revised superannuation scheme. The Molony Committee undertook a similar study for intermediate education. The government accepted the recommendations of the Killanin and Molony Reports, and on 5 April 1919, the Chief Secretary for Ireland, James MacPherson, drafted a bill to implement their recommendations. The bill was opposed by the Catholic hierarchy and not implemented. Eventually, after a considerable dispute and long negotiations, revised provisions for the remuneration of national teachers were agreed and became operative from 1 April 1920.

The pension regulations of 1898 were radically revised by the terms of new rules introduced in 1914, but the benefits were not as good as those enjoyed by civil servants and other public officials. Unfortunately for teachers, a revised scheme, based on the recommendations of Killanin, was not adopted by the Treasury before political events intervened.

Stage 2: 1922–2000

Independence in 1922 saw the transfer of the control of teachers' remuneration and pensions to the Department of Education. Teachers' remuneration and pensions developed in different ways during the following phases: 1922–1947, 1948–1967, 1968–1979, 1980–1995, and 1996–2000.

1922–1947

During the period 1923 to 1934 teachers' salaries were cut several times, amounting in total to approximately 20 per cent. The final salary cut imposed on national teachers in 1934 was accompanied by a revised pension scheme. From 1890 there had been difficulties with funding the pension scheme and its continued solvency was always in question. The government's solution was to convert it from a contributory to a non-contributory scheme. In addition, regulations were introduced which, with effect from 1 October 1934, obliged women to retire from the service after marriage.[5]

---

5 From 1926 female civil servants had been obliged to retire on marriage, and while the ban on married female teachers was removed in 1958, it was not removed for female civil servants until 1973.

By the end of the Second World War, the relative position of teachers' salaries had decreased, and it was generally accepted that the status of the teacher in society had seriously diminished. In response, the teachers of Dublin, supported financially by their colleagues throughout the rest of the country, went on strike in 1946. Following a seven-month strike, the teachers were eventually obliged to resume their positions. However, the strike had lasting political consequences.

1948–1967

Teachers played an active part in the general election of 1948, and Fianna Fáil, which had been in power for sixteen years, was displaced by a coalition government. For the next twenty years the memory of the 1946 strike and the militancy of the INTO ensured that teachers' salaries were sufficient to compensate for any price inflation.

Following the Roe Committee Report in 1949, teachers were granted an increase in salary, with effect from 1 January 1950, and additional pension benefits. In 1951 a Conciliation and Arbitration (C&A) Scheme was established as an independent forum to arbitrate on teachers' salaries and pensions.

1968–1979

Following the 1968 Ryan Tribunal Report on teachers' salaries, a common basic salary scale was introduced for all teachers, primary and post-primary. A points system, based on pupils' ages, was introduced which determined the rate of allowances for principals and vice-principals, and provided for a range of posts of promotion. In addition, national teachers' pension scheme was reconverted to a contributory one. In 1974, equal pay for men and women doing work of equal value was implemented for all employees in the public service.

1980–1995

The Salary Review Body Report of 1980 established a relationship between teachers' salaries and the salaries of other graduates in public service employment and introduced long-service scale increments, which became a feature of all public service salary scales within a few years.

A long sought-after objective of public service unions was achieved in 1983 when the government conceded parity of pensions, and full indexation was implemented from 1 February 1984.

In 1985 teachers and government came into open conflict over the payment of an Arbitration award. This campaign lasted for ten months, during which the Teachers United group established themselves as the strongest union group in the public service.

A radical change in the conditions of service of all public service employees was introduced by the government, with effect from 1 April 1995, when it declared that all new employees, including teachers, would be covered under full Pay-Related Social Insurance (PRSI).

1996–2000

In 1997 the teacher unions signed a significant agreement with the representatives of the Departments of Education and Finance. This agreement fundamentally altered how teachers were to be remunerated; it provided revised pension arrangements; and it radically altered in-school management structures. The most important element of this agreement was that the management structures in primary and post-primary schools would be different. The points system, which had determined the rate of allowances for principals and vice-principals and provided for a range of posts of promotion, was discarded in favour of a system whereby promotion posts would be determined by the number of teachers on the staff of a school. The pool of money available for promotion and qualification allowances was substantially increased. In order to receive this extra remuneration, teachers had to agree to procedures of flexibility and change, which resulted in savings and improved quality of the education service.

A Changing Negotiating Environment

Nearly all enhancements, amendments or revisions to remuneration and pensions schemes originated from changes achieved by civil servants. Only in 1968, 1981 and 1996 did teachers achieve conditions that were peculiar to teaching as a profession.

For the first 100 years any improvements achieved were the result of the findings of commissions and committees, and more particularly, of representations to politicians. By the end of the nineteenth century staff associations and trade unions had begun to come to the fore as a power in the field of industrial relations. While they were recognised as representatives of their members, negotiations were still ad hoc and at the pleasure of the Ministers. This format changed with the introduction of C&A Schemes, one for civil servants in 1946, and separate schemes for primary and secondary teachers in 1951. From that time, negotiations were conducted through established machinery in a formal structured manner, each area of employment dealing with its own employees.

From 1979 'National Wage Agreements' determined national wage and salary increases, and the agreement 'Sustaining Progress' continued this trend with effect from 2000.

The introduction of the Benchmarking Body fundamentally changed the C&A machinery that had been in use in the public service since the 1950s. While conditions of service claims can now be processed and minor claims may be considered, the main function of the Conciliation Council is to record national agreements on salaries and pensions that have been determined in other fora.

Public servants' pensions have been reviewed by the Public Service Pensions Commission and, while some of the recommendations have been implemented, many more are still under consideration.

Just as the new century begins, a new era for the determination of salary and pensions seems to be opening up. The implementation of the recommendations of the Benchmarking Body, the Pensions Commission, and pronouncements by Ministers for Finance in budget speeches will determine how remuneration and pensions will develop in the future. As a result, there is a high probability that future changes to the remuneration, pension and conditions of service of the different groups of public employees will be implemented contemporaneously.[6]

---

6 In answer to a question in the Dáil in June 2004, the Taoiseach, Bertie Ahern, stated that the Benchmarking project was not a once-off event and that another one would report in 2007.

1

The Establishment of Salary and Pension Structures for the Civil Service

An Historical Background

To fully appreciate the evolution and development of the remuneration and pensions of national teachers in Ireland, it is necessary, for reference and comparative purposes, to consider developments in the civil service.

The centralised bureaucracy, which became known as the civil service, commenced at the beginning of the seventeenth century with the centralisation of power. The privilege to select people to fill the ranks of the civil service was conferred on a small group of powerful men and, on some rare occasions, women. Procurement of a position became a matter of grace and favour, and this system of patronage became associated in the public mind with a variety of abuses leading to corruption and power-seeking. Notwithstanding these practices, by the end of the eighteenth century the civil service had been organised into departments with a structured system of salaries and avenues of promotion.

The period from the 1780s to the 1860s was a time of industrial expansion, social unrest, wars and colonisation, and a time of expansion of numbers in the public service. This combination of events resulted in a heavy drain on the public purse and severe fiscal problems for the government. Different governments tried to control expenditure by introducing reforms. Commissions, Select Committees and Treasury Committees were in almost continuous session, making recommendations on ways and means by which all pensions, salaries and emoluments paid out of public funds could be reduced without, at the same time, impairing the efficiency of public services. The implementation of many of the recommendations of these various commissions and committees consolidated the bureaucratic structure of the civil service, with contingent schemes regulating salaries and pensions.

By the last decade of the nineteenth century, trade unions were beginning to become more effective and the advances made by civil servants were used by other public service employees as a platform to achieve similar improvements. National teachers in Ireland were at the forefront in this battle. In 1879 they were successful in getting a statutory pension scheme, the first group of public employees in Great Britain, outside of the civil service, to achieve this.

Employees in the Civil Service

In 1780 the Commission on Public Accounts was established by the Prime Minister, Lord Frederick North, 'to inquire into the Fees, Gratuities, Perquisites and Emoluments received in certain public offices.'[1] The commission remained in force until 1787 and issued a number of reports which helped to stimulate the introduction of administrative reforms.[2]

As the 'Fees, Gratuities, Perquisites and Emoluments' of the various public offices remained so haphazard, and methods of dealing with them varied from department to department, in 1785, three commissioners were appointed to attempt to remedy the situation. They identified that corruption and wasteful practices were endemic, with numerous sinecure offices in existence. They recommended the establishment of a public service in which every officer should be paid a salary and be entitled to a provision upon retirement, 'not dependent upon caprice or accident, or arising from the perpetuation of abuses, but known and certain, free from the competition of individuals, or animadversion of the public'.[3]

Their recommendations removed dependence on the receipt of fees and commissions and ushered in the practice by which the income of civil servants was determined solely by means of a regulated salary.

This practice was further developed in 1807 when a Select Committee on Public Expenditure made a number of recommendations that were subsequently to become fundamental principles on which salaries and pensions would be based:

- It recommended the introduction of incremental salary scales.
- It was in favour of remuneration based on merit.
- It recommended that all allowances paid to retired officers should be classified as pensions and recorded as such.
- It was opposed to the payment of compensation for offices suppressed or abolished, or the payment of a pension where service was not actually given.
- It recommended that in all cases of superannuation, duration of service should be an essential requisite.
- It strongly commended the Customs' Officers Pension Scheme as the model for future schemes to deal with the issue of pensions.[4]

---

1   Lord Frederick North (1732–92), Prime Minister (1770–82)
2   The Act of 25 Geo. 3. c. 19
3   Gerald Rhodes, *Public Sector Pensions*, pp. 16–17. The principle of pensions for civil servants was introduced by the Superannuation Act of 1810.
4   Ibid., p. 18. In 1822 the civil servants vigorously opposed the introduction of the requirement to make contributions to their pension scheme.

The First Public Service Pensions

The first recorded contributory pension scheme for any group in the civil service was established when the government issued a Treasury Warrant on 1 February 1686, authorising the establishment of 'A Public Bank of Charity for Excise Officers'. This was followed by a pension scheme for Officers of the Customs in 1708,[5] and over the years other departments developed similar superannuation schemes for their employees.

Once the concept of the payment of a regular sum of money to a person on retirement was accepted, the development of pensions progressed in three stages.

In the first stage, employees of the Post Office and the Customs were allowed to transfer their jobs to personally nominated successors in return for an annuity or a lump sum payment from the person so nominated.

In the second stage, the authorities appointed the successor, and the pension paid to his predecessor was deducted from his salary.

In the third stage, the authorities appointed the successor and he was obliged to make regular contributions to a publicly organised fund out of which a pension had to be provided for the aged and infirm. The concept of the pension fund was thus established.

Sixty Years as Age for Retirement

The Treasury Minute of 1803 gave legal recognition to sixty years of age as an accepted and approved age for retirement. The important point of this provision was that while a person could retire at sixty, without proof of incapacity, retirement was not compulsory.

An Act of Parliament in 1809 extended a similar arrangement to Excise Officers. It also empowered the Treasury to grant to officers, who had ten years' service or more and who were incapacitated by age or infirmity, a pension of three-quarters of salary, averaged over the last seven years. This was the first instance where the concept of 'averaging salary' over a number of years was introduced for determining the amount of pension. The Act also permitted a pension of similar amount to officers disabled by accident, irrespective of length of service.

The First Superannuation Act, 1810

The Superannuation Act of 1810 introduced a standard scheme of superannuation for all employees in the civil service and provided a non-contributory, terminal type pension that became the foundation and forerunner of all modern pension schemes for public servants.[6] Although not compulsory, it recognised sixty years

---

5   It functioned throughout the eighteenth century and formed the basis of the first statutory comprehensive superannuation scheme for all civil servants established by the Superannuation Act of 1810. From evidence of Mr Hamel to the Select Committee of 1856.

6   A standardised unified system of salaries was not introduced until 1874.

as an approved age for retirement. In addition, it provided enhanced pensions for officers of sixty-five years of age or over who had forty years' service or more. The principles that pensions should be related to age and service and calculated upon the actual retirement salary and not on the average salary over a number of years were laid down. The Act also provided for superannuation allowances for persons who were less than sixty years of age, and allowed the State to remove from office, without causing undue hardship, officers who had become incapable of continuing to provide service due to old age or infirmity.

To Contribute or Not To Contribute

Whether or not an employee should contribute towards his pension caused serious difference of opinion between the Treasury and the civil servants for almost fifty years. It was finally resolved in 1859 when the civil servants were successful in having it decided that they should not have to contribute. This situation was to apply until 1995 when contributions became compulsory for new employees.

In the period from 1810 to 1820, superannuation and compensation charges increased at such a rapid rate that parliament passed an Act on 5 August 1822 proposing a standstill in salaries, amendments to eligibility and amounts of pension, and making contributions compulsory. The senior civil servants lobbied strenuously against the Act, claiming that the imposition of contributions on existing civil servants was a violation of their conditions of employment. On 24 June 1824, in opposition to the declared wishes of the government, they were successful in having parliament pass another Act removing the contribution conditions imposed by the 1822 Act. Furthermore, any contributions already deducted were returned.

The next effort made to introduce contributions occurred when a Treasury Minute issued on 4 August 1829 stipulated that new appointees to the service would have to make contributions.

With this change of approach (i.e. requiring only new entrants to make a contribution), the Treasury established a very important principle, the 'No Detriment Rule'. Henceforth, it now became an established principle in the public sector that new schemes or changes to existing schemes could only apply to new employees. Existing members would have to be given the option of joining the new scheme or remaining in the old scheme. The existing scheme would be closed to new members and classified as a 'Closed Scheme'.

Lords of the Treasury curbed pensions further when they redefined how the provisions of the 1822 Act should be applied. The Lords held that the Treasury had the ultimate power to fix the pension granted to a person within the scale in the Act.[7] This power was retained by the successors to the Treasury.

---

7 Treasury Minute, 21 June 1831

The Superannuation Act of 1834

The operation of the 1810 Act, and the various amendments to it, failed to establish a comprehensive and uniform scheme for all civil servants. In an attempt to remedy this situation, the Superannuation Act of 1834 was passed by parliament on 25 July 1834.[8] This Act was the first one devoted exclusively to the provision of superannuation for public servants and resulted in the establishment of a comprehensive superannuation scheme for all civil servants.

The contribution obligation on new officers appointed after 4 August 1829 was retained, and sixty-five remained the recognised age for retirement. An officer under sixty-five years of age could not qualify for a pension unless he could produce certificates from the head of his department and two medical practitioners claiming that, due to infirmity of mind or body, he was incapable of discharging his duties satisfactorily with diligence and fidelity. The scale of pensions was substantially reduced. Pension would now start at one-quarter of salary instead of one-third and the maximum pension that could be awarded was fixed at two-thirds.[9] The pension would be calculated upon the average amount of salary and other allowed emoluments and fees, received for the three years preceding the commencement of the pension.[10]

Review of First Pension Schemes, 1810–34

The formal structured pension scheme introduced in the civil service during this period became the benchmark for all schemes for employees in the general public service and, subsequently, for private sector schemes.

A number of fundamental principles were determined.

1   To contribute or not to contribute: The 1810 superannuation scheme was non-contributory, and when the government tried to make it a contributory scheme in 1822, this was overthrown by senior civil servants in 1824. However, the Treasury re-established its power in 1829 when it made contributions obligatory on new employees. This was not a complete victory as the very important principle, the No Detriment Rule, was established, and this still applies today.

2   Authority: In 1831 the Lords of the Treasury re-asserted their authority to use discretionary power in determining pensions and in granting them.

3   Age of retirement: The age of voluntary and compulsory retirement became an important factor. The 1810 Act established that a person could retire at sixty

---

8   Appendix V, HC 1857 (Sess. 2), Vol. 24

9   Current Revenue regulations allow a maximum pension of two-thirds of salary.

10 The principle of pension based on the average salary received over the last completed three years of service remained in force until the 1980s.

without having to submit proof of incapacity, and as a result sixty years of age became generally recognised as an approved age for retirement. The retirement age was raised to sixty-five in 1822 and this was retained in the 1834 Act.

4   Age and service: The principles that pensions would relate to age and service and that they would be calculated upon the average amount of salary, and other allowed emoluments and fees, received for the three years preceding retirement, were laid down.

5   Pension on disability: Another very important principle was established whereby pensions could be granted to persons of less than sixty years of age who had to retire due to physical or mental incapacity.

6   Amount of pension: The amount of the minimum pension was decreased from one-third to one-quarter, and the maximum possible was reduced from full pay to two-thirds.

7   Superannuation fund: A superannuation fund was not established and the superannuation scheme for civil servants became a 'pay-as-you-go' (PAYG) scheme.

A Major Review of the Public Service, 1853

By the middle of the nineteenth century regular schemes of salaries and pensions had become an established part of the terms and conditions on which civil servants were employed. However, the employment practices and salary structures in different departments were disparate and haphazard.

On 12 April 1853 Sir Charles Edward Trevelyan and Sir Stafford H. Northcote were directed to prepare a report on the consolidation and improvement of the civil service. While the stated objective of the study was to reorganise the civil service, the underlying objective was to curb expenditure.

On 23 November 1853 Trevelyan and Northcote submitted a report to parliament, 'The Organization of the Permanent Civil Service'. The report castigated the evil effect of patronage and proposed that entry to the service should be open to all through a unified competitive examination conducted by a Board of Examiners, that an entrance examination would not be applicable to positions for which a recognised professional qualification was essential, and that each successful candidate should be obliged to serve a probationary period. As expected, the report provoked considerable opposition, in response to which no immediate action was taken.

However, within a very short time, events were to occur that overcame all opposition and made the necessity for reform imperative. The Aberdeen Cabinet was defeated in the House of Commons when it resisted a demand for an inquiry into the incompetent organisation surrounding the disastrous events of the Crimean War (1853–56). The new Palmerston Cabinet, through its Chancellor of the Exchequer, Sir G. Cornwall Lewis, decided to implement the Trevelyan and Northcote Report in a modified and limited form. By an Order-in-Council, a Civil Service Commission was established to be responsible for the recruitment and employment of clerical grades in the civil service.

For the first time, entrance examinations were introduced, and the scholastic standard required for employment in the service was raised considerably. Regulations were laid down to ensure that candidates nominated for jobs were of suitable age, health, character, and had the knowledge to carry out their duties. Heredity, patronage and chance were replaced by competition, and opportunities for employment in the public service for educated young men from every social stratum became available. The foundation of the civil service as we know it today was established.

In 1853, when Trevelyan and Northcote were completing their report on the reorganisation of the service, the civil servants had submitted a memorial seeking amendments to their superannuation scheme. Trevelyan and Northcote did not refer to superannuation in their report. The establishment of the Civil Service Commission in 1855 gave the civil servants a further opportunity to seek amendments. As a result of pressure from them, the House of Commons, on 19 February 1856, appointed a Select Committee to consider the existing regulations respecting the granting of superannuation allowances and to recommend any changes to the system established by the Superannuation Act of 1834 that it deemed necessary.[11] While the committee made many recommendations, instead of proceeding with a bill based on its recommendations, the government, on 10 November 1856, appointed a Royal Commission to inquire once more into the operation of the 1834 Superannuation Act.

On 15 May 1857 the commission submitted its report with a series of documents relating to the subject. Its main recommendations were that:

- pensions for all civil servants should be non-contributory[12]
- voluntary retirement should be available at age sixty rather than sixty-five and compulsory retirement should apply to all officers at sixty-five
- pensions should be computed on sixtieths of salary for each year's service
- it was not expedient to establish a Superannuation Fund.

---

11 Select Committee to consider the existing regulations respecting the grant of superannuation allowances to persons who have held civil office in Her Majesty's Service, HC 1856, Vol. 9, p. 11

12 The pension scheme introduced in 1880 for national teachers in Ireland was contributory; it was converted to a non-contributory scheme in 1934 and converted back to a contributory scheme in 1968.

The Superannuation Act of 1857

The government, not being convinced by the commission's arguments against the contribution principle, drafted a bill encompassing all the other recommendations of the commission. However, before the bill could be brought before the House of Commons, a Private Member's Bill, with a single article proposing the repeal of Section 27 of the 1834 Act, was moved in the House. Section 27 obliged officers to contribute to their superannuation scheme by deductions from salary.[13] Despite being opposed by the government, the bill received widespread support and was passed on 4 August 1857. This campaign in the House of Commons was organised and promoted by civil servants.

The Superannuation Act of 1859

The government's bill finally passed the third stage in the House of Commons on 3 April 1859, and on 19 April it became the Superannuation Act of 1859.[14] The 1859 Act established the following as the main provisions for awarding pensions:

- pensions were to be non-contributory and based on one-sixtieth of pay for each year of service
- forty years' service would qualify for maximum pension
- maximum pension would be two-thirds of final pay
- ten years' service would qualify for a pension
- the recognised age of retirement should be sixty
- a person with ten years' service could qualify for a disability pension
- in special circumstances, if a civil servant was killed in the execution of his duty, a pension could be awarded to his wife and children.[15]

It established a principle that still applies to civil servants appointed before 6 April 1995: that the salary paid to civil servants is at a lower figure than it should be since, notionally, it comprehends a deduction having been made for superannuation purposes. If civil servants were obliged to make contributions then their salaries would have to be increased.

The principle of a notional contribution has operated to the disadvantage of civil servants. If their salaries had been increased, say by 5 per cent, and that amount then deducted from their salaries as a superannuation contribution, their subsequent pension would be assessed on a higher figure, thereby providing a higher pension and a greater retirement lump sum.[16]

---

13 20 & 21 Vic. c. 27, 17 August 1857
14 22 Vic. c. 26, 19 April 1859, HC 1884 (15), LVI, p. 125
15 The amount was regulated by Section 1 of Warrant 50 & 51 Vic. c. 71
16 Lump sum payments for male civil servants were introduced in 1909.

The passing of the 1859 Act marked a watershed in the long and extensive procrastination on the part of responsible authorities in recognising the entitlement to a pension.[17] Civil servants had proven that they were able to advocate for, and achieve, a just and equitable superannuation scheme. They proved to be the powerhouse that engineered the growth and expansion of superannuation schemes that apply in all public service employment and in many private occupations.

The Superannuation Act of 1859 strengthened the power of the Civil Service Commissioners, who had been appointed in 1855 to regulate the recruitment and employment of officers in the civil service. Under this Act, superannuation benefits were restricted to those who had been admitted to the civil service with a certificate granted by the Civil Service Commissioners.

The Playfair Commission, 1874

While the Treasury issued regulations based on the Trevelyan and Northcote Report, 1853, with regard to staffing, no reference was made to the salaries that should apply. Complaints about salary application injustices prompted parliament to establish a commission of inquiry into the structure of the civil service and the salaries paid to civil servants in England and Ireland.

This Royal Commission, under the chairmanship of Dr Lyon Playfair, published a report in December 1874 recommending a reorganisation of all departments in the service. It proposed a plan that set down the number of officers and clerks of every description that should be attached to each subdivision of each branch of each department, and the salary that each common category should receive. The recommendations of the Playfair Commission were implemented by Order of Council on 12 February 1876.

The Civil Administration in Ireland

Between 1700 and 1922 seventy-eight members of the English aristocracy were appointed as Viceroys or Lord Lieutenants of Ireland.[18] The Lord Lieutenant represented the Crown, and the Chief Secretary carried out the government's administration on his behalf.

The Lord Lieutenants had at their disposal an extensive range of patronage in the disbursement of posts and honours. They were open to supplication for the award of honours, sinecures, promotions, and pensions in the ranks of the nobility, within the armed forces, Church, judiciary, and the civil administrative structures. Many of them supplemented their income by selling offices within their patronage.[19]

---

17 22 Vic. c. 26, 19 April 1859
18 T. W. Moody and W. E. Vaughan (eds.), *A New History of Ireland*, Vol. 9, pp. 491–500
19 Joseph Robins, *Champagne and Silver Buckles*, p. 1

The Chief Secretary had a staff of officials and clerks to assist him in his administration. Patronage and the sale of offices were the accepted practice for obtaining public employment. Corruption was as prevalent in Ireland as it was in Great Britain.[20] These clerical employees were considered to be civil servants, and as such enjoyed identical conditions of service as those in the Crown's service in England. The Education Office of the Commissioners of National Education was specifically listed as an employment area covered by the 1834 Pensions Act.

The award of peerages and positions was often used as a means of dealing with political problems; the award of an honour often meant that a crucial vote was won.[21] The Union of Great Britain and Ireland became effective from 1 January 1801, when 162 members of the Irish Parliament, out of 303, voted in favour of the Act of Union. It has been estimated that one-and-a-half million pounds was spent on pensions and bribes to achieve this objective; twenty-four new Peers of the crown were created and titles of a higher degree were conferred on twenty-eight others who were already Peers.[22]

Robert Peel, in his service as Chief Secretary for Ireland from 1812 to 1818 under three Lords Lieutenants, resisted the use of patronage and endeavoured to introduce appointments based on merit. He subsequently served as Home Secretary and Prime Minister for two periods, and continued with this policy.

Although the authority of the Lords of the Treasury passed to the Department of Finance after independence, many of the rules and regulations laid down in the early nineteenth century continue to apply to this day.

---

20 Gerald Rhodes, *Public Sector Pensions*, p. 16

21 T. W. Moody and W. E. Vaughan (eds.), *A New History of Ireland*, Vol. 4, pp. 680–1

22 S. Ó Síochfradha, *The Educational History of Ireland*, p. 78

2

The Salaries and Pensions of National School Teachers, 1831–80

The Establishment of the National School System

Schools in Ireland, pre-1831

In 1824 clergymen of all persuasions in every parish throughout the country were asked to complete a survey of the schools in their parishes. A total of 11,823 schools were identified: 9,352 pay schools, 1,979 schools of Protestant Education Societies, 322 schools of Catholic teaching religious orders and Catholic Day Schools, and 170 others.[1]

There was no national system of teacher training or formal recognition of teachers, and a national curriculum was not taught in schools. The remuneration of teachers was haphazard and varied, and there was no reference to the retirement of teachers or to the payment of pensions to them. When they were no longer able to teach, they had to rely on their families to support them or depend on the parish provisions under the Poor Laws.[2]

'Pay schools' or hedge schools provided for the education of Catholic children, and teachers in these schools depended on the fees paid by the pupils.[3] The lowest remuneration recorded was £3 15s. 0d. per annum and the highest was £30. In almost every instance women were paid less than men, seemingly because the numbers attending their schools were, in general, fewer and they did not provide the same range of subjects as men. The schools of the Protestant Education Societies provided education for only a minority of the population. Teachers in these schools were provided with residences and received regular remuneration.[4]

---

1 Second Report of the Commissioners of Irish Education Inquiry, 1825–27, HC 1826–1827 (12), XII, Appendix No. 22, pp. 229–1331
2 More detailed information on the provision of schools and the remuneration and conditions of service of teachers prior to 1831 are considered in: Michael Moroney, TCD MLitt Thesis, 'The Remuneration of National Teachers, 1831–1900'
3 Patrick J. Dowling, *The Hedge Schools of Ireland*
4 First Report of the Commissioners of Irish Education Inquiry, 1825, HC 1825 (400), XII, pp. 39–40

Over a relatively short period, between 1775 and 1830, many schools were established in Ireland by various Catholic voluntary religious teaching orders of brothers and nuns.[5] These schools were established in cities and towns to provide free education for the children of the poor and were under the patronage of the bishop of the diocese.[6] Teachers did not receive any personal income and relied for funds on the goodwill and benevolence of parents for donations and some fee subscriptions.[7]

The Stanley Letter

In response to continuing pressure from the Catholic Hierarchy, Irish MPs and the people of Ireland, the Whig government decided to constitute a board for the superintendence of a system of national education in Ireland.[8] The government hoped that by providing a system of education for the children of all denominations together it would provide solutions to religious and political problems.[9]

On 9 September 1831 Thomas Spring Rice, Secretary to the Treasury, moved a vote in the House of Commons to place a sum of £30,000 at the disposal of the Lord Lieutenant of Ireland for the year 1831–32 to constitute a Board of Commissioners to oversee a new system of National Education.[10] The Chief Secretary for Ireland, Edward G. Stanley, would administer the system on behalf of the Lord Lieutenant.

The Chief Secretary wrote to the Duke of Leinster in October 1831 inviting His Grace to be President of the new Board of Commissioners of National Education and to take charge of a new system of elementary education for the people of Ireland.[11] The Duke accepted the invitation.

---

5   On 13 January 1837 the commissioners informed the Lord Lieutenant that the persons vaguely called 'monks' were not clergymen, but laymen who had devoted themselves to the education of children. Nevertheless, in official documents, they continued to refer to members of male teaching religious orders (Christian Brothers) as 'monks'. The Powis Commission did likewise.

6   By the end of the nineteenth century, convent schools numbered nearly 400, about three-quarters of which were managed by religious orders founded by Irish people.

7   First Report of the Commissioners of Irish Education Inquiry, 1825, HC 1825 (400), XII

8   Stanley Letter, HC 1831–2 (196), XXIX

9   F. S. L. Lyons, *Ireland Since the Famine*, p. 89

10 The Lord Lieutenant was the Queen's representative in Ireland and the head of the Irish Executive. His powers respecting the conduct of education in Ireland were quite wide. In spite of opposition in the House of Commons and the House of Lords the vote was adopted without division. £30,000 in 1830 had a value of £1,562,000 in the year 2000.

11 Letter from the Chief Secretary of Ireland to the Duke of Leinster, on the formation of a Board of Commissioners for Education in Ireland, HC 1834 (70) XL, 55, published in the *Dublin Gazette*, 8 December, 1831. It was reprinted in HC 1842, IX, 585. There are two versions of this letter: the first, written by Stanley, speaks of 'combined literary or

The Board of Commissioners of National Education

The new national school education system was not based on an Education Act but on the principles, ideals and general rules laid down in Stanley's Letter. Its administration was to be vested in the Commissioners of National Education, and they would have absolute discretion over the disbursement of all monies provided by parliament.

The first Board consisted of seven commissioners: three were members of the Established Church, two were Dissenters, and two were Catholics.[12] The Board was reconstituted in 1838, 1848, 1851 and again in 1861 when, in response to Catholic pressure, the principle of equality between the denominations was accepted. A National Board consisting of ten Catholics and ten members of other religious denominations was established, and the principle of equality was maintained until 1922 when the Board was abolished by the new Irish Government.

The Education Office

In 1835 Tyrone House, Marlborough Street, Dublin, was secured as the official head office of the Board of Commissioners, and the administration staff, the Training Department and the Model School were transferred there from their original quarters at the Army Accounts Department, 30 Merrion Street, Dublin.

The Education Office administration was carried out under the direction of the Secretary to the Board. The first Secretary, Thomas F. Kelly, a barrister and a member of the Established Church, was appointed with effect from 1 December 1831. On his resignation in 1838, two secretaries, one a Catholic and one a Protestant, were, with the permission of the Treasury, appointed by the commissioners. This dual appointment system was maintained down through the years and in most instances the posts were filled by promoting people from within the staff of the Education Office.[13]

---

11 *contd.* separate religious education'; the published version reads 'combined moral and literary education, or separate religious education'. The word 'moral' was inserted to meet Presbyterian objections. The second version, in effect, formed the basis for the establishment of the Commissioners of National Education. For an explanation of the circumstances leading to the alteration and for a textual comparison, see Royal Commission of Inquiry into Primary Education (Ireland), 1870, HC 1870 (c. 6), XXVIII, Part I, 1, 20–6

12 Constitution of the Board of Education: The Duke of Leinster (President); Dr Richard Whately, Archbishop of Dublin; Dr Franc Sadlier, Provost of Trinity College; Rev. James Carlyle; Robert Holmes; Dr Daniel Murray, Archbishop of Dublin; and Anthony Richard Blake. Report of Commission of Inquiry into Primary Education (Ireland), 1868–1870, (The Powis Commission), HC 1870 (c. 6), XXVIII, Vol. 1, Part I, 510

13 HMSO, *History of the Vote for Public (Primary) Education, Ireland, 1 January 1831–1 March 1895*, p. 37 (henceforth called *History of the Vote for Public (Primary) Education*)

With effect from 7 February 1833 the Rev. James Carlyle, one of the original seven commissioners, was appointed to the newly created full-time paid position of Resident Commissioner, a position analogous to the current Secretary General of the Department of Education and Science.

Funding

The £30,000 voted by parliament did not constitute additional money for the provision of education in Ireland as it was the same amount that had previously been given to the Protestant Education Societies. A grant of a similar amount was repeated for the year 1832–33. Local sources were expected to provide sufficient funds for the annual repair of the schoolhouse, to provide all necessary furniture, and to furnish a permanent salary for the Master.

Each year, from the establishment of the Board in 1831 up to 1849, the commissioners had to submit to the Lord Lieutenant, through the Chief Secretary, an estimate of the money required for the coming year. With effect from 1 April 1849 the government decided that the annual funds would go directly to the commissioners from the Exchequer through the Paymaster General instead of through the Lord Lieutenant. Under this new system the Education Office was obliged to tender monthly instead of annual accounts to the Audit Committee.[14] These new measures consolidated the Treasury's control over the disbursement of monies for education in Ireland.

The Remuneration of Teachers in National Schools, 1831–72

1831–39

Under the new national school system the Board of the Commissioners contributed only a small gratuity towards teachers' pay. Many teachers became dependent on this money as their sole income as most parents either would not or could not provide any contribution. Even with a contribution from local sources, teachers' salaries were insufficient to meet ordinary daily living expenses.

In 1833, because of difficulties in procuring local funding, school managers made representations to the commissioners seeking assistance towards the remuneration of teachers. The Treasury provided an extra grant-in-aid for the school year 1833–34 and authorised the commissioners to issue a gratuity to school managers of £5 per annum for each teacher. In this instance the Treasury did not differentiate between the amounts to be paid to male and female teachers. In all other subsequent salary revisions the commissioners maintained discrimination against women in the matter of pay.

---

14 From 1833 to 31 March 1849 the accounts of the commissioners had been presented annually to the Audit Department. The Audit Department reported to parliament on the income and expenditure of all the departments in the civil service. It was considered to be a public spending watchdog.

In 1835 the Treasury agreed to the provision of a gratuity of £10 per annum for male teachers and £8 for female teachers, for every 100 pupils enrolled.[15] The increased gratuity compounded the local contribution problem and encouraged more people not to contribute. Although the commissioners submitted requests to the government nearly every year for more money, these appeals were invariably unsuccessful.

1839–48

In 1839 the commissioners revised the system of payment and granted a salary increase.[16] Each inspector was instructed to bring teachers in his district together for the purpose of written and oral examinations so that they could be categorised for salary purposes. There were four salary categories: First Class, Second Class, Third Class, and Probationers. A salary figure was determined for each class, with men and women in the same class being paid different salaries.[17] With effect from 1 April 1839, salaries ranging from £20 per annum for a male First Class teacher to £10 per annum for a female Third Class teacher were sanctioned. Only a small proportion of teachers were categorised as First Class, the majority being categorised as Third Class. This apportionment of salary reflected the influence of the Treasury and was a ploy to keep the overall salary cost to a minimum.[18] Although this constituted the payment of 'annual salaries', the commissioners refused to accept the concept and persisted with the notion that this was the payment of a gratuity. Salary scales were not reviewed again until 1848.

1848–72

During the Famine and its aftermath people had to endure dramatic social changes, accompanied by a massive increase in the cost of living.

In 1847 the commissioners decided to grant teachers a salary increase and to revise the system of payment to teachers, in a manner similar to the 1839 arrangement. During the school year 1847–48 male teachers were brought together to take written and oral examinations. Based on the results of these examinations teachers were reclassified into one of seven categories for salary purposes.[19] A general examination of female teachers was carried out the following year.[20]

---

15 £10 in 1835 was equivalent in value to £587 in 2000.

16 Dr J. F. Murray in Tenth Report of the Commissioners of National Education, HC 1844 (569) XXX, 143

17 The Powis Commission, HC 1870, (c. 6) XXVIII, Vol. 1, Part 1, 320

18 Seventh Report of the Commissioners for the year 1840, HC 1842 (353) XXIII, 217, 4

19 Appendix No. 5 in *Fifteenth Report for the year ended 31 December 1848*, HC 1848, XXII

20 Appendix in Sixteenth Report for the year ended 31 December 1848–49, HC 1850, XXV, contains information on these examinations.

The seven categories to which teachers were assigned were as follows:

- First Class, First Division $[1_1]$
- First Class, Second Division $[1_2]$
- First Class, Third Division $[1_3]$
- Second Class, First Division $[2_1]$
- Second Class, Second Division $[2_2]$
- Third Class, First Division $[3_1]$
- Third Class, Second Division $[3_2]$[21]

The salaries awarded to male teachers with effect from 1 April 1848 ranged from £30 to £14 per annum, and for female teachers from £24 to £12. Lower rates of salary were laid down for assistants, probationary teachers, and needlework mistresses.[22]

Salaries paid to teachers were reviewed in 1849, 1851, 1852, 1855, 1859 and 1860. Notwithstanding the number of reviews, only the increase granted with effect from 1 April 1855 could be termed substantial: the increase for men varied from £2 to £10 per annum, and for women from £2 to £11.

From 1855, following the implementation of the recommendations of the Trevelyan and Northcote Report, new opportunities for employment in the public service for young men from every social stratum became available. The availability of these new employment opportunities had a serious impact on the recruitment of men to the teaching profession as they provided more attractive salaries and better conditions of service.[23] The commissioners tried to counteract this problem by offering higher salaries to male teachers, but the money made available by the Treasury was not sufficient for the purpose, and the feminisation of the profession accelerated.

On 4 December 1867 teachers in Belfast submitted a memorial to the commissioners requesting that it be forwarded to the Lords of the Treasury.[24] They sought an increase in their salary of at least 20 per cent. They claimed that the amount sought was barely enough to raise the purchasing power of their salaries to the level at which they had been when class and division salaries were originally introduced in 1848. They submitted the following table:

---

21 The numeral notation in the square brackets was often used in documentation from the commissioners to designate the different categories of teachers. 11 is read as 'First of First'; 13 is read as 'Third of First'.

22 Needlework mistresses were appointed in schools where there was an average attendance of about twenty girls and where no female teacher was working in the school. The commissioners appear to have left it to the discretion of the managers whether or not to employ needlework mistresses.

23 The Trevelyan and Northcote Report, 'The Organization of the Permanent Civil Service', HC 1854–1855, Vol. 30, pp. 375–6

24 Details of the memorial and the ensuing correspondence are published in the Powis Commission Report 1870, HC 1870 (c. 6), XXVIII, Part V, Section XII, 549

Increase in cost of living, Ireland, 1845–67

Product	1845	1867	Increase
oatmeal	12s. per cwt.	18s. per cwt.	50%
flour	30s. per sack	44s. per sack	47%
potatoes	1³/4d. per stone	6d. per stone	243%
beef	3d. per lb	6d. to 7d. per lb	100%
mutton	3d. to 4d. per lb	6d. to 7d. per lb	100%
pork	2³/4d. per lb	5d. to 6d. per lb	100%

The commissioners refused to forward the memorial 'purporting to come from the National teachers of Ireland seeking an increase to their salaries', and teachers did not receive any increase in salary during the period between 1860 and 1872.

Remuneration in Convent and Monastery Schools

After the establishment of the national school system in 1831, most of the schools staffed by monks and nuns applied to come under the aegis of the National Board. Initially, six schools of the Irish Christian Brothers joined but they withdrew in 1837 due to unacceptable intrusions by the Board's inspectors. In spite of a number of attempts to bring them back under the aegis of the Board, it was not until 1925 that the Christian Brothers became part of the national school structure again and began to receive State payments and grants. From 1831 to 30 September 1839 all teachers, religious or lay, were paid gratuities at the same capitation rate.

The commissioners' salary proposals of 1839 changed the method of payment from a capitation rate to an annual salary determined by the 'class' into which the teacher was placed. Each religious teaching community was given the option of retaining the original capitation method or adopting the new classification system. The majority of the religious communities opted to retain the old capitation system and thus two categories of schools were created for religious-run schools: 'Capitation Schools' and 'Classification Schools'.

Classification Schools

Under the new salary payment system all lay national schools and some religious order schools became 'Classification Schools' and remained under the control of a school manager, usually the local clergyman, and the patronage of the bishop of the diocese. Nuns and brothers in these schools received personal salaries, similar to lay teachers, and endorsed their pay orders and passed them over to the superior of the school.[25]

---

25 Patrician, Marist, and De la Salle Brothers were paid personal salaries.

Capitation Schools

The majority of the religious communities opted to retain the old capitation system of remuneration, which involved the payment of an annual sum called a 'Capitation Grant'. This grant was computed by multiplying the average daily attendance of all pupils by a stipulated capitation fee for each pupil. The capitation grant was deemed to be payment in full for all expenses incurred in conducting a school, including salaries for lay staff.

Elementary Education in Great Britain

The provision of money from public funds to establish a national school system in Ireland was quickly recognised by people in England as setting a precedent. A movement was initiated to have a similar provision made for education in England, and, in 1833, parliament voted a grant of £20,000 as aid to private elementary education societies.[26]

In 1839 the position was regularised and parliament sanctioned an annual grant for public education in Great Britain. An Education Department, which would be assisted by the Privy Council, was established to administer this fund.

In 1858 opponents of the State-aided voluntary education system succeeded in persuading parliament to establish a Royal Commission (the Newman Commission) 'to inquire into the present state of popular education in England, and to consider and report what measures, if any, are required for the extension of sound and cheap elementary instruction to all classes of the people'.[27]

The commission's main recommendation was to propose a 'payment-by-results' scheme for the primary schools of England and Wales. This scheme appealed to the Treasury and the government because it was perceived to promote a policy of accountability and value for money. Furthermore, it would help to provide a system of elementary instruction for large numbers at minimum cost. The quality of the education did not seem to be taken into consideration; as Robert Lowe so succinctly put it, 'The objective which we have in view is an increase, not of the quality, but of the quantum of education. We want not better schools, but to make them work harder'.[28]

---

26 Report of the Select Committee appointed to inquire on foundation schools and education in Ireland, HC 1837–38 (701), VII, 1

27 The Newman Commission, HC 1861, XXI, Part 1, 64–7. The Commission conducted a survey of salaries paid to teachers in England and Wales. It found that the average salary of a sample of 3,659 male certified teachers was £93 3s. 7d. (of whom 2,102 had, in addition, houses or house rents); the average salary of 1,972 certified mistresses was £62 4s. 10d. (of whom 1,035 had houses or house rents); uncertified masters' salaries averaged £62 4s. 11d.; uncertified mistresses averaged £34 19s. 7d.; certified infant mistresses averaged £58 3s. 8d.; and uncertified infant mistresses averaged £35 2s. The Commission's Report was published in six volumes in 1861.

28 Robert Lowe, *The Revised Code of the Regulations of the Committee of the Privy Council on Education*, p. 27

In August 1861 the government published a 'Revised Code' by which all direct payments to teachers and pupil-teachers were abolished. All existing annual grants were merged into a capitation grant paid to the manager for each pupil who was successful in the individual examinations. The small pension provision that had been available to teachers was abolished, although it was conceded that those in receipt of pensions would continue to receive them.[29]

The publication of the Code was followed by a vigorous and widespread campaign of opposition to the proposed changes, in which teachers played an active part.[30] The Revised Code did, however, satisfy the demands for retrenchment of public expenditure, and it answered the complaints by many groups and individuals that public money was being provided for the 'over-education' of pupils and teachers. It was adopted by parliament in May 1862 and implemented in schools.

The loss of augmentation grants to certified teachers and to pupil-teachers, and the non-availability of pensions, led to a decline in the calibre of entrants to the profession. There was a rapid decrease in the number of pupil-teachers entering schools; the number admitted fell from 3,092 in 1861 to 1,895 in 1864.[31] The government grant to training colleges was reduced from £113,242 in 1863 to £70,752 in 1867. Teachers' remuneration decreased and relations between inspectors and teachers deteriorated.[32]

The education problem became the leading question of the day, particularly during the 1868 election. Teachers canvassed candidates on scholastic registration, payment-by-results, pensions, and security of tenure[33] and spearheaded a movement towards the establishment of a national association for teachers. *The Education Reporter* campaigned for a national teachers' union in its first issue in April 1869,[34] and on 10 September 1870 the first conference of the National Union of Elementary Teachers (NUET)[35] was held in King's College, London.

The government responded to the educational ferment and political pressure and tabled an Education Bill on 19 February 1870. The Act became known as

---

29 Asher Tropp, *The School Teacher: The Growth of the Teaching Profession in England and Wales from 1800 to Present Day*, pp. 79–82

30 HC 1862, XLI. It contains over 300 letters and memorials addressed to the Lord President or Secretary of the Council of Education on the subject. A collection of the pamphlets may be viewed at the Library of the Ministry of Education.

31 HC 1870, XXII, Minutes of the Council, lxxxii

32 HC 1867–68, XXV, Minutes of the Council, 1867–8, viii

33 Asher Tropp, *The School Teacher: The Growth of the Teaching Profession in England and Wales from 1800 to Present Day*, p. 95

34 In Ireland, the *Irish Teachers' Journal* was founded in January 1868 and, from its first issue, campaigned for a national teachers' organisation. The Irish National Teachers' Association was established on 15 August 1868. It became the Irish National Teachers' Organisation (INTO) a few years later.

35 The NUET (National Union of Elementary Teachers) changed its name to the NUT (National Union of Teachers) in 1889, the name by which it is known to the present day.

Forster's Act after William Edward Forster, Vice-President of the Council.[36] The Act laid the foundations for a compulsory system of elementary education.

With the passing of the Education Act of 1870 and the establishment of the NUET the battle for satisfactory remuneration and a pension scheme entered a new phase. However, the government proceeded to implement a payment-by-results scheme into schools in Ireland in 1872.

The Case for Pensions for Irish National Teachers

Teachers had to overcome considerable difficulties and a long period of agitation before they achieved a national superannuation scheme. They had to progress from no payments on retirement, to *ex gratia* payments, to discretionary pensions, and finally to a statutory superannuation scheme that included all teachers.

By the middle of the nineteenth century a regular scheme of pensions had become an established part of the terms and conditions of the employment of civil servants.[37] Teachers were aware of this and aspired to similar conditions. However, the government did not recognise them as employees of the State, but rather of local management, and therefore not automatically entitled to a pension on retirement.

The first official recognition of the right of a teacher to a pension occurred on 13 December 1837 when a House of Commons Select Committee recommended that teachers should have a fixed and reasonable income, a comfortable residence, hope of promotion, and a contributory pension after twenty years' service.[38]

Treasury Minute, 25 August 1846

In a Treasury Minute issued on 25 August 1846, the Treasury signified that it was prepared to make provision for the granting of a strictly limited number of 'Code' pensions to teachers in England and Wales.[39] The provisions of the Minute were extended to teachers in Scotland but no reference was made to teachers in Ireland. All requests by the Commissioners of National Education in Ireland for an extension of the scheme to teachers in Ireland were ignored.

---

36 Mr William Edward Forster (1818–86) entered parliament in 1861. He was appointed Under-Secretary for the Colonies in 1865 and Vice-President of the Council in 1868. In 1880 he was appointed Chief Secretary for Ireland, incurring unpopularity because of the severe measures he used to maintain order. He resigned in 1882 and became an opponent of Gladstone's plans for Home Rule.

37 The Trevelyan and Northcote Report and the 1859 Superannuation Act

38 Report of the Select Committee appointed to inquire on foundation schools and education in Ireland, HC 1837–38 (701), VII. The committee was established in 1835 and published its report on 13 December 1837.

39 *Report of the Departmental Committee of the Superannuation of School Teachers*, HC Cmd. 1962, 1923, par. 4

Treasury Minute, 6 August 1851

By 1851 pensions granted to teachers in England and Wales were costing £12,000 and the Treasury was of the opinion that this was too much. It was also concerned that future expenditure on an open-ended scheme would continue to increase. Furthermore, there were many in the Houses of Parliament who were opposed in principle to granting any pensions.

On 6 August 1851 a Treasury Minute radically amending the 1846 scheme was issued. A limit was placed on the number and classes of pensions that could be granted, and the total amount that could be expended on pensions in any one year was restricted to £6,500.

Many teachers who would have qualified under the old rule would not now receive a pension. The Education Department used the inspectors to ensure that the quota of claimants for pensions was not exceeded. In 1853 Inspectors were exhorted to 'remember carefully' that pensions were intended only as 'the means of reconciling the claims of an individual with the good of the school'.[40]

The teachers objected to these curtailments and submitted petitions to the Committee of the Council on Education claiming that the 1846 Minute had been generally understood to mean that teachers would get a pension provided they gave long and faithful service.[41] The Education Department rebutted these claims by maintaining that the Minute never guaranteed a right to a pension and that it had always been made clear that pensions were to be discretionary and exceptional.

The commissioners, having failed to get a similar scheme for teachers in Ireland, decided, on their own initiative, to pay small discretionary gratuities, varying from £5 to £20, to teachers on retirement.

In 1854 a Select Committee of the House of Lords recommended that the commissioners should consider making available to teachers a superannuation scheme similar to that operating in other branches of the civil service. The commissioners proposed, as an alternative, that they should be empowered to grant reasonable gratuities to deserving teachers who had been in the service of the Board for a considerable number of years. It would appear that the Treasury consented to this, as £2,000 was allocated for this purpose in the Annual Estimates for 1855–56. This was the first provision for retiring gratuities to teachers in Ireland sanctioned by the Treasury.

The Civil Service Superannuation Act of 1859 was held not to apply to national school teachers because part of their salary derived from local sources and their certificates of employment were not obtained from the Civil Service

---

40 Committee of the Council on Education, Memorandum to Inspectors, 1853

41 For example, a witness to the 1872 Select Committee gave as the reason why teachers
   should have pensions: 'simply because I was distinctly promised the chance of one when
   I entered the profession', HC 344/1872, Question 711

Commissioners.[42] While many philosophical arguments were used to refuse pensions, the economic one that they would cost too much carried most weight.

Treasury Minute, 9 May 1862

On 9 May 1862 the Treasury ruled that teachers appointed from 1862 would be ineligible for pensions; it declared that its commitment to £12,000 under the 1846 Minute and £6,500 under the 1851 Minute was as much as it was prepared to provide. At that time financial reviews were being carried out across the public service but, while the axe fell on the restricted teachers' pensions, no cutbacks were applied to the civil service scheme.

For the next thirty years teachers who entered the teaching profession had no expectation of a pension. The teachers campaigned vigorously and offered to contribute to a scheme, but without success. In this fight they were supported by many inspectors who urged a pension scheme as a means of attracting suitable people to become teachers. Retirement gratuities, such as they were, continued to be applied to teachers in Ireland in a manner more or less similar to that which applied to teachers in England.

Retirement gratuities awarded to teachers in Ireland, 1863–67

	1863	1864	1865	1866	1867
Old Age					
Number of vacancies	8	8	20	12	21
Number of gratuities	8	6	17	12	19
Sickness or Infirmity					
Number of vacancies	34	43	60	57	88
Number of gratuities	16	22	36	29	45
Number dismissed		1			1
Total Gratuities	24	29	53	41	65
Total Leaving Service	563	573	659	694	705

Only 4.2 per cent of the 563 teachers who left the service in 1863 qualified for a retirement gratuity; this increased to 9.2 per cent of the 705 retirements in 1867.

---

42 Bill to amend the law concerning superannuating and other allowances to persons having held civil offices in the public service, HC 1859 (2nd Sess. 1.) II, 787. Amended in committee (33rd Sess. 1.) II, 795

The Status of the Teacher in Ireland

In Ireland, applicants (men of seventeen years and women of sixteen years) for admission to the service of the Board as teachers had to have references showing them to be persons of Christian sentiment, of exceptional moral character, and free from such physical or other defects as would in any way interfere with their usefulness.[43]

The great majority of teachers were untrained as the training facilities were totally inadequate.[44] At first a restricted number of male teachers, who were already in positions in schools, were called for training, and in 1842 a training establishment for women was opened in the grounds of Tyrone House. Over the years other arrangements were made to provide trained teachers: pupil-teachers and monitor-teachers were recognised, and Model Schools were established. The first Model School was established in 1833, and between 1849 and 1867 a further twenty-six were established in large towns throughout the country. Every Model School produced six male and two female 'trained' teachers every year.

Although the teacher continued to be held in high esteem by his/her local community, in the world of officialdom he/she was less highly regarded. The commissioners considered teachers to be on the lowest rung of the ladder and laid down a detailed set of rules and regulations that ordered the teacher's life, work and behaviour.[45] Teachers were issued with a document entitled 'Twelve practical rules for the teachers of national schools', which barred them from participating in elections other than to vote, and from attending fairs, markets and political meetings.[46] These rules remained largely unchanged throughout the century.

Teachers also suffered from insecurity of tenure: they could be hired and fired at the whim of the school manager. There were many instances of teachers being dismissed for spurious and unjust reasons.[47] They did not achieve the right of appeal against unfair dismissal until 1873.

The Irish National Teachers' Organisation, 1868

Prior to the 1840s there is little available evidence to indicate that teachers met to express their grievances, but following the central examinations in 1839, for

---

43 Teachers, their Classification and Salaries, 15 July 1867. See Powis Commission, Section XII
44 Second Report of the Commissioners of National Education, 1834–35, HC, 1835 (300) XXXV, 35
45 Appendix A in all annual reports of the Commissioners of National Education, Ireland, 1832–1900
46 Appendix XVII to the Thirteenth Report of the Commissioners of National Education, 1846, HC 1847 (832) XVII, 187
47 David W. Miller, *Church, State and Nation in Ireland 1898–1921*, pp. 32–4

salary placement purposes, a change took place. The new procedures allowed a teacher, having served for a particular length of time in a 'class', to gain promotion to a higher grade following an examination and the recommendation of the inspector. This led to the practice of teachers coming together to help each other to prepare for the examinations. The 1839 method of salary placement and promotion was applied again in 1848, and this may have given teachers further encouragement to meet.

Reports of meetings of isolated groups of teachers began to appear in the newspapers. Anonymous letters appeared occasionally in the newspapers calling attention to teachers' grievances regarding pay and conditions of service, and some individuals wrote to the Commissioners of National Education voicing their complaints.[48]

These letters and reports were noted by the inspectors and the commissioners, and teachers were threatened with penalties if they engaged in correspondence in public journals about the system of national education.[49] While these threats did restrain teachers from publicly voicing their dissatisfaction, groups of them persisted in holding meetings and in establishing local associations to promote their interests. It is evident from commissioners' reports that, from the early 1850s, attempts were being made to organise a central national association or organisation from the scattered local teachers' associations.[50]

In November 1857 the 'National Teachers' Association for Ireland' was inaugurated at a meeting of teachers in Coleraine. They drew up a petition seeking redress of their grievances and forwarded it to the Board. It was ignored.

On 29 January 1859 teachers in Dublin organised a 'congress' that consisted of 'deputies' representing teacher associations from Edenderry, Tullamore, Ballina, Dundalk, and other parts of the country. This congress prepared a memorial, which was presented to the Chancellor of the Exchequer in 1861. Nothing positive resulted from the memorial.

In 1863 teachers in Dublin, inspired by a teacher-activist Jeremiah Henly, founded the 'Central Teachers' Association' by combining associations in Dublin and the surrounding areas.[51] The activists in Dublin saw that the teachers nationally would not give allegiance to a central organisation unless it was led by a person from outside the teaching service who would not be threatened by

---

48 See *The Irish Times*, 21 October 1863, for an example of an anonymous letter from a teacher in Co. Mayo

49 T. J. O'Connell, *A Hundred Years of Progress*, pp. 1–2

50 Ibid., pp. 1–3

51 Henly played an important role in the establishment of the INTO in 1868. He was subsequently appointed Professor of Mathematics in Kildare Street Teacher Training College. He was a regular contributor to the *Irish Teachers' Journal* and its successor *Irish School Weekly*, in which he wrote under the pen name 'Beta'. Professor Henly was known for his trenchant views in favour of teachers.

the expected opposition.[52] Vere Henry Louis Foster, a former diplomat and an activist in social affairs, particularly education, was identified as such a person.

The Irish Teachers' Journal

In 1867, Robert M. Chamney, Henly, and Vere Foster agreed to publish a monthly journal, the *Irish Teachers' Journal*. The decision to launch this publication proved to be the catalyst for the establishment of the Irish National Teachers' Organisation (INTO).

The first issue of the journal, which was published in January 1868, contained a long letter from Vere Foster. He presented a set of proposals for the alleviation of the hardship being experienced by teachers. He advocated that salaries should be increased substantially and paid monthly instead of quarterly and that teachers should have pensions similar to those enjoyed by officers in other branches of the civil service. He encouraged teachers to come together to form 'Teachers' Associations' in order to promote their cause.

Teachers throughout the country began to form associations, and Vere Foster's list of proposals was adopted as policy and the basis for agitation on a united front.

In the second issue of the journal, in February 1868, teachers were again urged to continue forming local associations, and a framework was laid down as to how such associations might work. The establishment of a central organisation was also promoted and details of the purpose and duties of such a body were given.

The editorial in the March issue of the journal promoted a central unified organisation that would have the strength to achieve teachers' objectives.

A government decision, in January 1868, to appoint a Royal Commission (the Powis Commission) to carry out a general inquiry into the system of primary education in Ireland provided a further incentive for the establishment of a central teachers' association.[53] The appointment of this commission aroused great interest and excitement among teachers as it was perceived as a possible opportunity to remedy the problems of remuneration and conditions of service. Many local teachers' associations began to prepare petitions and memorials to be submitted for consideration by the commission.

The First Teachers' Congress, 15 August 1868

On 20 June 1868 the Dublin Central Teachers' Association decided to hold an educational conference in Dublin on 15 August to consult members on the possible contents of a memorial for presentation to the commission. It was

---

52 T. J. O'Connell, *A Hundred Years of Progress*, p. 4
53 The Powis Commission, HC 1870 (c. 6), XXVIII, Vol. l, Part 1, 159

intended that the memorial should deal mainly with the question of salaries and conditions of service, but it was also decided to speak against the likely introduction of a payment-by-results scheme into schools in Ireland, similar to the situation in Great Britain. Thirty associations were represented at the congress and many of the remaining associations sent contributions to help defray the expenses incurred.[54] Vere Foster was invited to attend and preside, but he was unable to do so due to other commitments.

James Kavanagh, secretary of the Dublin Central Teachers' Association, addressed the conference. He explained that the objective of the conference was 'to consolidate the various teachers' associations at present in existence so that the national teachers might form a solid phalanx in order to obtain their just rights'.[553] Papers dealing with salaries, pensions, and teachers' residences were presented at the conference.

At a private session of the conference the 'Irish National Teachers' Association' was founded as a nationwide teachers' organisation, and James Kavanagh was appointed its secretary. The main objectives of the new association were to procure a substantial salary increase and a pension scheme for teachers.

The next congress was held on 29 and 30 December of the same year, and representatives of seventy-one local associations and of two county associations, Kildare and Donegal, attended.[56] Vere Foster attended and was elected the first President of the new Irish National Teachers' Association. Delegates adopted a constitution and a set of rules for it. Shortly after its foundation the word 'Association' was dropped in favour of 'Organisation' and the title 'Irish National Teachers' Organisation' (INTO) was adopted.

The Powis Commission, 1868–70

By 1868 the National Education system had been in operation for nearly forty years. It had expanded to 6,586 recognised national schools, with 918,344 pupils taught by 13,611 recognised teachers. The annual parliamentary estimate for national education had increased from £30,114 in 1833 to £360,195 for the year 1868–69. This ever-increasing bill and the heavy reliance on central funding were matters of dissatisfaction and recurring concern to the Treasury and the government. The government, as a matter of policy, was continually seeking economies and efficiency in the public service generally.

---

54 The *Irish Teachers' Journal*, September 1868, for the names of some of the delegates who attended the congress on 15 August 1868. In England the first conference of the NUET was held in King's College, London, on 10 September 1870.

55 T. J. O'Connell, *A Hundred Years of Progress*, p. 8

56 *The Irish Teachers' Journal*, February 1869, for a list of the delegates who attended the congress held on 29 and 30 December 1868

Furthermore, there had been developments in education in England, Wales and Scotland where payment-by-results schemes had been introduced.

The Lords of the Treasury were anxious to have similar revisions introduced in Ireland, the main objective being to have the amount of public money being expended reduced. In order to carry out its objectives, the government appointed a Royal Commission in 1868, the Powis Commission, named after its chairman, Earl Powis.[57]

The Powis Commission was asked to inquire into five main areas of concern: denominational teacher training, the instruction afforded in primary schools, salaries and mode of payment of teachers, the workings of the Board of National Education, and religious teaching under the Rules of the Board. Pensions were not referred to in the terms of reference.

The commission sat for two years and carried out an exhaustive inquiry into all aspects of the national education system in Ireland. Ten assistant commissioners surveyed different sections of the existing system and submitted reports.

Patrick Keenan, one of the two Chief Inspectors for national schools, was requested by the Royal Commission to prepare a scheme of payment-by-results for schools in Ireland.[58] He submitted a memorandum on 28 April 1868 detailing a payment-by-results scheme for implementation. He advocated that the introduction of such a scheme would result in an increase in the attendance of scholars and ensure more effective teaching by teachers; that money should be provided from the local rates for the payment of teachers; and that on retirement they should receive a pension.[59]

Vere Foster, at the invitation of the commission, conducted a survey of teachers' associations on a number of specific questions. He tabulated the replies and forwarded them, with a comprehensive covering report, to the commissioners in April 1869. He stated, 'I have appended in full all the replies which I have received from Associations and from teachers ... so as not to be liable to a charge of partiality.'[60] He removed all references to names or localities. In his report he commented that the pittance given to teachers was so miserably inadequate that the best teachers were resigning for other posts or emigrating and that it would require an increase of at least 100 per cent to put them on a level with teachers in England. He suggested that if pay in Ireland was higher, better results could be commanded. He also recommended that liberal retiring allowances should also be provided for teachers, 'for how can any teacher, with the grim walls of a prison workhouse looming in the distance, be expected to devote his whole time and attention to his duties?'[61]

---

57 The Powis Commission, HC 1870 (c. 6), XXVIII, Vol. 1, Part 1, 159
58 Patrick Keenan's Memorandum in Parliamentary Papers, HC, 1870, XXVIII, Part III, 89–105
59 MCNEI 28 February 1871
60 Ibid., p. viii
61 Vere Foster Report, pp. x–xi

Other interested parties, including bishops, clergymen, inspectors, professors from the training college, and teachers submitted memoranda and/or gave oral evidence to the commission. The INTO was successful in having four representatives, one from each province, appear before the commission. They submitted written statements and gave oral evidence.

This was the first time that teachers had been given an opportunity to present evidence of their grievances before a public forum. They optimistically expected the Royal Commission to make favourable recommendations.

Memorial, 31 March 1869

On 31 March 1869 Vere Foster led a deputation of national teachers to present a memorial, signed by 3,385 signatories, to the Chief Secretary. The meeting discussed the inadequacy of salaries, the absolute necessity for pensions, and the utter ruin which the introduction of a payment-by-results scheme would bring on the national school teachers of Ireland.[62]

Teachers objected in particular to the unsatisfactory system of awarding retirement gratuities. They organised a vigorous campaign and lodged complaints with the Royal Commission regarding retirement gratuities. In response to this campaign, and prior to the publication of the commission's report, the Treasury was obliged to concede revised conditions to the scheme with effect from 1870. Henceforth, it was determined that all teachers would be entitled to a retiring gratuity, and that the gratuity would equal one year's salary for every ten years of completed service.[63] While the change was substantial in comparison with what had applied previously, it was still a once-off payment based on a low salary.

The 1871 Memorial

In 1871 Foster, assisted by his brother, the Rev. Sir Cavendish Harvey Foster, led a deputation of teachers to present another memorial; it was addressed to the Right Honourable William Ewart Gladstone MP, First Lord of the Treasury, and to Right Hon. C. P. Fortescue, Chief Secretary for Ireland. In this memorial, which covered the same points as those raised in the 1869 memorial, teachers specifically requested a large increase in salaries and pensions to bring them into line with all other public servants under the Crown.

The deputation was sympathetically received but no promise of redress was forthcoming. The rejection of this petition led to a great outcry in the public press. Public meetings were held throughout the country at which the treatment of the teachers was strongly denounced.

---

62 *The Irish Teachers' Journal*, Vol. 1, 1 May 1869, p. 106
63 T. J. O'Connell, *A Hundred Years of Progress*, p. 258

The Powis Commission Report, 1870

In its report, which was published in May 1870, the commission made a total of 129 recommendations.[64] Some of the recommendations were given immediate attention while others were implemented over the succeeding years. The recommendations that were implemented had a profound effect on the general development of the primary school system in Ireland in the later part of the nineteenth century. They concluded that the salaries of teachers in national schools were insufficient to secure the best candidates. It adopted the scheme proposed by Keenan and proposed a new basis for the payment of teachers. Henceforth, the remuneration of a teacher should consist of two elements: a fixed class-salary and an additional payment-by-results element. It recommended that the seven 'classes' for salary purposes should be reduced to three.

The Commissioners of National Education, the inspectorate and the Catholic bishops welcomed the introduction of the new scheme. At a meeting on 14 January 1871 the commissioners resolved to submit proposals to the Treasury, in the estimates for 1872–73, for a 50 per cent increase in the remuneration of teachers based on the principle of a payment-by-results scheme.

The Treasury was not prepared to accept the commissioners' proposals as they would have increased the cost of elementary education by approximately 25 per cent. It did adopt Keenan's main proposal on the introduction of the payment-by-results scheme, but it rejected his recommendations that money should be provided from the local rates, that teachers on retirement should receive a pension, and that the regulations concerning local management should be changed.[65]

The Revised Salary Structure, 1 April 1872

After considerable discussion and some dispute with the commissioners, the Treasury introduced a payment-by-results scheme and a new basic salary structure, with effect from 1 April 1872.

The new classification of teachers was as follows:

- First Class, First Division [1_1]
- First Class, Second Division [1_2]
- Second Class [11]
- Third Class [111]
- Probationers

---

64 The report traces the historical development of the system of national education from its inception in 1831 to 1870. It reports on the role of the manager, the curriculum and proficiency of the pupils, the publication of schoolbooks, and the remuneration and training of teachers.

65 MCNEI 28 February 1871

Teachers were assigned over the different categories: 9 per cent were listed in First Class, 25 per cent in Second Class, 49 per cent in Third Class, and 17 per cent as probationers. This re-designation placed two-thirds of the teaching force in Third Class or lower, again with the purpose of keeping the amount of money required at its lowest level. A Third Class male teacher was awarded £24 per annum; a First Class, First Division male teacher got £52, more than double. Female teachers fared even less well: the respective figures for female teachers were £20 and £42. The restructuring of the salary scales did not alter, to any great extent, the budgetary provision for the payment of teachers.

Programme of Instruction and Result Fees, 1872

The full results scheme was introduced in all schools in Ireland with effect from 1 September 1872. The commissioners sent a document to all schools entitled 'Programme of Instruction & Examination for National Schools & Scale of Result Fees'. The Board issued specific instructions for inspectors regarding the organisation of the annual examination of individual pupils in each grade, and a scale of fees was set down for payment of a fee to the teacher for every successful pupil in each subject.

While the experience of operating the results scheme in England was used to determine the curriculum to be introduced and the fees to be paid in Ireland, there was a fundamental difference between the two schemes. On their appointment, teachers in England were given set salaries, determined by the school board, and the income from the result fees and the local contributions went to the school management. In Ireland, the teacher was paid a basic salary every quarter by the commissioners and paid an annual sum based on result fees for successful pupils in their examination. Teachers' incomes, therefore, varied from year to year.

A 'Contract of Employment' Agreement for Teachers, 1873

As part of the package, the Treasury informed school managers that payment of result fees would be sanctioned only on condition that teachers were offered 'contract of employment' agreements.[66] Catholic managerial bodies vehemently opposed this as they wished to retain the power to hire and fire teachers without hindrance.[67] Eventually, in February 1873, a compromise was reached between the commissioners and the managerial bodies, and the principle of a contract of employment was adopted. The teaching profession hailed this agreement as the 'Teachers' *Magna Carta*'. A teacher could no longer be summarily dismissed or obliged to discharge non-professional offices against his/her will, without extra remuneration.

---

66 The Powis Commission, HC (c. 6 III), XXVIII, Vol. 1, Part 1, 522–45. Recommendation No. 65

67 T. J. O'Connell, *A Hundred Years of Progress*, p. 43

The Powis Commission and Pensions for Teachers

The question of pensions for teachers was brought to the attention of the Powis Commission by Vere Foster's report, through submissions from the INTO, by local teacher associations and by other interested parties. However, the majority of the commissioners regarded it as 'contrary to public policy that the instructors of the people should be servants of the Government', and considered the pension proposal to be 'entirely at variance with our national traditions' and consequently rejected the motion.[68] This was in conformity with the position of the government and the Treasury, and an acceptance of the concept that thrift should be encouraged and that people should make provision for themselves and their dependants and not become a burden on society.[69]

Review

After forty years of operation, the national school system had over 6,900 schools staffed by 9,600 teachers and 4,000 monitors; the original £30,000 grant had become £480,000. Over that period of time, pay had moved from an annual gratuity of £10 for men and £8 for women to an average annual salary of £30 for men and £25 for women. Teachers' living conditions had not improved and their general conditions of employment did not compare to those enjoyed by teachers in Great Britain.

The end of this period was marked by a radical change in the education system: teachers' involvement in the system was changed following the establishment of the INTO in 1868, and the introduction of the payment-by-results scheme in 1872 radically altered both the curriculum and the method of remuneration of teachers.

Through the operation of a centralised organisation, the INTO began to have an effect on the commissioners and the Treasury. Campaigns were organised locally and nationally, delegations were sent to Westminster, and some victories were achieved.

The true effectiveness of the INTO during the next twenty-five years was demonstrated when parliament was obliged to pass five Acts which dealt specifically with the remuneration of teachers and their conditions of service.

---

68 *Irish School Weekly*, 23 August 1930
69 *Golden Rules for Teachers*, circulated by the commissioners

3

Developments in Salaries and Pensions, 1872–1900

Remuneration and Pensions, 1872–80

The restructuring of the basic salary in 1872, and the addition of the result fees, did not address the remuneration problem of teachers. The basic salary had changed little and teachers had to depend on result fees for any additional income. To make matters worse, the basic salary was paid every quarter and the result fees were issued only once a year. All payments for teachers were sent to the school managers. In a few instances, the manager put the payments in the post for the teacher, but in most cases teachers had to attend at the residences of their managers to collect their payments. This method of payment placed teachers in a very subservient position and was resented by them. They endeavoured to have it changed, but without success.

The Result Fees

The application of the results scheme was very unpopular among teachers. Most of the money went to the large schools in towns, and in particular to schools conducted by the religious orders. Teachers in small rural schools were at a serious disadvantage due to the small numbers on rolls and the irregularity of attendance by the pupils. As a result of recommendations from the inspectors, the commissioners introduced a revised programme with a revised scale of result fees with effect from 1 September 1873.

Initially, the fees were allocated among the school staff according to the following formula:

- In a school conducted by a principal and one assistant, two-thirds of the fees went to the principal and one-third to the assistant.
- In a school conducted by a principal and more than one assistant, one half of the fees went to the principal and the balance was divided equally among the assistants.
- Result fees for needlework and for extra subjects taught during ordinary school hours were placed in the common fund and divided among teachers.
- Result fees for subjects taught outside ordinary school hours were paid to the teacher who gave the extra tuition.

In 1875 the method of allocating the fees was revised. The new arrangements stipulated that the principal teacher should receive twice as much as any assistant. For example, in a school with a principal and three assistants, the principal got two-fifths and each of the assistants got one-fifth.

The National School Teachers (Ireland) Act, 1875

From the beginning of the establishment of the national education system the Treasury aspired to have education placed as a charge on the local rates, but without success. Acts of Parliament in 1870 and 1872 had made provision for significant contributions from local rates to English and Scottish schools.
In Ireland the result fees estimate for 1874–75 had been £120,000, and on 10 December 1874 the National Commissioners recommended to the government that the grant for 1875–76 should be £240,000.[1]

The government refused to accept the request and submitted alternative proposals to parliament. It made available £189,174 but proposed that it should be apportioned as follows: (a) £65,064 for additional salaries, (b) £60,000 for unconditional 'payment-by-results' fees, and (c) a further grant-in-aid of £64,110 towards result fees, on condition that the Guardians of the Poor Law Unions would make a contribution of an equal amount from the local rates.

Under this system result fees would be provided from three sources, each of them providing one-third of the total amount: the Non-Contingent Moiety, without any conditions attached; the Contingent Moiety, which was conditional on an equal amount being provided by the Guardians; and the Local Rates Moiety, which would have to be raised by the Guardians from the local rates. It was intended that the three moieties should exceed £180,000, but it never reached that figure. These proposals, with revised salary scales, became law in August 1875 when parliament passed The National School Teachers (Ireland) Act, 1875.

Teachers were now only guaranteed the basic salary and one-third of the result fees, payment of the other two-thirds was conditional.

The Problem with the Local Rates Moiety

The Boards of Guardians of Poor Law Unions were not in favour of increasing local rates to provide one-third of the result fees for teachers in national schools in their respective unions. Invariably, the Guardians were the largest landowners in the district and they themselves would be obliged to pay it. With the government insistent that the payment of the Contingent Moiety would have to be matched by a corresponding contribution from local sources, the payment of two-thirds of the fees was in jeopardy.

---

1 HMSO, *History of the Vote for Public (Primary) Education*, p. 3

Every year teachers had to address meetings of Boards and canvas Guardians to persuade them to become contributing unions. In the majority of cases the teachers were unsuccessful as most unions decided not to contribute. The fact that it was not compulsory on a Board of Guardians to become a contributory union proved to be a fatal flaw.[2] Only teachers in contributing unions received the full amount of result fees due to them, and teachers in non-contributing unions received only one-third. This caused great dissatisfaction and unrest among teachers and managers in the non-contributory unions, and resulted in agitation and continuing campaigns to achieve equity.

Review of the 1875 Act

The government's attempt to transfer responsibility for part of teachers' remuneration to local sources was unsuccessful because the 1875 Act was not compulsory. It was not compulsory because the government was not prepared to impose it on the Guardians, the large property owners.

In the year 1875–76 the largest number of unions (70 out of 163) opted to become Contributing Unions; only thirteen unions opted in for the year 1880–81. Eventually, clauses were included in The Local Taxation (Customs and Excise) Act, 1890 and The Irish Education Act, 1892, which effectively repealed the 1875 Act.

Year after year, the amount that parliament had to provide for Irish education continued to rise; the amount required in 1860 had been £270,722 and it reached £1,145,721 by 1900.

Miscellaneous Developments in Remuneration, 1876–78

The Abolition of Commission on Book Sales, 1876

From 1863, teachers in national schools who paid for books and school requisites in advance had been allowed to charge a commission of 20 per cent on their sale in school. The Treasury Committee of 1873–74 argued for the abolition of the scheme and, in spite of opposition from the commissioners, the Treasury abolished it from 1876. This commission had been a source of considerable income for many teachers and its loss brought about a severe reduction in their remuneration.

The Intermediate Education (Ireland) Act, 1878

The position of national teachers was further exacerbated by some of the provisions of The Intermediate Education (Ireland) Act, 1878. National teachers were specifically excluded from earning fees under the provisions of this Act, in

---

2   Consequently, the 1875 Act became known as 'The Permissive Bill'.

spite of the fact that children in national schools could compete for exhibitions and prizes under its terms.

Revision of the Method of Payment of Teachers, 1878

In order to reduce costs the Treasury changed the system of salary payment to teachers from postal orders to money orders with effect from 1 January 1878. Under this method the managers received teachers' salaries on a fixed day every quarter, instead of varying dates as previously. This method of issuing salaries reduced the cost to central funds by about £200.[3]

Pensions for Teachers in Ireland, 1870–80

Retirement Gratuities in Ireland, 1873–1879

With effect from 1870 the Treasury conceded that all teachers were entitled to a retiring gratuity equal to one year's salary for every ten years of completed service. However, between 1 January 1873 and 1 January 1879, only 359 retiring gratuities were paid.[4] The majority of the gratuities were less than £200 and, of those, about 50 per cent were less than a £100.

Causes of withdrawal	Trained	Untrained	Total
Resigned to enter the civil service	6	36	42
Resigned for domestic duties	18	43	61
Commercial pursuits	7	10	17
Collegiate or religious vocation	4	13	17
Age or ill-health	13	10	23
Retiring gratuities	26	12	38
Teaching in non-recognised schools	3	4	7
Other pursuits	17	8	25
Emigrated	10	16	26
Dismissed	8	21	29
Died	12	37	49
Lunatic asylums	3	4	7
Totals	**127**	**214**	**341**

3   HMSO, *History of the Vote for Public (Primary) Education*, p. 108

4   The teachers' names, the names of their schools, and the amount of gratuity each one received are listed in Returns of Retirement Gratuities for National Teachers, 1873–79, HC 1881 (259) LXXIII, 235

The reason for the small number of gratuities was because the majority of teachers left the service for reasons other than normal retirement. Seven hundred and forty-five teachers left the service during 1875–76 and, yet, only thirty-eight got retirement gratuities. The inspectors conducted a survey and identified the reasons for leaving in the case of 341 teachers:[5]

Ages of Teachers

In 1877 the commissioners investigated the ages of teachers in the service as it had become apparent that teachers invariably served to an advanced age before retiring. It was established that, due to great carelessness with record keeping in the Education Office, teachers, with comparatively few exceptions, had represented themselves as being younger than they really were; the average difference amounting to nearly two years. This information was used by the new Teachers' Superannuation Office when it commenced registering teachers for the new pension scheme in 1880: all teachers wishing to join the pension scheme had to produce proof of age.

The INTO Campaign for a Pension Scheme

From the time that they were first paid by the commissioners in 1831, teachers had sought a pension scheme similar to the one enjoyed by civil servants. However, the Treasury consistently claimed that teachers were not public servants but rather the employees of local management, and therefore not entitled to a superannuation scheme.

In 1877 the government submitted a proposal to the INTO for the resolution of the pension question on the basis of deferred annuities. On 7 May 1878 James Lowther, the Chief Secretary for Ireland, accepting a motion proposed in the House of Commons, stated that pensions should be conceded to teachers in Ireland, that proposals had been submitted to an actuary, and that the government was only waiting for his report before making a decision on the subject.[6]

Congress was due to be held on 30 and 31 December 1878 and, in order to intensify its campaign, the Central Executive Committee of the INTO (CEC)[7] sent a requisition – signed by the city members, the Lord Mayor elect, the High Sheriff, the members of the Town Council, several MPs, magistrates, deputy lieutenants, merchants, and notables of all sorts – to the Lord Mayor to convene a meeting of the citizens on the subject of teachers' grievances. The meeting was

---

5 Forty-second Report of the Commissioners of National Education for the year ended 31 December 1875, HC 1876, XXIV

6 Letter from John Ferguson, President INTO, published in *Irish Teachers' Journal*, 18 May 1878

7 The Central Executive Committee of the INTO will be designated as the CEC throughout.

convened on 7 December by the Lord Mayor as he had very strong views on teachers' grievances.

The government finally succumbed to the pressure and The National School Teachers (Ireland) Act, 1879 was passed by parliament on 15 August 1879. Under the Act teachers of Ireland were granted a statutory pension scheme with effect from 1 January 1880. A Teachers' Pension Fund was established from which all future pensions and gratuities would be paid to teachers on retirement.

While the provision made by the Act was a big advance, the actual amounts paid as pensions were very small: the amount depended on the teacher's age, the number of years of completed recognised service, and the teacher's 'class' for salary purposes. It could be as high as £71 or as low as £15 for a man, and £58 to £12, respectively, for a woman.

Nevertheless, after only ten years in existence the INTO had achieved one of its main objectives. The teachers in the United Kingdom did not get a statutory pension scheme until 1898.[8]

The National School Teachers (Ireland) Act, 1879

Under the terms of the Act a capital sum of £1,300,000 was appropriated from the Irish Church Temporalities Fund to establish a 'Pension Fund' – a perpetual endowment to provide reversionary pensions for national teachers in Ireland, i.e. the money would not be sourced from central funds.[9]

The Commissioners of Church Temporalities were responsible for the management of the Irish Temporalities Fund, and if they were unable to provide the sum required from the funds under their control, Section 8 of the Act gave them power to borrow it.[10]

It was stipulated that all 'classed' teachers entitled to benefit under the Act would be obliged to contribute to the scheme and that such contributions would be lodged to the fund.[11] The amount of the contribution was not specified, but the government retained power, under a schedule to the Act, to determine contributions as conditions required.[12] Contributions paid by teachers who died in service would be repaid, with interest, to their legal representatives.

---

8 When teachers in England did get a pension scheme in 1898, they paid lower contributions for greater benefits.

9 This money was part of the surplus money that became available in Ireland as a result of The Irish Church Act, 1869. (The Irish Church was disestablished under this Act.) The *Oxford English Dictionary* defines 'reversionary' as having an entitlement to get back. It could be understood to mean a 'contributory' pension.

10 The Commissioners of Church Temporalities in Ireland, four people nominated by the government, formed a corporate body established under The Irish Church Act, 1869.

11 The term 'classed teachers' meant such principal and assistant teachers of model or ordinary national schools as received salaries from, and were classed according to, the regulations of the Commissioners of National Education.

12 The National School Teachers' (Ireland) Act, 1879, s. 4

The Commissioners for the Reduction of the National Debt were directed to invest the capital sum of £1,300,000 with the Irish Land Commission at a yield of 3 per cent per annum. It was estimated that the annual interest of £39,000 would be sufficient to meet three-quarters of the annual liability of the pension fund and that teachers' contributions would be responsible for the other one-quarter.

The compulsory retirement age for male teachers was fixed at sixty-five, and for females at sixty. Only with the special permission of the Commissioners of National Education could this requirement be avoided.

The Administration of the Pension Scheme

A new office under Treasury direction, the National Teachers' Superannuation Office, was given responsibility for administering the pension scheme. Henceforth all teacher appointments, resignations, promotions, etc., had to be notified to this office.

Eligibility for Pensions

All 'classed' principal and assistant teachers who were in the service of the Commissioners of National Education at the time of the passing of the Act on 1 August 1879 were allowed five years to exercise the option to join or decline to join the pension scheme. A teacher declining to join the new scheme remained eligible for a retirement gratuity under the old scheme of 1870.

All teachers entering the service from 1 January 1880 were compulsorily enrolled in the scheme, but they would not be entitled to a pension until they had completed ten years' service.

Four grades of pensions were provided: First Class, First Division; First Class, Second Division; Second Class; and Third Class. The basic contribution and pension were determined on the salary of the Third Class Teacher; teachers in a higher class could make extra contributions that would give them an entitlement to a higher pension rate appropriate to their 'class'.

It was laid down in the Act that the total number of teachers allowed to secure pension privileges at any one time could not exceed 5,300 males and 5,400 females (these were called the 'Standard Numbers'). The numbers were limited to the different 'classes' as follows:

	Males	**Females**
First Class, First Division	150	130
First Class, Second Division	410	350
Second Class	1,850	1,550
Third Class	2,890	3,370
Total	**5,300**	**5,400**

The overall totals could not be exceeded; if a teacher wished to retire and the number for the year had been reached he or she had to wait until a vacancy occurred. The same rule applied to the numbers for each class/division, except in one particular case: the number in any class might be exceeded provided the total of the standard number in it and the classes above, taken together, was not exceeded.

Pensions on Compulsory Retirement

A male teacher retiring at sixty-five years of age or upwards, or a female teacher retiring at sixty years of age or upwards, was entitled to a pension appropriate to his/her 'class', provided he or she had paid the contribution of that 'class'; if not, the pension was set at the highest 'class' for which contributions had been paid. Service after the age of sixty-five for males and sixty for females, even if specially permitted, did not qualify for pension purposes.[13]

Maximum Pension

The maximum pension that teachers in the different classes could achieve, all conditions being fulfilled at their highest value, were as follows:

Class from which retiring	Males – £	Females – £
First Class, First Division	88	63
First Class, Second Division	60	47
Second Class	46	34
Third Class	35	25

Male teachers aged fifty-five or upwards, or female teachers aged fifty or upwards could qualify for voluntary pensions. The amount of pension depended on the number of years of completed service and the teacher's class for salary purposes. A pension could be as high as £79 or as low as £15 for a man; the corresponding figures for a woman were £58 and £12.

Pensions were paid quarterly by the Paymaster General on production of a signed declaration form, provided by the Education Office, which provided proof of the existence and identity of the claimant. Arrangements were made for local encashment of the payment orders.

Pension or Gratuities on Disability

Male teachers over thirty and under fifty-five years of age and female teachers over thirty and under fifty years of age, who were compelled to retire through

---

13 HMSO, *History of the Vote for Public (Primary) Education*, p. 128

illness, could qualify for the payment of a gratuity, or, if they preferred, a small disablement pension, according to set scales.[14] To qualify for a disablement gratuity or disablement pension, teachers would have to satisfy the commissioners on two conditions:

- that they were permanently incapacitated through infirmity of mind or body for further service as a national school teacher
- that, if they had been able to serve to compulsory retirement age, they would have been entitled to a pension under the normal provisions of the Act.

Refund of Contributions

A teacher who was dismissed or quit the service, other than by death or receipt of a pension, had his/her contributions refunded to him/her. A teacher who had been dismissed or who had quit the service and re-entered the service had to repay any money received and, in addition, contributions for the period spent out of service. Arrangements could be made to have the payments spread over one or two years.

'Special Gratuities' to Teachers

The small number of teachers who declined or omitted to join the new pension scheme and remained entitled to retirement gratuities under the 1870 regulations did not have to pay pension contributions.[15]

Pensions for Members of Religious Communities

In 1839 and in subsequent years the majority of the conductors of religious-run schools opted to remain as capitation schools; this decision had serious pension consequences for teaching staff in these schools. The Act stipulated that only teachers who had been paid personal salaries from the Commissioners of National Education would be eligible for a pension, meaning that both the lay and religious teachers in capitation schools were ineligible for any pension as they did not receive personal salaries.

New Basic Salary Scale from 1 January 1880

New salary scales were introduced, with effect from 1 April 1880, which helped to compensate teachers for the contributions they were now obliged to make to the new pension fund.[16] The salaries, with the old figures in brackets, were as follows:

---

14 Male teachers over fifty-five and female teachers over fifty would qualify for a voluntary pension.

15 HMSO, *History of the Vote for Public (Primary) Education*, p. 106

16 The extra amount, when eventually granted, came to £42,650. Treasury Letters, 5562, 5/4/1880, and 7514, 1/5/1880

	Males – £	Females – £
First Class, First Division [1_1]	70 (58)	58 (48)
First Class, Second Division [1_2]	53 (44)	43 (36)
Second Class	44 (38)	34 10s/(30)
Third Class	35 (32)	27 10s/(25)

These salary scales were not reviewed again until 1892 and, in the meantime, teachers' financial position deteriorated.[17] They felt particularly aggrieved with regard to the inequality between their pay and the pay of teachers in English and Scottish schools. Teachers in Ireland fared very badly in a report, given to parliament in 1885, which compared the average income, from all sources, of male national school teachers in Ireland, and of certified masters in England, Wales, and Scotland.[18] The INTO used this information when making its claim for revised salaries.

Remuneration and Pensions, 1880–1900

During the years 1880–1892, due to vigorous campaigns conducted by the INTO, parliament had to pass a number of Acts that had a profound influence on the remuneration and, consequently, on the pensions paid to teachers. The Acts were as follows:

1　The Local Government Act (England), 1888
2　The Probate Duties (Scotland and Ireland) Act, 1888
3　The Local Taxation (Custom and Excise) Act, 1890
4　The Irish Education Act, 1892

The Local Government Act (England), 1888, and the Probate Duties (Scotland and Ireland) Act, 1888

Under these Acts it was provided that the income received from Probate Duties should be shared between England/Wales, Scotland and Ireland for the purpose of relieving local taxation (local rates) from the obligation of providing funds for education. It was resolved that the Probate Duties collected would be divided among the countries in the following manner: 80 per cent for England/Wales, 11 per cent for Scotland, and 9 per cent for Ireland (a ratio of 80:11:9).[19] This division was assessed as being the proportional contribution

---

17 Irish Education Act, 1892, HC 1892 IV, 645
18 Return of the average income from all sources of male national school teachers in Ireland, and of certified masters in England and Wales, and in Scotland, HC 1884–85 (105) LXI
19 This ratio became known as the 'Goschen Ratio'.

made by each country to the Imperial Exchequer. Even though the Acts were passed in 1888, Ireland did not receive its first allocation of Probate Duties until 1892, when The Irish Education Act, 1892 was passed by parliament.

The Local Taxation (Custom and Excise) Act, 1890

This was described as 'An Act for the distribution and application of certain duties of Customs and Excise, and for other purposes connected therewith'.[20] It empowered the government to distribute among the teachers in England/Wales, Scotland, and Ireland, again in the ratio of 80:11:9, the total amount of revenue raised by the Custom and Excise Service from excise duties on goods. These monies were additional to the annual estimates for education passed by parliament.

The first contribution made to Ireland was for the school year 1890–91 and it amounted to £78,000. The Commissioners of National Education distributed the money in three ways:

1   Teachers in non-contributing unions were paid grants that were approximately equivalent to the amount received by teachers in contributing unions. This portion of the grant was popularly known as the 'Whiskey Money'.[21]

2   The Boards of Guardians in the Contributing Poor Law Unions were refunded part of the money that they had collected from the local rates and which had been paid to teachers in the schools in their district.[22]

3   The remaining money was given to the Irish Intermediate Board of Education. This Board used the money to awards prizes, bursaries and grants.

These provisions did not ameliorate the problem of teachers' salaries, and the INTO intensified its campaigns. Membership of the organisation had increased and it had become more influential and effective in its representations on behalf of teachers. It lobbied Irish MPs to put pressure on the government to respond to the demands of the teachers in Ireland.

The Irish Education Act, 1892

In response to this campaign, and in order to implement the provisions of The Probate Duties (Scotland and Ireland) Act, 1888, the government introduced The Irish Education Act, 1892. This was the first major piece of legislation to deal exclusively with the remuneration of teachers in Ireland. It incorporated a

---

20 The Local Taxation (Custom and Excise) Act, 1890
21 T. J. O'Connell, *A Hundred Years of Progress*, p. 150
22 The Unions were refunded £17,759 for the school year 1890–91. In 1893–94 result fees raised from the rates amounted to £21,912, and the Guardians were refunded £17,303.

radical statutory provision in that the government finally assumed responsibility for the total remuneration of teachers.

The Act had three main provisions:

1   With effect from 1 October 1892, the government agreed to pay the Contingent Moiety of the Result Fees irrespective of any contribution from the Board of Guardians.
2   The government agreed to distribute Ireland's share of The Probate Duties (Scotland and Ireland) Act, 1888 to the teachers of Ireland through an annual 'School Grant' in accordance with the Fourth Schedule of the 1892 Act. The Act stated that the amount of the School Grant was to be £210,000 or 'of such other amount as parliament may determine'.
3   The government agreed to partially abolish – in most cases totally – School Fees with effect from 1 October 1892.[23]

Fourth Schedule of the 1892 Act

With the concurrence of the Treasury, the commissioners allocated the first school grant of £210,000, with effect from 1 April 1892, to the different categories of teachers in the manner described in the Fourth Schedule of the Act as follows:

1   Under Clause 1, the existing rates of class salaries of principal and assistant teachers were increased by 20 per cent. The grant to capitation schools was increased by 3s. 6d. per pupil per annum.
2   Under Clause 2, assistant teachers who were classed higher than Third Class and who were of five years' standing or more were granted an annual bonus. The bonus for men was £9 and for women £7 10s.[24]
3   Clause 3 introduced revised methods for the payment of teachers previously paid under the Modified Aid to Small Schools Scheme.
4   Clause 4 set down in detail the distribution of the balance of the School Grant, almost half the amount, through the payment of the 'Residual Capitation Grant'. The 'Residual Capitation Grant' was distributed to all schools 'as nearly as possible in proportion to the number of children in average daily attendance in the year'. In this manner teachers got their full entitlement to result fees and compensation for lost school fees.

The passing of The Irish Education Act, 1892 marked a major achievement by the INTO. It was the final step in the process of removing national teachers from

---

23 Section 18 of the Act provided for an additional parliamentary grant to compensate teachers for the loss of the school fees.

24 This special annual bonus to assistants, of £9 and £7 10s., continued to be paid until 1917.

dependence on local sources for the payment of any portion of their salaries. Henceforth, the total remuneration paid to teachers would be provided from the Exchequer. The result was that the annual estimate for teachers' remuneration increased by about 25 per cent.

'The Equivalent Grants Affair'

The Probate Duties (Scotland and Ireland) Act, 1888 stipulated that the duties collected should be divided among the countries in the ratio of 80:11:9. Even though the probate duties collected increased every year, the Treasury tried to maintain the Irish grant in subsequent years at the figure paid in 1892, while the amount paid to England/Wales increased. The failure to increase the grant in the following years caused a serious dispute between the Commissioners of National Education and the Treasury, with the latter maintaining that it was empowered under Section 18 (1) of The Ireland Education Act, 1892 to determine the School Grant as it saw fit.[25]

In the three years 1893–96 Ireland received only the original figure of £210,000 each year. If the proportionate principle had been preserved Ireland should have received £248,962 in 1894–95.[26] Every year the commissioners sought both the proportionate amount and the arrears for the previous years and the controversy became known as 'the equivalent grants affair'.

Finally, in 1895, the Treasury was prevailed upon to concede the proportional principle and to pay the arrears. It agreed to pay £108,000 as arrears for the three previous years but on condition that £13,000 went to convent and monastery schools and the rest went to the Teachers' Pension Fund. The commissioners accepted this offer.[27]

While the commissioners were successful in getting the money, the teachers did not get any of it. This action of the commissioners could not be interpreted as a true reflection of their relationship with the Treasury during the nineteenth century; Akenson's opinion would appear to be accurate: 'the equivalent grants affair was the only time in the years from 1870 to 1900 that the commissioners stood up to the Treasury on an important issue'.[28]

The Rise of Staff Organisations within the Civil Service

Civil servants also consolidated their influence and power during this period. A Superannuation Act was passed by parliament in 1887 which gave authority to:

---

25 The Ireland Education Act, 1892, Fourth Schedule
26 Sixty-second Report of the Commissioners of National Education, 1895, p. 34
27 MCNEI 16 February 1897
28 D. H. Akenson, *The Irish Education Experiment: the National System of Education in the Nineteenth Century*, p. 339

- pay a gratuity or an allowance to a civil servant who had been injured
- grant a retiring allowance to persons removed from office who were considered 'not fit or proper'
- award a compassionate grant on retirement to a person not entitled to superannuation
- distribute money, not exceeding £100, to dependents who had not taken out probate
- prohibit the payment of two incomes from the public purse, one of which was a public service pension, by providing for the forfeiture, suspension, or deduction, of any sums granted to officers in the army or navy who were in receipt of a pension or retired on half pay, and who were in full-time employment.

In 1888, responding to representations from civil servants claiming a salary review, the government appointed a Royal Commission to inquire into the pay and conditions of employment in the different offices of the Civil Establishments at home and abroad.[29] The commission made a number of recommendations that had a profound effect on the conditions of service of civil servants. It characterised promotion by seniority as a great evil, and recommended promotion by merit. A new salary scale structure was introduced; seven hours was fixed as being the length of the standard work day, and civil servants were granted entitlement to sick leave and annual leave.

Many of these new conditions of service became the aspirations of teachers and some of them, when achieved, were highly beneficial.

The Teachers' Pension Scheme, 1880–1900

INTO Agitation for Improved Pensions

A number of regulations issued under the Act of 1879 caused considerable disquiet to teachers. One regulation stipulated that if a teacher was dismissed for any reason whatsoever, he or she ceased to be entitled to a pension. Teachers were very aggrieved over this provision since it placed unprecedented power in the hands of school managers. Continuous efforts were made by the INTO to have this power removed.

Teachers also continued to express dissatisfaction with the levels of pensions. Resolutions were adopted at successive INTO congresses seeking improvements and changes.

---

29 The Ridley Commission; First Report, HC 1887 (c. 5226) XIX. 1, Second Report, HC 1888 [c. 5545] XVII, Third Report, HC 1889 (c. 5749) XXI. 1

The First Quinquennial Valuation of the Pension Fund, 31 December 1884

The first actuarial valuation of the pension fund was carried out in 1885 based on the fund as at 31 December 1884. For the period 1879–84, the following pensions and gratuities had been granted:

Pensions	Average		Average	
	Males	**Rate**	**Females**	**Rate**
At compulsory ages	184	£47	84	£39
Voluntary retirement	116	£80	67	£2
Disability	10	£12	6	£9
	310		**157**	

This actuarial valuation was to be the only one that ever showed a surplus, in this case of some £200,000.[30] On considering the report and in light of the surplus, the government decided to reduce the contributions by 10 per cent and to amend a number of benefits. Henceforth, forty years' service after the age of twenty-one for men or eighteen for women would qualify for a full pension. Men could retire on a full pension any time after the age of sixty-one, and women could retire on a full pension any time after the age of fifty-eight, as long as forty years' recognised service had been completed. The New Rules came into effect from 1 January 1886.

The Second Quinquennial Valuation, 31 December 1890

The second actuarial valuation, carried out in 1891, showed the pension fund to be in deficit, and it was estimated that without remedial action the fund would become insolvent. In March 1892 parliament was obliged to vote a supplementary sum of £90,000 for education in Ireland, and the Treasury assigned the money to the pension fund. Irish teachers were not pleased with this. They claimed that this sum was the proportionate amount of the fee grant due to them as part of their remuneration for 1891–92 and that it should not have been assigned to the pension fund.

The Third Quinquennial Valuation, 31 December 1895

The third actuarial valuation of the fund, as of 31 December 1895, was published in 1897 and showed that the actuarial deficiency had reached £1,200,000. The actuary advised the Treasury that, with a deficit of that

---

30 Report of the First Quinquennial Valuation of the National Teachers' Pension Fund, HC
    1884–85 (286) LXI, 461. Ordered by the House of Commons to be printed 23 July 1885.

magnitude, drastic steps would have to be taken to forestall the collapse of the fund. A vote-in-aid of the pension fund for £95,434 was passed in a Supplementary Estimate in February 1897. A further sum of £18,000 was voted later that year, and it was agreed that a similar sum would be granted as an annual grant-in-aid.[31] It was recognised, however, that in order to resolve the problem, the pension rules would have to be changed.

The Irish Teachers' Pension Rules of 1898

Parliament passed The National School Teachers (Ireland) Act, 1897, which authorised the Treasury to issue new rules. 'The Irish Teachers' Pension Rules, 1898' were implemented by the Lord Lieutenant with effect from 1 January 1898, and all previous rules were revoked. For all intents and purposes, a new pension scheme was introduced; new contribution rates and pension tables were substituted for those hitherto in force.[32]

The new rules applied to all classed teachers then in the service, with the exception of those teachers who had opted out under the 1879 Act. All teachers joining the service would come under the new rules. Pension benefits previously enjoyed by teachers were considerably curtailed and rates of contributions were increased, on average, by nearly 15 per cent.[33] These pension contributions and any interest accruing thereon, together with such other sums as the Treasury might direct from time to time, were to be lodged to 'The Teachers' Contribution Account'. All other sums, such as interest from the original capital sum, interest from other investments, and any sums voted by Parliament, would be lodged to 'The Endowment Account'.

The government gave a categorical undertaking, similar to the undertaking in the 1879 Act, that it would assume the responsibility of ensuring that 'The Endowment Account' portion of the Fund would be kept solvent.[34] The history of the operation of the scheme was to show that the government did not fulfil this commitment, and the fund remained in deficit up until 1934 when it was converted into a non-contributory scheme by the Saorstát government.

Teachers protested strenuously against the imposition of the new rules, but without success. Irish MPs at Westminster challenged the proposals on behalf of Irish teachers, but their representations were also unsuccessful. Eventually, the

---

31 Treasury Letters, 8 July 1897, No. 10, 205 / 97, and Treasury Circular of August 1897
32 Rules for the Administration of the Teachers' Pension Fund, 22 November 1897
33 A letter from 'An Mainséalach' published in *Irish School Weekly*, 24 November 1928. 'An Mainséalach' was Eamonn Mansfield, an INTO activist, and a recognised expert on the Teachers' Pension Scheme. He was sacked as a teacher in 1913 and served as General Secretary INTO (temporary) for a short period during 1914–15.
34 This commitment was confirmed by the Chancellor of the Exchequer, Sir Michael Hicks-Beach, when replying to the debate in the House of Commons in July, 1898. HC, July 1898, Hansard, Vol. LXI. Col. 1243 to 1248

INTO brought a Petition of Right to the courts seeking that the increased contributions required of them under the new rules should be declared illegal. By a unanimous judgement of the Irish Court of Queen's Bench, on 29 November 1899, the Petition was dismissed.

New Pension Rules

The new pension rules were significantly different to the old rules.

'Standard Numbers'

The 'Standard Numbers' were abolished.[35] All existing teachers who had been excluded from joining the scheme or contributing for a higher category of pension could, if they desired, pay for pensions corresponding to their classification and thereby qualify for a higher pension.

Service

Recognised service for pension was changed from 'service on retirement on age' to 'retirement on service given', with the consequence that future pensions would show a considerable reduction.[36] Forty years' service would continue to qualify for maximum pension, but if a teacher made contributions for more than forty years, he/she could only count forty years for pension purposes.

The Determination of Ordinary Pension

It was declared that a teacher on retiring from the service (at sixty-five or upwards for a male and at sixty or upwards for a female) would be entitled to an ordinary annual pension of a fixed amount depending on his/her classification. The pension would consist of two portions:

1   an annual sum, deducted from the Teachers' Contribution Account, in respect of the contributions made by the teacher to that fund, and
2   an annual sum three times that amount to be deducted from the Endowment Account.

The maximum pension for a First Class male teacher was reduced from £88 to £60; and for a First Class female teacher from £63 to £47; Second Class teachers' pensions were reduced to £46 and £34 per annum; and Third Class teachers' pensions to £35 and £25.

---

35 Under the 1879 Act the total number of teachers allowed to secure pension privileges at any one time could not exceed 5,300 males and 5,400 females (these were called the 'Standard Numbers').
36 *Irish School Weekly*, 24 November 1928, letter from 'An Mainséalach'

Disablement Pensions

Gratuities to teachers incapacitated through ill-health were replaced by Disablement Pensions, and the qualifying age was raised from thirty to thirty-five years of age.

Death in Service

On the death of a teacher in service the amount of the pension contributions paid by the teacher would be repaid out of the Pension Fund to his/her legal representative, with compound interest at 2.5 per cent per annum.

Related Developments

The Elementary School Teachers (Superannuation) Act, 1898

This Act, which was passed on 8 August 1898 and recognised as a victory for the NUT, sanctioned the establishment of a universal, compulsory, contributory, deferred annuity superannuation scheme for elementary school teachers.

Although the scheme also applied to teachers in Scotland, the Act specifically stated that its provisions did not apply in Ireland.

Civil Service Pension Schemes

Civil servants had achieved a statutory pension scheme as early as 1810. This had been superseded by the 1859 scheme, and by the end of the century they had developed a sophisticated structured scheme.

While the civil servants were enhancing their pension provisions, progress towards developing a definite system of pensions for employees in occupations outside the civil service was slow. This was because the puritan philosophy of self-provision still remained in vogue in Victorian England, particularly among the ruling classes.

A number of events helped to weaken this philosophy: the extension of the franchise in 1867 and 1885; the increasing strength of the trade union movement, which by 1895 included about one-fifth of all adult male workers; a change in public attitudes to an acceptance that people had to be provided for when they could no longer work.[37]

By the end of the nineteenth century the sophisticated pension of civil servants had become the aspiration of all other employees in the public sector, and the far-off dream of most of those in the private sector.

---

37 E. Halévy, *History of the English People in the Nineteenth Century*, Vol. 5, p. 211. Some unions provided a system of benefit, including pensions, for their members, for example, the Amalgamated Society of Engineers. See Report of the Royal Commission on the Poor Law, 1909, pp. 311–12.

Review at the End of the Century

The Expansion of the National School System, 1831–1900

From the date of its establishment in 1831 to the end of the nineteenth century, the national school system in Ireland expanded rapidly. By the end of the school year 1899–1900 there were 8,670 national schools. All denominations had complete control over the provision of schools for their own congregations and provided schools in locations where required; every parish in Ireland had at least two Catholic national schools and some of them had as many as four. The average number of children attending school daily was 584,005.

Supply of Teachers between 1866 and 1900

During the period from 1866 to 1900 a number of factors had considerable influence on teacher supply. The most important of these were the salary reviews, the extension of the length of training, changes in the enrolment requirements for new appointments, the introduction of a pension scheme, and the official sanctioning of denominational training colleges. In 1866, 900 teachers were appointed to the service, but every year thereafter until 1893 the numbers dropped and did not begin to rise again until 1899, when 578 teachers were appointed.[38]

Although teachers in Ireland benefited from considerable increases in remuneration and improved conditions of service during the period 1868 to 1900, the average remuneration still lagged behind the average remuneration of teachers in Great Britain.[39] However, fewer teachers were leaving the service because the improved conditions had made the position of the 'national teacher' more desirable.

The INTO at the End of the Century

The development and strengthening of the national school system was accompanied by the emergence of teachers' and managerial organisations.[40] A crucial factor in teachers' achievement of improvements in their conditions of employment was the establishment of the INTO in 1868. With the INTO, the teachers now had a Central Executive Committee and a central administration to determine policy in the pursuance of legitimate objectives. The teaching

---

38 HMSO, *History of the Vote for Public (Primary) Education*, p. 64. During the school year 1899–1900, of the 578 principals and assistants appointed for the first time, 282 had been trained and 296 were untrained.

39 HMSO, *History of the Vote for Public (Primary) Education*, p. 90. The salary figures are taken from the reports of the Commissioners of National Education for the relevant years.

40 Séamus Ó Buachalla, *Education Policy in Twentieth Century Ireland*, p. 28

profession became increasingly militant and the INTO became an active force in the political scene and succeeded in raising the status of the teacher in society.

INTO Campaigns

At a very early stage the leaders in the INTO recognised that the Commissioners of National Education had no real power. The central power of the Lords of the Treasury over the national school system and over the remuneration of teachers was, to all intents and purposes, almost absolute. It was clear, therefore, that political activity was the only way to get concessions. To achieve its objectives, the CEC organised campaigns on a number of fronts and became increasingly sophisticated at organising them. The following strategies became the template for all campaigns:

1   Local associations were formed in every town throughout the country, and teachers were encouraged to join the organisation.
2   Members were kept informed of developments by their district representatives at association meetings.
3   Local associations were encouraged to hold public meetings and to have local dignitaries and people of influence address them.
4   Every campaign was publicised extensively by the distribution of relevant information through the local and national press; local associations ensured that local newspapers were kept fully briefed, and the writing of letters for publication was encouraged.
5   The CEC lobbied officials in the Education Office, the Resident Commissioner, the Commissioners of National Education, the Chief Secretary, and the Lord Lieutenant.
6   Relations with Irish MPs were established, and the MPs were canvassed extensively and lobbied by teachers in their constituencies. Irish MPs were constantly encouraged by the INTO to pressurise the government to reform the education system in Ireland.
7   Members of the CEC went to London to lobby members of the government.
8   Common fronts were established with other interested parties; on some occasions joint lobbying was carried out with representatives of teachers from Scotland, England and Wales.

INTO Strategy

From the late 1860s up to the end of the century, control of government in Britain passed between the Conservative Party and the Liberal Party. The INTO used this instability, the general unrest in the Irish countryside due to the Land League agitation, and the growing influence of nationalism, to achieve some of its demands.

In 1873 teachers won security of tenure when school managers were obliged to give teachers contract agreements of employment. Even with this protection the INTO, on a number of occasions, had to defend teachers threatened with summary dismissal by school managers, often for spurious and unjust reasons.[41]

Campaigns organised by the INTO resulted in parliament passing The Irish Education Act, of 1892. This Act was a major achievement by the INTO; it dealt exclusively with the remuneration of teachers and granted teachers a considerable increase in income.

The Turn of the Century

The 'payment-by-results' scheme went out of favour in England and Scotland and was abandoned in 1895. Teachers in Ireland used this, and the inequality in the salary and conditions of employment of national teachers in Ireland in comparison with those in Great Britain, to put pressure on the English Parliament to establish a Vice-Regal Commission to report on the Educational System under the Commissioners of National Education in Ireland. The Belmore Commission published its report in 1898. Its recommendations sounded the death-knell of the 'payment-by-results' scheme and resulted in the introduction of a new method of computing teachers' remuneration. It also resulted in a radical revision of the school curriculum.

During the next two decades the INTO would be involved in many disputes with the Education Office, the Resident Commissioner (William Joseph Myles Starkie),[42] the Commissioners of National Education, the Treasury, and the government. As in the past, goals would not be reached nor advances made without confrontation and strife.

---

41 David W. Miller, *Church, State and Nation in Ireland 1898–1921*, pp. 32–34

42 Starkie was a distinguished Catholic academic and a former President of Queen's College, Galway. E. Brian Titley, *Church, State, and the Control of Schooling in Ireland, 1900–44*, p. 17

4

The Starkie Regime up to 1914

The New Rules and Regulations, 1900–1

Introduction

Starkie's period of rule encompassed the transition from rule by the commissioners and Westminster to that by the government of the Irish Free State. His implementation of Treasury policies was marked by considerable disruption in the education sphere and dissatisfaction among teachers.

Even though he was to subsequently claim that he had been assured by Lord Cadogan, the Viceroy, and Gerald Balfour, Chief Secretary, of the enthusiastic support of the government for a revision of the Irish education system, not enough money was provided. It may have been the intention to provide the money for education in Ireland but it was sequestered for other purposes.[1] An extended Boer War and an increasing public service created enormous financial difficulties for the government.[2]

These problems were compounded by the dictatorial rule of Starkie, who appeared to have had complete control delegated to him by the Board. His vigorous promotion of the new rules and regulations engendered much comment and criticism in the national daily newspapers from school managers, from the INTO and from teachers, whom he characterised 'as ignorant and malevolent';[3] and he refused to meet deputations from the INTO. Because of cutbacks, restrictions on promotions, the non-award of increments, and changes in conditions of employment, the Starkie regime marked a period of general unrest in the teaching profession.[4]

The Treasury

The influence of the Treasury was evident in every matter concerning the financing of education and, particularly, whenever a revision of the conditions

---

1 'The history of Irish primary and secondary education during the last decade', an inaugural address delivered on 3 July 1911 by W. J. M. Starkie on the occasion of the inauguration of university extension features in the Queen's University, Belfast
2 Thomas Pakenham, *The Boer War*, p. 512
3 Dill Committee Report, CEC Report, Congress 1913, p. 37
4 INTO, *A Plan for Education*

of employment or a restructuring of teachers' salaries was under consideration; every opportunity was availed of to keep costs to a minimum and to use control of the purse-strings to bring about changes in the system of education in Ireland.

Position of the INTO at the Beginning of the Century

Although the CEC was successful in getting a pension scheme and increased salaries for all teachers, paradoxically, less than half of the 13,000 teachers in the service were subscribing members of the organisation. There were a number of reasons for this situation:

1   The concept of joining trade unions was fairly new.
2   A number of people could not afford to pay the subscription, or did not want to.
3   Many of the Catholic hierarchy were opposed to trade unions, and a number of them were particularly opposed to teachers being members of the INTO.

In 1900 the bishops exhorted teachers not to join the organisation, attributing anti-clericalism and the promotion of secularism to its leaders. The CEC was accused of not having a correct and becoming attitude towards the bishops and priests of the Church, and of no longer being in harmony with the principles of faith, or with their duties as members of the Catholic Church.[5]

The view expressed by the hierarchy appears to have had an effect because within a matter of weeks the CEC issued a circular stating that 'any other position than that of a correct and becoming attitude towards the Bishops and Priests of Ireland shall never find sympathy, favour or toleration with us'.[6]

Notwithstanding these differences, the INTO was supported by the bishops and the school managers in many of its battles with the commissioners and the Treasury; but in matters of power and control over schools, of which they were patrons, the Catholic hierarchy brooked no interference.

Report of the Belmore Commission, 1898

On 25 January 1897 parliament appointed a Vice-Regal Commission, with Somerset Richard, Earl Belmore, as chairman, to inquire into and 'report on the educational system under the Board of National Education in Ireland'.

The main recommendations of the commission were accepted, and in April 1900 the Resident Commissioner issued 'The New Rules and Regulations, 1900–1', in which:

---

5   Pastoral Letter issued by the Catholic Hierarchy, published in the *Irish Teachers' Journal*, 6 October 1900, p. 4
6   INTO Circular, October 1900

- a new, radically revised, curricular programme was promulgated
- the results scheme was replaced by a system of whole-class inspection
- a completely new method for the computation of teachers' remuneration was introduced, and
- a new scheme for the promotion of teachers was implemented.[7]

The 'Provisional' Remuneration of Teachers from 1900

Salaries and Promotion

Early in 1900 the Education Office issued a circular with details of 'provisional' revised salary scales, a new method for computing salaries and a new promotional procedure that purported to incorporate into one payment all the previous separate payments.

It was proposed that the system of categorising teachers in 'classes' for salary purposes would be abolished and that, henceforth, they would be categorised into 'grades'. A teacher's salary would consist of a basic salary determined by the grade attained and, in addition, the payment of a capitation grant.

Under the 'grade' system, no teacher in a school with an average attendance less than seventy pupils could be promoted to the First Section of First Grade. In addition, if enrolment fell below thirty, the salary of the teacher would be reduced, even if this happened due to circumstances beyond the teacher's control.

Teachers appointed before 1 April 1900 would receive a 'consolidated salary', which would determine their grade for salary purposes. Teachers appointed after 1 April were given a considerably lower rate of pay, £52 for men and £39 for women. Teachers could no longer gain promotion by passing an examination and all teachers appointed as principals in the future would have to be trained.

Assistant Teachers

Under new Rule 9, no assistant teacher appointed after 1 April 1901 would be eligible for promotion beyond Third Grade and he or she would not receive the 1892 bonus of £9 for men and £7 10s. for women. Furthermore, Rule 20 stated that the initial salary of an assistant promoted to principal would only be that of an assistant.

While the opportunity for employment as an assistant was improved by a reduction in the average attendance required for the appointment of an assistant from seventy to sixty, this was nullified by other adverse conditions:

- the yearly average attendance would be substituted for quarterly averages
- the number of days of vacation would be reduced from forty to thirty per year

---

7 Revised Programme of Instruction in National Schools, published in an appendix to the Annual Report of the Commissioners of National Education, 1902, HC 1903, XXI

- the days on which the average attendance was under one-third of the monthly averages would have to be deducted from the vacation entitlement.

Reaction to the 'Provisional' Salary Proposals

The word 'provisional' was used in the title of the circular on salary proposals, and the Education Office indicated that these proposals would apply until such time as permanent structures could be prepared and issued.

As the implementation of these proposals would affect every teacher and have implications for every school, the INTO, the Catholic and Church of Ireland Archbishops of Dublin, school managers' associations and individual commissioners objected strenuously to the Education Office, and an acrimonious public dispute ensued.

The Church of Ireland authorities were very aggrieved as 75 per cent of the schools under their management had an average attendance of less than seventy, and the majority of teachers in their schools would be permanently excluded from attaining the maximum of the proposed salaries.

The Education Office proceeded to implement the new salary system but, due to both the number and the variation of the old payments, the computation of the average salary proved very difficult. The figure arrived at was, in most cases, a cause for great dissatisfaction.

Starkie was obliged to reconsider the situation. At the beginning of April 1901 he issued New Rules and Regulations, 1900–1, to operate retrospectively from 1 April 1900.[8] The commissioners were optimistic that the revised retrospective proposals would resolve the problems regarding teachers' pay.

The New Rules and Regulations, 1900–1

The revised rules set down in great detail the official code governing administration of the system of education in schools. The code was arranged under five section headings:

Section I:	Rules Applicable to all Principal and Assistant Teachers
Section II:	Rules Specially Applicable to Principal and Assistant Teachers Appointed on or after the 1 April 1900
Section III:	Rules Specially Applicable to Principal and Assistant Teachers Appointed Prior to the 1 April 1900
Section IV:	Rules Applicable to Convent and Monastery Capitation Schools and to Special Teachers
Section V:	Rules Applicable to the Examination, Inspection, and Organisation of the Schools Programme

8 Office of National Education (March 1900), New Scheme of Payments to Teachers and of Examination and Organisation of National Schools

Salaries and Promotion

As in 1900, different salary structures and conditions of employment would apply to teachers appointed before and after 1 April 1900. All principal and assistant teachers (except teachers in convent or monastery schools paid by capitation rate) were assigned to one of four 'grades' for salary and promotional purposes: First of First Grade, Second of First Grade, Second Grade or Third Grade. The concept of granting incremental credit was introduced when a special Continued Good Service Salary was created to facilitate the payment of triennial increments as a supplement to a teacher's grade salary. Teachers would also receive an Annual Residual Capitation Grant, which would be determined by the grade attained by the teacher.

The New Salary Structure

Grade Salary

The grade salary was dependent on the average attendance in the school:

- Third Grade: an average attendance of between twenty and twenty-nine pupils
- Second Grade: an average attendance of between thirty and forty-nine pupils
- Second of First Grade: an average attendance of between fifty and sixty-nine pupils
- First of First Grade: an average attendance of seventy-plus pupils

The salaries for men varied from £56 for Third Grade to £139 for First of First Grade, and the respective figures for women were from £44 to £114. Teachers could also endeavour to qualify for 'Continued Good Service Triennial Increments'.

Continued Good Service Salary

The concept of granting incremental credit was already in place in all other government employments, but the principle was to operate in a different way for teachers. Only teachers in schools with an average attendance of twenty pupils or more could qualify for a triennial increment.[9]

The number of increments in the different grades varied between one and three, and the value of the increments varied between £7 and £12 for men and between £7 and £9 for women.

The Annual Residual Capitation Grant

The amount of the Annual Residual Capitation Grant given to a school was governed by the average attendance in the school, and it was apportioned

---

9 In effect, the award of 'Continued Good Service Salary Triennial Increments' was at the discretion of the inspectors.

between the principal and the assistants according to an established scale. In a school with an average attendance of eighty and a staff of a principal and one assistant, the principal got 60/80 and the assistant got 20/80. In a school with an average attendance of 230 and a staff of a principal and four assistants, the principal got 90/230 and each assistant got 35/230.

Small Schools

Teachers in schools with attendance of under thirty pupils had their remuneration restructured:

1   Schools with an average attendance under ten: teachers received a capitation grant of £1 15s. and a Residual Capitation Grant for each pupil in average attendance. The capitation grant was £3 10s. for schools on islands remote from the mainland.
2   Schools with an average attendance of ten and under twenty pupils: teachers received a fixed salary of £44 per annum (the rate for a Third Grade female principal), together with an Annual Residual Capitation Grant (1900) for each pupil in average attendance, but they were not entitled to Continued Good Service Salary. It was stated that it was desirable that teachers in these schools should be women.
3   Schools with an average attendance of twenty and under thirty: teachers were paid the same salary as assistants, i.e. the salary for a Third Grade principal.

Assistant Teachers

The average attendance required for the appointment of an assistant was reduced from seventy to sixty. Male assistant teachers were granted a fixed salary of £56 per annum, with the possibility of rising to a maximum of £77 by triennial Continued Good Service Increments of £7, and female assistants were granted a fixed salary of £44 per annum, rising by triennial increments of £7 to £65. These salary scales and increments were the same as those awarded to Third Grade principals. Further, assistants in the service before 1 April 1900 were entitled to the 1892 long-service bonus of £9 or £7 10s., which would give a maximum salary of £86 per annum for men and £72 10s. for women. Assistants were also entitled to a share of the Annual Residual Capitation Grant.

Capitation Convent and Monastery Schools

The conductors of capitation convent and monastery schools received annual capitation grants (exclusive of the Residual Capitation Grant) in lieu of all emoluments from the State for work done during ordinary school hours. Three rates of capitation grant were introduced with effect from 1 April 1900, namely, 25s., 30s., and 35s. per pupil.

Additional Subjects

Payments at specified rates were offered for approved extra subjects taught before or after regular school hours. Not more than two extra subjects would be paid for without the special sanction of the Board. The teachers had to be approved by the inspector to be competent to teach the subject, and the pupils had to pass a test administered by him. The approved subjects and fees were as follows:

Subject	Fee per Pupil
Irish Language	10s
French	5s
Latin	5s
Mathematics	10s
Instrumental Music	5s

Preliminary Circular to Inspectors

The Education Office issued a confidential circular to inspectors which laid down in great detail the inspectors' duties in applying the new rules, regulations and salary conditions.[10]

T. J. O'Connell recounts that under the authority granted by this new code, the inspectors inflicted something like a reign of terror on teachers.[11] It gave them effective control over the awarding of increments and the sanctioning of promotion by operating a system of reprimands and adverse reports against teachers.

The Implementation of the New Salary Arrangements

Salary Scales

A number of anomalies became apparent when the new salary scales were applied.

1   The new basic salary rates were fixed at too low a level, with the result that the average salary of a male principal teacher with two years' training and three years' service, who received £73 10s. 2d. pre-April 1900, was £63 4s. 9d.; the figures for females were £52 17s. 1d. and £50 13s. 3d., respectively.

2   Inter-graded teachers: Where the figure of the consolidated salary did not coincide with any point in the new salary scales, the teacher was placed between points.

10 Office of National Education (April 1901) Preliminary Confidential Circular to Inspectors, New Scheme of Payments to Teachers and of Examination and Organisation of National Schools

11 T. J. O'Connell, *A Hundred Years of Progress*, p. 405

Thus, a man with a consolidated salary of £75 was placed in Grade III and had to wait for a further three years for an increase of another £2 to bring him to the maximum of the grade.

3　New appointments: Teachers who changed school or who were first appointed during the first three years of the implementation of the new scales, 1900–03, had problems with their salary placement.

Regrading

Before 1900 a teacher in a school with an average attendance of thirty-five could reach First of First Class. Under the new system, irrespective of inspectors' reports or ability, an average attendance of

- seventy was required for promotion to the First Division of Grade I
- fifty was required for promotion to the Second Division of Grade I
- thirty was required for promotion to Grade II.

This system resulted in many teachers being ranked lower than they had been under the class system. Only 10 per cent of principals could ever reach the top of Grade I, and a teacher who had been in Class I pre-1900 could now find him/herself placed in Grade II or even in Grade III because the consolidated salary was less than the maximum of these grades, and the new average attendance regulations prevented advancement.

Increments

Grave dissatisfaction was expressed regarding the number of increments, their value and the varied number of years between each increment in the different grades, which resulted in teachers taking a considerable number of years to reach the maximum of the salary scale.

Principals and Promotion

From 1 April 1900 promotion from a lower to a higher grade, which had been available by examination and service, would now depend on (a) training, (b) position in school, (c) ability and general attainments, (d) good service, and (e) seniority.

As well as the efficiency rating, principals seeking promotion had to overcome two further obstacles: a system of average attendance and standard numbers. With the standard numbers the commissioners could determine, from time to time, the number of teachers in every grade above the Third Grade. When the fixed number for a grade was reached, a teacher could be promoted but the extra salary would not be paid until a vacancy occurred due to the death or resignation of a teacher in that grade. Such promoted teachers became the 'paper promoted' teachers.

Assistants and Promotion

A trained teacher, appointed prior to 1 April 1900 and placed in the Second Class, was now placed in Grade III, and the opportunity for promotion was reduced.

Assistants appointed after 1 April 1900 were not eligible for promotion beyond Third Grade unless they were trained, even though their qualifications were equal to those of the principal.

The appointment of Work Mistresses, Industrial Teachers, or Junior Literary Assistants was discontinued and a new class of teacher, called a Manual Instructress could be appointed to give instruction in needlework, kindergarten, hand-and-eye training, and object lessons at the capitation rate of £1 for every girl in average attendance.

The New Salary Placements

Officials in the Education Office experienced considerable difficulty applying the new salary provisions, and it took over two years to implement the new system in full. Many teachers disputed their placements and complained that the calculations had been incorrect and that all their entitlements had not been included in their emoluments.

The INTO sought redress for teachers' grievances through every means available: negotiation, direct representation, and appeals to MPs. In reality, less than 1 per cent of complaints were re-examined and only a small number had their special problems resolved; the rest were ignored or not responded to satisfactorily.

This salary format for the payment of teachers was to remain in operation for twenty years and while some of the anomalies were removed or their effects ameliorated, most of them remained unresolved.

The Revised School Programme

Difficulties arose with the implementation of the new programme because of the number of subjects offered and the scarcity or, in the case of some subjects, the complete absence of teachers competent to teach them. While organisers were appointed to give short-term courses at various centres, and some experts were brought over from England to give courses in kindergarten, drawing and science, the amount of in-service training was inadequate. Complaints by teachers eventually compelled the Board to issue a Revised Programme of Primary Instruction to schools in 1904.[12] The school programme was revised for a third time in 1914 and remained in place until 1922.

---

12 The Education Office, *The New Curriculum*

Education and Teachers, 1900–14

Attempts to Reform Irish Education

By 1900 the government was facing political and practical problems in Great Britain, with demands to provide post-primary education facilities for the great number of pupils who were completing elementary schools. In response, the Conservative government introduced the Education (England) Act, 1902,[13] under which a Local Education Authority (LEA) was established in each county or county borough council area to provide a comprehensive scheme of education under a single central authority. LEAs had power to levy a rate for education, and up to 50 per cent of education costs were raised in this manner.

Chief Secretary Wyndham, 1904

In Ireland, the sharing of responsibility for financing the school system by central and local bodies was never satisfactorily resolved from the Treasury's point of view, and most of the money continued to come from central sources. Government circles considered that the reformed English educational system could provide a blueprint for possible action in Ireland.

In 1904 Chief Secretary Wyndham proposed a restructuring of the whole Irish education system, but these plans were strongly and successfully opposed by the Catholic Church and Irish MPs.[14]

The Dale Report, 1904

In March 1902 F. H. Dale, an inspector from the Board of Education in London, was appointed to carry out an inquiry into the Irish national school system.

In his report, Dale drew attention to 'certain radical defects in the general conditions under which the schools work and in their organisation, which are bound both to impair the efficiency of any syllabus of instruction however well devised, and to render the expenditure of public money on education wasteful and unproductive.' He was critical of the 'deplorable' lack of local interest in primary education and advocated local authority funding for national education. He found that the instruction in Irish national schools 'compared favourably with that of similar English schools in point of accuracy, but very unfavourable in point of intelligence of method and aim of teachers'[15] This report was ignored by the Resident Commissioner.

---

13 It became known as the Balfour Education Act. Arthur James, 1st Earl of Balfour, was Prime Minister between 1902 and 1905. He had been Chief Secretary for Ireland (1887–91) and earned the nickname 'Bloody Balfour' from the Irish; he had been an opponent of Home Rule and had instigated a regime of coercion and repression.
14 State Paper Office, Dublin Castle, CSORP 1904 10032
15 Report of F. H. Dale on Primary Education in Ireland, 1904, HC 1904 (Cd 1981), XX, 947

Junior Assistant Mistresses

In 1906 sanction was granted for the appointment of a new class of teachers, Junior Assistant Mistresses (JAMs). They could be appointed in one-teacher schools, with an average attendance of between thirty-five and forty-nine pupils, to teach the regular programme to the junior classes, singing to all the pupils where required, and needlework to the girls. They were appointed at a salary of £24 per annum.

The Irish Councils Bill, 1907

The Irish Councils Bill of 1907, introduced into parliament on 7 May 1907 by the newly appointed Chief Secretary, Augustine Birrell, proposed the amalgamation of eight of the forty-five boards which administered government grants, putting them under the control of a central council.

The Roman Catholic hierarchy saw this as the long-threatened Irish education reform bill and objected strongly to it. Public meetings were held to protest against it and at the Irish Party Convention on 21 May 1907 a proposal by John Redmond, leader of the Irish Party, that the bill be rejected was passed unanimously. Shortly afterwards the government withdrew it.

Increments and Promotions, 1906

A confidential circular, dated 6 March 1906, was issued to inspectors setting down 'special regulations' governing the award of the triennial increments. These special regulations were promoted by the commissioners, on the instructions of the Treasury, to save money.[16]

Clear evidence began to emerge that the inspectors were abusing the system to deny teachers increments and promotion. A teacher could not be promoted unless three successive annual reports from the inspector marked 'Good' had been received.

Complaints lodged with the Board and Starkie, alleging that inspectors were using unjustifiable reasons to deny the award of increments, did not receive any sympathy and were invariably dismissed.[17] The denial of increments had serious consequence for retiring teachers as pensions were computed on reduced pay.[18]

16 INTO, *Eighty Years of Progress*

17 Catherine M. Mahon, Presidential Address, INTO Congress, 1914

18 Information from Memorandum of Irish Teachers' Pensions, furnished by the INTO to the commissioners at their request in 1920. Due to inflation, a pre-war pension of £41 had only the purchasing power of £16 1s. 6d. in 1922.

Augustine Birrell, Chief Secretary for Ireland, 1906–1916

In the general election in the spring of 1906 the Liberals won a sweeping victory and replaced the Tories.[19] James Bryce was appointed Chief Secretary for Ireland and replaced by Augustine Birrell early in 1907.

On 18 April the Chancellor of the Exchequer provided £200,000 in his budget for 'necessitous school areas in England'. A sum of £500,000 was made available to Scotland for similar purposes, but nothing was provided for Irish education.

In November the CEC submitted a comprehensive memorandum to the Chancellor setting down particulars of the INTO claims, which were estimated to cost £500,000.[20] The commissioners submitted proposals that were estimated to cost £133,000 and recommended that most of the money should be allocated on a capitation basis, without differentiation as to the payment for men or women.[21] These proposals were not acceptable to the INTO as principals of large schools with greater attendance would get most of the money.

The Birrell Grant, 1908

In April 1908 the Treasury wrote a confidential letter to the commissioners informing them that Birrell had obtained a supplementary grant of £114,000 and advising them on how it wished the money to be divided. It proposed that £100,000 of the grant would go to principals in schools with an attendance of thirty-five or over and that the remaining £14,000 would be given as a bonus to the principals of schools with an attendance of seventy or over.[22]

The CEC issued a press statement on 29 June protesting 'in the strongest possible manner against the inadequacy of the supplementary estimate and against the method of its allocation'. It was in favour of an equal distribution of the grant.

The supplementary estimate was finally moved in the House of Commons by Birrell on 2 July 1908 and was fiercely attacked by the Irish MPs, both Nationalist and Unionist. Faced with such formidable opposition, Birrell was eventually compelled to withdraw his estimate, promising that he would again consult with the commissioners.

The Lord Lieutenant requested the assistance of the commissioners in drawing up a scheme that would embody the principle of a capitation grant while ensuring that assistants would get some share of the grant and no teacher would be ruled out.

In response, at a specially convened meeting on 21 July, the commissioners recommended that the grant should be distributed under four headings:

19 Herbert Henry Asquith was Liberal Prime Minister from 1908 to 1916.
20 *Irish School Weekly*, 14 December 1907, p. 540
21 MCNEI 1907, 19 November, p. 435
22 T. J. O'Connell, *A Hundred Years of Progress*, p. 162

1   First, the grade salaries of all teachers (principals and assistants) would be increased by an annual supplement at the following rates:
    - £10 to teachers (male and female) in Grade I1.
    - £8 to teachers (male and female) in the Grade I2.
    - £7 to teachers (male and female) in the Grade II
    - £6 to teachers (male and female) in the Grade III
    - This proposal was in effect a recommendation of an equal pay award to female and male teachers in each category. The commissioners estimated that this recommendation would absorb £82,687 of the proposed £114,000 grant.

2   Second, those convents and other schools paid solely on the capitation system would receive 'an annual supplemental capitation grant of five shillings per unit on the average attendance in augmentation of the present scale of capitation grants'. It was estimated that this recommendation would cost a further £13,000.

3   Third, principals of large schools would be rewarded in exactly the same manner as had been suggested originally and these awards should be contingent on satisfactory inspectors' reports. This recommendation would cost £11,000.

4   Fourth, 'an annual grant of £4 in augmentation of the present scale of salaries' would be paid 'to junior assistant mistresses with two years' efficient service'. This new feature, estimated to cost approximately £3,313, was probably included to satisfy the Chief Secretary's request that all teachers be included under the grant.[23]

On 31 July, INTO representatives, accompanied by Irish MPs, both Nationalist and Unionist, met with Birrell. They thanked him for his personal efforts in securing the £114,000 but expressed their disappointment at its inadequacy. Birrell promised to give favourable consideration to the INTO equal division plan.

The Treasury, not being in agreement with all of the commissioners' proposals, re-submitted a revised plan for the distribution of the £114,000 grant:

1   £92,976 of the total grant was to go as a supplement to the grade salaries (principals and assistants) at the following rates:
    - £10 to teachers (male and female) in Grade I1.
    - £10 to teachers (male and female) in the Grade I2.
    - £7 to teachers (male and female) in the Grade II.
    - £7 to teachers (male and female) in the Grade III.

2   £17,000 was to go in extra capitation grants to convent and other schools paid solely on capitation.

3   £4,024 was to go in grants of £4 to the salaries of Junior Assistant Mistresses with two years' efficient service.[24]

---

23 MCNEI 1908, p. 293

24 *Irish School Weekly*, 1 August 1908, p. 765

This equitable distribution of the grant was generally acceptable to all teachers. The commissioners, however, were not pleased and passed a resolution protesting strongly against the revised plan.

Review of the Birrell Grant

The Birrell Grant was the only general salary increase given to teachers between the introduction of the new scales in 1900 and the award of the first war bonus from 1 July 1916.[25] It was an equal pay award, giving men and women in each grade the same amount, and it established a precedent for the payment of equal war bonuses in 1916.

In the negotiations the INTO, recognising that the commissioners' influence had declined, had by-passed them and gone directly to the powerbase in London to secure its objective of equal distribution.

Promotion of National Teachers, 1908

In June 1908 all inspectors were instructed to enforce the regulation limiting the number of teachers who could be promoted to a higher grade for salary purposes. They were instructed that promotions could not be sanctioned unless a vacancy occurred in that Grade, due to the demotion, resignation or death of a teacher who had been at that Grade.[26]

In January 1909 the commissioners sent out a circular setting down the principle for the determination of seniority of assistants. This principle applies to the present day, i.e. the order of seniority of assistants is determined by the length of unbroken service in the school in which they are employed.[27]

Teachers were further exasperated in 1912 when the commissioners introduced a rule prohibiting, except under special sanction, the promotion of men who had not been trained in a recognised training college.

Congress 1912

A decision was made at Congress 1912 to mount a major political campaign demanding a public inquiry into the whole question of national education in Ireland.[28] Matters came to a head when Eamonn Mansfield, Vice-President of the INTO and principal of Cullen National School, Co. Tipperary, was summarily dismissed by the commissioners on 15 October 1912. He had made a speech protesting against the treatment of teachers by a new inspector; the

---

25 T. J. O'Connell, *A Hundred Years of Progress*, p. 164
26 Office of National Education (June 1908) Notice to Managers and Teachers of National Schools
27 Office of National Education (June 1909) Circular to Managers and Teachers of National Schools
28 CEC Report to Congress 1912

speech was published in *The Clonmel Chronicle*. Demands by the Education Office for a retraction and an apology were not complied with and Mansfield was dismissed.

The INTO entered into a public campaign seeking Mansfield's reinstatement, but all requests were ignored. Mansfield was appointed General Secretary of the INTO in 1913 and held this position until 1915 when his teaching position was restored.[29]

Vice-Regal Committee of Inquiry in 1913 (The Dill Committee)

Teachers' dissatisfaction with salary placement and promotion procedures became so serious that, under pressure from the Irish MPs, the government established a Committee of Inquiry in January 1913, under the chairmanship of Sir Samuel Dill, Professor of Greek in Queen's University, Belfast, to inquire and report on the methods adopted by the inspectors when awarding increments and recommending the promotion of teachers, and the facilities for appeal and means of access to the Board that were allowed to teachers.[30]

The committee's report condemned Starkie's administration, finding grave defects in the organisation of the inspectorate and in relations between inspectors and teachers. Evidence showed that in the course of a year upwards of 900 appeals against inspectors' reports were sent to the Resident Commissioner's office, where most of them were ignored.[31] The teachers were elated in that they had been vindicated, and the INTO claimed that it was the most damaging indictment against practically everything that had been done for the past fourteen years.[32]

The committee presented a long list of recommendations referring to promotion, grading and changes in the inspectoral system.[33]

The commissioners were distinctly hostile to the report and they issued a statement supporting Starkie, the Education Office officials and the

29 He led the negotiations on the 1913 Pension Rules revision and was the author of the INTO memorandum on pensions sent to the commissioners in 1920.

30 Vice-Regal Committee of Inquiry into Primary Education (Ireland), 1913 (Dill Committee), Final Report HC 1914 (Cd 7235) XXVIII, 1081. Professor Jeremiah Henly of Kildare Street Training College was appointed to the commission. He had played an important role in the establishment of the INTO in 1868 and had continued to write in the *Irish Teachers' Journal* under the pen name 'Beta'. Starkie objected to his appointment, but without success. See T. J. O'Connell, *A Hundred Years of Progress*, pp. 406, 454, and the confidential evidence submitted by Starkie to the commission. It is worth noting that the time span between the foundation of the INTO in 1868 and the Dill Committee in 1913 is forty-five years.

31 Catherine M. Mahon, Presidential Address, INTO Congress, 1914

32 Editorial, *Irish School Weekly*, 7 February 1914

33 Vice-Regal Committee of Inquiry into Primary Education (Ireland), 1913 (Dill Committee), Final Report HC 1914 (Cd 7235) XXVIII, 1081

inspectorate. The only concession they were prepared to make was that if the money was made available by the Treasury, the Board would consider the following recommendations:

- that increments should be paid annually rather than triennially and that they should be automatic in the absence of an adverse report
- that promotions should be more rapid
- that additional inspectors should be appointed.

The commencement of the First World War on 4 August 1914 resulted in the suspension of negotiations on proposals for increased salaries.

National Teachers' Pensions 1900–14

From 1 January 1900 teachers were, in everything but name, truly public servants; the government had assumed their total remuneration and their pension scheme was a vital element in their conditions of employment. However, these conditions were not as good as those for civil servants. The pensions paid to the lowest civil service grades were higher than those paid to teachers.[34]

The objective of the INTO was to get a similar scheme for its members and, notwithstanding the ongoing difficulties between teachers and the Resident Commissioner, the government was influenced by a number of factors to grant teachers a revised scheme to come into effect from 1 October 1914.

Average Pensions, 1907

Teachers' average pension figures for the year 1906–07 were as follows:[35]

Pension	Male, Average			Female, Average		
	£	s	d	£	s	d
Compulsory	47	0	0	36	3	10
Voluntary	35	17	7	23	17	0
Disability		6	17	6	4	5 0
Overall average	38	12	9	28	10	0

34 *The Return of Civil Service Superannuation and Retirement Allowances, 1904–5*, a volume of some 100 pages, from which extracts were published in *The Schoolmaster*, 17 December 1904, p. 1222

35 CEC Report to Congress 1909: voluntary retirements numbered 59, 25 males and 34 females; disability retirements numbered 20, 8 males and 12 females.

Teachers were very dissatisfied with regard to their low pensions and this dissatisfaction was added to when male civil servants were granted extra benefits under the Superannuation Act of 1908; civil servants were now entitled to gratuities on death in service and a lump sum on retirement. However, to ensure that this new benefit would not incur extra Exchequer expenditure, pensions would henceforth be assessed on eightieths of the retirement salary and the payment of a lump sum instead of being calculated on sixtieths and no lump sum.

Estimates, 1912

Early in 1912, Lloyd George promised an INTO deputation that he would consider putting the Pension Fund on a sound financial basis at an early date. The subsequent estimates provided a sum of £25,000, in addition to the £18,000 annual grant, and it was further agreed to provide an amount equal to 15 per cent of the expenditure from the fund during the previous year.[36] This was not sufficient to meet the claims made but it was equivalent to the sums voted for similar purposes in England and Scotland.

The New Pension Scheme, 1914

The CEC established a Pensions Sub-Committee to negotiate a new scheme with the Chancellor of the Exchequer. After several months' delay, discussions commenced in June 1913 and, following long and arduous negotiations, rules for a revised scheme were agreed.

The INTO had finally achieved one of its main objectives: a superannuation scheme for teachers based on the principles that underpinned the civil service scheme. Pensions would now be based on the actual service given by the teacher and computed on his/her average annual salary for the three completed years prior to retirement.[37] However, the pension would be calculated on eightieths, no lump sums would be paid, and the scheme would be contributory.

All previous rules and regulations were withdrawn and the new scheme became operative with effect from 1 October 1914. The provisions were also made available to teachers who had retired on or after 1 April 1900.[38]

---

36 INTO, *Teachers' Pension Fund: Report of the Actuarial Investigation*, 1926

37 In a letter addressed to the President of the INTO on 12 December 1913, H. P. Hamilton, Secretary to the Treasury, set down the terms which the Chancellor, Lloyd George, was prepared to concede by way of a final offer to resolve teachers' pension problem. *INTO Report of the Actuarial Investigation*, p. 27

38 Even though the terms of the scheme had been agreed before the First World War commenced in August 1914, the date for the commencement of the scheme was delayed to 1 October. The late date was to have disastrous consequences for Irish teachers when it came to the implementation of the Pensions (Increase) Act of 1920.

A: The Pension Accounts

The Teachers' Pension Fund would continue to comprise of 'The Teachers' Contribution Account' and 'The Endowment Account', as laid down in the Act of 1898.

It was agreed that the premium would be a percentage of the average salary of the teacher as at the end of the previous school year, and having been determined would remain unaltered for a period of five years. The percentage would vary depending on the teacher's grade, and would be as follows:

1   5 per cent from teachers in First Grade, First Division
2   4.5 per cent from teachers in First Grade, Second Division
3   4 per cent from teachers in Second Grade
4   3.5 per cent from teachers in Third Grade.[39]

The following table sets out the rate of contribution for the first premium period:

Grade	Average Salary			Contribution			
	1913–14			**Rate**		**Amount**	
	£	**s**	**d**	**per cent**	**£**	**s**	**d**
Men:							
First Grade, First Division	192	1	10	5	9	12	4
First Grade, Second Division	149	14	0	4.5	6	15	0
Second Grade	120	3	5	4	4	16	4
Third Grade	84	4	8	3.5	2	19	0
Women:							
First Grade, First Division	158	6	9	5	7	18	8
First Grade, Second Division	125	19	2	4.5	5	13	8
Second Grade	102	7	8	4	4	2	0
Third Grade	69	10	7	3.5	2	9	0

B: Eligibility

All serving teachers had to sign a form signifying that they wished to opt in or out of the new scheme. Teachers temporarily out of the service at the date of commencement were treated as existing teachers. Service by a teacher in any of the naval or military forces of the Crown during the war would be considered service for the purposes of the Rules.

---

39 Pension Rules and Regulations, 1914

Teachers who had retired between 1 April 1900 and 1 October 1914 were given the option of joining the new scheme. If they joined their recalculated pensions would apply from the 1 October 1914. Teachers who had retired on or before 31 March 1900 were not allowed to join the new scheme.

C: Service

Service for pension purposes was considered to be any period after the age of eighteen years for which the teacher received salary. Ten years' service remained as the minimum period for the award of a pension and forty years' service was required for the maximum pension. All teachers would have to retire on the last day of the quarter in which they reached their sixty-fifth birthday. The 'normal' retiring age for women remained at sixty, but women classified as 'efficient' could continue to sixty-five.[40]

Service as a monitor, a JAM, or a lay assistant in a convent or monastery school, or as a teacher in an industrial or workhouse school, or in any school outside of Ireland could not be considered for pension purposes.

A teacher who left the service for any reason, or was dismissed, and who was not entitled to a pension, could claim the return of contributions made, but no interest would be paid.

Where a teacher retired from the service prior to the compulsory retirement age of sixty-five and received a pension, if he/she re-entered the service the pension ceased. On retiring a second time, service prior to the first retirement and during the second period of employment was used in calculating the new pension.

D: Pensions

Ordinary Pensions

A teacher's pension would be calculated at the rate of one-eightieth of average annual 'income'[41] for the three years ending on 31 March prior to retirement, multiplied by the number of 'completed years of service',[42] up to a maximum of 40 years' service. The maximum pension was, therefore, equivalent to one-half of the average income over the last three completed years of service.[43] It was determined that the minimum pension paid to a teacher should be £13 per annum.

No gratuities of any kind would be payable to any teacher on retirement, nor could pensions be commuted for a lump sum, as was sometimes allowed under

---

40 In practice, extensions were given as a matter of course.

41 Income included actual salary, capitation and extra fees; it did not include evening school fees or the value of a free residence.

42 A 'completed year' did not mean a calendar year. A completed year of service could be made good by a period of service during the following school year.

43 Pension Rules and Regulations, 1914

previous pension regulations. This provision did not affect the payment of gratuities on death in service.

Voluntary Retirement Pensions

A teacher who had reached fifty-five years of age and who had thirty-five years of recognised service could retire 'voluntarily' and be granted a pension based on eightieths of the average income. A teacher with ten years' service could retire at sixty years of age and qualify for a pension.

Disablement Pensions

A teacher over the age of thirty-five and under fifty-five if a male, and fifty if a female, deemed incapable of discharging his/her duties due to an infirmity of mind or body that was likely to be permanent, could qualify for a 'Disablement Pension'. The Disablement Pension consisted of one-eighteeth of annual income (calculated as above) for each completed year of service.

A Disablement Pension could be assigned partly to the institution or person having care of the teacher and partly for the benefit of the wife, husband or relatives of the teacher.

Inability Pension

An Inability Pension, based on eightieths, could be awarded to a teacher who was over fifty years of age and was removed from the service owing to an inability to discharge his/her duties efficiently.[44]

Death in Service

On the death of a teacher in service, the amount of the pension premiums paid by the teacher would be repaid out of the Pension Fund to his/her legal representative, with compound interest at 2.5 per cent per annum.[45] If a teacher died so soon after retiring on pension that he had not drawn by way of pension an amount equal to the amount of his premiums plus compound interest, the balance necessary to make up this amount would be paid to the next-of-kin.

E: Claims

A claim for any type of pension had to be submitted to the Superintendent of the Teachers' Pension Fund within one year of leaving the teaching service.

---

44 A Disability or Inability Pension could be reduced if the circumstances which led to the infirmity or inefficiency had been in whole or in part due to the teacher's own negligence.

45 Pension Rules and Regulations, 1914

The 1914 Rules

The benefits of the new pension scheme were not as good as those enjoyed by civil servants and other public officials, but they were considerably better than those under the 1898 rules. The male civil servant scheme had the following advantages over the teachers' scheme:

- it was non-contributory
- on retirement civil servants could get a maximum pension of half of the retirement salary and a lump sum of one-and-a-half years' salary, which together were deemed to be equal to a pension of two thirds of salary
- civil servants retiring on disability got a pension and a lump sum
- on death in service a gratuity was paid to the estate
- special benefits were paid to civil servants compelled to retire with less than ten years' service.

Under the new rules teachers had to pay an increased premium, and the period of contributions was extended from forty years to the date of retirement. Even though teachers could now pay forty-five years' contributions, only forty years would be counted for pension purposes.

Fixing teachers' contribution as a percentage of salary ensured that as salaries increased the amount transferred to the 'Teachers' Contribution Account' also increased. No provision was made for an automatic increase of contribution by the government to 'The Endowment Account' to cover increased pension liabilities. The funding problem of the Pension Fund continued to persist and, in order to resolve the problem, the Saorstát government converted the teachers' superannuation scheme into a non-contributory scheme in 1934 and assumed liability for all pension payments.

Review of the Period 1900–1914

New rules and regulations were issued in 1900 which changed the manner in which schools were organised and radically changed every aspect of teachers' lives:

- a new curriculum was issued for every class
- the system of inspection was changed
- very little in-service training was provided
- the provision of equipment and aids was inadequate
- a new method of computing teachers' remuneration was introduced, which left many teachers dissatisfied
- a new system of promotion was implemented which was perceived to be a numbers' game rather than one based on ability.

The vigorous implementation of the new rules and regulations by Starkie's administration engendered very bad relations between teachers, inspectors and the Education Office. In his defence Starkie claimed that he was not adequately financed to implement the new schemes justly and fairly.

A number of significant developments occurred during this period: for the first time, and not without a strong fight by women, an equal pay award was made; and the Teachers' Pension Scheme, while still not as good as the civil servants' scheme, was radically improved.

5

War and Progress, 1914–22

Teachers' Salaries in Ireland, 1915–22

Introduction

The onset of the First World War, which commenced on 4 August 1914 and lasted until 1918, was used as an excuse not to implement a salary increase that had just been negotiated for teachers, even though they were paid wages 'at which a dust man would turn up his nose'.[1]

Civil servants were similarly affected: a report, published on 2 April 1914, recommending increased salaries was not implemented.

War Bonus for Irish Teachers, 1916

However, as the war progressed, and the cost of living continued to rise, war bonuses had to be paid. Civil servants were paid their first bonuses with effect from 1 July 1916: four shillings a week for men and two shillings for women.

It was some time later, and only after a dispute, that the government conceded a bonus to teachers on the same terms that had been granted to civil servants. Even then the CEC was not prepared to accept the disbursement formula proposed by the government because women, the majority of INTO membership, were not treated as equal to men. Responding to pressure from the INTO, MPs, the managerial bodies, and the Board of Commissioners, the government eventually introduced a scheme of bonuses that were graded as to income, with one very important distinction: women and men in the same category were paid at the same rate. As was the case for civil servants, teachers with a salary exceeding £3 per week did not get any bonus.[2]

At the special request of the INTO, the capitation rate paid to capitation convent and monastery schools was proportionately increased.[3] Pensioners did not receive any increase.

---

1   *Irish School Weekly*, 10 November 1923, p. 135
2   The Eighty-Second Report of the Commissioners of National Education, 1915–16
3   T. J. O'Connell, *A Hundred Years of Progress*, p. 170

Monthly Salaries

In December 1916 the commissioners acceded to teachers' requests and introduced monthly payment of salaries, a change from quarterly payments introduced in 1850.

School managers, however, would not agree to direct payment, and teachers had to continue to attend at their residences to collect their salary cheques.[4] Finally, on 9 April 1918, and in spite of objections from managerial bodies, the commissioners sanctioned the direct payment of salaries to teachers.

The Duke Grant

In 1917 a sum of five million pounds was made available to finance the Fisher Act, which was aimed at revising the education system in Great Britain. A proportionate amount was provided for Scotland and, as nothing had been assigned for Ireland, the CEC claimed that the education system in Ireland should be treated in a similar manner. Further, the CEC proposed that a major portion of the money assigned should be used to increase salaries, abolish the grading system, remove all barriers to normal promotion and, in a revolutionary move, introduce a common basic salary that would apply to all national teachers.

In the meantime, early in January 1917, civil servants were granted a second war bonus, and the CEC sought a similar one for teachers. The government responded by stating that a large permanent increase in salary was being prepared and that teachers had to decide which claim they wished to process, the salary increase or the bonus. The CEC decided to concentrate on securing a substantial permanent increase in salaries.

It was not until July 1917 that the Chief Secretary, Duke, read out the government's salary proposals in the House of Commons. This was a departure from the usual practice of publishing such proposals as a White Paper. The proposed grant amounted to £381,000 – less than half of what had been expected.

When the White Paper, containing details of the Duke Salary Grant Scheme, was eventually published on 15 December 1917, it contained the following proposals:

- new grade salary scales, giving substantial increases to some and very little to others, would be applied retrospectively to 1 April
- promotion to second grade was provided for assistants
- the maximum salary for JAMs was increased from £28 to £52
- standard numbers were abolished
- increments were converted from triennial to annual
- the capitation grant for principals of schools with an average attendance of over sixty was increased
- 'Highly Efficient' principals of larger schools would get supplemental salaries.

---

4   In 1924 it was conceded that pensions should be paid monthly.

The contentious salary grading system and the promotion rules remained unaltered.

The CEC rejected the proposed distribution of the money as being 'so inequitable as to be fantastic' and engaged in a public controversy. Even while the dispute was in progress, the commissioners proceeded to transfer teachers to the new payment scheme with, as they claimed, 'a minimum of friction and delay'.[5]

All teachers were granted a new war bonus of eight shillings per week with effect from 1 January 1918. Taking the Duke award and the war bonuses into consideration, over a two-year period the average salaries of principals and assistant teachers increased as follows:

		31 March 1916			31 March 1918		
		£	s.	d.	£	s.	d.
Principals:	**Men**	115	19	11	142	5	6
	Women	92	13	9	114	5	9
Assistants:	**Men**	83	11	4	86	11	2
	Women	70	2	3	82	18	3

The Arbitration Board

Because the salaries of public officials in England were not being reviewed and the bonuses paid were based on very poor pre-war salaries, considerable unrest ensued. In 1917 the government responded by establishing the Civil Service Arbitration Board to consider claims from civil servants and other government employees for increased remuneration. This committee was specifically debarred from hearing claims from teachers.

In an effort to placate teachers, A. W. Samuels, Solicitor General for Ireland, announced in March 1918 that a committee was to be established to inquire into the system of salaries of all Irish teachers.[6] This was welcomed by the CEC, which was successful in negotiating the following procedures:

- two separate committees would be established, one for primary and one for secondary teachers
- the INTO would be consulted on the terms of reference
- nominees of the INTO would be on the committee for primary teachers

---

5   Eighty-Fourth Report of Commissioners for 1917–18, HC 1919, XXI
6   In May 1918 Duke was appointed Lord Justice of the Appeal Court. He was succeeded as Chief Secretary for Ireland by Edward Stott.

- the committee would not be bound by the Duke Scheme
- the committee would be free to make any recommendations it thought advisable.

Five months later, on 12 August 1918, the government announced the names of the seventeen people appointed to the committee: four were INTO appointees and three were members of the Principal Teachers' Union. Lord Killanin, a member of the National Board, was appointed chairman. The terms of reference gave the committee a mandate to review the system governing the salaries of teachers in national schools.[7]

Because of the government's delay in naming the committee, on 27 July 1918 the CEC submitted a claim to the Arbitration Board for an increase in their war bonus. When the claim came up for consideration the Treasury contested the right of teachers to be heard by the Board as they were deemed to be non-eligible. As the Board had not given a decision by September, the CEC called upon its members to withdraw from work on Wednesday, 2 October 1918.[8]

On the morning of the strike the Treasury conceded and the Board subsequently introduced a bonus award giving all men twelve shillings and sixpence and women ten shillings a week, backdated to 1 July 1918. While the CEC was not satisfied with the award, it accepted it because two important principles had been established:

1 Access to the Arbitration Board had been achieved.
2 Equality with civil servants with regard to future bonus awards had been established.

Civil servants were awarded another bonus in November 1918, and teachers were awarded two bonuses, one from 1 January 1919 and the other one from 1 June; in all cases men and women were paid at different rates.[9] Claims that the Arbitration Board should recommend permanent scale salaries for teachers were turned down.

The Killanin Committee, 1919

The Killanin Committee held its first meeting in September 1918 and submitted its signed unanimous report on 26 February 1919. Many of the principles sought by the INTO had been conceded by the committee. It recommended a considerable salary increase for all teachers, to be implemented through a

---

7 Report of the Vice-Regal Committee of Inquiry into Primary Education (Ireland), 1918, HC 1919 (Cmd 60) XXI, 741 (The Killanin Report)

8 The pledge to strike was signed by 11,587 teachers. INTO membership for the previous year (1917) was recorded as 10,511. T. J. O'Connell, *A Hundred Years of Progress*, p. 184

9 *Irish School Weekly*, 6 March 1920, p. 714

revised incremental salary scale structure and, in addition, a scheme of extra allowances for qualifications and responsibility.

It also recommended a completely revised superannuation scheme. It was considered by both sides that the settlement of the pension question was very much bound up with the settlement of the salary question.

In addition, the committee recommended that:

- a local education rate should be levied
- local education committees should be established with responsibilities for the maintenance, heating and cleaning of national schools
- local school committees should be established to have the right to provide medical and dental care, school meals, school books, and transport for necessitous children.

In the field of education it recommended:

- the co-ordination of the existing systems of education
- the provision of scholarships
- special schools for children with disabilities
- continuation schools for young people whose education had been neglected
- improved teacher residences.[10]

The Molony Committee, 1919

Another vice-regal committee, under the chairmanship of the Rt. Hon. Thomas F. Molony, Lord Chief Justice of Ireland, was appointed to review the remuneration and conditions of service of teachers in intermediate schools.

The Molony Committee submitted its report to Dublin Castle on 4 March 1919, within a week of the presentation of the Killanin Report. It recommended significant improvements in teachers' pay and conditions, and many radical proposals for the operation of the intermediate education system. It proposed that a Central Authority should be established to co-ordinate the three branches of education under a system of educational administration similar to that in operation in England.[11]

The Education (Ireland) Bill, 1919, (The MacPherson Bill)

The Chief Secretary for Ireland, James MacPherson, lauded the Killanin and the Molony Reports as 'two admirable reports which had been prepared on primary

10 John Coolahan (1979) *The Education Bill of 1919, Problems of Educational Reform*, Proceedings of the Education Studies Association, pp. 10–31

11 Report of the Vice-Regal Committee on the Conditions of Service and Remuneration of Teachers in Intermediate Schools, and on the Distribution of Grants from Public Funds for Intermediate Education, 1919

and intermediate education in Ireland'.[12] While the government accepted the reports, it insisted that the recommendations would require a parliamentary Act for their implementation. The CEC sought the immediate implementation of the recommendations that did not require legislation, but without success.

On 9 May the government established a departmental committee of five experts to draft a comprehensive bill addressing the whole education system in Ireland.[13] The Education (Ireland) Bill was published on 29 November 1919 and promoted in the House of Commons as 'the most comprehensive single effort at legislation for first and second level in the history of Irish education.[14]

The Freeman's Journal described the bill as 'an impudent proposal from more than one point of view'. *The Irish Independent* considered its introduction at this stage as singularly inopportune.[15]

The Provisions of the MacPherson Bill

Part I of the bill proposed a Department of Education, under the control of the Chief Secretary, which would take over the duties of the existing three branches; Part II proposed the establishment of local education committees for each county and county borough; Part III dealt with the remuneration of teachers; Part IV dealt with new financial arrangements for the funding of Irish education.

While Part III dealt with the remuneration and superannuation of teachers, it did not contain any reference to the long-awaited increase in salaries. However, at a meeting on 10 December 1919, the Chief Secretary reassured the CEC when he gave them particulars of proposed new salaries which were substantially better than those in the Killanin Report.

Section 18 of Part III was also of great importance to the INTO as it made it obligatory on the new Department of Education to frame a superannuation scheme similar to the schemes introduced in England and Scotland.

The bill also marked a radical change in the financial arrangements for Irish education by the establishment of a special 'Irish Education Fund'. This, and the establishment of the Department, removed 'the veto power of the Treasury which had for so long been a stranglehold on national and intermediate education'.[16]

---

12 Hansard, 5th Ser., Vol. 115, 5 April 1919
13 Bonaparte Wyse was chairman of the committee. The other members were Butler of the Intermediate Board, Fletcher of the Department of Agriculture and Technical Instruction, Alexander of the Scottish Education Department, and Bennett, late Chief Inspector of the English Board of Education.
14 Hansard, November 1919, A Bill to Make Further Provision with Respect to Education in Ireland and for other purposes connected therewith, HC 1919 (214) I; 'The MacPherson Bill'
15 T. J. O'Connell, *A Hundred Years of Progress*, p. 296
16 John Coolahan (1979) *The Education Bill of 1919, Problems of Educational Reform*, Proceedings of the Education Studies Association, pp. 10–31

The bill was opposed by the Catholic Hierarchy, and the Catholic Clerical Managers Association issued a statement declaring as a fundamental principle 'that the only satisfactory system of education for Catholics is that wherein Catholic children are taught in Catholic schools, by Catholic teachers, under Catholic control'.[17]

The bill was supported by the INTO, the Church of Ireland House of Bishops, the General Assembly of the Presbyterian Church, the Association of Irish Schoolmistresses, the Provost of Trinity College and heads of many Protestant schools.[18]

The CEC welcomed the financial provisions of the bill as they contained many improvements that the organisation had sought and would lead to an improvement in the financing of Irish primary education.[19]

Newspapers adopted editorial stances that reflected different political and sectarian attitudes. Control of school management was identified as a main area of controversy. *The Irish Times, The Northern Whig, The Northern Newsletter,* and *The (London) Times* supported the bill. *The Freeman's Journal, The Evening Telegraph* and *The Irish Independent* opposed it.

A very bitter campaign against the bill was waged from platforms, pulpits and newspapers. The Irish Parliamentary Party was successful in preventing its second reading in the House of Commons on 16 December 1919.[20] The bill was withdrawn on 22 December with the promise from Bonar Law that the government intended to proceed with the measure in the next parliamentary session.[21]

The controversy continued into 1920 and a new bill, a slightly amended version of the old bill, was given a first reading on 24 February 1920. However, as time elapsed it became obvious that the implementation date of 1 April would not be met. MacPherson resigned as Chief Secretary in early April, giving 'ill health' as the reason. He was succeeded by Sir Hamar Greenwood.[22]

The Irish Teacher's Salary Position

The CEC had a problem: the Killanin Report had been published in the first week of March 1919 but the new salary scales and pension scheme had still not been introduced in April 1920.

The CEC response was to lodge a claim with the Treasury seeking arrears for the new salaries that should have come into effect from 1 April 1919, and the

---

17 *Evening Telegraph*, 24 January 1920
18 *The Irish Times*, 15–19 December 1919 and 21 January 1920
19 *Irish School Weekly*, 24, 31 January 1920
20 The Irish Parliamentary Party did badly in the 1918 general election; only four of its members were successful. Sinn Féin won 73 of the 105 seats.
21 Hansard, 5th Ser., Vol. 123, col. 324
22 *The Irish Times*, 3 April 1920. MacPherson had replaced Stott and he was now replaced by Hamar Greenwood.

implementation of the new scales from 1 April 1920. It threatened to apply directly to the Arbitration Board to determine permanent salary scales if its claim was not conceded by 16 June.[23]

On 18 June 1920 the Treasury stated that while it was prepared to allow the matter of an interim grant to go before the Arbitration Board, it would not concede that teachers had any right to appear before the Arbitration Board to have a case for a permanent salary heard. The CEC rejected this offer, finalised negotiations on the payment of the interim grant and, by threatening a general strike, got the right to present the INTO claim for a permanent scale of salaries to the Arbitration Board.[24]

The Arbitration Board Report was signed on 29 November 1920 and its findings were accepted by the Treasury, the commissioners and the INTO. The teacher agreement was signed just in time: ten days later the 'Geddes Axe' fell and all further increases in wages or salaries were stopped and any negotiations then in progress were suspended indefinitely.[25]

The new salary provisions for national teachers were based on the principles laid down in the Killanin Report of 1919 and became operative from 1 April 1920.

The Salary Agreement, 1920

The main provisions of the 1920 'Salary Agreement' radically changed the 1900 salary structure. Its main elements were as follows:

Common Normal Basic Salary Scale

The system of classifying teachers into grades for salary purposes was abolished.

1   A common 'normal' basic salary scale was introduced for all trained teachers, principals and assistants, and progression up the scale to its maximum by annual increments would be automatic in the absence of an adverse report from an inspector. The normal scale for trained male teachers would commence at £170 and rise by seventeen annual increments (sixteen of £12 and one of £8) to a maximum of £370; the normal scale for trained female teachers would commence at £155 and rise by fifteen annual increments (fourteen of £10 and one of £5) to a maximum of £300.

2   Existing masters of schools with an average of twenty to twenty-nine pupils would be placed on a scale commencing at £170 and rising by fourteen increments of £12

---

23 Eighty-Fifth Report of the Commissioners of National Education, 1918–19
24 O'Connell has also acknowledged that the INTO negotiating team received considerable assistance from the NUT. T. J. O'Connell, *A Hundred Years of Progress*, p. 188
25 *Irish School Weekly*, 23 October 1920, p. 226. The public finances were causing concern and the government had established a Departmental Committee on National Expenditure, presided over by Sir Eric Geddes, which recommended a series of financial cutbacks. The 'Geddes Axe' fell on 9 December 1920.

to a maximum of £338. In future, men appointed to schools with this average attendance would be placed on the same salary scale as women.

3   Teachers with special qualifications would be entitled to annual bonuses in addition to scale salary.

4   No further war bonuses would be paid and the ones currently being paid would be incorporated into the new salary scales.

Probation and Diploma Salary Placing

The following procedure for completion of probation and placement for salary purposes was laid down:

1   On appointment, a teacher would be placed on the minimum point of the salary scale and remain there until probation regulations had been completed.

2   To satisfy probation regulations and merit the award of the Diploma, a teacher would be required to serve a minimum of two years' service and receive two successive satisfactory annual reports from an inspector.

3   On being awarded the Diploma the teacher would be given two increments and placed on the third point of the scale, but no arrears would be paid. Irrespective of how long it took to complete probation, only two increments would be awarded.

4   Untrained teachers would be awarded two increments on satisfactorily completing the probationary requirements.

Supernormal Scales

1   Principals rated 'Highly Efficient' who had reached the maximum of the normal scale could qualify for placement on 'supernormal' scales, each with five increments (a different scale for men and women), depending on the size of the school. Schools would be divided into five categories depending on their average attendance as follows: Category I, 20–29; Category II, 30–49; Category III, 50–119; Category IV, 120–239; Category V, 240 pupils and over. The maximum of the supernormal scales ranged from £320 to £460 for men and from £320 to £360 for women.

2   All teachers in First Grade, where length of service warranted it, would be placed on the supernormal scale.

3   Principals in Second Grade classed in inspectors' reports as 'Highly Efficient' for each of the three years ending on 30 June 1920 would be eligible for placement on the supernormal scale warranted by length of service.

4   Assistants rated 'Highly Efficient' who had reached the maximum of the normal scale could qualify for placement on the supernormal scales for principals in the category of schools with an average of thirty to forty-nine pupils.[26]

---

26 Final Report of the Killanin Committee, Vol. I, HC 1919 (Cmd 60) XXI, 741, Vol. 11, Summaries of Evidence, Memoranda and Returns, HC 1919 (Cmd 178) XXI, 789

Capitation Payments in Classification Schools

1   Existing principals of schools with an average attendance under thirty would receive an unchanged capitation fee of five shillings per pupil. Principals appointed to such schools in future would not be eligible to receive a capitation grant.

2   Principals of schools with an average annual attendance of between 30 pupils and 120 pupils would receive an annual capitation grant of ten shillings for each pupil between the ages of three and fifteen years.

3   Principals of schools with an average annual attendance in excess of 120 pupils would receive an annual capitation grant of five shillings for each pupil between the ages of three and fifteen years.

Vice-Principals

1   Vice-principals would be recognised in schools with an average annual attendance of 160 pupils and receive, in addition to their salary as assistant teachers, an annual capitation grant of five shillings for each pupil between the ages of three and fifteen years in excess of 120, up to a limit of 280.

2   A second vice-principal would be recognised in a school with an average annual attendance of 360 pupils and receive, in addition to his/her salary as assistant teacher, an annual capitation grant of five shillings for each pupil between the ages of three and fifteen years in excess of 280, up to a maximum of 440.

Convent and Monastery Capitation Schools

During negotiations the INTO had demanded that all teachers in schools under the management of religious orders should be treated in a manner similar to teachers in lay schools. The following provisions were agreed:

1   Capitation rates paid to the conductors of convent and monastery capitation schools were increased to an amount equal to the total amount paid to teachers in classification schools with a similar average attendance.

2   Lay assistant teachers in convent and monastery schools would be paid salaries identical to teachers of a similar standing in classification schools. However, trained and untrained assistants, recognised on or before 1 April 1905, could only count one year of service as a lay assistant as equivalent to half a year for salary placement purposes. (This salary placement problem arose because prior to 1920 lay assistant teachers were paid by the conductors of capitation schools and did not have fixed salary scales or security of tenure.)

Untrained Teachers

1   Special scales were recommended for untrained teachers:
   (a) All untrained teachers appointed before 1 April 1905 were eligible, after placement for salary purposes, to earn increments in normal or supernormal scales on the same conditions as trained teachers.
   (b) Untrained teachers appointed after 1 April 1905 and before 1 January 1921 were placed on a salary scale with twelve increments as follows: the first four years would not count for increments, the second four years would count for half increments, and the third four years would count for full increments.
2   No untrained teacher appointed after 31 March 1905 could receive a higher placing than the sixth increment of the normal scale, i.e. four years uncounted, four years' half increments, and four years' full increments. After twelve years an untrained female teacher could proceed to a maximum of £215; if she was rated 'Highly Efficient' she could proceed to a maximum of £300. After twelve years an untrained male teacher could proceed to a maximum of £242; if he was rated 'Highly Efficient' he could proceed to a maximum of £370.
3   The appointment of men as untrained teachers was discontinued. Untrained teachers appointed from 1 January 1921 were placed on a scale ranging from £130, by increments of £5, to a maximum of £155. (It was INTO policy that all teachers should be trained and this scale was pitched low to try to discourage the appointment of untrained teachers.)[27]
4   Special scales were recommended for JAMs, rising from £110 by eight annual increments of £5 each to a maximum of £150.[28]

Extra and Special Subjects

1   Bilingual Fees: The bilingual fees of four shillings, eight shillings and ten shillings were increased to eight shillings, ten shillings and twelve shillings, respectively.
2   Mathematics: The fee for both branches of mathematics was increased from five shillings to ten shillings, but the minimum amount of time to be devoted to each branch of the subject was increased from forty to forty-five hours in the school year.
3   Rural Science and Horticulture: The higher grant for schools with over sixteen pupils was increased from £7 10s. to £13.

The Application of the New Salary Scales

The increases in salaries granted to teachers in England in the 1918 Burnham Reports were paid over three years. A 'carry-over' system was adopted so that the teachers would be on the defined maximum at the end of the three-year period.

27 *Eighty Years of Progress*, INTO Booklet, 1948
28 JAMs were first appointed in 1906. No special qualifications were required other than a good primary education.

It was agreed that a similar formula should apply to the increase granted to teachers in Ireland. The first phase would be paid from 1 April 1920, the second phase from 1 April 1921, and all teachers would have reached their proper placing on the normal and supernormal scales by 1 April 1922.

Understanding and applying the new salary structure caused severe problems for many teachers as various increments and allowances had to be taken into consideration.

Salary Increments

There were five different types of increments:

1 The Normal Increment: this was the regular increment on the normal scale.
2 The Supernormal Increment: this was the regular increment on the supernormal scale, sometimes referred to as the 'higher increment'.
3 The Special Increment: sometimes referred to as the 'acceleration increment' – a teacher who was passing through the normal scale, who was rated 'Highly Efficient' and had received three very favourable inspector reports in a five-year period, could be awarded this increment in addition to the ordinary increments of the scale. A special increment could not bring the teacher beyond the maximum of the normal scale.
4 The 'Standard' Increment: this was the amount of the 'carry-over' to be added to the current year's salary and bonus.
5 The 'carry-over' increment: this was the balance of the carry-over which was to be added on from 1 April 1921 and from 1 April 1922.

Salary Placement

The 'proper placing' of a teacher was defined as 'the salary to which he or she would have attained on 1 April 1920 ... had the new scale been in operation during the whole period of his/her recognised service'.

The INTO head office had to deal with hundreds of queries regarding salary placement. For many weeks successive editions of *Irish School Weekly* carried examples setting down how the system worked.[29]

Notwithstanding the difficulties of understanding the application of the salary structure and the placement system for salary purposes, teachers recognised that during the four-year period from 1916 to 1920 the CEC had achieved considerable improvements: monthly salaries, direct payment of salaries, annual increments, rapid promotion, the abolition of standard numbers, war bonuses, several 'average' concessions, full equality for teachers in religious-run schools, and the 1920 salary agreement.[30] However, the CEC still had the problem of getting the Killanin pension recommendations implemented.

---

29 *Eighty Years of Progress*, INTO Booklet, 1948
30 T. J. O'Connell, *A Hundred Years of Progress*, p. 197

While the salary position was being resolved it had not been possible to make any progress on the pension question. By now the political situation in Dublin had become very tense and the Education Bill had been formally withdrawn on 13 December 1920 without a second reading.[31] The CEC turned its attention to seeking the implementation of the Killanin pension recommendations.

Teachers' Pensions, 1918–22

The value of the Irish Teachers' Pension Fund on 31 December 1918 was £2,918,658. Income was insufficient to meet future liabilities and keep the fund solvent. This problem was compounded by the fact that the actuarial valuation due in 1918 or 1919 did not take place. The implementation of the Killanin Committee pension proposals of 1919 would have changed the revised pension rules of 1914, but this did not happen.

The War Bonus and Pensions

Initially, a Statutory Order was issued by the Treasury in 1916 declaring that the war bonus was not pensionable.[32] This meant that teachers retired with diminished pensions because all income was not taken into consideration and, as there was no mechanism for a review of pensions once awarded, they had to endure a serious loss of income for the remainder of their lives. Their position was severely aggravated by an increasing cost of living.[33]

In 1920 it was agreed that 50 per cent of the bonus could be taken into consideration but, even though this improved the situation, teachers' pensions were not calculated from their full salary.[34] After considerable unrest the Treasury allowed teachers who retired after 1917 to count 75 per cent of the war bonuses, but only on condition that they paid 4 per cent of the 75 per cent as a premium.

Civil servants and local authority officers were treated better than teachers: they did not have any deduction made from their war bonus as a pension contribution.

The Pensions (Increase) Act, 1920

The Pensions (Increase) Act, 1920 authorised the payment of graded increases, with effect from 1 April 1920, to civil servants, elementary teachers, national teachers and members of the Royal Irish Constabulary (RIC) and the Dublin

---

31 John Coolahan (1979) *The Education Bill of 1919, Problems of Educational Reform*, Proceedings of the Education Studies Association, pp. 10–31
32 Statutory Rules and Orders, 1916, No. 939, Treasury Chambers, 27 December 1916
33 *Irish School Weekly*, 14 May 1927
34 *Irish School Weekly*, 13 March 1920

Metropolitan Police, as long as they had been in receipt of pensions before 4 August 1914.

An income limit was placed on eligibility for a pension. An unmarried pensioner in receipt of a pension of more than £150 a year or a married pensioner with a pension of more than £200 a year could not receive any increase. The following graded increases were sanctioned:

- an increase of 50 per cent on an existing pension not exceeding £50 a year
- an increase of 40 per cent on an existing pension exceeding £50 but less than £100 a year in the case of an unmarried person, or £130 a year in the case of a married person
- an increase of 30 per cent on an existing pension exceeding £100 but less than £150 a year in the case of an unmarried person, or exceeding £130 a year but less than £200 a year in the case of a married person

Part II of the Schedule allowed that pensions granted on or after 4 August 1914 could be increased by an amount sufficient to make the increased pension equal to the amount to which the pre-war pensions might have been increased under Part I of the Schedule.

The following interpretations were laid down:

- the expression 'unmarried' included a widow or widower having no children under sixteen years of age dependent on him or her
- the expression 'means' in the case of a married person included the means of both husband and wife.
- where a person was in receipt of more than one pension, the aggregate of the pensions had to be used to determine the limits that would apply.[35]

The Pensions (Increase) Act and Teachers in Ireland

The Pensions (Increase) Act of 1920 was not applied to pensioned teachers in Ireland in the same way as to other beneficiaries. Their eligibility to the full benefit of the increases was affected not only by the 'Means Barrier' but also by a 'Time Barrier'. Consequently, only a few pensioners got the full increase, some got a portion of the increase, and many got no increase.

The 'Means Barrier'

If a teacher pensioner could satisfy the 'Means Barrier' of £150 a year if unmarried or £200 a year if married, he or she had still to satisfy the 'Time Barrier'.

---

35 The Pensions (Increase) Act, 1920, quoted in Garry Sweeney, *In Public Service: a History of the Public Service Executive Union, 1890–1990*

The 'Time Barrier'

Although the revised National Teachers' Superannuation Scheme was agreed in 1913, it was not implemented until 1 October 1914, and the Treasury ruled that it was a post-war scheme for the purposes of the Pensions (Increase) Act, 1920. The Treasury's interpretation of the Act had the following results:

- teachers granted pensions before 1900 under the 1879 Act would benefit in full from the pension increases
- teachers granted pensions after that date, and who got revised pensions under the 1914 scheme, would have their increases assessed on the pensions they had received under the 1897 rules and not on the revised pensions they had received under the 1914 rules
- the majority of teacher pensioners who retired after 4 August would not qualify for any increase, and the small number who could benefit only got a portion of the increase.[36]

In addition to being excluded from full benefit under the 1920 Act, the vast majority of retired teachers suffered again when the 'Geddes Axe' fell on 9 December 1920; this imposed an embargo on all increases until further notice.

The Proposed Pension Scheme for Irish Teachers, 1921

No changes occurred to the 1914 pension scheme until 1 April 1920 when the rates of contribution were increased as follows:

- Teachers in First Grade, First Division: 5 per cent
- Teachers in First Grade, Second Division: 4.5 per cent
- Teachers in Second Grade: 4 per cent
- Teachers in Third Grade: 4.5 per cent

Shortly afterwards the rate was converted to a flat rate of 4 per cent for all teachers with the addition that all other payments and allowances were liable for deduction.

The Negotiated Scheme

All parties had expected that the pension recommendations of the Killanin Committee would be implemented after the resolution of the salary issue. Unfortunately for teachers, the salary question was not resolved until 29 November 1920 and the MacPherson Bill, which contained pension provisions, had been withdrawn.

---

36 *Irish School Weekly*, 4 September 1920

In 1920, in an effort to expedite matters, the CEC submitted a memorandum on pensions to the commissioners and lodged the following claims:
Those teachers who retired prior to 1 April 1919 should receive:

- an addition of £1 per annum for each year served
- a minimum pension of £1 per week.

That for teachers in the service:

- the pension scheme should be non-contributory
- all service as a teacher should be recognised for pension purposes
- any contributions made to the Pension Fund should be returned
- a lump sum, based on thirtieths and up to a maximum of one-and-a-half years' salary, should be awarded on retirement.[37]

The CEC was seeking the same conditions that had been granted to Scottish teachers and argued that teachers in Ireland had a stronger claim.

Early in 1921, following intensive discussions, representatives of the INTO and the commissioners agreed terms of a pension scheme, based on the recommendations in the Killanin Report, and similar to the civil service scheme.

With foreboding as to the political situation, the negotiated pension scheme was forwarded to the British government for immediate implementation. A deputation from the CEC had a very unsatisfactory meeting with the Chief Secretary, Sir Hamar Greenwood, and, as feared, was told that the settlement of the pension question was no longer a matter of concern for the Imperial Parliament.[38]

With the signing of the Anglo-Irish Treaty in December 1921, and the implementation of the salary agreement of 1920, it became the responsibility of the Irish Free State government to implement the remaining recommendations of the Killanin Committee.

Civil Servants and Teachers in Great Britain, 1918–22

School Teachers (Superannuation) Act, 1918

In 1918 one of the first pieces of legislation introduced for the sympathetic consideration of parliament was a School Teachers (Superannuation) Bill, granting teachers a pension scheme similar to one enjoyed by civil servants.[39]

---

37 Memorandum of Irish Teachers' Pensions, furnished at the request of the commissioners by the INTO, 1920
38 The CEC deputation to London were Harbison, Mansfield and Maher. CEC Report to Congress 1922
39 The School Teachers (Superannuation) Act, 1918

The Education (Scotland) Superannuation Act of 1919 made similar provisions for teachers in Scotland.

The legislation converted the English and Scottish schemes from being 'money-purchase' schemes with fixed benefits and fixed contributions to non-contributory unfunded 'pay-as-you-go' schemes. Contributions made by English and Welsh teachers under the 1898 Act were refunded or could be retained for additional benefits under the form of Deferred Annuities corresponding to the contributions paid. Scottish teachers had all contributions paid under the 1912 scheme refunded and, in addition, all of their rights were preserved.

The 'old guard' was the only group of teachers who did not benefit from the new scheme. These were teachers who had commenced teaching before 1862, and as they were now on very restricted pensions, the NUT opened a 'Thanks-Offering Fund' for them in recognition of their long fight for a pension scheme.[40]

The National Whitley Council, 1919

Even after the establishment of the Civil Service Arbitration Board in 1917, civil servants had great difficulty getting regular salary reviews. The government was prevailed upon to establish The National Whitley Council in 1919 to 'consider the cost of living and its effects upon the salaries of civil servants, whether permanent or temporary'.

The council's recommendation that a cost-of-living bonus be paid as a supplement to basic pay was adopted; the bonus was to be revised every four months during the first twelve months and every six months from 1 March 1921. The cost-of-living index of 100, as at 1914, was adopted as the base point for the award of any subsequent bonus; the bonus could increase or decrease by 1/26 for every five full points by which the average cost of living rose or fell. Variations of less than five full points in either direction were ignored.

The Burnham Committee Salary Scales, 1920

In the early autumn of 1919 the government established a structure of three Standing Joint Committees to secure the orderly and progressive solution of the salary problems of elementary, secondary and technical teachers.[41] Lord Burnham was appointed chairman of the three committees.

In November 1919 the Burnham Committee for elementary teachers produced a 'Provisional Minimum Scale' to come into effect from 1 January 1920. Two months later it produced its first formal report setting down

---

40 Asher Tropp, *The School Teacher: The Growth of the Teaching Profession in England and Wales from 1800 to Present Day*, p. 213

41 Report of the Departmental Committee of the Superannuation of School Teachers, HC 1923, par. 17

permanent salaries for teachers under the Schedule of Standard Salary Scales. The Board of Education accepted the report on condition that the increases were implemented in three equal instalments from 1 April 1920, 1 April 1921, and 1 April 1922. While most LEAs accepted the new salaries, problems arose in a few of them and prolonged bitter strikes ensued.

The Burnham scales granted significant salary increase to teachers. The following table sets out how average salaries for male and female teachers were increased:

	Average Salary as on 31 March			
Total: all categories	**1914**	**1920**	**1921**	**1922**
Men	139	260	319	326
Women	82	168	207	215
Men and Women	97	189	233	241

Teachers' Pensions in Great Britain

The School Teachers (Superannuation) Act, 1918 and the Education (Scotland) Superannuation Act, 1919 conferred considerably improved superannuation benefits on teachers in Great Britain. However, within a very short period of time it became apparent to the government that the financial consequences of these improvements had been seriously underestimated. On 9 May 1922 a Superannuation Bill was introduced imposing a 5 per cent levy on the salaries of all teachers in respect of superannuation benefits. The Teachers (Superannuation) Act, 1925 re-converted teachers' pension schemes to contributory schemes.

Review of the Period 1918–1922

Following the war, it was apparent that a major review of the conditions and remuneration of all employees paid from the public purse was required. It is of significance for comparative purposes to record how teachers in Ireland, teachers in Great Britain and civil servants got major salary and pension revisions during the period 1918–22.

Civil servants got the Arbitration Board in 1917 and the Whitley Council in 1919; teachers in England got the Burnham Committee in 1920; teachers in Ireland got the Killanin and Molony Committees. However, it was apparent that teachers in Ireland were not as fortunate as their colleagues in Great Britain in terms of both salary and pension advancements.

Salaries

Civil servants got a remuneration packet that guaranteed a bonus review every six months based on the cost-of-living index. Teachers in Great Britain got the Burnham Committee, to which salary claims could be referred for determination.

During the 1920 salary negotiations the CEC was offered the bonus/salary structure but decided to persist with its policy of seeking a substantial increase in the basic salary. While this objective was successfully achieved, the process had a serious flaw in that it did not include any mechanism for periodic reviews.

During the period from 1922 to the end of the Second World War both teachers and civil servants were adversely affected by economic circumstances, but teachers suffered more. Their salaries were cut on six occasions by a cumulative 20 per cent and they got one salary increase of 5 per cent in 1938 and some bonuses during the war. The civil service indexed bonus was reviewed every six months and it increased or decreased as the situation warranted. Only new entrants to the service had their basic salary reduced on a number of occasions. The bonus system lasted until 1 November 1946, when it was replaced by consolidated salary scales.

Pensions

The amendment to the civil service superannuation scheme in 1909 added to the advantages that civil servants had over all other groups. They now had entitlements to lump sum payments on retirement and death.

Teachers in Ireland got some increased benefits in their 1914 scheme; however, while contributions were increased substantially they still did not have an entitlement to lump sum payments. A revised superannuation scheme had been negotiated but, in spite of the best efforts of the INTO, it was never implemented. An actuarial valuation of the Pension Fund was not conducted in 1919 and its funding problems continued. Teachers in Ireland did not benefit from The Pensions (Increase) Act, 1920 to the same extent as teachers in England.

The Anglo-Irish Treaty made provision for the transfer to the Irish Government of the liability and administration of the salary structures and pension schemes of previous employees of the Crown. Pensioners in Great Britain got further increases under the Pensions (Increase) Act of 1924 but the Saorstát government did not pass comparable legislation, and pensioners in Ireland did not get any increases.

An actuarial report published in 1928 disclosed that the Pension Fund was underfunded to a sum in excess of £4 million. In 1934, when introducing a further salary reduction in teachers' salaries, the government converted the teachers' superannuation scheme into a non-contributory one as a remedy for the serious deficit in the pension fund. Teachers did not get a lump sum on retirement until 1950.

6

The First Years of Independence, 1922–29

The Education System of Saorstát na Éireann, 1922

The First Dáil

The Representation of the People Act, 1918 broadened the basis of parliamentary representation and broke the link between property and franchise. The right to vote was extended to age twenty-one with a condition of six months' residency. Women over the age of thirty were given the vote, but they had to be local government electors or the wives of these electors. The Irish electorate increased from 701,475 in 1910 to 1,936,673 in 1918. The general election of 1918 was a triumph for Sinn Féin; it won 73 of the available 105 parliamentary seats.[1]

Twenty-seven Sinn Féin MPs came together in Dublin on 21 January 1919, constituted themselves as an independent parliament, Dáil Éireann, and provisionally established a republic.[2] They drew up a provisional constitution which provided for a prime minister and 'aireachtaí' (ministers) in charge of finance, home affairs, foreign affairs, and defence. At a second session on 1 April 1919, attended by fifty-two members, de Valera was elected President and the following portfolios were assigned: home affairs, finance, defence, foreign affairs, labour, local government, industries, and agriculture. The first Minister for Education, J. J. O' Kelly (An Sceilig), was appointed by the Dáil on 26 August 1921.

The Anglo-Irish Treaty was signed on 6 December 1921, and on 7 January 1922 de Valera and his supporters withdrew from the Dáil following the vote on the Treaty.[3] On 9 January a provisional government was established under

---

1 John A. Murphy, *Ireland in the Twentieth Century*, p. 28. The Unionist Party won twenty-six seats, Sinn Féin won seventy-three, and the Irish Party won only six, down from eighty. This was a clear rejection of British authority in Ireland.
2 Dáil Éireann is the Assembly of Ireland. The majority of the new MPs were either in jail or on the run from the British military forces. Joseph Robins, *Champagne and Silver Buckles*
3 The Anglo-Irish Agreement was approved by sixty-four votes to fifty-seven.

Michael Collins, and Fionán Lynch was appointed Minister for Education.[4] De Valera refused to recognise the provisional government and appointed his own cabinet with Michael Hayes as Minister for Education. The Irish Free State came into existence on 16 January 1922 when the provisional government formally accepted the transfer of power in Dublin Castle.

The people of Ireland had achieved the right to elect from among their fellow citizens those whom they wished to have as leaders in a parliament situated in Dublin.

The First Education Administration

Fionán Lynch formally assumed responsibility for education affairs on 1 February 1922 and took over responsibility for the supervision of three separate Boards of Commissioners:

1 The Board of Commissioners of National Education
2 The Board of Commissioners for Intermediate Education
3 The Board of Commissioners for Endowed Schools

Seosamh Ó Néill (Joseph O'Neill) was appointed Chief Administrative Officer of the three boards and Pádraig Ó Brolcháin (Patrick Bradley) was appointed Chief Executive Officer for the National Board.

On 31 January 1922 Ó Brolcháin convened a meeting of the Board of Commissioners of National Education and informed them that they were being disbanded.[5] Thus the Board, which had been in existence since 1831, ceased to exist.

On 26 October 1922 the Dáil passed its first Act, the Constitution of the Irish Free State (Saorstát Éireann) Act. It declared that:

• Irish was the national language of the Irish Free State
• the English language would be equally recognised as an official language
• all citizens had the right to free elementary education.

The Department of Education was formally established in June 1924 under the Ministers and Secretaries Act (1924), and the administration of all educational services came under the control of a State Ministry and State Parliament.[6] The State, through the Department of Education, would maintain control over the

---

4 For evidence that effective power was assumed by the Ministers of the provisional government, *The Irish Independent*, 19 January 1922, and *The Irish Times*, 1 February 1922. The records of the Department of Education list Fionán Lynch as Minister for Education from 1 April 1922.
5 *The Irish Times*, 1 February 1922
6 D. H. Akenson, *A Mirror to Kathleen's Face*, p. 32

national school system and the curriculum taught in national schools, and the
Department of Finance would maintain control over the conditions of service
and the payment of teachers.

The Irish Question

On achieving independence, and in response to the considerable public
nationalistic fervour, the government felt obliged to promote national
regeneration. This political objective was to be furthered by the restoration of
the Irish language, the responsibility for which was passed on to national school
teachers.[7] The methods used to achieve the restoration, and the rewards and
penalties system used, had serious consequences for the conditions of service of
many teachers. Some teachers, such as teachers in Gaeltacht schools, were
promoted and received special bonuses, while others were demoted and suffered
a loss of salary increments.

Public Notice No. 4, issued on 1 February 1922, declared that, from the 17
March 1922, 'the Irish language be taught, or used as a medium of instruction,
for not less than one full hour each day in all National Schools where there was
a teacher competent to teach it'.[8]

The First National Programme Conference, 1922

On 6 January 1921 representatives from the INTO and a number of other
organisations came together to draft a National Programme of Primary
Instruction. The conference's report, issued on 22 January 1922, was
provisionally adopted by the Minister for Education and became operational for
all national schools on 1 April 1922.[9] Irish was made a compulsory subject and
the fees for the teaching of Irish as an 'extra subject' were withdrawn.

While the First National Programme was amended in 1926 and 1934, its
objective, structure and content remained unchanged up to 1971, when the 'New
Curriculum' was issued.[10]

The Recruitment of Teachers

Prior to independence, seven teacher training colleges had been receiving grants
from the Commissioners of National Education. In 1922 St Mary's Training
College, Belfast, passed to the jurisdiction of the Minister of Education for
Northern Ireland. In the Irish Free State, recruitment through the monitorial
system was terminated in 1925; the non-denominational teacher-training

---

7   John Coolahan, *Irish Education: History and Structure*, p. 41
8   Public Notice No. 4, Ministry of Education, 1 February 1922
9   National Programme of Primary Instruction, 1922
10 John Coolahan, *Irish Education: History and Structure*, pp. 38–40

establishment at Marlborough Street was closed with effect from 1 September 1928; and the remaining five denominational training colleges continued under the control of the State.

The Establishment of the Preparatory Colleges

In furtherance of the State policy of restoring the Irish language, all trainees had to reside in the training colleges and Irish was made the colloquial language.

In 1926 the Department of Education established seven Preparatory Colleges, three for Catholic boys, three for Catholic girls, and a co-educational one for Protestant boys and girls.[11] Preference for admission to the colleges was given to students from the Irish-speaking districts, the Gaeltachts. Irish was the medium of instruction and it was the language used by students during all domestic and social activities.[12] From the outset the scheme was opposed by the INTO and the inspectorate.[13]

The Inspectorate

Teacher rating predated Saorstát Éireann, and it was probably applied most vigorously during the Starkie regime. During the reign of the Commissioners of National Education, inspectors supervised teachers, ensured that the rules and regulations were complied with, and had the final word on whether or not a teacher should continue to be paid, promoted or be demoted.

Although some changes did occur after independence, particularly in the curriculum, little changed in the operation of the inspection system. The day-to-day administration was still under the control of the officers who had served under Starkie, and the old teacher 'merit mark' system continued.

A teacher was deemed to be 'Highly Efficient', 'Efficient' or 'Inefficient'. Salary placement was dependent on the category achieved: a demotion from a 'Highly Efficient' rating to an 'Efficient' rating meant the loss of an increment on the supernormal scale, while demotion from 'Efficient' to 'Inefficient' meant the loss of an increment on the ordinary scale.

Not alone could a bad rating mean the loss of an increment but it could also affect one's chances of promotion. Teachers were suspicious about the operation of the merit mark system due to the fact that the percentage of 'Highly Efficient' both nationally and within each inspectoral district always seemed to come out at about 28 per cent, and the less than 'efficient' scarcely ever exceeded 10 per cent.

The actual percentages were as follows:[14]

---

11 Dáil Debates, 24 February 1926
12 Rules for National Schools, Department of Education, August 1932
13 Séamus Fenton, *It All Happened, Reminiscences*, p. 93
14 *Irish School Weekly*, 5 March 1927

Year	Highly Efficient	Efficient	Inefficient
1923–24	28%	62%	10%
1924–25	28%	63%	9%
1925–26	28%	62%	10%

The statistical constancy of the grading of so many teachers 'was a source of wonder if not of admiration to the individuals concerned'.[15] It appeared that no matter how efficient a teacher was, he/she could not be graded higher unless a vacancy in the higher grade occurred due to a death, resignation, retirement, or another teacher's downgrading.

The retention and the method of implementation of the merit mark system remained as one of the main causes of constant tension in relations between the administration, the inspectorate and teachers. It gave rise to serious discontent in the teaching profession.

The Report of the Committee on Inspection, 1927

A unanimous report by 'A Committee of Inquiry into the Inspection System', established by the Minister, was well received by the delegates at the 1927 INTO Annual Congress.[16]

The report identified the chief defect of the inspection system: 'too little attention was attached to the directive and specifically educational aspect of inspection in comparison with its aspect as a controlling agency'.[17]

In March 1928 the Department issued a circular to managers, teachers and inspectors implementing a new inspection scheme with effect from 1 August 1928. It provided an Appeals Board for teachers against unfavourable reports issued by inspectors. It also included a proposal by the Minister to introduce a Primary Certificate Examination; the first examination was held in 1929. This examination was always viewed with disfavour by teachers and its abolition in 1967 was welcomed by all. The new inspection system still retained the merit mark rating system of 'Highly Efficient', 'Efficient' and 'Inefficient'.

Relations between the inspectorate and teachers were further strained by a circular issued by the Department in 1929 instructing inspectors to make the award of the rating 'Highly Efficient' or 'Efficient' largely dependent on the proficiency of the teacher in the use of Irish as a teaching medium.[18] The INTO

15 T. J. O'Connell, *A Hundred Years of Progress*, p. 416

16 The chairman was Rev. L. J. McKenna; he had also been the chairman of the Second National Programme Conference. *Irish School Weekly*, 8 October 1927

17 Report of the Committee on Inspection in Primary Schools, 1927

18 Circular to Managers, Teachers and Inspectors on Teaching through the Medium of Irish, Department of Education, July 1931

was outraged that a teacher's salary should be dependent on use of the Irish language.

While it existed, the rating system was one of the greatest sources of grievance for INTO members. Records of teachers' annual inspection reports bear testimony to the level of inspectoral supervision and the harshness of conditions and penalties imposed on teachers in operating the system.

Developments in the Irish Civil Service from 1921

The Saorstát government guaranteed that the system of remuneration and the terms of pension regulations governing the British civil service would continue to be applicable to the Irish civil service.[19] The method of remuneration introduced for civil servants in March 1920 gave them a basic salary and a twice-yearly bonus determined on the increase or decrease in the cost-of-living index.[20] In addition, retired civil servants were entitled to a six-monthly review of the bonus element that was used in the calculation of their pensions.

National teachers had been offered a similar system for the determination of remuneration but they had opted to accept a consolidated salary scale in their 1920 salary negotiations.[21]

Civil servants were awarded substantial increases in the bonuses for 1920, 1921 and 1922 due to increases in the cost-of-living index. Teachers had to depend on the instalment increases to their basic scale salary to compensate them for the increase in the cost of living.

The cost-of-living index peaked at 165 on 1 March 1921 and declined almost continuously to an index of 60 in 1936. Consequently, the cost-of-living bonus paid to serving civil servants was reduced at each review date, as were the pensions of retired civil servants. During this period the pay and pension bill for the civil service declined significantly and resulted in savings in public finances.[22]

Transfers

At the time of independence, there were about 21,000 civil servants in Ireland who were administering the affairs of the Crown; half of them worked in the Post Office. Those who were not prepared to serve under the new government were granted special concessions, such as added years. Those who remained in

---

19 Article 10 of the Treaty and Article 78 of the Constitution fulfilled these commitments.
  Gerard Hughes, *The Irish Civil Service Superannuation Scheme*, p. 7
20 This bonus is not to be confused with the war bonus.
21 Teachers appointed on a whole-time basis by the Technical Instruction Committees
  adopted the civil service method of determining remuneration.
22 Gerard Hughes, *The Irish Civil Service Superannuation Scheme*, p. 114. Data on civil
  service pay and pensions and average industrial earnings and consumer prices are given
  in Table 1.1, p. 13.

the Irish service were guaranteed no less favourable terms than if they continued to serve in the English service. They were referred to as 'transferred officers'. The inherited civil service bureaucracy was staffed almost entirely by 'former functionaries of the United Kingdom'[23] and they brought with them the imperial civil service structures and procedures. This meant a continuation, almost without change, of the practices, precedents and prejudices of the previous regime.

Notwithstanding the terms of the Treaty, one of the first acts of the Saorstát Government was to abolish the negotiating machinery that had existed prior to 1922; the Civil Service Arbitration Board and the National Whitley Council were discontinued. The Civil Service Regulation Act, 1924 gave the Executive Council power to appoint Civil Service Commissioners who would control entry into the service. It gave the Minister for Finance power over the classification, remuneration and other conditions of service of all permanent and temporary employees in the service.

The tight grip that successive governments were able to maintain on expenditure for the civil service and public employees, during the inter-war period, was possible because salaries, pensions and other conditions of service were determined by the Minister for Finance without reference to any external body.

Superannuation Acts

Much of the pension legislation relating to the civil service, which was passed between the First and Second World Wars, was concerned with the interpretation and implementation of the superannuation scheme as it applied to transferred officers.[24]

The Superannuation Acts of 1929, 1936, and 1942 ensured that civil servants, and members of the RIC who resigned or were dismissed during the period 1916–1923 because of their nationalist sympathies, would be no worse off as regards the application of the Superannuation Code than had their service not been broken.[25]

Officers who were appointed to the civil service for the first time were accorded the same pension conditions as those who had transferred in. Efforts by civil service staff associations to improve the terms of the superannuation arrangements were met by an attitude of financial stringency on the part of the government because of the economic situation in the country.

---

23 D. H. Akenson, *A Mirror to Kathleen's Face*, p. 31
24 Ronan Fanning (1978) *The Irish Department of Finance 1922–58*, Dublin: Institute of Public Administration, p. 190, quoted in Gerard Hughes, *The Irish Civil Service Superannuation Scheme*, p. 112
25 DEPD, Vol. 63, col. 1134, quoted in Gerard Hughes, *The Irish Civil Service Superannuation Scheme*, p. 113

Civil Servants' Salary Revisions, 1926

In 1926 the Minister for Finance, Earnest Blythe, introduced a revised contract of employment for future entrants into certain grades of the civil service. The new contract had benefits and disadvantages, the principal new arrangements being as follows:

1 'Differentiated scales' as between married men and single men were introduced.
2 Single men would be placed on salaries reduced by about 25 per cent.
3 Women and single men up to the age of twenty-five would be paid the same salaries.
4 Once they were married men would get a substantial increase.
5 An allowance of £10 a year would be paid for each child up to a maximum of £60.
6 Women, who were obliged to retire when they married, would receive a gratuity subject to the following conditions: teachers with six years' service or more would receive a marriage gratuity of a month's pensionable emoluments for every year served, up to a maximum of twelve months' pensionable emoluments.[26] (A regulation was introduced in 1924 which declared that female civil servants holding established posts would be required on marriage to resign from the civil service.)[27]

Heretofore, all men had been paid the same rate, and the introduction of 'differentiated scales' as between married and single men was strenuously opposed. The civil service campaigned against it for many years.

Teachers, 1922–29

In contrast to the esteem in which they were held in their communities, relations between national teachers and educational authorities in Ireland were never good. Their major objective, at all times, was to have their status within society confirmed and the valuable work they carried out recognised by the receipt of satisfactory remuneration and good conditions of service. These objectives were very difficult to attain as their pay was controlled by politicians who were always endeavouring to control public expenditure. There was no established negotiating machinery nor was there any agreed procedure whereby one could seek redress. Very often salary reviews were intermingled with administrative reforms, curricular revisions, and the implementation of recommendations from various commissions or committees.

Under the British regime, the INTO had been involved in a continuous campaign to improve the status and salaries of teachers, and its objectives were

---

26 *Irish School Weekly*, 15 August 1925
27 Circular 24/24, Department of Finance, 9 May 1924

no different under the new government. These ongoing battles became more intense during the first decades of the new State because of salary cuts and adjustments made to conditions of employment. These salary reviews and changes were interwoven with curricular reform, in particular government policy on the Irish language, the role of the inspectorate in implementing the rules and regulations of the Department of Education, and teacher training.

Four phases in relations between governments, respective Ministers for Education, and the INTO can be identified:

Phase 1	1922–1932, Cumann na nGael Governments
Phase 2	1932–1948, Fianna Fáil Governments (The pivotal event during this period was the 1946 teachers' strike.)
Phase 3	1948–1985, Coalition and Fianna Fáil Governments
Phase 4	1986–2000, Coalition Governments

The Salary Cut, 1923

The Irish Free State came into existence on 16 January 1922 and the provisional government became responsible for the payment of the third instalment of the 1920 Salary Agreement, which fell due for payment on 1 April 1922.

The War of Independence, followed by the Civil War, had resulted in severe damage to the economy through loss of production, destruction of property and increased security costs.[28]

The urgent requirement to provide resources for the huge task of reconstruction, in conjunction with a zealous desire by the government to live within its means, resulted in the imposition of stringent controls in spending by the Saorstát Government, which was determined 'to adopt a policy of rigid opposition to any extension of State activity which involves a burden on the Exchequer and is not of proved urgency in the public interest'.[29]

On 2 November 1923 Blythe, the Minister for Finance, proposed a reduction of 10 per cent in the salaries of all public servants, including national teachers, and a cut of one shilling per week in the old age pension; the latter left a particularly bitter legacy.[30]

The reduction was applied to the salary scales of all serving national teachers, but civil servants continued to benefit from the scales granted in 1918 and the vagaries of the cost-of-living bonus.[31] However, new scales, which were the old scales reduced by 10 per cent, were introduced with effect from 1 November

28 James Meenan, *The Irish Economy Since 1922*, p. 53
29 Joseph Brennan, Secretary of the Department of Finance, Memorandum from
   Department of Finance, 23 April 1923, File 208, Department of Education Archives
30 Dáil Debates, Vol. 2, November 1923, p. 672
31 Circular 44/24, Department of Finance, 21 November 1924

1924 to apply to new entrants to the service and those who were promoted within the service.[32]

The resentment of teachers over the unequal imposition of the salary cut was to remain for several decades. Editorial comment in nearly all of the daily newspapers condemned the government's action and supported the teachers in their reaction.[33] The CEC called a Special Congress for Saturday, 24 November 1923, and organised a campaign whereby every TD was lobbied by a deputation of teachers from his own constituency to protest against the cut and forestall the danger of further cuts.

As pensions were calculated on the average salary of the last three years of service, teachers retiring during the payment of the instalments and after 1 November 1923 had their pensions calculated on much reduced salaries.

The Northern Ireland Government honoured the 1920 Salary Agreement in full. However, new salary scales for teachers were introduced with effect from 1 January 1926, which reflected a 7 per cent reduction.

A Legal Challenge to the 'Cut'

The INTO supported a High Court challenge to the legal authority of the government to cut salaries. Mr Justice Meredith ruled on the 29 July 1924 that while the government had the legal right to make a cut in teachers' salaries there was no evidence to show that this particular cut had been properly made. The teacher-plaintiff was awarded the costs of the High Court action.[34]

The government appealed the verdict and the Supreme Court concurred with the High Court judgment and the costs of the appeal were again awarded to the plaintiff.[350] However, as the judgment did not rule against the authority to make the cuts, only the manner in which they were made, the cuts were applied and teachers' position remained the same.

In the course of his statement to the Dáil on 25 March 1926, Blythe announced that while he had no intention of restoring the 10 per cent, he would make no further cuts in teachers' salaries.

The next range of cutbacks was applied to the general education field in 1929. They were as follows:

1 The evening continuation schools in Dublin and other parts of the Free State were closed from the end of March.
2 The special fees paid to national teachers for classes outside school hours, teaching mathematics, gardening, etc., from which teachers derived substantial income, were withdrawn.

---

32 Ibid.
33 Editorial, *Irish School Weekly*, 17 November 1923
34 *Irish School Weekly*, 2 August 1924; the plaintiff was Martin Leydon, a teacher in the Central Model School, Marlborough Street, Dublin
35 *Irish School Weekly*, 2 January 1926

3   Summer courses in Irish for national teachers were discontinued.

4   The subsidy for winter Gaelic League classes was withdrawn.

5   Summer courses for secondary teachers in art, science, mathematics and Irish were also discontinued.

Pensions 1922–1926

The Historical Position of the Pension Fund

The development of the pension scheme for national teachers, from independence up to the year 2000, can be divided into four phases:

1   From independence to 1934
2   From 1934 to 1950, the Roe Committee
3   From 1950 to 1968, the Ryan Tribunal
4   From 1968 to 2000.

In 1918 a new and improved superannuation scheme was introduced for teachers in England and Scotland. In 1921, the CEC and the commissioners had agreed a new pension scheme but due to the political situation it did not come into operation.

The main differences between the teachers' 1914 scheme and that enjoyed by civil servants were as follows:

• The civil service scheme was non-contributory.

• Male civil servants were entitled to a lump sum, in addition to a pension, on retirement, but their pensions were based on eightieths.

• Female civil servants were entitled to a pension based on sixtieths but no lump sum.

• All teachers' pensions were based on eightieths with no lump sum.

Under the British Pensions Increases Act, 1920, teacher pensioners in Great Britain had their pensions increased by 30, 40 or 50 per cent, but the vast majority of Irish teacher pensioners were excluded from the full benefit of this Act.

During the years immediately following the changeover of government the CEC realised that the probability of getting sanction for the new pension scheme was remote. Consequently, as a matter of policy, it pressed for the full implementation of the terms of the 1920 Act for retired teachers.

In May 1922 General Michael Collins, Minister for Finance, promised a deputation from the CEC that he would correct the situation by having the necessary legislation passed in the Dáil. However, this did not happen until July 1923. Even then it did not fully correct the position; it left a large number of teachers disaffected, either because they received little benefit or no benefit at all. Under the Act, increases would be assessed on 'existing pensions', payable on 6 August 1920. The increases payable were:

- 50 per cent where the pension was £50 per annum or under
- 40 per cent where the pension exceeded £50 but did not exceed £100 in the case of a married person
- 30 per cent where the pension exceeded £100 but was less than £150 per year in the case of a single person, or exceeded £130 but was less than £200 in the case of a married person.

The Monthly Payment of Pensions, 1924

On 11 October 1924 the Minister for Education signed an order whereby payment of pensions was changed from quarterly payments to monthly payments, with effect from 1 October 1924. The first monthly pension was issued in November 1924.

Service as a Monitor, Pupil Teacher, Lay Assistant, JAM

Service as a lay assistant in a capitation school, as a JAM, monitor, pupil-teacher, or as teacher in an industrial school was not regarded as 'service' for pension purposes. This was a major cause of concern for the INTO. The salary settlement of 1920 had granted lay assistants in capitation schools personal salaries and had recommended that their service should be deemed pensionable. The CEC, at every occasion possible, pressed to have lay assistants and JAMs included in the pension scheme.

Except for a small number of men employed in Christian Brothers Schools, all of the lay assistants were women.[36]

In June 1926 the Minister for Education, Professor O'Sullivan, in response to the repeated claim by the INTO that lay teachers and JAMs should be included in the pension scheme, stated that:

- as no actuarial valuation of the pension fund had been carried out since 1913, the Minister for Finance would arrange for one to be carried out at an early date
- until that report became available no decision would be taken about the inclusion of any extra teachers in the pension scheme.

However, when the actuary's report was published in January 1929, the probability of any concession was removed.

---

36 There were over 1,800 JAMs and approximately 600 lay teachers in Convent and Monastery National Schools who got no pension or gratuity of any kind on retirement.

Teachers in Northern Ireland and the Pension Fund

Following partition, the assets of the Pension Fund were divided between the Northern and Southern administrations, and each jurisdiction became responsible for the teachers in its employment.

When the actuary's report on the Teachers' Pension Fund was published in January 1929, Eamonn Mansfield, an INTO activist and expert on the scheme, raised many questions on the contents of the report. He queried, among other items, the manner in which the amount transferred to Northern Ireland was computed. He claimed that the fund was incorrectly distributed in the ratio of 32:68 and not in the ratio of 27:73, which was the proportion of pensioners, North and South, at the date of allocation on 1 February, 1922.[37]

The reply of the Minister for Finance in the Dáil on 3 July 1929 does not clarify how the Saorstát's portion of the assets, 68.2 per cent, was determined, but it seems to suggest that it was a compromise between contributions made and liabilities incurred.

The Government and the Pension Fund, 1927–30

All of the actuarial valuations of the Pension Fund, except the first one in 1885, declared that the fund was in deficit, on some occasions seriously so.

The 1897 Act[38] had divided the Pension Fund into two separate accounts, 'The Teachers' Contribution Account' and 'The Endowment Account'. The Teachers' Contribution Account was always up-to-date as contributions were deducted from salaries, and if it was found to be insolvent contributions were increased. Notwithstanding a categorical undertaking to keep 'The Endowment Account' solvent, the government did not fulfil its responsibility in this regard. Clearly, the deteriorating position of the Pension Fund, with its increasing deficit, was caused by the Endowment Account not receiving the proportion due from the Exchequer.[39] The amount of money required continued to increase year after year but the condition of the national finances meant that the Saorstát government was not in a position to deal with it.[40]

The Appointment of an Actuary, 1927

In January 1927 the Minister appointed the British Government's actuary, Epps, to examine the Teachers' Pension Fund as at 31 December 1926. On this occasion, the CEC decided not to seek the appointment of an actuary on its own

---

37 *Irish School Weekly*, 15 March 1929
38 National School Teachers (Ireland) Act, 1897; the pension rules to implement the provisions of the Act were issued in 1898
39 The required funding ratio was 1:3.
40 National School Teachers' (Ireland) Fund, Statement of Accounts for 1927

behalf but to wait for the publication of the report and then, if it was thought necessary, appoint one to examine the report and 'give such expert opinion on the various matters raised as the INTO would think necessary'.[41]

The Actuarial Valuation Report, 1929

The actuary submitted his report to the government in November 1928. In his valuation he did not differentiate between the Teachers' Contribution Account and the Endowment Account; he valued the assets and liabilities of the fund as a single unit.

The CEC suspected that this method of assessing the fund was at the behest of the government, as on all other occasions the funds had been valued separately. If the separate account method had been used the insolvency of the fund would have been attributed to the failure of the government to make good its required contribution to the Endowment Account. The actuary reported that the fund was in deficit to the sum of £4,210,364 and that it was growing at compound interest.[42]

He estimated that to make good the deficiency, either of the following contributions would be required:

   (a) in addition to the existing State contribution, an annual Exchequer contribution of
     £212,000 for forty years

or

   (b) an increase of 8.5 percentage points in existing teacher contributions of 4 per cent,
     making a total of 12.5 per cent.

The Minister for Finance sent a copy of the report to the INTO and followed it with a letter on 7 January 1929, outlining the government's position:

-    ... in the present position of the national finances ... the Government cannot entertain the possibility of further financial assistance to the Fund beyond that involved in existing commitments
-    ... the government is not obliged to make good the deficiency and the teachers should do so by increasing their annual contribution from 4% to 12.5%.[43]

The Minister's proposal was completely unacceptable to the CEC. The suggestion that teachers should contribute one-eighth of their salaries over the next forty years to make good a deficiency for which, as they saw it, they were not responsible, triggered strong protest.[44] As far as the CEC was concerned the

---

41 *Irish School Weekly*, 1 December 1928
42 CEC Report to Congress 1932
43 *Irish School Weekly*, 13 July 1929
44 CEC Report to Congress 1932

deficiency was in the Endowment Account and the responsibility for making that solvent rested with the State.

The CEC submitted the report to its own actuary, Dr Howell, who concluded that Epps's figures were accurate. He suggested that the fund should be reassessed to take account of the two years that had elapsed since 31 December 1926.

The actuary's report was circulated to all INTO Branches and published in full in *Irish School Weekly*, 23 February 1929. It was the main topic at the 1929 Easter Congress in Waterford. The delegates resolved that there should be no compromise on the pension question as the historic obligation to maintain the solvency of the Fund rested with the government.[45]

The Government's Position

At a meeting with a CEC deputation on 8 August 1929, Blythe conceded that the teachers should not be asked to make up the entire deficiency, but they should have to pay some of it.[46]

At a meeting that evening the CEC decided to hold a Special Delegate Conference on 1 November and to organise special information conferences for members in thirteen centres throughout the Saorstát on 21 and 28 September.

The INTO Special Delegate Conference, November 1929

The delegates at the INTO Special Delegate Conference, on 1–2 November 1929, passed some resolutions and decided on an intensive publicity and lobbying campaign which resulted in:

- every elected public representative being approached in his constituency by deputations of local teachers
- County Council and Corporation meetings being addressed by local teacher leaders
- the arrangement of public meetings which were addressed by local dignitaries, bishops, school managers and members of the CEC.

Intensive publicity was generated in *Irish School Weekly* and in the daily newspapers. In addition, meetings were held with the Ministers for Finance and Education, but no progress was made.

---

45 *Irish School Weekly*, 13 April 1929
46 T. J. O'Connell, *A Hundred Years of Progress*, p. 262

Review of the Period, 1922–29

National teachers had suffered very badly under the British regime in the matter of salary, pensions and conditions of service; they had expected that under a national government things would be different.

Many teachers had been active participants and, in many cases, leaders in the fight for independence; Lloyd George had called the rebellion in Ireland 'the revolt of the teachers'. A number of national teachers held high profile positions in the political parties. In addition, teachers were influential and powerful figures in their own areas. There was not a parish in the country that did not have two or more national schools. Teachers were very involved in social, religious, and sporting activities, and were often the secretary or chairman of committees associated with these activities. However, they were not treated on a par with other public servants.

The following may explain why this was so:

- The national finances were in a precarious state and the political situation was very unstable.
- A number of fractious general elections took place and it was not until after the general election of June 1927, when Fianna Fáil deputies took their seats in the Dáil for the first time, that a truly democratic system of government and opposition came into operation.
- It may have been thought that national teachers, being dispersed throughout the country, would not be able to organise a cohesive opposition to the cuts or that teachers would be prepared to suffer the cuts for the sake of the country 'in this its time of need'.
- The inherited civil service bureaucracy continued the traditions of the previous regime.

The economic situation was to be exacerbated by the Stock Market Crash in 1929, which had repercussions throughout the world. The position of national teachers was to deteriorate further under the Cumann na nGael governments, and, as will be seen, the situation did not improve under the succeeding Fianna Fáil governments.

7

Salaries and Pensions, 1930–34

The Economic Crisis

Between 1929 and 1931 the World Economic Trade Index dropped by 59 per cent, affecting economic activity and trade in every country throughout the world.

In response the Minister for Finance, Earnest Blythe, told a CEC deputation that he could hold out no hope of conceding any claims for improvements in salaries, allowances, pensions and conditions of service.

The discomfort of teachers was further increased when, in 1931, the Minister made the award of salary increments dependent on their proficiency in Irish.[1]

The Pension Fund

The INTO Easter Congress of 1930 adopted a resolution instructing the CEC to enter into negotiations with the government on the basis that 'the retention of a Pension Fund need not be the basis for a settlement'. This proposal, which was a fundamental departure from the previously held position,[2] was submitted to the Ministers for Education and Finance.

However, despite constant representations by the CEC, public meetings, and questions in the Dáil, no progress was made on the Pension Fund question.

The INTO Offer in November 1931

Blythe introduced a Supplementary Budget in the Dáil on 6 November 1931 to make good a budgetary imbalance of £900,000. He proposed to recover £450,000 of the deficit by increasing income tax and increasing tax on petrol, and to recover the remaining £450,000 by reducing the salaries of public servants and national teachers by 10 per cent.

In the light of this proposal, the CEC held an emergency meeting on 9 November 1931 and decided to offer the Minister an alternative proposal: it would recommend to its members a salary cut of 5 per cent, which, with the

---

1 Circular to Managers, Teachers and Inspectors on Teaching through the Medium of Irish, Department of Education, July 1931. *Irish School Weekly*, 27 January 1934
2 *Irish School Weekly*, 17 May 1930

4 per cent pension contribution would make a total cut of 9 per cent, if the government was prepared to:

- convert the pension scheme into a non-contributory one
- include lay assistants and JAMs in the pension scheme
- take full responsibility for the payment of pensions to all teachers
- give an undertaking that any cuts would be subject to review
- apply any proposed salary cuts to all public servants.

In a letter on 5 December 1931 the Minister submitted the following counter-proposals to the INTO:

- teachers' salaries should be reduced by 6 per cent
- the State would accept liability for the payment of all teachers' pensions
- the existing rights of teachers to the return of pension contributions would be preserved
- JAMs and lay assistants in convent and monastery schools would be included in the pension scheme
- terms with regard to back service and other details would be the subject of further discussions.[3]

The CEC recommended the deal at a Special Delegate Conference, held in Dublin on 19 December 1931, and the government's proposal was accepted by 212 votes to 121.[4] However, before the deal could be implemented the government was dissolved on 29 January 1932, and a general election was called for 16 February.

The General Election, February 1932

By this time the world-wide economic crisis was seriously affecting Ireland. Exports of meat and dairy produce had dropped sharply and there was a big fall in the price of cattle and sheep. Many factories had closed and unemployment figures had risen by 50 per cent.[5]

During the election campaign these economic difficulties were exploited by Fianna Fáil. Teachers' salaries and pensions also became a very live issue, with Fianna Fáil spokespersons denouncing the CEC for betraying their Pension Fund. In a speech at Rathmines Town Hall, Eamon de Valera promised civil servants that if his party was returned to power, salaries of £300 or £400 would not be subject to any cut and that civil servants would have an Arbitration Board

---

3 CEC Report to Congress 1932, p. 47
4 CEC Report to Congress 1932, p. 44
5 John A. Murphy, *Ireland in the Twentieth Century*, p. 74

to deal with matters between the service and the government.[6] Shortly afterwards he stated that the same principle would apply to national teachers.[7]

Fianna Fáil secured 72 of the available 154 seats[8] and de Valera formed a coalition government with the Labour Party and three Independent deputies.[9] De Valera was elected President of the Executive Council and he appointed Tomás Ó Deirg as Minister for Education and Seán MacEntee as Minister for Finance.

On 15 March 1932, in response to questions in the Dáil on proposed salary cuts, MacEntee stated:

> As far as the lower grades of the Civil Service and the lower ranks of the Gardaí are concerned we hope to leave them immune from any economies that may be made ... Everything else will be cut before the standard of living of the lower grade Civil Servants and Gardaí is reduced. I cannot go further than that.[10]

He did not refer to national teachers.

The INTO Annual Congress, 1932

Even though the government's proposals had been endorsed at the Special Conference in December 1931, opposition to the deal grew among INTO members. In the 1932 elections for the CEC 'virtually every member of the executive who had negotiated the Blythe agreement was defeated'.[11]

The delegates at Congress adopted a resolution repudiating the decision of the Special Conference and rejected the proposals put forward by the previous government. They also agreed that the CEC would not have to consider itself tied either to the continuation or abolition of the Pension Fund.[12]

The CEC and the New Government

On 20 May 1932 a deputation from the CEC met the Minister for Finance, Seán MacEntee, and the Minister for Education, Tomás Ó Deirg, to discuss the question of teachers' pensions. The CEC deputation found that the proposals for consideration did not differ very much from those forwarded by Blythe. The

---

6 *The Irish Press*, January 1931
7 *The Irish Press*, 16 February 1932
8 Three of the newly elected Fianna Fáil TDs were members of the INTO: Breathnach, Rice and O'Rourke; at the time the INTO was affiliated to the Labour Party.
9 Fianna Fáil was to remain in government for the next sixteen years. John A. Murphy, *Ireland in the Twentieth Century*, p. 75
10 Dáil Report, 15 March 1932
11 T. J. O'Connell, *A Hundred Years of Progress*, p. 265
12 Ibid., p. 267

deputation was asked to accept the Blythe proposals 'as the basis of negotiation'.[13]

Following extensive negotiations between the two sides, the following proposals were tabled by the government:

- the proposed salary cut would be reduced from 6 per cent to 5 per cent, making a total deduction of 9 per cent
- pensionable income would remain unchanged
- the 4 per cent pension contribution would continue to be refundable
- the salary cut in the case of lay assistants would be 9 per cent
- the salary cut in the case of JAMs would be 6 per cent
- JAMs and lay assistants could join the pension scheme and get two-thirds recognition for service given before 1 April 1932
- the 'cuts' would take effect from 1 August 1932 and continue in operation for one year, when the position would be reviewed
- the State would accept responsibility for the future payment of all pensions.

INTO members rejected the offer by a ratio of 13:1, and the CEC maintained an extensive campaign against the proposals: advertisements were placed in the daily newspapers and up-to-date information on teachers' salaries and pensions was circulated to TDs, County Councillors, and other people in prominent and representative positions.

The INTO had great difficulty arranging meetings with the Minister for Education and many requests for meetings were turned down. Almost two years were to pass before MacEntee would again meet a CEC deputation.[14] A number of requests to the Taoiseach for meetings were also turned down.

Inquiries and Legislation

Inquiry into Temporary Reductions

Following the general election the government established a Committee of Inquiry into Temporary Reductions in the Pay of Public Servants.[15] The committee decided that it would not receive any oral evidence, and invited interested parties to make written submissions. The CEC submitted a comprehensive document on the following subjects:

- Salaries under the British Regime
- The 1920 Salary Scales

13 *Irish School Weekly*, 4 June 1932
14 T. J. O'Connell, *A Hundred Years of Progress*, p. 267
15 The committee was established in September 1932; it became known as 'The Cuts Committee'.

- The Ten Per Cent and Other Cuts
- The Training of Teachers
- The Income of Teachers
- The Probationary Period
- The Incremental Scales
- The Lower Paid Grades
- A Comparison With Other Employments
- Teachers' Pensions
- Previous Proposals for Reduction of Salary
- What of the Future?[16]

While it was known that the committee submitted a majority and a minority report to the government in October 1932, neither report was published nor were any of the recommendations made known. Newspaper reports, believed to be well-founded, claimed that the majority report recommended substantial cuts to the pay of army personnel and teachers but not to the pay of civil servants. A request from the CEC to President de Valera in June 1932 to receive a deputation was answered on 10 October by the President, stating that no useful purpose would be served by receiving a deputation, particularly as a special committee was considering the pay of all public servants.[17]

The General Election in January 1933

In January 1933 de Valera called a snap general election,[18] during which the INTO interviewed the leaders of the different political parties. President de Valera informed the deputation that he would abide by the spirit of his declaration made at Rathmines during the previous election.[19]

Fianna Fáil won seventy-seven seats, an overall majority; Cumann na nGael won forty-eight seats,[20] Labour eight seats, the Centre Party eleven seats, and

---

16 At that time a national teacher at the age of thirty was lucky if he/she was earning £230 per annum; a bank clerk was in receipt of £270 free of tax, a clerk in the Dublin Corporation received £255. From an INTO statement submitted to the Committee of Inquiry into Temporary Reductions in Pay of Public Servants, 1 October 1932

17 *Irish School Weekly*, October 1932

18 In the autumn of 1932 a group of farmers and independents founded the Centre Party under the leadership of Frank MacDermott and James Dillon. It was pledged to move away from Civil War politics, to try to secure all-Ireland security by a conciliatory Northern policy, and to give strength and cohesion to those concerned about the economic state of the country. See John A. Murphy, *Ireland in the Twentieth Century*, pp. 77–8

19 *Irish School Weekly*, 28 January 1933

20 In September 1933, Cumann na nGael, the Centre Party and the National Guard merged to form Fine Gael, with the head of the Blueshirts, General Eoin O'Duffy as its leader. W. T. Cosgrave was leader of the party in the Dáil.

Independents nine seats. John A. Murphy attributes Fianna Fáil's success to the announcement made by de Valera in the middle of the campaign that the land annuities that farmers had to pay under the Land Acts would be halved. A record 81 per cent of the electorate turned out to vote and the result confirmed the personal ascendancy of de Valera in Irish politics.[21] De Valera was elected President of the Executive Council and MacEntee and Ó Deirg were re-appointed as Ministers for Finance and Education, respectively.

Three members of the INTO were elected as Fianna Fáil TDs, including Cormac Breathnach who was Vice-President of the INTO.

Public Services (Temporary Economies) Act, 1933

On 30 March 1933 the government introduced the Economies Bill in the Dáil, the ostensible objective of which was to compel all those paid from public funds to contribute their share to the financial needs of the country. It proposed to make deductions from salaries paid to all public sector employees during the financial year commencing 1 April 1933.

However, it was not proposed that the cuts would be applied in a similar manner to the different groups in the public service. The cuts would be applied to teachers and civil servants as follows:

Teachers:

- a percentage deduction on an ascending scale, commencing with a deduction of 5 per cent on the first £175 of annual remuneration and an increasing percentage deduction on every next £25 thereafter up to 8 per cent on any amount over £450
- a 1 per cent per annum reduction in the salaries of untrained teachers and JAMs (Their maximum salary was £139 10s. per annum.)
- a 6 per cent reduction in all personal allowances and grants, including grants for teaching cookery and laundry, grants to teachers in Fíor-Ghaeltacht schools and in Special Irish Schools outside the Gaeltacht
- a 7 per cent reduction in the capitation grants to Convent, Monastery, and Fosterage schools.

Civil Servants:

- no deduction where the salary did not exceed £300 per annum; 2 per cent on the next £100

Where the annual salary exceeded £400:

- 2 per cent on the first £400, plus
- 2.5 per cent on next £100 or part thereof, plus

---

21 John A. Murphy, *Ireland in the Twentieth Century*, p. 78

- 3 per cent on next £100 or part thereof, plus
- 4.5 per cent on next £100 or part thereof
- up to plus 25 per cent from a salary in excess of £1,600

In addition to being angered at the severity of cuts for teachers, INTO members were angered by the publication on 30 March of an unsigned memorandum by the Department of Finance, which purported to show that national teachers were leniently treated in the matter of cuts in their salaries in comparison to civil servants; that the cuts imposed on teachers were not as severe as the December 1931 cuts proposed by Blythe; that 6,000 teachers would fare better; and that nearly 8,000 would be no worse off.[22] The actual situation was that 2,000 of the group of 6,000 teachers were JAMs and untrained teachers, whose maximum salary was £139 10s. per annum, and who would have to take a cut of 1 per cent.

The bill was rushed through its second reading in the Dáil on the following day, 31 March 1933.

The Dáil Debate

During the debate in the Dáil, de Valera reiterated that he had kept his promise to civil servants not to cut low salaries, but he made no reference of his promise to national teachers.[23]

MacEntee made no attempt to justify the cuts and claimed that the INTO's campaign against the cuts was inspired by political motives and animated by a spirit of opposition to the Fianna Fáil government. He declared that 'the Government was dealing with unreasonable men' and that it was not possible to deal with the organisation.

It was stated on a number of occasions during the debate that unless teachers were prepared to negotiate a settlement on the pension question, on the terms laid down by the government, a scheme would be imposed. MacEntee stated that he was prepared to meet the INTO to discuss the matter.[24]

It would appear that the invitation to meet was a ploy used by the Minister to ensure the passage of the Economies Bill in the Dáil because when the CEC requested meetings with MacEntee, the requests were ignored.[25]

INTO One-Day Strike, 26 April 1933

The situation was exacerbated when civil servants were granted an increase in their cost-of-living bonus. The CEC called a one-day strike for 26 April to

22 Memorandum to the press from the Department of Finance on 30 March 1933. The Blythe proposals had been accepted by the Special Conference on 19 December 1931, but rejected by the 1932 Annual Congress.
23 Dáil Report, 31 March 1933
24 Dáil Report, May/June 1933
25 Letter from the Department of Finance, *Irish School Weekly*, 15 April 1933

protest against the discriminatory treatment of national teachers by the government. On the day of the strike teachers organised public protest meetings in many centres throughout the country. Reports in the newspapers generally conceded that abstention from school on that day was practically nationwide.[26]

Teachers who went on strike had their salary for that day deducted from their pay cheques, and the day was discounted in the calculation of their pension entitlements. This had serious consequences for a number of teachers as the loss of that single day resulted in the loss of a year's credit for pension purposes. The INTO made up for the loss suffered by these teachers out of its own funds.[27]

By the end of June the Economies Bill had been passed in the Dáil. The salary deductions to be made from the three groups were laid out in the Schedule to the Act. The following table sets out the deductions that applied to the different services:

Percentage Salary Reductions, 1933

£	Present Income %	National Teacher %	Army To £300 %	Civil Servant Excess £300 %
Less than 100	–	4	Nil	2
Less than 175	5	4.443	Nil	2
175–200	5.25	(100–200) 4.5	Nil	2
200–225	5.5	4.66	Nil	2
225–250	5.75	4.8	Nil	2
250–275	6	4.9	Nil	2
275–300	6.25	5	Nil	2
300–325	6.5	5.15	–	2
325–350	6.75	5.3	–	2
350–375	7	5.4	–	2
375–400	7.25	5.5	–	2
400–425	7.5	5.65	–	2.03
425–450	7.75	5.8	–	2.06
450 and over	8	6	–	2.08
500	8	6+++	–	2.1++

26 T. J. O'Connell, *A Hundred Years of Progress*, p. 268

27 Some years later the method for calculating pension service was changed to a system whereby service up to the last day of a quarter was taken into consideration. It was not until the 1980s that it was agreed that every day served should be counted as service recognised for pension purposes.

On an income of £300, a teacher had 6.5 per cent deducted, an army officer 5.15 per cent, and a civil servant nil.[28] The respective figures for reductions on a salary of £450 per annum were: a teacher, 8 per cent; an army officer, 6 per cent; and a civil servant, 2.08 per cent. The deduction for teachers was capped at 8 per cent on salaries of £450 or over as very few teachers had an income in excess of that figure; the maximum of the highest supernormal scale for men was £414. The Minister for Finance recovered two-thirds of his £280,000 budget deficit from teachers.

A New Cut

The cuts sanctioned by the Economies Act ceased on the 31 March 1934 and, with the exception of national teachers, all public servants were restored to the salary position they had prior to 1 April 1933. In addition, teachers had another salary cut imposed with effect from 1 April 1934, the sixth salary cut, making a total reduction of approximately 20 per cent between 1923 and 1934. A new pension scheme was also introduced.[29]

Civil Servants and the Brennan Commission

Dissatisfaction in the civil service over the cost-of-living bonus adjustments and consequent reductions in pensions, combined with a desire among staff associations to return to the Whitley Council system for determining their pay, led to the government establishing a 'Commission of Inquiry into the Civil Service' in 1932, under the chairmanship of Joseph Brennan. The Brennan Commission issued an interim report in 1934 and a final report in 1937.

The interim report noted that it was common practice in the community that women were paid at a lower rate to men, but that it was beyond the scope of the commission to investigate this matter. It did comment that the wage of the average man tended to be influenced by the fact that, unlike the average woman, he was usually the head of a dependent household. It did recommend that no arrangement should be made whereby the award of an independent Arbitration tribunal should be recognised either legally or *de facto* as finally binding upon the Executive Council or upon the Minister of Finance and that superannuation ought to be excluded as a matter for consideration at Arbitration.[30]

In the final report the commission recommended that:

- the bonus element in the remuneration package should be abolished by being consolidated with the basic salary[31]

---

28 The 'Economy' Bill Statement by the INTO CEC
29 Document issued by the INTO Strike Committee in 1946
30 The Brennan Commission Interim Report, presented to the Minister for Finance on 5 February 1934. Published in *Ireland*, Department of Finance, 1934, pp. 19–22.
31 This recommendation was not implemented until 1 November 1947.

- the normal retirement date should remain unchanged at sixty-five
- an actuarial investigation of the pension scheme should be carried out to ascertain the extent of the pension liability
- pensions should be contributory and a Pension Fund established out of which pensions would be paid without any further burden on the taxpayer
- the cost of the introduction of pensions for the widows and orphans of civil servants should be actuarially investigated.

Revised Rules and Regulations for National Schools, 1934

The Government's Proposals

During the second half of 1933 and at the beginning of 1934 rumours and speculation were rife in the newspapers regarding an early settlement of the teachers' pension question. The INTO was of the view that a lot of this speculation was leaked or inspired by official sources.[32]

On 23 February 1934 the CEC received a memorandum from the Department of Education setting down new salary scales and the government's proposals for the settlement of the pension question for national teachers. It also declared that a marriage ban, which had been proposed for implementation from 1 October 1933, would now become operative from 1 October 1934.

The memorandum was accompanied by a letter inviting the CEC to send representatives, 'should they so desire', to a meeting on the following day, 24 February 1934, for clarification 'lest any point of importance had been overlooked in the formulation of the new salary scales'.[33] The CEC deputation was met by a group, led by the Ministers for Finance and Education, which made it clear that it was not prepared to deviate from the proposals submitted and that it was the government's intention to place their proposals before the Dáil at an early date.

The CEC refused to endorse the proposals and stated that it was not prepared to recommend their acceptance to the teachers.

The government processed the proposals through the Houses of the Oireachtas, where they were adopted. The necessary Statutory Orders were signed and new salary structures, linked to new pension arrangements, came into operation with effect from 1 April 1934.

The Revised Normal Salary Scales

A completely new book of 'Rules and Regulations for National Schools' was issued by the Department of Education. It laid out the structure and organisation of the primary education system as it would be administered by the Department.

The main provisions of the revised salary structure were as follows:

---

32 *Irish School Weekly*, 20 January 1934
33 T. J. O'Connell, *A Hundred Years of Progress*, p. 269

- The new salary structures showed a 9 per cent reduction in the previous salary received by a teacher, an actual salary cut of 5 per cent and the retention by the government of the 4 per cent pension contributions that teachers had made previously. The normal salary scale for male principals and assistants of £333 was reduced to £303 and all other scales were proportionately reduced.
- The maximum of £139 10s. payable to untrained teachers was reduced by 6 per cent to £131. Untrained teachers appointed prior to 1 April 1905 were eligible to receive salaries applicable to trained teachers.
- The salaries and emoluments payable to all JAMs were reduced by 6 per cent, with a new maximum of £127.
- Increments would to be granted annually to eligible teachers, provided no adverse rating was received from the inspector.
- Grants, allowances and bonuses were reduced by between 5 and 9 per cent.

Supernormal Salary Scales

The maximum rates for the five categories of supernormal scales, each with five increments, were as follows:

	Average Enrolment	Maximum for Men	Maximum for Women
Category I	20–29	£301	£262
Category II	30–49	£340	£270
Category III	50–119	£352	£278
Category IV	120–239	£364	£286
Category V	240 and over	£377	£295

A school would be promoted to a higher category if it held the required higher average attendance figures for two successive calendar years, effective immediately. A school which failed to maintain the required average attendance figures for two successive calendar years would be demoted to a lower category. Assistants eligible for placement on supernormal scales were placed in Category II (30–49).

Annual Capitation Grants

In normal circumstances, an average attendance of at least twenty pupils would have to be maintained to warrant the continuing recognition of a school by the Department of Education.

From 1 April 1934 only children between four and eighteen years of age could be enrolled in a national school. It was no longer necessary to keep a separate Roll or Report Book segregating pupils 'over 15'.

The capitation rates paid to principals were reduced by approximately 10 per cent, but it was to be paid for all eligible pupils on rolls.

Convent and Monastery Schools Paid by Capitation

The Residential or Annual Capitation Grant previously paid to the conductors of convent and monastery capitation national schools was merged with the regular capitation grant and these grants were reduced by approximately 5 per cent of the net amount available.

Security of Tenure of Teachers in National Schools

The historic right of a manager to dismiss teachers without reason or good cause, merely by giving them three months notice or paying them three months' salary in lieu, was a constant source of trouble, and in some instances led to the perpetration of injustices. Some relief from this practice had been achieved by the adoption by the Catholic Hierarchy of the 'Maynooth Resolution' in 1898. While its terms had been amended in 1916, the position was not completely satisfactory and it was revised again in 1934. Henceforth, a Catholic Manager could not dismiss a teacher or serve him/her with notice of dismissal until the prior consent of the bishop had been obtained and after the teacher and/or his/her representative organisation had been heard in the teacher's defence by the bishop.

In 1935 a procedure analogous to that of the 'Maynooth Resolution' was negotiated between the INTO and most of the other Religious Teaching Orders with regard to lay teachers employed in their schools.

All of these arrangements gave a Catholic teacher virtual security from unjust dismissal by a school manager.

Other Changes

A new revised curricular programme was introduced, the main changes being:

- Where the teacher was sufficiently qualified, all work in infant classes was to be entirely through Irish.
- If the teacher was not sufficiently qualified, Irish was to be taught as a subject to infants and to be used as much as possible as a medium of instruction.
- The higher Irish course, as set down in the 1926 programme, was to be taught in all schools.

The revival of the Irish language was to be the responsibility of the national teacher and its achievement brought about through the imposition of a compulsory educational programme in primary schools.[34]

---

34 *The Sunday Tribune*, 22 February 1998

In addition to revised salary scales, revised conditions of service and a new curricular programme, a new non-contributory pension scheme was introduced and the rules for the operation of the Marriage Ban were officially promulgated.

The National School Teachers' Superannuation Scheme, 1934

During the fifty-four years in which the Pension Fund had been in existence there had been difficulties with its funding. The new 1934 scheme, which came into effect from 1 April 1934, was proposed as the solution to this funding problem. This new scheme had advantages and disadvantages for both the government and for teachers.

The advantages for the government were:

- It removed from the government the obligation of making good the deficit in the Teachers' Pension Fund.
- The teachers' pay-bill was reduced by 4 per cent.

The main disadvantage was that the continuing liability for national teachers' pensions would have to be met from Central Funds.

The advantages for teachers:

- Teachers now had a scheme similar to civil servants but without lump sum payments on retirement.
- The scheme was non-contributory and the government would henceforth be responsible for the payment of pensions to all national teachers.

The disadvantage was that the reduced salary scales resulted in correspondingly reduced pensions and, due to the three-year average rule, impacted in full on pensions awarded after 31 March 1937.[35]

The General Conditions Governing Award of a Pension

Pensions would be paid on the same basis as before, and the method of calculation for voluntary and compulsory retirement in relation to salary, age, and service remained unchanged.[36]

'Salary' for the purpose of calculating pension was defined as all monies received by the teacher from the Department of Education for duty as a national teacher, with the exception of:

---

35 The revised salaries introduced from 1 April 1934 reduced trained teachers' salaries by 9 per cent.

36 In addition to a pension, teachers in England and Northern Ireland received a lump sum equivalent to one-and-a-half times salary; teachers in the Saorstát did not receive any lump sum.

- gratuities for the instruction of pupil-teachers
- payment in respect of candidates for the Preparatory College Entrance Examinations
- special allowances to teachers in schools for Irish-speaking children outside the Gaeltacht
- the value of a teacher's residence
- any payment granted after 1 April 1934, which the Minister would declare to be excluded.

The Basis of Calculation of a Pension

A teacher had to have at least ten years of recognised service to qualify for a pension.

No male teacher could serve beyond the end of the quarter in which he reached his sixty-fifth birthday, or female teacher her sixtieth birthday. The pension would be equal to one-eightieth of the average annual salary for the three years preceding the date of retirement multiplied by the number of completed years of pensionable service up to a maximum of forty.[37]

The maximum pension that could be awarded to any teacher was one half of the average annual salary paid to him/her for the three years ending on the 31 March immediately before the date of retirement.

Completed Years of Service

Only completed years of service could be counted in determining the amount of pension, but every day on which service was given could be counted towards making up a complete year. For instance, if a teacher lost a day's salary for any reason in the school year 1 July to 30 June, recognition for that year would be lost, but if he/she served for one further day in the next school year he/she could use that day to complete the year's service.

Other Provisions

Voluntary retirement:
There were two classes of voluntary retirements:

- A teacher with at least ten years of recognised service could retire voluntarily at age sixty, and claim a pro rata pension.
- A teacher with at least thirty-five years' pensionable service could retire voluntarily at age fifty-five and claim a pro rata pension.

---

37 National School Teachers' Superannuation Scheme, 1934

Application for a pension:
As a rule, application for a pension had to be made within one year after the date of retirement.

The new scheme made no provision for the continuance of reciprocal superannuation arrangements with Northern Ireland and consequently these arrangements ceased as from 1 April 1934.

Pensions for lay assistants, JAMs and other teaching posts:
Lay assistants and JAMs were entitled to membership of the pension scheme with effect from 1 April 1934, but only two-thirds of recognised service given prior to 1 April 1934 and all service given after that date would count as pensionable service. A Manual Instructress got the same pension rights as a JAM.

Teachers in Industrial Schools or Work Mistresses were not included in the scheme. Service given in an Industrial School, a Workhouse, a Fishery School, or in any school outside Ireland was not recognised for pension purposes.[38]

Death gratuity:
A death gratuity[39] would be paid provided the teacher had given not less than five years' recognised service.

Disablement and inability gratuity:
A disablement gratuity equal to one-tenth of the average annual salary multiplied by the number of years of service would be paid.[40]

A teacher who had attained the age of fifty and was removed from the service because of 'inability to discharge the duties of a teacher efficiently' could be awarded a pension of one-eightieth of his/her average salary for each year of pensionable service.

Service interrupted for political purposes:
A new provision was made in the regulations whereby any period which the Minister for Education, with the concurrence of the Minister for Finance, deemed to be an interruption of service owing to political causes could be reckoned as pensionable service.

Teachers who rejected the 1914 rules:
The forty or fifty teachers who had not exercised their option to come under the 1914 Pension Rules were allowed to become members of the new scheme, but

---

38 An amendment was introduced to the scheme in 1941 to give relief to some of these teachers.

39 A grant to the estate of a teacher on his/her death while in the teaching service.

40 Under the 1914 Rules a teacher with less than ten years' service who became unable to serve owing to disablement of mind or body could only claim the return of pension premiums.

only half the service given prior to 1 April 1934 and all service given after that date would be counted as service for pension purposes.

Teachers who had withdrawn their premiums:
A teacher who had left the service prior to 1 April 1934 and had withdrawn his/her premiums and who re-entered the service after 1 April 1934 could repay these premiums with compound interest at 2.5 per cent, and all service before and after the break in service would count for pension purposes. If he/she did not avail of this option, the service before the break, for which premiums had been withdrawn, would not be counted in future pension calculations.

A pensioned teacher who died shortly after retirement:
Provision was made for the exceptional occasion when a pensioned teacher died after retirement and had not drawn as pension a sum equal to what his representatives would have received had he/she died on the last day of his/her service. An amount equal to the difference between what he/she had drawn in pension and the amount to which his/her representatives would have been so entitled would be paid to them.

The Teachers' Pension Fund:
As the government had assumed responsibility for the payment of pensions there was no longer a need for the Teachers' Pension Fund established under the 1879 Act. Consequently, the government issued a Statutory Order winding it up as and from 1 April 1934.[41]

Review of the New Pension Scheme

The 1934 scheme was put forward by the government as the resolution of the 'teachers' pension question' but teachers did not consider it so. The main extra benefits were:

- For the first time lay assistants and JAMs were entitled to pensions.
- The conditions for the award of death gratuity, death benefit, and disablement gratuity were improved and brought into line with those awarded to civil servants.
- Female teachers obliged to retire on marriage would be awarded a gratuity.
- Teachers with thirty-five years' pensionable service retained the right to retire at age fifty-five and claim a pension.

While the pension scheme was an improvement on the 1914 scheme, the INTO was not prepared to accept it and considered the question of salary and pensions still unresolved for the following reasons:

41 National School Teachers' Pension Fund (Winding-Up), 1934, Statutory Rules and Orders, 1934, No. 43

- Teachers had been the victims of discrimination in the various salary cuts.
- The new scheme was not retrospective: no provision was made for the award of a pension to any JAM or lay assistant who had retired from the teaching service before 1 April 1934.
- The new scheme made no provision for the continuance of reciprocal arrangements with Northern Ireland.
- The concession of the payment of a gratuity to women on compulsory retirement on marriage had a serious disadvantage, i.e. the payment of a marriage gratuity removed eligibility for a pension in the future.
- Teachers wished to have a pension scheme similar to the civil service scheme. The amount of pension payable to male and female teachers was one-eightieth of the average annual salary; male civil servants appointed after September 1909 were paid an annual pension of one-eightieth of annual salary and emoluments, together with a lump sum up to a maximum of one-and-a-half times emoluments.[42]
- The reduced scales of salary introduced on 1 April 1934 resulted in a corresponding reduction in the rate of pensions that teachers would receive who retired after that date. The pensions of teachers who retired prior to 1 April 1934 were, on average, 9 per cent higher.

Another major deficiency of the pension arrangements was that there was no mechanism for reviewing a pension once it was granted. The vagaries of the cost of living were ignored, and the longer the retiree lived the more precarious his/her standard of living became, particularly during the war years.

No Pension Increase Act was passed during the period from 1932 to 1948 when Fianna Fáil was in power. When the Inter-party Government came to power in 1948, the Minister for Finance announced in his first budget speech that pensioners who had retired prior to 31 October 1946 would be granted increases in their pensions with effect from 1 April 1949.

Every INTO Congress adopted resolutions seeking improvements in the benefits paid to pensioners and there was constant pressure on the CEC to achieve a scheme similar to the one enjoyed by civil servants. The battle for the restoration of the cuts would continue through public meetings, and the canvassing of bishops, school managers, TDs and public representatives.

The Marriage Ban

From the foundation of the National School System, under the Commissioners of National Education in 1831, female teachers, married and single, were

---

42 The civil service pension scheme was improved in 1975 retrospectively to 1 June 1973. One of the improvements was a revised basis for calculating the lump sum based on three-eightieths rather than one-eightieth of pay for each year of service. (See *Ireland*, 1977, pp. 28 and 31)

recognised and employed in national schools. Female teachers who married and became pregnant were facilitated by being allowed to take Maternity Leave under Rule 92(j), the Sick Leave rule.[43] Lay women employed as teachers in convent schools were, as a rule, obliged to retire on marriage.[44]

The commissioners issued a revised Rule 92(j), with effect from 1 July 1911, under which a pregnant married woman was obliged to absent herself from school for a period of three months during the period before and after childbirth, and to employ and pay a substitute for such portion of this period as was not included in the usual school vacation. This rule was subsequently amended such that 'all women teachers, who were in the service on 30 June 1911, married or unmarried, were exempt from the operation of the revised rule and … the period of absence for those who entered the service after that date was reduced from three to two months'.[45]

The Proposed Marriage Ban

During the early 1930s many young teachers were unemployed, mainly due to the fact that the number of teachers coming out of the training colleges exceeded the number of vacancies available. In this context the idea of a marriage ban was considered, the rationale being that if women were obliged to retire on marriage then vacancies would be created to absorb unemployed teachers.[46]

On 1 January 1932 the General Secretary received a letter from the Department of Education intimating that it was proposing to introduce a marriage ban.[47]

The Cumann na nGael Government was in power at that time, but before the proposal could be implemented a general election took place. A Fianna Fáil/Labour government came to power in March 1932 and the CEC submitted a memorandum objecting to the ban on economical, educational and ethical grounds. At a meeting with the Minister for Education on 27 May 1932, the case against the proposed ban was argued under the following headings:

- the regulation would be unconstitutional
- the ban would result in inefficiency
- the ban would involve the State in extra expense
- married women were especially suited to teaching young children
- parents favoured married women as teachers

---

43 Rules of the Commissioners of National Education, Rule 92(j)
44 T. J. O'Connell, *A Hundred Years of Progress*, pp. 275–7
45 Office of National Education, Circular, November 1912, Hansard, Vol. 42, No. 112, Col 2653–55
46 A Marriage Ban had been introduced in the civil service in 1924.
47 T. J. O'Connell, *A Hundred Years of Progress*, p. 280: Letter from the Secretary of the Department of Education, 1 January 1932, to T. J. O'Connell

- there was no demand for such a regulation
- the regulation would mean fewer marriages
- the arguments for the regulation were devoid of substance.[48]

While the new government did not appear to have a different view from the previous government on this subject, the Minister stated that he would place the views of the INTO before his colleagues when the matter came up for consideration.[49]

On 2 December 1932 the Secretary of the Department of Education wrote to the INTO stating that the government felt that there were strong reasons for the introduction of a regulation requiring female teachers to retire on marriage and, accordingly, all female national teachers appointed for the first time to a school in the Saorstát, as principal, assistant, or junior assistant mistress on or after 1 October 1933, would, on marriage, cease to be eligible for recognition in any capacity in a national school.[50]

Some of the reasons put forward to justify the ban were as follows:

- If married female teachers continued to work this would result in some loss, either to the school or to the home.
- Local irritation or jealousy was accentuated in a district by the comparatively large incomes received in households where the married couple were both teachers, or where a female teacher was married to a farmer or shopkeeper.
- The existing rule obliging a teacher to absent herself for two months on the occasion of childbirth resulted in a loss of teaching resources, even when a fully qualified substitute was employed. This problem was compounded by the difficulty of getting a qualified substitute.
- On their marriage female teachers were, on average, about thirty-one or thirty-two years of age and had thus given ten years' service before being required to retire. The amount saved on salaries by appointing replacement teachers at the minimum of the scale would be adequate to cover the cost of training additional teachers or any other expenditure incidental to the change.[51]

Representations were made to the bishops, to TDs, and managers, but it was clear from correspondence that the government was aware before announcing the proposed ban that the move would not be opposed by the bishops or the managerial authorities.[52]

---

48 T. J. O'Connell, *A Hundred Years of Progress*, p. 281
49 INTO Memorandum, Objections to Proposed Regulations Compelling Women Teachers to Retire on Marriage; the full text was published in *Irish School Weekly*, 4 June 1932.
50 T. J. O'Connell, *A Hundred Years of Progress*, p. 282
51 Ibid., pp. 281–2
52 *Irish School Weekly*, 17 June 1933

When a Fianna Fáil government came to power in 1933, a deputation from the INTO met the new Minister for Education to again make its case for the non-implementation of the Marriage Ban.

The Minister did not hold out any hope that the ban would not become operative and was therefore asked to ensure that it should not apply to any person who had actually entered the preparatory or training colleges before the Rule was published.[53] The introduction of the marriage ban would affect three groups of women:

- Students who had entered the training colleges in 1933 and 1934 and would not qualify until 1935 and 1936.
- Students who had entered the preparatory colleges in 1929, 1930, 1931, or 1932, and having entered the training colleges would not qualify until 1935, 1936, 1937, or 1938.
- Students who went to training colleges in Great Britain and Scotland and, on being trained, came back to Ireland and took up teaching posts.

The Minister promised to give some consideration to the students then in their second year in the Training Colleges, but that was as far as he was prepared to go. This consideration was not given. It was not until 1981 that some compensation for the deprivation of pensionable service was successfully negotiated for these women.

The Marriage Rule

The conditions applying to the operation of the marriage ban were as follows:

- All female teachers who entered the service for the first time on or after 1 October 1934 had to retire on marriage, except in the case of women who finished their training course before that date but had not been permanently appointed.
- Women compelled to retire under this rule could act as substitutes for a period not exceeding six months in any one school year.
- Women compelled to retire under this rule and who subsequently become widows could be re-admitted to the service subject to certain specified conditions.
- A female teacher with a minimum of seven years' recognised service would, on retirement on marriage, become entitled to the payment of a lump sum, a marriage gratuity; the amount due would be based on the number of completed years of recognised service and the salary on the date of retirement.
- Seven years' service was required to qualify for a gratuity and the maximum that could be received was one year's salary.

---

53 *Irish School Weekly*, 14 October 1933

Review of the Marriage Ban

The marriage ban, for the period it remained in operation, had serious consequences for women in the teaching force, not least of which was eligibility for pension.[54] The main consequences for women were:

- Women were denied the right to continue in their chosen profession following marriage.
- Women who married were denied the right to continue to earn a salary and the opportunity to accumulate recognised service for pension purposes.
- As the marriage gratuity was a payment contingent on the years of recognised service given, it was deemed to remove any future eligibility for pension, and that service could not be counted subsequently in any future pension calculations.
- Many married women continued to give service in schools as substitutes, temporary teachers and supernumeraries, but service given in these capacities was not recognised for pension purposes.

Although the marriage ban was rescinded on 30 June 1958, it took many years of processing claims through the Teachers' Conciliation Council and other fora before the problems resulting from the ban were reasonably resolved. It was agreed in 1973 that temporary service given during the marriage ban should be recognised for pension purposes with effect from 1 July 1971.

---

54 The Marriage Ban remained in operation for twenty-four years. It was revoked with effect from 1 July 1958 by the then Minister for Education, Jack Lynch.

8

Period of Upheaval, 1935–48

1935–1940

The National Education Commissioners (Transfer of Functions) Order, 1935 completed the transfer of power to a Minister for Education of the Irish Free State.[1]

The Economic War, 1934–38

A bitter economic conflict took place between Ireland and Great Britain from 1934 to 1938, which became known as 'The Economic War'. It had been agreed under the terms of the Treaty that land annuities, due under the terms of the Land Acts of the late nineteenth and early twentieth centuries, would continue to be paid to the British Government, but De Valera refused to pay them. The British Government retaliated by imposing a substantial tariff on Irish agricultural produce entering the British market. Counter-measures were taken by Dublin against British imports and the financial-constitutional dispute developed into the prolonged 'economic war' between the two countries. Irish imports fell by one-half and Irish exports by three-fifths.[2]

To mitigate the effects of the 'war', the government promoted a policy of independence and self-sufficiency by encouraging the development of indigenous industry, placing tariffs on imports, and maintaining a constraint on expenditure in the fields of education and health.

Eventually, the threat of war in Europe made it desirable that the differences between the Irish and British governments should not continue, and the Economic War ended with the signing of the Anglo-Irish Agreement by De Valera and Neville Chamberlain on 25 April 1938. Ireland was subsequently to become a major supplier of foodstuffs to Great Britain during the war.

Unemployed Teachers in the 30s and 40s

During the 1930s there were many young unemployed teachers. With effect from 1 October 1934, as part of a package of retrenchments, a marriage ban was

---

1 Saorstát Éireann: Statutory Rules and Orders, National Education Commissioners (Transfer of Functions) Order, No. 264, 2 August 1935
2 John A. Murphy, *Ireland in the Twentieth Century*, pp. 76–8

introduced to relieve the unemployment situation. In another move, on 26 September 1936, Tomás Ó Deirg, the Minister for Education, placed a limit on the number of students entering the training colleges. Employment opportunities could have been created by the Department if it had amended the enrolment numbers for the appointment or retention of teachers, but this was not done due to financial restraints.

During this period the CEC continued its campaign for the restoration of the salary scales of 1920 and the removal of the marriage ban.[3] Bishops, school managers, TDs and public representatives were canvassed by local teachers; public meetings were organised throughout the country;[4] and a Special Congress, attended by branch representatives, was held on 30 January 1937 where resolutions were adopted endorsing the actions of the CEC.

The Minister for Education regarded the INTO's position as 'simply incomprehensible'. He reiterated the government's contention that 'the 1934 scales were not cuts but an essential element in the settlement of the pensions problem'.[5]

The Salary Increase, 1938

By 1937 it was generally recognised that the effects of the Great Depression were abating and that there were increasing signs of prosperity in the country. Financial returns to the government had improved and there were increases in commodity prices. Between 1934 and 1938 the cost-of-living index increased by twenty-two points and civil servants were granted an increase in excess of 10 per cent in their cost-of-living bonus.[6]

Teachers did not receive any offer until 12 April 1938, just prior to the 1938 INTO Congress, when Ó Deirg announced that the government had decided to grant an increase of 5 per cent on all teachers' salaries with effect from 1 April 1938 and, as the problem of unemployed teachers had not abated, that female teachers would have to retire from teaching on reaching the age of sixty years or on completing thirty-five years of recognised service.[7] Salary scales for untrained teachers and JAMs were also increased by 5 per cent, as were all bonuses, allowances and rates of capitation paid to the conductors of capitation schools.

Delegates at Congress were not happy with the increase as national teachers had not received the same increase as civil servants and they were still receiving less than they did under the 1920 agreement. The relevant comparative figures are as follows:[8]

---

3 T. J. O'Connell, *A Hundred Years of Progress*, p. 203
4 CEC Report to Congress 1938
5 Dáil Debates, Vol. 66, 1 April 1937, p. 269
6 CEC Report to Congress 1937, p. 38
7 Letter from the Department of Education in *Irish School Weekly*, 30 April 1938
8 The maximum quoted is that for 'Highly Efficient'. The 1920 figures are gross, before the deduction of the 4 per cent pension contribution. The 1934 and 1938 scales are net as they were not subject to any deduction for pension purposes.

	1920 Scale		1934 Scale		1938 Scale	
	M £	F £	M £	F £	M £	F £
Minimum	170	155	140	128	147	134
Maximum	370	300	303	246	357	284

The delegates re-instructed the CEC to continue agitating for the restoration of the 1920 scales and to organise a regional strike to further the campaign.

In May 1938 de Valera was defeated by one vote in the Dáil and he dissolved the government. The INTO endeavoured to make the retirement of women at sixty an issue during the general election in 1938, but without success. Fianna Fáil was returned with a fifteen seat majority.[9] The early retirement regulation remained in force until 1948.

Following Congress 1938, the CEC focused on the implications of the new regulations for teachers. Some were affected by the salary revisions, others by revised appointment and retention numbers, and all female teachers were affected by the compulsory retirement at age sixty. No progress was made during the year on achieving any changes or revisions to any of the new regulations.

The Lost Increments – The McEnaney Judgment

In June 1930, in furtherance of State policy on the promotion of the Irish language, the Department of Education issued a regulation declaring that increments would be withheld from teachers who were under thirty years of age on 1 July 1922 and who did not possess a certificate to (a) teach Irish or (b) give instruction through the medium of Irish.[10]

In 1939 the CEC challenged this rule in the High Court. Ignatius McEnaney, of Monaghan Branch INTO, was selected to take the action as the named plaintiff in a test case. He had taught Irish and had been rated 'Highly Efficient', but he had failed to obtain the Teastas Dhá-Theangach (Bi-lingual Certificate), although he had sat the examination on more than one occasion.

A judgment was issued on 9 April dismissing the case and awarding costs against the plaintiff, McEnaney. The CEC appealed the verdict to the Supreme Court. On 17 December 1939 the Supreme Court ruled that the salary increments had been withheld without lawful justification and it awarded costs, both for the appeal and the original High Court hearing, against the Minister and in favour of the plaintiff.

The INTO demanded that the retained increments should be refunded. While McEnaney received his increments and the costs, it was not until the end of

---

9 This government served the maximum term and remained in power until 1943.
10 The power to withhold increments was subsequently included as Rule 77 of the Department of Education Rules and Regulations of 1932.

April 1941 that the government finally decided to regard the McEnaney judgment as a test case and agreed to refund increments to all teachers concerned. However, these teachers did not receive their refunds until 1955.

Pensions Review

During the period 1923 to 1935 teachers' salaries were reduced on a number of occasions with the result that teachers going out on retirement received lower pensions. Although salaries were increased by 5 per cent from 1 April 1938, the three years' average salary rule meant that only teachers retiring after 1 April 1941 got the full benefit of that salary increase in their pensions.

There was no machinery in place to allow for a periodic review of the pension awarded. Once calculated, it remained at that figure for the teacher's lifetime. With the increasing cost of living, pensioners on a fixed pension were unable to maintain their standard of living.

In 1940, 1942, and 1943 several amendments to national teachers' pension scheme were passed. The 1940 amendment had a number of sections: Section I concerned a small group of teachers who had given service in specific schools that promoted the Irish Language; Section II gave recognition to military service given by some teachers; Section IV put into effect the consequences of the 1938 regulation that required women to retire at age sixty. The 1942 amendment concerned lay teachers employed in Reformatory National Schools or Industrial National Schools; they were granted recognition for such service for salary and pension purposes. The 1943 amendment allowed averaging to be carried out for a number of lay literary teachers (employed in Reformatory National Schools or Industrial National Schools) who did not have three years' recognised service to be averaged for pension purposes. The amendment also allowed women to add non-recognised service, such as temporary assistant or supernumerary, to a minimum of five years' recognised service, to qualify for a marriage gratuity.

The War Years

The Start of the Second World War

The Second World War commenced on 1 September 1939 and lasted for six years. The government declared a 'State of Emergency', under which it assumed the power to control and regulate the economic affairs of the country by means of issuing 'Orders of the Government'. Rationing of essential commodities and press censorship were enforced for the duration of the war. Ó Deirg was Minister for Education for most of the war period; Seán T. Ó Ceallaigh served for a short period, and de Valera served as Taoiseach/Minister for Education for seven months in 1940.

The cost-of-living index increased from a figure of 173 in 1938 to 284 in 1943. Teachers were the only group of public servants that did not receive any increase in remuneration during this period, even though the INTO applied on a number of occasions for a war bonus.

Congress 1940 adopted the following resolutions:

- demand an immediate increase in salaries to compensate for the rising cost of living
- establish agreed machinery to make adjustments to compensate for fluctuations in the cost of living.

This remuneration resolution was a departure from previously established INTO policy. From 1923 the INTO had been seeking the restoration of the 1920 salary scales, but by 1940 a restoration of the cuts would have been insufficient to compensate for the intervening increase in the cost of living.

On 22 April 1940 the CEC submitted a claim to the Taoiseach/Minister for Education seeking an immediate increase of fifteen shillings per week for all teachers 'to meet immediate necessities caused by the great increase in the cost of living which has taken place during recent months'.[11]

Even though it was common knowledge that civil servants had been awarded an increase in their bonus with effect from 1 January 1940, the Taoiseach refused to meet a deputation from the CEC to discuss the salary claim. The Secretary of the Department of Education wrote to the CEC stating that the INTO claim would cost £500,000, 'an additional burden on the community which it would not be possible for the government to justify'.[12]

On 26 June 1940 the Minister for Finance issued the Civil Service (Stabilisation of Bonus) Regulations, 1940, which came into force on 1 July 1940. These regulations stabilised the civil service bonus from 1 January 1940 based on the cost-of-living index figure of 85, which was actually the figure for the quarter ended 31 December 1939.[13]

Ó Deirg met a deputation from the ASTI on 9 April 1941 to discuss a salary claim and stated that 'increased salaries to teachers at the present moment would definitely be opposed by the Department'.[14]

The Wages Standstill Order, 1941

The Emergency Order No. 83, known as the Wages Standstill Order, was passed by the Dáil in May 1941. This Order gave the government power to freeze wages, salaries and pensions, except in accordance with the emergency bonus

---

11 CEC Report to Congress 1941
12 Ibid.
13 Circulars 1/40, 6/40, 12/40, and 13/40, Department of Finance
14 John Coolahan, *The ASTI and Post-Primary Education 1909–1984*, p. 150

arrangement. Strikes were made illegal by the removal of workers' protection under the 1916 Trades Dispute Act. Notwithstanding the Standstill Order, civil servants and the Gardaí got bonus increases with effect from 1 January 1942. This strengthened the feeling among teachers that they were being discriminated against.

The Minister met a deputation from the CEC on 5 June 1942. While he agreed to place teachers' views before the government, he held out no hope that their demands would be met.[15] However, it would appear that the representations had an effect on the Minister. In a memorandum to the Taoiseach on 8 August 1942, he expressed the urgency of their case and pointed out that refusal to increase remuneration to national teachers would have grave results and might seriously impair work being done in schools.[16] In the same letter a history of the salary cuts in national teachers' salaries was outlined, and a comparison with salary scales in Northern Ireland was made.

Emergency Bonus for Teachers in National Schools, 1943

Frustration and disappointment led to the inauguration by the CEC of a campaign seeking redress on the salary issue. Branch resolutions were sent to TDs, to the Minister, and to the local press. Public meetings were held in Dublin, Cork, Galway and elsewhere. Arrangements were in train to progress the campaign when the Department of Education published a large notice in the daily national newspapers on the morning of 19 December 1942, stating that the government had decided to award an emergency bonus to all teachers.

A bonus of seven shillings per week for men and five shillings per week for women was granted, to become operative from 1 January 1943. The bonus was restricted to teachers whose total remuneration did not exceed £398 17s. per annum.[17]

The notice also declared that the emergency bonus would be a pensionable emolument. This was an important concession.

The CEC expressed its disappointment about the award on the grounds that:

- the INTO had not been consulted about the bonus
- the amount of the bonus was inadequate and not equal to awards made to other groups
- it was the first increase in remuneration that teachers had received since 1938
- all other groups had received more frequent increases

15 SPO, 12036/A
16 Memorandum from Minister for Education to Government Regarding Teachers' Claim for Increased Remuneration, 8 August 1942, SPO, 10236/A
17 The figure of £398 17s. was the basic salary of a civil servant at £5 per week plus a cost-of-living bonus of £137 17s.

- the award was discriminatory; both male and female teachers should receive the same amount
- the award was discriminatory in imposing a gross income limit above which it did not apply.

Teachers were also aggrieved about the manner in which they were notified of the award. They were the only group of public employees who were notified by an advertisement in the daily national newspapers. It was stated that it was done in this way because of a paper shortage and that it was not intended to issue any circular to teachers on the matter.

Placing the notice in the daily newspapers used up considerably more paper than sending a circular to every individual teacher. Circulars on other matters had been sent, and continued to be sent, to schools through the post.

At this time the INTO was in the middle of a public campaign against the government over pay. It would appear that the government used the strategy of announcing the emergency bonus in advertisements in the national newspapers to attempt to defuse the INTO campaign and to influence public opinion against teachers. It was calculated to show that the teachers were being accommodated by the government and that they were malcontents, at a time when the country's economic circumstances were so grave.

Fianna Fáil was returned to office in the general election of July 1943, and the Labour Party increased in strength from nine to seventeen seats. The INTO continued its campaign of public protest meetings to highlight their claims.

Pressure from teachers and public service and local government employees resulted in a bonus of three shillings per week being granted with effect from 1 January 1944. The CEC described the award as 'a stupid, pointless kind of bonus for it has no relation at all to the increased cost of living on which it is avowedly based'.[18] Serious dissatisfaction was expressed by delegates at Congress.

In a snap general election, held in May 1944, Fianna Fáil was returned with a strong overall majority. The Labour Party had split into two factions, Labour and National Labour, as a result of a dispute between William O'Brien of the Irish Transport and General Workers Union (ITGWU) and James Larkin of the Federated Workers Union (FWUI), and lost a total of five seats.[19]

In July 1944 Ó Deirg, in answer to a Dáil question, stated that a new salary scale for teachers was under consideration, to be put into effect when the Emergency ended. However, he qualified this in a letter to the INTO on 10 August 1944 when he said that it could only be considered in accordance with government policy towards the various classes of persons paid from the public purse.[20]

18 Editorial, *Irish School Weekly*, 5 February 1944
19 The Labour Party and the National Labour Party reunited in 1950.
20 *Irish School Weekly*, 26 August 1944

Support for the teachers' cause came from an unexpected source. The Catholic Hierarchy, at its general meeting in Maynooth on 10 October 1944, passed a resolution recommending to the sympathetic consideration of the government the claim for an increase in the remuneration of national teachers. The resolution was forwarded to the government.[21]

In November 1944, 26,000 civil and local authority servants received increases in their ordinary cost-of-living bonus, ranging from 7s. 9d. to £1 3s per week, with an additional emergency bonus of one shilling per week. The teachers were awarded one shilling per week but nothing more. The award was described as contemptuous and insulting by the INTO.[22]

Following its meeting on 9 December, the CEC informed the Minister for Education that the only proposals that would be acceptable to teachers in the matter of salary scales would be those arrived at as a result of negotiations between the government and the INTO, and such other interests or bodies as might properly claim to have a voice in the formulation of such scales.[23]

Cost-of-Living Index

The CEC submitted a claim to the Minister for a revision of the salary scales and pensions of national teachers. It presented a memorandum setting down teachers' case based on a cost-of-living index of 100 in 1922, with the following information:[24]

Year/August	Index
1938	173
1939	176
1940	206
1941	228
1942	284
1943	296
1944	296

To maintain purchasing power, a teacher's salary would have to be as follows:

- £100 in 1939 would have required an increase of £70.
- £200 in 1939 would have required an increase of £140.
- £300 in 1939 would have required an increase of £210.

21 Letter from Most Rev. Dr Staunton, Joint Secretary to the Hierarchy, to Ó Deirg, 17 October 1944, SPO, S10236/B
22 T. J. O'Connell, *A Hundred Years of Progress*, p. 210
23 Ibid., p. 210
24 By 1947 the cost-of-living index had increased to 319.

Furthermore:

- £100 in 1939 had a purchasing power of £59 in 1944.
- £200 in 1939 had a purchasing power of £118 in 1944.
- £300 in 1939 had a purchasing power of £177 in 1944.

The total amount received by teachers from emergency bonuses during that period was £28 12s. by men and £23 4s. by women.

Pensioned Teachers

It was claimed that the Teachers' Pension Scheme was the worst in the public service, and that about 70 per cent of pensioners were receiving less than £3 per week. The following table sets out the number of pensioners receiving different amounts:

Amount	Number
under £1 per week	320
between £1 and £1 10s.	136
between £1 10s. and £2	230
between £2 and £2 10s.	679
between £2 10s. and £3	792
over £3	955

Pensioners, some of whom had retired in the early 1930s, had not received any increases in spite of the increase in the cost of living during the war. Teachers in Great Britain and Northern Ireland had received increases as follows:

- pensions under £100, an increase of 30 per cent
- pensions under £200, an increase of 25 per cent
- pensions under £300, an increase of 20 per cent.[25]

In December 1944 the Cabinet rejected teachers' claim with a vague promise that the remuneration of teachers, along with other classes of public servants, would be open to reconsideration after the Emergency.[26]

With effect from 1 January 1945 civil servants got increases varying from £22 to £77 per annum, and Gardaí got increases ranging from 10 per cent to 12 per cent.[27] The government justified these increases by claiming that these salaries

25 INTO, *Brief Outline of Teachers' Case for Increased Remuneration*
26 Cabinet Minutes, 19 December 1944, Item 1, GC 4/39, SPO, S10236B
27 INTO Pamphlet – The Case for Increase in Remuneration of National Teachers 1945,
    SPO 310236B

had been stabilised in 1940 when the cost-of-living index was at 85, whereas the general Standstill Order was made in 1941 when the index figure had risen to 110. It was deemed just and fair that these public servants should have their salaries calculated on the figure of 110 instead of 85.

Notwithstanding these substantial increases, at a meeting with teachers on 24 March 1945 Ó Deirg offered nothing to the INTO but the promise to bring their representations before the government.[28] He was, however, fully aware of the seriousness of the situation. In a letter to the Taoiseach he referred to the urgent need for some relief, to the Hierarchy's intervention, and to 'fears of a serious degree of discontent among teachers'.[29]

At the 1945 INTO Congress in Galway, Tom Frisby, in his Presidential address, accused the government of showing disregard amounting almost to contempt for the Hierarchy and warned it against forcing the teachers into revolutionary action that might have repercussions far beyond the educational service.[30]

The following day an editorial in *The Irish Press* described Frisby's speech as deplorable and as being an ultimatum to the government.[31] Delegates at Congress responded by unanimously passing a motion of confidence in the stand taken by Frisby.

A group of teachers, mainly from the Dublin Branch, was successful in getting Congress delegates to elect a 'Propaganda Committee' to organise and pursue a vigorous campaign, in co-operation with the CEC, to achieve a salary increase. Congress also decided to disaffiliate the INTO from the Labour Party as it was perceived that the link was proving to be a source of embarrassment and a liability.[32]

In response to a telegram from Congress, de Valera met a deputation from the CEC on 18 April. The meeting was unsatisfactory as he claimed that his hands were tied by the Standstill Order in the matter of salary. He justified the substantial increases to the civil servants and Gardaí 'as righting a wrong caused by a promise made to them before the enactment of the Standstill Order'.[33]

Teachers staged a protest in the Public Gallery of the Dáil on 27 April 1945. Leaflets were distributed and the Gardaí were called to clear the gallery. In the resumed debate, Ó Deirg reiterated the argument of the Department of Finance, that a rise for teachers would be tantamount to abandoning the policy implemented by the Standstill Order.[34]

---

28 *Irish School Weekly*, 5 May 1945
29 Letter from the Secretary of the Department of Education to the Secretary of the Taoiseach, 27 March 1945, SPO, 10236B
30 *Irish School Weekly*, 7 April 1945
31 Editorial, *Irish Press*, 4 April 1945
32 *Irish School Weekly*, 21 April 1945; this motion had been on the Congress agenda for a number of years. The INTO formally registered as a trade union and affiliated to the Labour Party in 1918.
33 Confidential Report of Meeting on 18 April 1945, SPO, S10236/B
34 Dáil Debates, Vol. 97, 2 May 1945, p. 118

At its meeting on 28 April 1945 the CEC mandated the Central Propaganda Committee 'to pursue all work in connection with the salary campaign'.[35] The committee lobbied, canvassed, circulated pamphlets, arranged publicity, and organised meetings.

Support for teachers was voiced at the General Synod of the Presbyterian Church, by Church of Ireland bishops at a meeting on 8 June,[36] and by the Catholic Clerical Managers Association.[37]

The Minister's Salary Offers

At a meeting held in the Mansion House on 6 October, Dublin teachers voted in a secret ballot by 999 to 47 to strike, if and when called upon to do so by the CEC. A plan of campaign was drawn up and it was agreed to establish a number of subcommittees to oversee the special procedures that would operate during the strike. It was agreed that

- a strike fund would be established
- all INTO teacher members in Dublin would come out on strike
- teachers on strike would receive strike pay equal to 90 per cent of their existing salaries
- the other INTO members throughout the rest of the country would contribute 10 per cent of their salaries in monthly payments for the strike fund
- arrangements would be made in every INTO branch to collect the 10 per cent strike levy
- a Roll of Honour Fund would be established as a second method of collecting sufficient funds. All members were requested to make a voluntary contribution of a minimum of £5 to the fund.[38]

At a meeting with Ó Deirg on 16 November 1945, the CEC was presented with an elaborate scheme, in which all the principles and suggested reforms embodied in the Galway Congress salary scales were ignored.[39] The CEC was further incensed at finding that the allowance for a 'Highly Efficient' inspector's report was set at £2 per annum. This was seen as an insult and contributed to the rejection of the Minister's proposed scales. Two further meetings produced some minor adjustments but they were deemed to be insufficient.

It subsequently became known that the Minister had submitted to government, on 24 September 1945, salary scales that had much higher

---

35 *Irish School Weekly*, 5 May 1945
36 *Irish School Weekly*, 19 May 1945
37 *Irish School Weekly*, 28 July 1945
38 In accordance with the undertaking given, all donations to the Roll of Honour Fund were refunded to the contributors in 1950.
39 T. J. O'Connell, *A Hundred Years of Progress*, p. 212

maximums. The government rejected the Minister's recommendations.[40]

In a letter to Ó Deirg, dated 10 December 1945, the CEC threatened that strike action would commence on 17 January 1946 unless he was prepared to increase his offer. The threat was withdrawn the following day on the advice of His Grace, Dr Charles McQuaid, Archbishop of Dublin. He attempted to find a compromise between the teachers and the government. In spite of receiving the letter of withdrawal, Ó Deirg did not move any closer to meeting teacher demands.

At a meeting on 18 January 1946 the Minister informed an INTO delegation that no further improvements could be made. A special delegate conference in the Mansion House on 9 February 1946 urged the CEC to make further representations to the Minister and 'to submit the eventual final offer to all the members in the State, who would decide by referendum whether the offer should be accepted or rejected.[41] An amendment calling for a strike on 26 February was defeated but it was agreed that if the government offer was rejected, Dublin teachers would be called out 'within a period of 10 days after the result of the referendum became known'.[42]

Further representations were fruitless and the government's final offer was duly put to individual INTO members in a postal ballot. The result of the vote was announced on 9 March 1946: 9,121 ballot papers had been issued and 8,522 (94%) valid votes were returned; 3,773 voted for acceptance, 4,749 favoured rejection – a majority of 976. A letter signed by T. J. O'Connell, General Secretary of the INTO, was issued to all INTO members in the Dublin Branch instructing them to come out on strike on Wednesday morning, 20 March 1946.

The 1946 Strike

On 11 March O'Connell sent a letter to the Minister informing him of the result of the referendum and of the decision of the CEC to call the Dublin teachers out on strike on 20 March.

Dr McQuaid wrote to the Minister on 14 March acknowledging his failure to fashion a compromise between the parties, and stated:

> There seems to be inevitability about this matter which will cause it to work itself out to the bitter end. And when the end will have been reached it will be only a question of starting where one might have started before.[43]

---

40 Memorandum for Information of Taoiseach from Secretary of the Department of Education to the Secretary of the Taoiseach, 23/5/1946
41 T. J. O'Connell, *A Hundred Years of Progress*, p. 212
42 Ibid., p. 212
43 Letter from Dr John Charles McQuaid to the Minister for Education, 14 March 1946, SPO 10236B

On 14 March a letter from the Minister was published in the daily press questioning the result of the ballot and the mandate to strike. The Minister's letter was considered unnecessarily provocative and removed any possibility of stopping the strike.

Dr McQuaid was angry about the government's intransigence in not recognising the plight of teachers and ignoring his efforts to resolve the situation. On the morning of the strike the daily newspapers published the text of a letter from the Archbishop to O'Connell, supporting the INTO in its stand.[44] The Archbishop stated:

> Your Organisation must have no doubt that the clerical managers of the city and the religious superiors have full sympathy with the ideal of a salary in keeping with the dignity and responsibility of your profession as teachers. Further, every member of your Organisation must now clearly be aware of my desire that you should obtain the best salary possible in our circumstances, and of my unremitting efforts to secure such a settlement of your problems as would keep negotiations open and avoid the decision to declare a strike.[450]

Support from this source was a great boost to teachers, but it was resented by the government. It has been claimed that it created a rift between Dr McQuaid and de Valera that was never reconciled.[46] Less than 1 per cent of teachers did not answer the call to come out on strike, which involved 140 schools and 1,200 teachers. So commenced a bitter and acrimonious strike that was to last for seven-and-a-half months, and the repercussions of which were to last for many years.

De Valera and the government set their minds steadfastly against any concessions to the teachers. One month into the dispute, the government rejected an approach from Dr McQuaid to act as mediator in the dispute; other offers of mediation were also turned down. Eventually, after seven-and-a-half months, Dr McQuaid intervened to create a situation that facilitated the teachers in calling off the strike and resuming their teaching positions on 30 October.

Dermot Keogh depicts this defeat of the teachers by the Taoiseach as a pyrrhic victory 'where wiser elements in Fianna Fáil might have prudently reflected on the line: One more such victory and we are lost'.[47]

The circumstances in which the strike ended, together with events that occurred and things that had been said during it, left a residue of bitterness, resentment and frustration. Many teachers who had been 'traditionally regarded as the backbone of Fianna Fáil' resigned from the party as they felt betrayed.[48]

---

44 *Irish School Weekly*, 7 April 1945
45 T. J. O'Connell, *A Hundred Years of Progress*, p. 218
46 Ronan Fanning, *Independent Ireland*, p. 158
47 Dermot Keogh, *Twentieth-Century Ireland: Nation and State*, p. 167
48 Ibid., p. 166

The salary scales, proposed by the Minister on 8 December 1945 and rejected by teachers in March 1946, were applied by the government with effect from 31 October 1946. The scales were as follows:

	Married Men	Single Men	Women	JAMs
Efficient minimum	220	220	200	150
Efficient maximum	485	380	340	196
Efficient	525	416	376	212

No progress was made at a meeting with the Minister on 22 November to discuss changes and adaptations to the application of the new scales. The claim that the strike period should be allowed for increment and pension purposes was rejected.

The Minister, while not hopeful that the government would give favourable consideration to the cause of pensioners, said he would raise the question again.

The Memorandum to the Government on 23 May 1946

A memorandum from the Secretary of the Department of Education to the Secretary of the Taoiseach, dated 23 May 1946, showed that the Minister for Education was aware that the salary position of national teachers was very bad. This memorandum became available only when the time-span of cabinet confidentiality had elapsed.[49] It showed:

- the 1938 salary scales for teachers without the emergency bonus
- the salaries claimed by the INTO in its submission of 9 December 1944
- the salaries that the Minister presented to the government on 24 September 1945 (the salary scales he wished to offer to the teachers)
- the salaries officially proposed to the INTO on 16 November 1945
- the second and final offer to the teachers on 8 December 1945
- the salaries, net of pension contribution, paid to teachers in Northern Ireland at that time
- the estimated cost of each proposal.

This document is very important on a number of counts:

1 It indicated that the Minister for Education was aware that the salary position of national teachers was very bad. He proposed that the minimum point of the basic

---

49 Memorandum from the Secretary of the Department of Education to the Secretary of the Taoiseach, 23 May 1946, SPO, S10236/C; Eugene P. McCormick, *The INTO and the 1946 Teachers' Strike*

scale for a married man should be increased by 36 per cent, and that the maximum point should be increased by 71.4 per cent. In the final offer by the government, the minimum point was increased by 49.7 per cent and the maximum point by 52.5 per cent.[50]

2 He proposed that the minimum point of the basic scale for a woman should be increased by 49.3 per cent, and that the maximum point should be increased by 55 per cent. In the final offer by the government the minimum point increase remained the same at 49.3 per cent, and the maximum point was increased by 31.8 per cent.

3 The INTO claim of December 1944 had two scales, one for married men and a common scale for single men and women; this was a departure from the 1938 salary agreement which had two scales, one for men and one for women. Both offers by the government, in November and December 1945, proposed three salary scales, a scale for married men, one for single men, and one for women. The government's offer of December was the salary scale imposed at the termination of the 1946 strike.

The following table sets out the minimum and the maximum of each of the basic scales:

	Married Men		Single Men		Women	
	Min.	**Max.**	**Min.**	**Max.**	**Min.**	**Max.**
1938 Scales	147	318	147	318	134	258
INTO Claim 9/12/44	350	650	300	600	300	600
Minister to Gov. 24/9/45	200	545	200	400	200	400
First Offer 16/11/45	200	485	200	380	180	324
Final offer 8/12/45	220	485	220	380	200	340
Northern Ireland	264	522	264	522	237	427

Review of the Period 1935–1948

During this period many of the young teachers leaving the training colleges failed to secure permanent teaching posts for a number of years. Some of them got positions as supernumeraries, substitutes or temporary teachers, others took up work in other occupations, and some emigrated. These teachers lost incremental credit and recognised service for pension purposes and, subsequently, when they came to retire they did not have sufficient service for maximum pension. The problem became known as 'The Unemployed Teachers

---

50 The percentage increases would be reduced somewhat if the emergency bonuses were absorbed into the increase. The bonuses are ignored for clarification purposes.

in the 30s and 40s'. It was not until 1974 that a concession of added years for pension purposes was achieved for them. Nothing could be done about salary lost due to the delay in reaching the maximum of the salary scale.

Following a very acrimonious strike the government had imposed its own salary revision in 1946. The strike had ended badly for teachers and left very bad relations between the two parties.

A comparison of the salaries granted in 1920 and the salaries of December 1945 is as follows:

	Married Men		Single Men		Women	
	Min.	Max.	Min.	Max.	Min.	Max.
1920 Scales	170	370	170	370	155	300
Final offer 8/12/45	220	485	220	380	200	340
Percentage Increase	29.4	31.1	29.4	2.7	29.0	13.3

While the increases offered in 1945 seem to be very large, they did not make up for the deterioration that had occurred since 1923. From a base of 100 in 1922, the cost-of-living index had increased to 296 in 1944, an increase of 196 per cent. The percentage increase in teachers' salaries varied from 2.7 to 31.1 per cent. The pre-1946 group of single men was particularly aggrieved because, of the three groups, it had received the least.

The situation was further aggravated when the government sanctioned the payment of a bonus to teachers who had remained at work throughout the strike; they numbered 316 nuns, 121 brothers, 52 lay women and 11 lay men. On average, they received £11 14s.[51]

The situation for pensioners was particularly severe. Between 1939 and 1944 the purchasing power of £100 had fallen to £59, and standards of living had plummeted.

Civil servants were successful in changing the method used to determine their pay, from a cost-of-living index bonus method to consolidated salary scales, with effect from 1 November 1946. The consolidated salary was arrived at by adding to the basic salary a figure equivalent to a cost-of-living bonus calculated on an index of 270 referenced to a base of 100 in 1922, coupled with the withdrawal of emergency bonuses.

In addition, the government introduced a Conciliation and Arbitration Scheme for civil servants. There was no plan to make a similar provision for national teachers.

From the INTO's perspective the strike did much to restore professional morale among teachers, and it strengthened its power. It was now on its way to

---

51 Dermot Keogh, *Twentieth-Century Ireland: Nation and State*, p. 172

becoming a major force in industrial relations and in the political field. Changes took place in its leadership: T. J. O'Connell retired at Congress 1948 and David J. Kelleher, a member of the CEC for the previous fifteen years and President for the year 1946–47, was elected as his successor, becoming General Secretary-Designate on 1 September 1948. Another of the strike leaders, Seán Brosnahan, was elected President for 1947–48 and became General Treasurer in 1961 and General Secretary in 1968.

The repercussions of the strike were to last for many years. Lord Longford and T. P. O'Neill were of the opinion that it was 'a strike which went a long way towards undermining the goodwill which de Valera had won by his success in maintaining neutrality'.[52]

The last general election had been held in May 1944 and it was generally expected that the next general election would be held during 1948. INTO activists prepared for the election on the basis that any government was an improvement over a Fianna Fáil government. It has been readily conceded by most authorities that the teachers' strike had a profound affect on the outcome of the 1948 general election.

---

52 Lord Longford and T. P. O'Neill, *Eamon de Valera*, p. 428

9

Seeking Status, 1948–68

The First Inter-Party Government, 1948–51

Fianna Fáil was returned as the largest single party (68 seats out of 147) in the general election of 1948 but lost its overall majority.[1] John A. Murphy gives the following reasons for the defeat of Fianna Fáil:

> Fianna Fáil had been in power without interruption since 1932, and there was a general feeling, typical of post-war moods elsewhere, that it was time for a change. Fianna Fáil, still harping on its neutrality policy accomplishments, seemed to be out of touch with the realities of wages and prices. Discontent with the cost of living found expression in the activities of a militant housewives' association and in a number of bitter strikes, particularly that of the primary teachers who were heavily represented in the new Clann na Poblachta party.[2]

Fine Gael, Clann na Poblachta, Labour, National Labour, Clann na Talmhan and some Independents agreed to form an Inter-party Government on the basis of a general ten-point programme.

General Richard Mulcahy, Fine Gael, was appointed Minister for Education. The teachers had a much better relationship with both the Minister and the government than they had ever had with Fianna Fáil. Within a very short period the INTO achieved a number of very important concessions from the government.

Salary

1 The 1938 regulation obliging women to retire at age sixty was rescinded.
2 A rent allowance, similar to the one paid to married men, was granted to widows.
3 Service given by a trained teacher as a supernumerary or substitute would count for increments when the teacher was later appointed to a permanent post.

---

1 Fianna Fáil won sixty-eight seats, Fine Gael thirty-one, Labour fourteen, National Labour five, Clann na Talmhan seven, Clann na Poblachta ten, and there were twelve Independents.
2 John A. Murphy, *Ireland in the Twentieth Century*, p. 117

4   The Minister declared that the principle of Arbitration for persons paid by the State had been accepted by the government.

5   The Minister established a committee to examine and report on the salaries and pensions of teachers in national schools.

'Highly Efficient'

At an INTO convened conference of interested parties on 24–25 February 1948 delegates adopted a resolution accepting 'merit marks' if the 'highly efficient' rating was abolished. This proposition was accepted by Minister Mulcahy even though it was estimated that the cost of abolishing the rating would be £80,000 for the first year of operation.[3]

Pension Increases for Retirees as from 1 April 1949

In his budget for 1949, the Minister for Finance granted the following increases, from 1 April 1949, to pensioners who retired prior to 31 October 1946, subject to a number of conditions:

- 50 per cent on pensions up to £2 per week
- 40 per cent on pensions between £2 and £3 per week
- 30 per cent on pensions over £3 per week.[4]

National School Teachers' Superannuation (Amendment) Scheme, 1949

The national teachers' superannuation scheme was amended as follows:[5]

1   The period during which a teacher was on strike, from 19 March 1946 to 31 October 1946, would be recognised for incremental and pension purposes.[6]

2   Two-thirds of every period of full-time service given as a lay teacher in a Christian Brothers' school prior to 1 January 1927 would be recognised as pensionable service.[7]

3   Service given after the last day of the quarter in which a teacher reached the age of sixty-five years would not be recognised as pensionable service.

---

3   Letter from the Minister for Education, dated 6 October 1949, CEC Report to Congress 1950. The abolition of the rating 'highly efficient' would raise the possible maxima of salary scales for about 70 per cent of teachers, by £36 per annum for women and single men, and by £40 per annum for married men, as well as raising the value of annual allowances.

4   The Pensions (Increase) Act, 1950

5   Statutory Instrument No. 423, 1949

6   Letter from the Minister for Education, dated 25 March 1949

7   The Christian Brothers had opted out of the National School system and did not formally come back as a Capitation School under the Department of Education until 1 January 1927. From that date lay teachers employed in these schools were paid directly by the Department and their service was recognised for pension purposes. This amendment allowed for two-thirds of previous service to be recognised for pension purposes.

4   Where a teacher retired on pension and took up a position in a post paid out of public funds, the pension would be abated by the amount that the total of the pension and the new remuneration exceeded the salary on which the teacher's pension had been calculated. (This amendment was to prevent a retired teacher being paid out of public funds a total income greater than he/she had had as a teacher.)

5   In the calculation of a teacher's annual average salary for the purposes of awarding a pension, teachers whose salary was based on the new scales introduced on 31 October 1946 would have periods of service given before and after that date taken into account, as if the new salary scales had been in operation during both periods. (This amendment enhanced the averaging process for teachers who retired any time up to three years from 1 October 1946.)

6   The date of marriage of a female teacher would be construed to mean the date of her retirement immediately preceding her marriage, except when the date of marriage coincided with the date of retirement. (This amendment covered situations where the date of marriage and retirement did not coincide, as when a marriage took place during summer vacation.)[8]

The Roe Committee's Reports on Teachers' Salaries, 1949

Early in 1949 Richard Mulcahy, in fulfilment of his promise to improve relations with teachers, established a Committee on National Teachers' Salaries 'to consider salaries and other grants, including provisions on retirement, to be paid to teachers in national schools', and to recommend new salary scales and amendments to the teachers' pension scheme.

The Roe Committee comprised of eighteen members: Judge Roe (chairman), five officials from the Departments of Finance and Education, six representatives of the INTO, and six independent members. A Minority Report signed by the five civil servants and a Majority Report signed by the other members were presented to the Minister for Education on 18 May. The main recommendations in the Majority Report were as follows:

1   There should be a common salary scale for single men and women.
2   Female teachers, principals, vice-principals and privileged assistants should receive the same rate of allowance as single men.
3   Married men should receive a higher salary which incorporated an annual marriage allowance.
4   On marriage, men should receive a lump sum gratuity.
5   Additional bonuses should be paid for university honours' qualifications.
6   Teachers should be granted a pension scheme similar to the one enjoyed by civil servants.

---

8   The Statutory Instrument was signed on 21 December 1948 by Richard Mulcahy, Minister for Education, and Patrick McGilligan, Minister for Finance.

In their Minority Report the five civil servants objected to the principle of equal pay for men and women on social, economic and professional grounds. They advocated that the existing three separate salary scales should continue because, given that the majority of teachers were women, the introduction of a common scale would prove too expensive and would, in general, give teachers higher salaries than the majority of civil servants.

In the Majority Report the members saw no satisfactory reason for a differentiation between the remuneration paid to men and women but recommended that married men should receive an annual gratuity incorporated into the common scale to help them to provide for a wife and family.

The Majority and the Minority Reports both recommended that teachers should have the same pension provisions as civil servants.

The Minister's Counter-proposals

In spite of INTO requests for the immediate retrospective implementation of the recommendations of the Majority Report, four months were to elapse before the Minister responded with the government's proposals. He accepted all of the principles in the recommendations but stated that the government, with regret and in light of the present economic circumstance, could not approve the proposed salary scales. He put forward a revised scheme of salary scales for implementation with effect from 1 April 1950. The new scales, while retaining the initial scale points recommended by Roe, had a greater number of increments to reach considerably reduced maximum points.

The recommendation that single men and women should receive the same salary and allowances remained unchanged, as did the recommendation that teachers should be granted the same superannuation conditions as were enjoyed by civil servants. The bonus paid to teachers holding Honours Degrees or the Honours Higher Diploma was increased by £10.

The CEC expressed its dissatisfaction with the scales offered and the proposed date of implementation. Teachers felt discriminated against because the following groups had received increases: civil servants in September 1948, Gardaí in January 1949, and the army in September 1949. Following a series of meetings and representations, the Minister agreed to a number of concessions, which he signified were his final ones. He agreed that:

- the new salary scales and other grants, and the revised pension arrangements would be brought into operation with effect from 1 January 1950 instead of 1 April 1950 as previously proposed
- female teachers in the service on 1 January 1950 would retain the right they had under the 1934 rules, whereby a gratuity equivalent to one year's salary would be paid to their legal personal representative on death in service.

Review after Roe

Salary

The revised salaries introduced by the Minister were a severe disappointment to the INTO as publication of the Roe Committee's reports had raised expectations. However, some progress had been made: women were now on the same scale salary as men, albeit single men.

A comparison between the 1938 scales and those of 1950 shows that the minimum of married men's scale increased by 104 per cent and the maximum by 81 percent; the scale for women increased by 87 and 74 per cent, respectively; and the scale for single men by 70 and 42 per cent, respectively.

A Comparison of the Salary Scales for National Teachers, 1938–1950[9]

	Minister's Scales 1/4/38	Minister's Scales 8/12/45	Roe's Scales	Minister's Scales 1/1/50	Increase 1938–1950 £	% Increase
Married men	£	£	£	£	£	%
Minimum	147	220	300	300	153	104.1
Increments			18	20		
Maximum	318	485	650	575	257	80.8
		A marriage gratuity of £75				
Single men						
Minimum	147	220	250	250	103	70.1
Increments			17	20		
Maximum	318	380	535	450	132	41.5
Women						
Minimum	134	200	250	250	116	86.6
Increments			17	20		
Maximum	258	340	535	450	192	74.4
JAMs						
Minimum	98	150	250	250	152	155.1
Increments			18	16		
Maximum	133	196	425	310	177	133.1

---

9 The table shows the relative salary positions, both in monetary and percentage terms, in 1938 and 1950.

Position of Single Men

Of all groups, single men felt most aggrieved. The minimum point of their salary scale was increased by the lowest percentage of all groups, and the maximum point was increased by approximately half that of married men.[10] They organised themselves into an action group and as a result of representations by the CEC, the Minister, with effect from 1 April 1951, granted pre-1949 trained teachers an extra increment, a twenty-first increment, to be paid when the maximum of the salary scale was reached. During the following years several attempts were made to establish a separate teachers' union group for single male teachers, but without success. The special increment was increased at every salary review up to 1968.

Superannuation

The breakthrough on the superannuation provisions was of major importance: teachers had at last achieved their objective of a superannuation scheme similar to the one enjoyed by civil servants; they had moved from retiring on half pay to retiring on half pay with a tax-free lump sum of three times the pension.

In the resolution of the superannuation provisions women came to the fore as a powerful interest group. They were offered the same provision that applied to female civil servants, i.e. pension based on sixtieths and no lump sum. They demanded the same conditions as men; they were not prepared to be set aside with a pension only. Following strenuous representations, the government was obliged to grant the same pension provisions to men and women.[11] Women in the civil service did not get these provisions until 1954.

However, as the new benefits only applied to teachers who were in the service on or after 1 January 1950, those who retired before that date felt very aggrieved and the CEC had to fight a long campaign to get some compensation for them.

Civil Service Conditions of Service

With effect from 1 November 1946 revised salary scales were introduced in the civil service which were arrived at by consolidating basic pay and the cost-of-living bonus. This was followed by the establishment of a Civil Service Conciliation and Arbitration (C&A) Scheme, a new concept for the determination of salary and pension improvements.

Over the next twenty years many amendments were made to the civil service pension scheme and they invariably permeated down to all public employees:

---

10 Salary scales, differentiated on marriage, had been introduced in the civil service in 1926, but single male teachers were not treated in a similar manner.

11 The National School Teachers' Superannuation (Amendment) Scheme, 1950, Statutory Instrument No. 180 of 1950. Signed by the Ministers on 12 July 1950.

- The Superannuation Act of 1954 removed discrimination in pension benefits payable to female civil servants and introduced death-in-service benefits.
- The Superannuation Act of 1956 allowed male civil servants to allocate part of their pension in favour of a pension for dependents (wife or one dependent).
- The Superannuation and Pensions Act of 1962 made pensions portable within the agreed public sector network or designated employments.[12]
- The Superannuation Act of 1964 enabled the relevant Minister, with the permission of the Minister for Finance, to implement amendments to superannuation schemes by means of Statutory Instruments rather than by Acts of the Oireachtas.
- The Pensions (Abatement) Bill of 1965 provided that where a public service pensioner was re-employed, his/her pension would not be abated unless the new employment was that from which the pensioner had retired.
- In 1968 the Widows' and Orphans' Contributory Pension Scheme was introduced. This ensured cover for the surviving spouse and dependents of an officer who died while in the service.

There was, however, one major flaw in all pension schemes: there was no established procedure for a review of a pension once it had been determined. Pensioners were dependent on the goodwill of the Minister for Finance for any increases granted to compensate for increases in the cost of living. This problem was not resolved until 1983 when full indexation of pensions to current pay levels was achieved.

C&A Schemes for Teachers

By 1951 it was clear that the government was not prepared to change its position on the revised salary scales introduced for national teachers with effect from 1 January 1950. In response, the CEC sought to establish a recognised C&A Scheme that would give the INTO a forum for the resolution of salary and pension disagreements with the government.

The CEC submitted a draft C&A Scheme for teachers to the Minister for Education, General Mulcahy, on 23 September 1950, and after lengthy discussions a scheme came into effect from 1 March 1951.[13] While this scheme was deemed to be a temporary one for one year, it was a watershed in industrial relations between the government and the INTO.

In future, all claims regarding salary, allowances, and superannuation had to be processed through the Conciliation Council. If the government accepted the report its findings were implemented. When the sides failed to reach agreement,

---

12 Gerard Hughes, *The Irish Civil Service Superannuation Scheme*, pp. 10–11
13 Agreement: C&A Machinery in Connection with the Salaries and Other Emoluments of Teachers in National Schools

the claim, as long as it was not a pension claim, could be referred to an Arbitration Board.

The INTO 1951 Salary Claim

The INTO lodged its first claims with the Conciliation Council in May 1951. It was a comprehensive collection of salary and pension claims, many of them a long time outstanding. The salary claims were as follows:

1   that all teachers' salaries should be substantially increased to compensate for the rise in the cost of living
2   that special consideration should be given to single male teachers appointed before 1946
3   that allowances for principals, vice-principals and privileged assistants should be increased
4   that allowances for qualifications should be increased
5   that rent allowances should be increased and that the scheme should be extended to include widows
6   that the method of computation of the marriage gratuity should be revised
7   that married men and widowed teachers should receive children's allowances at a rate similar to that which had been conceded to civil servants and army officers.

The claims for amendments to the superannuation scheme were as follows:

1   that all teaching service, including service as substitute or supernumerary, whether in Ireland or any other country, or interrupted service arising from teachers being engaged in national service, should count for pension and lump sum purposes
2   that pension and lump sum should be based on salary on retirement, as applied in the civil service
3   that teachers with thirty-nine years of recognised service should qualify for maximum pension and lump sum
4   that the lump sum should be calculated on twenty-sixths instead of thirtieths
5   that women who had been obliged to retire on marriage should be compensated
6   that women who had been obliged to retire before the age of sixty-five should be compensated
7   that a teacher's widow should receive the pension that her husband would have received had he lived
8   that all service pre-1934 given by JAMs and lay assistants in capitation schools should be recognised in full for pension purposes
9   that the pensioners who did not accept the 1914 scheme should be recognised as members of the present scheme
10   that teachers who retired before 1 January 1950 should be granted a lump sum.

That same month, following the general election, Eamon de Valera was elected Taoiseach with the help of Noel Browne and a number of Independent TDs.[14] General Mulcahy was replaced as Minister for Education by Sean Moylan, and McGilligan was replaced as Minister for Finance by Seán MacEntee.

The first meeting of the Conciliation Council took place on 11 June 1951, and after a number of meetings the Official Side presented its final salary offer and stated that it was not prepared to go any further. Salaries were increased by approximately 12 per cent, allowances were increased by 7.5 per cent, and the civil service children's allowance scheme was extended to teachers, widows of teachers and teacher widows.[15]

On 12 July the CEC considered the report from the negotiators and decided to accept the offer, mainly due to the instability of the political situation.

The INTO 1952 Salary Claim

Agreement was recorded on the following claims at a meeting of the Conciliation Council on 8 February 1952:

- The list of academic qualifications that qualified for an allowance was extended and some allowances were revised.
- The salary of a trained teacher serving as a JAM was increased with effect from 1 November 1951.
- Revisions were made to the rules regarding the placement of certain categories of teachers on the salary scales for trained teachers.
- The method for calculating the retirement benefits of civil servants was conceded. Henceforth, from 1 January 1952, retiring salary would be defined as the sum of the annual rate of scale salary on the last day of pensionable service and the average annual amount of allowances for the last three years ending on the last day of the relevant quarter.
- An *ex gratia* grant was conceded to a small number of teachers who had not opted into the 1914 or 1934 pension schemes.

The Appointment of an Arbitrator

A number of claims had not been disposed of and the CEC requested the appointment of an arbitrator. The Minister prevaricated and stated that 'as the present scheme comes to an end on 29 February ... the appointment of a

---

14 Fianna Fáil gained only one seat in the general election; De Valera ruled with a minority government for almost three years.

15 The Conciliation Council consisted of a chairman, a serving civil servant nominated by the Minister for Education; four representatives on the Official Side, two from the Department of Finance and two from the Department of Education; and four representatives from the INTO.

chairman of the Arbitration Board during the currency of the Agreement would not appear to arise'.[16]

Efforts to have the C&A Scheme re-established were unsuccessful. It appeared to the CEC that operations and responses under Fianna Fáil governments had not changed.

Congress 1952 had instructed the CEC to take High Court proceedings against the Minister, challenging the constitutionality of the introduction of different salary scales for married men and single men in November 1946.[17] When the CEC pressed for the re-establishment of the C&A Scheme, the government claimed that negotiations could not proceed as the court decision might affect the whole pattern of salary scales. The INTO refused to withdraw its support for the two plaintiffs. In early July 1953, after a six-day hearing, both cases were dismissed with costs. The verdict was appealed to the Supreme Court, again without success.

Salary Increases, 1 April 1953

In his budget speech in 1953, the Minister for Finance announced salary increases for all those employed in the public service, to come into effect from 1 April 1953. The increases for national teachers were as follows: £25 on the first £230 of existing salary, plus £1 for each £22 of the existing salary in excess of £230. All allowances were increased by 5 per cent except children's allowances, where the allowance for each eligible child was increased by £2.[18]

Pension Claims, 12 May 1953

At a meeting with the Minister on 12 May 1953, an INTO deputation presented the following pension claims:

1   All pre-1934 service given by JAMs and lay assistants in capitation schools should be recognised in full for pension purposes.

2   All teaching service given in secondary and vocational schools should count for pension and lump sum purposes.

3   The one-day strike absence in 1933 should be recognised for pension purposes.

4   All teaching service, including service as substitute or supernumerary given in Northern Ireland, England and Scotland, should count for pension and lump sum purposes.

---

16 CEC Report to Congress 1952
17 *O'Callaghan and Ó Cinnéide v. the Minister for Education and others, Irish School Weekly*, 12 and 19 September 1953
18 In the period from 1939 to 1953 the expenditure on salaries and pensions for national teachers had almost doubled, and the major portion of that had occurred in the three years 1950–53. In 1939, the expenditure for 11,424 teachers had been £3,663,056 and in 1953 it was £7,145,400 for 10,613 teachers.

The Minister promised to give consideration to claims two and three, he asked for an explanatory memorandum on claim one, but showed no sympathy for claim four.[19]

Later that year the Minister agreed to pay an *ex gratia* lump sum to teachers who had retired before 1 January 1950; payment of the balance of the gratuity was not conceded until April 1960.[20]

Salary Parity

With effect from 1 October 1952, vocational teachers were granted salary scales that brought them into line with those paid to secondary teachers. The CEC approved of this and requested the Minister to treat national teachers in a similar manner so that all teachers with minimum qualifications should be paid the same salary. The Minister requested a detailed memorandum on the claim.

For the next fifteen years, the quest by the CEC to achieve parity of salaries between teachers in the three teaching sectors was to be a consuming objective and the cause of considerable inter-union discord.

The Second Inter-Party Government, 1954–57

The Fianna Fáil minority government of the period 1951–4 was as unsuccessful as its coalition predecessor in dealing with the chronically depressed economy.[21] In the general election of 1954 Fianna Fáil won sixty-five seats, a loss of four, and now stood at its lowest strength since 1932; Fine Gael won fifty seats, a gain of ten; and Labour won nineteen, a gain of three. Though Fine Gael and Labour had fought the election independently of one another, Declan Costello formed his second coalition Inter-Party Government. The three Clann na Poblachta deputies supported but did not participate in the government. On 2 June 1954 the new government took office with Costello as Taoiseach, General Mulcahy as Minister for Education, and Gerard Sweetman as Minister for Finance.

At a meeting on 17 December 1954 the Minister responded to INTO claims as follows:

- He could not accept the principle of parity in salary for all teachers.
- He could not ban the entry of untrained teachers into the profession as it might affect teacher supply but, as from July 1956, and for every year after that, sixty extra trained lay female teachers would enter the service.

---

19 CEC Report to Congress 1954
20 Statutory Instrument No. 255 of 1953. Pension concessions were also granted to secondary teachers. Their pension contribution was increased from 2.5 per cent to 5 per cent, beginning from the school year 1954–55. The minutes of the ASTI Convention of 1960 recorded that 26 per cent of lay secondary teachers were still outside the pension scheme.
21 John A. Murphy, *Ireland in the Twentieth Century*, p. 136

- As the marriage ban was government policy there was no intention of removing it.
- The government was of the view that the 1934 Pension Scheme was a generous settlement and that there was no hope of pre-1934 service being recognised.

The Lost Increment

Arising from the McEnaney judgment[22], delivered on 17 December 1939, a number of teachers in the service before 1 June 1930 were due a refund of increments. This case was finally brought to a conclusion in 1955 when, following INTO pressure and advice received from the Attorney General, the Department refunded the increments that had been withheld since 1930.

Teachers were still unhappy about the merit mark system and the use of competency in Irish as a determining factor. Following a number of conferences and discussions an agreement was reached.

- Henceforth, merit marks would be discontinued except in the case of teachers (a) on probation or (b) who were rated 'Unsatisfactory'.
- The rating 'Satisfactory' would be given, where warranted, even if oral Irish was weak, 'unless the weakness was the result of the negligence of the teacher'.[23]

Judge Conroy Arbitration Award

After two years of representations, meetings and memoranda, the terms of a new C&A Scheme were finally agreed and signed on 11 December 1954.[24] The way was now open for disputed salary claims to be referred to an arbitrator.

On 12 February 1955 an INTO claim seeking parity of salaries was referred to the Arbitration Board. Judge J. C. Conroy was appointed chairman and he issued his findings in September 1955. He did not concede the principle of parity but he did grant a salary increase with effect from 1 October 1955 and recommended that the salary differentials that had existed in 1946 should be restored. The percentage ratios between the maximum of the scale for single men and women had been:

Secondary Teachers	Vocational Teachers	National Teachers
100%[25]	89.8%	89.6%

---

22 See Chapter 8
23 A circular, issued by the Department of Education in 1959, set down new rules for the guidance of inspectors in their work in schools.
24 Eventually, three different C&A Schemes were agreed, with the Irish National Teachers' Organisation (INTO) in 1954, with the Association of Secondary Teachers Ireland (ASTI) in December 1955, and with the Vocational Teachers' Association (VTA) in 1957.
25 John Coolahan states that the basic salary paid varied from £200 to £300, *The ASTI and Post-Primary Education 1909–1984*, p. 156

A salary increase awarded to all public servants, except secondary teachers, from 1 November 1955 left the percentage ratios between teachers, assuming a £200 school salary for secondary teachers, as follows:

Secondary Teachers	Vocational Teachers	National Teachers
100%	100%	95.2%

INTO Conciliation Council Claims

On 12 September 1956 the INTO submitted five claims to the Conciliation Council. At subsequent meetings the Official Side was not prepared to make any offer on four claims but it responded to Claim No. 15, which concerned amendments to the pension scheme, as follows:

- It was prepared to concede that service given after the age of sixty-five would be recognised for increments but not for pension.
- It would not accept as pensionable any teaching service that was not paid for by the Department.
- It could not allow added years for teachers unemployed in the period between 1915 and 1940, since added years were not granted in respect of any group remunerated from voted funds.
- It would not allow a further option to the pre-1914 teachers to opt into the scheme since they had refused in 1914, 1918 and 1921.[26]

The INTO requested the appointment of a chairman to the Arbitration Board to hear the non-pension claims on which the Conciliation Council had failed to reach agreement.

On 3 January 1957, at a meeting requested by the Ministers for Finance and Education, a CEC deputation was requested, due to economic circumstances, not to proceed to Arbitration with claims of a substantial nature. The Ministers stated that similar representations were being made to all groups who were paid from the public purse. At its meeting on 5 January the CEC agreed to refrain from proceeding to Arbitration but stressed that it would exercise that right if the situation warranted it.

On 11 January 1957 the national newspapers carried a report that Kevin Liston SC had issued a finding awarding secondary teachers a two-element increase in remuneration. This award widened the salary gap and disrupted the relativities that Judge Conroy had recommended.

On 27 January 1957 Dave Kelleher, General Secretary INTO, wrote to the Minister for Education expressing amazement and shock at the announcement. He stated that the CEC felt that it had been misled by the Ministers but would

---

26 Conciliation Council Report, 5 December 1956

nonetheless stand by the commitment given on 5 January. However, he concluded by saying that suitable action would be taken at an appropriate time.

In an effort to defuse the situation, special Conciliation Council meetings were arranged during February and March to consider the outstanding INTO claims. On 2 March 1957 the Conciliation Council recorded agreement on claims Nos. 17, 19, 20, 21, 23, 26, and 28, and disagreement on claims 18, 22, 24, 25, 27, and 29.

Claims 19, 20, 21, and 23 granted recognition to the following for incremental purposes from 1 January 1957: (1) service given by trained teachers as JAMs, (2) service given between their two years of training by ex-members of religious communities, (3) service given by national teachers in secondary or vocational schools, and (4) from 1 October 1956, service given by teachers after they had reached the age of sixty-five.

Claims 26 and 28 were important concessions with regard to superannuation. Claim 26 acknowledged any recognised service as a vocational or secondary teacher as pensionable service under the National Teachers' Superannuation Scheme. Claim 28 granted that service up to the end of the school year, 30 June, instead of up to the end of the quarter in which the teacher reached the age of sixty-five, could be counted as pensionable service.[27]

Fianna Fáil Governments, 1957–68

In the general election of March 1957 Fianna Fáil was returned with an overall majority of ten, having won seventy-eight seats. Fine Gael lost ten seats, and Labour seven. This election ushered in a sixteen-year period of Fianna Fáil government. Jack Lynch was appointed Minister for Education and Dr Jim Ryan as Minister for Finance.

The INTO re-submitted its claim for parity to the Conciliation Council on 16 August 1957.[28] At a meeting on 13 September with the new Ministers for Finance and Education, CEC representatives were requested to continue the undertaking given to the previous Ministers in January, and not to proceed with major cost claims as the economic situation in the country had not changed. The delegation responded explaining that:

- the commitment given to the previous Ministers had been given without the knowledge that a status award was contemplated for secondary teachers
- the CEC considered the withholding of this information a breach of faith
- the commitment would not have been given if the information had been known to them, and due to all the circumstances the parity claim was being processed.

---

27 Statutory Instrument No. 247 of 1959
28 Claim No. 30

The Ministers responded by stating that the Official Side would be directed not to make any offer at conciliation and if an award was made at Arbitration it could not be implemented as there was no money available and, in the circumstances, there was no point in having discussions on the appointment of a chairman to the Arbitration Board.

At a further meeting on 15 December it was stated that the government considered it inappropriate for the principle of parity to be the subject of Arbitration. The INTO protested as this was considered to be tantamount to setting aside the established negotiation machinery. It was eventually agreed that the Ministers would set up a conference to consider the principles governing teachers' salaries.[29]

Cost-of-living Salary Claim, 1958

As national teachers had not received a salary increase since November 1955 and, in the meantime the cost-of-living index had increased by sixteen points, on 20 February 1958 the CEC submitted a salary claim for an increase for 12.5 per cent. Kevin Liston SC was appointed arbitrator in September and his report was issued on 11 October 1959. National teachers were awarded an overall increase of 6 per cent on scale salaries and on principals' and vice-principals' allowances, with effect from 1 September 1958. No increase was awarded on all the other allowances.

Removal of the Marriage Ban, 1958

The rule requiring women to retire on marriage was revoked by Jack Lynch, Minister for Education, with effect from 1 July 1958. He outlined his reasons for the removal of the ban during his speech in the Dáil:

> I would like to stress that I am satisfied that on balance the long-term effect of the rule has been an adverse one, both educationally and socially. One aspect in this connection is that women teachers are being forced to retire at a time when they are reaching the peak of their teaching efficiency. Another aspect which might not be immediately obvious is that the provision of trained teachers in remote rural areas should prove an effective step in preventing emigration or migration of parents from these areas.[30]

In June 1958 a separate agreement was reached with the Conference of Convent Primary Schools to 'accept the decision of the Minister for the good of the State'.[31]

---

29 CEC Report to Congress 1959
30 Revocation of Rule 72 (1) of Department of Education's Rules, January 1958. CEC Report to Congress 1959. The marriage ban was not revoked for civil servants until 1 July 1973.
31 Letter from Sister M. Ita O'Connor, President CCPS, to D. J. Kelleher, 9 June 1959

Women who were in temporary appointments had their positions confirmed as permanent and those who had been obliged to retire were free to resume their teaching careers. The number of married women returning to work caused problems for teachers leaving training colleges and some unemployment occurred.

Subsequently, the CEC negotiated an agreement which enabled women to repay their marriage gratuities and thereby ensure that service given before marriage would be taken into consideration for superannuation purposes on eventual retirement. In 1973 the CEC was successful in having the temporary service as assistants and principals given by married women during the operation of the marriage ban recognised for pension purposes.

The Teachers' Salaries Committee

On 20 March 1958 Jack Lynch informed the CEC that he intended to establish a committee with the following terms of reference: 'To examine and report on principles which might guide the Minister for Education in determining the relationship between the remuneration payable to trained National Teachers, recognised Secondary Teachers and permanent whole-time Vocational Teachers respectively.'[32]

When the committee met for the first time on 8 January 1959 the Minister for Education advised that it was being asked to issue findings regarding a solution to the parity of salary question.[33]

The final report of the Salaries Committee, presented to the Minister for Education on 29 July 1960, consisted of a Minority and a Majority Report. The Majority Report recommended three salary scales, the highest one for secondary teachers, the next highest for vocational teachers, and the lowest one for national teachers. The implication for the CEC was clear: primary teachers were considered inferior in both quality and qualification.[34] If the proposed salary relationship was accepted, it would make the attainment of INTO parity policy impossible.

The reports' recommendations were not implemented and the C&A Scheme continued to operate as it had previously done.

Salary Increase, 1 January 1960

In 1959 Seán Lemass became Taoiseach[35] and Patrick J. Hillery was appointed Minister for Education. Lemass set about implementing the First Programme of

---

32 Letter to D. J. Kelleher from T. Ó Raifeartaigh, Secretary, Department of Education, 20 March 1959
33 CEC Report to Congress 1959
34 John Logan (ed.), *Teachers' Union: the TUI and its Fore-Runners in Irish Education, 1899–1994*, p. 171
35 Seán Lemass led Fianna Fáil to victory in the general elections in 1961 and 1965.

Economic Expansion, which was a comprehensive rational plan for the economy as a whole and provided a framework for its radical expansion. In the five-year period from 1958 to 1963 national output increased by nearly one-quarter and the purchasing power of wages rose by one-fifth.[36]

As the cost-of-living index had increased by sixteen points since 1955, on 30 November 1959, the INTO lodged a claim seeking an increase in salaries of 14 per cent. Agreement was reached giving an increase of slightly less than 5 per cent, with effect from 1 January 1960.

Retirement Lump Sum and Pre-1950 Teachers

In 1953 the CEC had successfully negotiated an *ex gratia* grant for teachers who had retired prior to 1 January 1950 and had continued to seek the balance deemed due.[37] Finally, with effect from 12 April 1960, the Minister agreed to pay the balance due to any eligible person currently in receipt of a pension, or to a widow whose husband would have been entitled to such grant.[38]

Pension Claims

The following pension claims were heard at Conciliation Council meetings on 1 September and 21 October 1961:

1   Full pension credit for pre-1934 service should be granted to certain teachers.
2   Service given by JAMs and lay assistants in Convent and Monastery schools should be recognised in full for pension purposes (the Roe Committee had recommended this).
3   Teachers trained between 1930 and 1940 who were unemployed for a period should be granted added years for pension purposes.
4   Fractions of a year in excess of completed years should be taken into account in the calculation of pension and lump sum.

It was agreed, without any commitment, that further discussion should take place on the first claim, but no offer was made on the other three claims. For tactical reasons the INTO withdrew these claims rather than have disagreement recorded. If disagreement was recorded the claims could not be resubmitted for a further three years.

At a Conciliation Council meeting on 24 December the Official Side conceded that pre-1934 service would be recognised for pension but not for lump sum; this restriction appears to have been retained to save money. Retired teachers' pensions were increased and teachers still in the service were to get

36 John A. Murphy, *Ireland in the Twentieth Century*, p. 144
37 Section 11 of Statutory Instrument No. 255 of 1953
38 Statutory Instrument No. 156 of 1964

full recognition on retirement. Although the claim was not conceded in full, teachers accepted it because a resolution to this problem had been sought by the INTO for twenty-seven years.[39]

Seán Brosnahan, the newly elected General Treasurer of the INTO, was elected to Seanad Éireann in November 1961.[40] In one of his first speeches he claimed that pensioners should receive increases on a par with the increases granted to those still serving.[41] This was a claim for the indexation of pensions, and it was to figure in all public service union negotiations until it was finally achieved in 1983.

Notwithstanding the problem that existed between the INTO, ASTI and the VTA with regard to the parity of salary question, three meetings were convened in November and December 1962 to discuss problems being experienced with the different superannuation schemes. The three parties agreed to make representations to the Department on the following matters:

- early voluntary retirement at sixty years of age
- the adjustment of pensions in line with salary increases
- the provision of 'added years' in cases of disability after thirty years of service
- resolution of the problem of 'effective days lost'.[42]

Arbitration Award, November 1961

Following another general election in October 1961, Seán Lemass led a minority government, which John A. Murphy regards as arguably the best administration in the history of the State.[43] Dr Hillery was re-appointed Minister for Education.

A series of leapfrogging settlements in the salaries of teachers occurred during Lemass's period in power, and the parity question was still a matter of contention between the teacher groups.[44] The Official Side tried to introduce the Teachers' Salaries Committee in salary negotiations on a number of occasions, but this was strongly opposed by the INTO. The CEC representatives warned them that if they persisted with this 'there was no prospect that the INTO would participate in a common C&A Scheme for national, secondary, and vocational teachers'.[45]

---

39 Ibid.
40 Michael P. Linehan retired from the post as General Treasurer/ Assistant General Secretary, INTO, on 30 June 1961. Seán Brosnahan, Dublin City District Representative on the CEC, was elected unopposed to fill the vacancy from 1 July 1961.
41 CEC Report to Congress 1962
42 John Coolahan, *The ASTI and Post-Primary Education 1909–1984*, p. 199
43 John A. Murphy, *Ireland in the Twentieth Century*, p. 142
44 Leapfrogging occurs when the success of one group with a claim is used by another group as the basis for a successful claim on behalf of its members.
45 CEC Report to Congress 1963, p. 22

The Arbitration Board, with Liston as chairman, granted national teachers revised salaries with effect from 1 November 1961. This award brought the percentage ratio between the maximum of the scale for single men and women to:

Secondary Teachers	Vocational Teachers	National Teachers
100%	97.1%	89.4%

The differential for vocational teachers had decreased from the full parity of 1952, and the percentage ratio for national teachers had reached its lowest point ever. Nevertheless, leapfrogging continued: secondary teachers got an Arbitration award in March 1962, and vocational teachers got one a few months later.

The Mangan Arbitration Dispute

In response to these salary movements the CEC presented a 'Status Salary Claim' at a Conciliation Council meeting on 28 September 1962. Disagreement was recorded on 30 October 1962 as the Official Side was not prepared to make any offer. The CEC, however, delayed submitting it to Arbitration until after 30 November 1962 when Liston's term as chairman expired. A new chairman for the three separate Arbitration Boards was not agreed until 22 February 1963 when Frederick Mangan was appointed.

Board negotiations began on 2 April and the chairman issued his findings on 10 April 1963. The CEC was very disappointed with the chairman's report and his award.[46]

The government declared that it was prepared to implement the new scales with effect from 1 April 1963 but the CEC set about getting the Arbitration findings set aside and having the claim re-heard. Meetings were held with the Minister on 1 May and 1 August and with the Taoiseach on 14 September 1963, and extensive correspondence was exchanged between the parties.

The situation was not helped by an award made to the Gardaí by the same arbitrator which gave a Garda £148 more than a teacher at the initial point of the common salary scale.

As the matter was not being resolved, the INTO called a Special Regional Conference of branch delegates for 28 September 1963. Among the resolutions passed at the conference were:

- that a campaign of regional strikes should be organised
- that the INTO should withdraw from the C&A Scheme
- that a system for the collection of levies from members to finance the strike should be put in place.

---

46 CEC Report to Congress 1964, p. 19

On 30 September 1963 the INTO gave six months' notice to the Minister of its intention to withdraw from the C&A Scheme. Further meetings took place between officials in the Departments and the CEC. Everybody was aware that a resolution to the problem had to be found or a situation similar to that which had led to the 1946 strike episode would develop. It was eventually conceded that the INTO could re-submit its claim to the Conciliation Council. Following meetings of the Council on 11 and 15 November 1963 revised salary scales were offered to national teachers.[47]

- The number of increments in each trained salary scale was reduced from twenty to seventeen.
- Rent allowances would be absorbed into the salary scales, which meant they would be taken into consideration in computing pension and lump sum.
- Teacher widows were granted a special allowance of £50 in lieu of the rent allowance.
- Salaries for other teachers would be proportionally increased.
- The new scales would be implemented with effect from 1 September 1963.

The Official Side also stated that they had the highest authority to confirm:

1 that the offer was without prejudice to any ninth-round adjustment (the Ninth National Wage Round was under negotiation at that time.)
2 that the government was not opposed to the principle of further improvements for national teachers to be achieved over a reasonable period as general adjustments in the salaries of public officials were made.

The offer was accepted by INTO members in a ballot, 5,905 for and 3,066 voting against. By 1 November 1961 the relativity of scale salaries of national teachers to those of secondary teachers had decreased to 89.4 per cent, lower than it had been in 1946; this award restored the relativity back to the 1955 figure of 95 per cent.[48]

Following Mangan

On 12 February 1964 the CEC submitted a claim seeking a status salary award in addition to the 12 per cent ninth-round increase.[49] The CEC, without going to Arbitration, accepted an offer made by the Official Side to be paid from 1 February 1964.

---

47 National Teachers' Conciliation Council Agreed Report, 1963, CEC Report to Congress 1964, p. 19
48 Department of Education Archives: Memorandum for 1964 Arbitration, quoted in John Coolahan, *The ASTI and Post-Primary Education in Ireland, 1909–1984*, p. 243
49 The Ninth National Wage Round became operative from 1 February 1964. CEC Report to Congress 1965, p. 11

However, an obstacle was created before the award could be implemented. The Official Side stated that it was not prepared to apply the status element of the award, only the 12 per cent ninth-round award, to the £50 special allowance granted to widows in September 1963. The CEC was reluctant to accept the award without first consulting widow representatives on the matter. They agreed that the offer would be acceptable to them on condition that henceforth they would be entitled to a pro rata increase in future salary awards. The CEC, having received an assurance that widows would be considered as a special category in future negotiations, agreed to accept the offer.

School Salaries for Secondary Teachers

The Department of Education's regulations stipulated that managers of secondary schools had to pay, to a prescribed minimum number of its teaching staff, a basic salary of not less than £200 per annum. The incremental salary scale from the Department and the basic £200 was deemed to be the standard salary for secondary teachers and constituted their pensionable salary. In 1964 an agreement was negotiated between the ASTI and the Catholic Headmasters Association (CHA) whereby school authorities would pay secondary teachers an additional non-pensionable amount of 12.5 per cent of the married standard salary as part of the basic salary and that those already in receipt of higher salaries would not suffer.[50]

This agreement was kept confidential for a considerable time but it eventually entered the public domain.[51] The INTO considered this increase to be a disturbance of the existing relativities between teachers' salaries and lodged the following status claim on 2 November 1964:

> That the salaries of national teachers be revised to compensate for disturbance in relationships (a) with salaries of secondary teachers which had been increased as a result of new contracts with Conductors of secondary schools on the rate of basic pay, and (b) with salaries paid to Executive Officers and Staff Officers in the civil service.

The VTA also reacted angrily to the 'secret award' and made efforts to regain the position lost.

Before the next Conciliation Council meeting could be arranged, the Minister, Dr Hillery, invited representatives of the three teacher organisations to a meeting on 27 January 1965. He stated that he was disturbed that teachers, who had got status awards the previous year, had now lodged further claims. He

50 John Coolahan, *The ASTI and Post-Primary Education in Ireland, 1909–1984*, p. 244. Teachers in some schools were paid in excess of the agreed minimum basic salary.
51 The Ryan Tribunal in 1968 was to record: 'We have no doubt that the agreement had divisive effects within the teaching profession.' Tribunal Report on Teachers' Salaries, 1968, p. 15

said that he had got a policy declaration from the government that the status of teachers should be improved and that, in furtherance of that objective, he had secured a further million pounds for distribution to teachers. He requested the teachers' organisations to process their claims through conciliation and 'not rock the boat'.[52]

The CEC acceded to the Minister's request and attended a meeting of the Conciliation Council on 11 February 1965 where revised salary scales were offered by the Official Side. It was stated that a similar percentage increase, approximately 8 per cent, was being offered to secondary and vocational teachers.[53] However, the offer to national teachers was conditional on the acceptance by them that the school day should be extended by half an hour. The CEC representatives were not prepared to accept the scales offered or the condition attached. They withdrew after requesting a meeting with the Minister.

A further meeting of conciliation was arranged where the condition regarding the extension of the school day was withdrawn, the salaries offer remained unchanged, and the date of implementation was changed to 1 November 1964.[54] At a meeting on 20 February the CEC unanimously rejected the offer and decided to seek the appointment of an arbitrator. In response to this request, the Minister indicated that the government would be more inclined to appoint a common arbitrator for all three teacher groups. The INTO insisted on its right under its own scheme to have an arbitrator appointed to consider its own claim.

Following a general election in April 1965 Seán Lemass was appointed Taoiseach of another Fianna Fáil government, and George Colley was appointed Minister for Education.

On 12 July the chairman of the Arbitration Board, Sandys, issued his findings. This Arbitration award differed marginally from the offer made at the Conciliation Council on 11 February and the date of implementation was changed from 1 November 1964 to 1 December 1964.[55]

In the meantime, the ASTI and VTA had both processed claims for salary increases through Conciliation and on to Arbitration. The award made by the arbitrator to secondary teachers was based on the assumption of a standard school salary of £200 per annum; the new agreement negotiated with the CHA was not in the public domain. Vocational teachers received an arbitrator's award with effect from 1 January 1965.

These salary scales established by Arbitration in 1964 were to have consequences for the common basic salary scales recommended by the Ryan Tribunal in 1968.

---

52 CEC Report to Congress 1965, p. 9
53 Approximately £700,000 would be going to the primary sector.
54 On 13 February the ASTI had accepted an offer made to them.
55 CEC Report to Congress 1966, p. 2

Tenth Round Salary Claim

In September 1965 the Minister for Education asked the teacher unions for opinions on the possibility of having a common basic scale of salaries for all teachers. He indicated to them that, in addition to a common basic scale, there would also be recognition for length of training, academic qualifications, and extra responsibility and status in relation to the holding of particular posts. In response the INTO submitted a memorandum detailing its policy on parity.

Under the terms of the Tenth National Wage Round the government announced that, due to economic circumstances, no claim for an increase would be entertained from public servants earning £1,200 per annum or more, and that the increase would be £1 per week with effect from 1 June 1966.[56]

The CEC endeavoured to get an exemption for teachers from this salary restriction at a Conciliation Council meeting on 27 September 1966 by applying for the increase for all teachers irrespective of salary limits, marriage or sex. The Official Side responded by saying that even though the civil service unions and the VTA had already accepted the terms, it was prepared to waive the inclusion of allowances in the calculation of the income limit of £1,200, if the INTO was willing to accept the salary formula that had been accepted elsewhere. When it was agreed that the INTO could enter a claim on behalf of teachers with salaries in excess of £1,200 should other groups exceed the income limit, the offer was accepted.

Another cause of dissension arose between the INTO and the ASTI when the Department gave full incremental recognition for previous service to national and vocational teachers who fulfilled registration requirements and transferred to secondary teaching.[57] The ASTI objected to this as it gave national teachers an incremental advantage over secondary teachers. National teachers were appointed after two years' training and secondary teachers were appointed after a four-year period.

Salary Claim, 1967

At a Conciliation Council meeting on 26 January 1967 the upper limit of £1,200 was removed and the award was made retrospective to 1 June 1966.

In processing the claim the Official Side indicated its preference for a unified teaching profession and a common salary scale and allowances for the three groups of teachers. The CEC representatives promised to bring this suggestion back to the organisation for consideration.

---

56 Lemass resigned as Taoiseach in 1966 and was succeeded by Jack Lynch. Donogh B. O'Malley was appointed Minister for Education from 13 July 1966. Jack Lynch led Fianna Fáil to victory in the general election in November 1966. Donogh O'Malley was re-appointed Minister for Education.
57 Circular M44/66, Department of Education

This award was the culmination of a process that, in a relatively short period of time, had considerably improved national teachers' salaries. The following table shows the improvements:

	Married Men		Women, Single Men	
	Min.	**Max.**	**Min.**	**Max.**
November 1959	445	900	375	715
June 1966	822	1,542	659	1,229
Increase	377	642	284	514
Percentage increase	85%	71%	76%	72%

John A. Murphy states that 'both pay and pensions increased more than consumer prices and the increase in average pay was nearly 40 per cent more than the increase in prices.'[58]

Untrained Teachers – Transfer to Trained Scale

In the early 1960s, there were over 2,500 untrained teachers and JAMs in the school system, approximately 18 per cent of the total teaching staff of 14,000. These teachers were on a lower scale than trained teachers and the CEC had been discussing their conditions of service with the Department of Education for a number of years. In November 1965 the Department proposed that a series of summer training courses should be made available for them over three successive summers. Following satisfactory completion of the summer course an untrained teacher would be deemed 'trained' and transferred to the trained salary scale. The CEC initially objected to the scheme but following negotiations on some of the details, the Department's scheme was accepted.

Pension Claims

During the 1960s the government increased public service pensions on six occasions, and a number of amendments were introduced to the National School Teachers' Superannuation Scheme. The following amendments were agreed with effect from 15 June 1967:

- Paragraph 8 of Statutory Instrument No. 423, 1949, which provided for the abatement of pension where a teacher was employed as other than a national teacher, was revoked.
- Where a teacher retired and died before applying for a pension, the estate would receive the pension for the relevant intervening period as if an application had been submitted.

58 John A. Murphy, *Ireland in the Twentieth Century*, p. 144

- Where a person had a pension as a secondary or vocational teacher, the number of years reckonable for pension under the scheme could not, when added to the number of years of service on which the previous pension had been based, exceed forty.
- A person who re-entered national teaching service on or before 5 November 1951 was permitted to reckon for superannuation service one-half of his/her whole-time service with the Irish Folklore Commission.[59]

The resolution of some pension claims often took many years; they were presented on a regular basis at Conciliation Council but the Official side was not prepared to make any offer. The following were such perennial pension claims:

- recognition of service lost by teachers in the 1930s and 40s
- recognition for supernumerary service
- recognition for service given as a member of a religious community
- recognition for temporary service during the marriage ban
- recognition for gratuity purposes of service given as lay assistants and JAMs.

These claims originated in the 1950s and the last of them was not resolved until 1996.

Review of the 1960s

The changes in teachers' perceptions and the desire for the development of a more orderly and rational way of dealing with teachers and schools have to be considered in the context of the major economic changes that were occurring in the country. Seán Lemass came to power as Taoiseach in 1958 and introduced the First Programme for Economic Expansion, which spearheaded a massive upturn in economic expansion in the country. In the words of John A. Murphy:

> ... Lemass epitomised the new Ireland as well as being in large measure its architect ... for seven years he was to direct energetically the transformation of the economy, if not of society as a whole.[60]

Gross National Product (GNP) rose by over 4 per cent per annum and the despair and gloom engendered by unemployment and emigration in the 1950s, which had over-shadowed the country, began to dissipate. Protectionism as a policy was discarded and free trade and an openness to challenge were encouraged. People responded to the new challenges with optimism for the future and a demand for changes in every aspect of life.

---

59 Statutory Instrument No. 45, 1967
60 John A. Murphy, *Ireland in the Twentieth Century*, pp. 141–2

Factories were opened, houses were built, and emigrants began to return home. The 1966 census recorded that the population had grown by nearly 25 per cent; the proportion of the population in the younger age groups increased, with a particularly high increase of 62,000 in the 20–24 age group.

Enrolment in primary schools increased at a rapid rate, and structures in post-primary education were expanded and rationalised. In May 1963 the Minister for Education, Dr Hillery, announced that the government intended to:

- establish some State comprehensive schools which would offer a curriculum combining the academic and technical traditions
- introduce a new Common Intermediate Certificate which would further erode the prevailing post-primary bipartite system
- introduce a new Technical Leaving Certificate to parallel the academic one.

In January 1966 the Minister for Education, George Colley, announced that the government was committed to the concept of comprehensive education. Vocational and secondary schools were urged to develop similar programmes and to pool their resources and teacher supply so that pupils in any district would have available to them the widest range of curricular options.

In September 1966 the Minister for Education, Donogh O'Malley, announced that from the following school year it was the government's intention to make post-primary education free for all children and that a free transport system would be provided to facilitate maximum participation for all eligible school children.

These developments, and the difficulties of resolving teacher remuneration problems over the previous twenty years, were a major inducement in seeking a single unified teaching force with a common basic salary and access to a common C&A Scheme.

Parity of Pay

From the early 1950s, there had been an almost continuous stream of claims from the different organisations, all being processed through their own C&A Schemes. There had been salary claims, status claims and Arbitration claims, claims for increased responsibility allowances, claims for qualification allowances, claims for rent allowances, claims for children's allowances, and superannuation claims, either catching up with or leapfrogging the gains of another group.[61] Only in a few instances had the government been successful in having claims heard by a common arbitrator.

The length and intensity of the Mangan award dispute may be seen as a watershed in the way the government considered the machinery available for the

---

61 John Coolahan, *The ASTI and Post-Primary Education in Ireland, 1909–1984*, p. 244

resolution of teacher remuneration claims. It soon became obvious from the manner in which the Official Side responded at C&A hearings that a common scheme of C&A was favoured as a much more efficient way of accommodating claims from the different teacher groups.

It was also obvious that this objective could not be achieved unless the question of parity of salaries was resolved. Without parity the INTO would not join a common scheme and the ASTI would not join because its preferential salary position would be placed in jeopardy.[62]

Whether the Official Side was responding to the strength of the INTO or accepting the inevitability of parity if a common C&A Scheme was to be secured, its attitude towards the implementation of parity began to change. It now appeared to be in favour of the principle, with due recognition being granted for length of training, qualifications and responsibility of a post held.

On 6 October 1967 the Minister for Education, Donogh O'Malley, announced that the government had decided to establish a Tribunal on Teachers' Salaries. The Ryan Tribunal conducted a full review of the remuneration and conditions of service of national, vocational and secondary teachers. Its recommendations were to lead to a radical restructuring of the whole teaching profession at first and at second level.

---

62 INTO statement issued to the Sunday papers of 10 May 1964, with reference to the ASTI action in advising its members not to engage in the work of examining or superintending at the Certificate Examinations.

10

The Breakthrough, 1968–78

The Ryan Tribunal on Teachers' Salaries, 1968

The establishment of separate Conciliation and Arbitration Schemes for the different teacher groups in the 1950s resulted in a series of salary settlements, one leapfrogging the other. In an attempt to rationalise the situation, the Minister for Education, Donogh O'Malley, announced on 6 October 1967 that the government had decided to establish a Tribunal on Teachers' Salaries.[1] The ASTI did not want to participate at first because by so doing it would be accepting a commitment to the principle of a common basic salary scale for all teachers. Following assurances from the Minister that, in the event of dissatisfaction, it could revert to its own C&A Scheme, it agreed to participate.

The tribunal was appointed on 15 December 1967, with Professor Louden Ryan, Professor of Political Economy, Trinity College, as chairman.[2] The terms of reference were:

- to recommend a common basic salary scale for teachers in national, secondary and vocational schools
- to recommend what appropriate additions might be made to the basic scale in respect of qualifications, length of training, nature of duties, etc.

In its submission to the tribunal the INTO sought that:

- the salary position of teachers should be improved
- there should be one integrated teaching profession with a common basic salary for teachers possessing the minimum qualifications required to serve in national, secondary or vocational schools

---

1   Donogh O'Malley announced in September 1966 that from the following school year free post-primary education and its accompanying school transport scheme would be available for all eligible school children.
2   The other members were Ernest Benson, employers' representative from the Labour Court, Cathal O'Shannon, trade union representative from the Labour Court, Maurice Cosgrove, General Secretary of the Postal Workers Union, and Louis Fitzgerald, former Assistant Secretary in the Department of Finance; Art Ó Callanáin, an officer from the Department of Education, was appointed secretary.

- compensation should be given for length of training, age of entry, and qualifications, by placement on the salary scale at different points
- widows should be paid at the same rate as married men
- unpromoted teachers should receive a long-service increment
- qualification allowances should apply only in respect of degrees and diplomas above primary degree pass level
- there should be free movement of teachers from one branch to another
- there should be a common contributory superannuation scheme
- no distinction should be made in regard to the age-level of pupils in determining posts of responsibility.

The ASTI and the VTA submitted their own proposals.

The Tribunal Report

Donogh O'Malley died suddenly on 10 March 1968 and on 26 March 1968 Brian Lenihan was appointed Minister for Education. The tribunal held twenty meetings and presented its report to the Minister on 23 April 1968.[3] The tribunal was in favour of the development of a single profession of teaching and to that end recommended:

- a common course of professional training for all entrants to the teaching profession
- a common basic salary scale
- a common scheme of allowances for principals and vice-principals
- a common scheme of allowances for posts of responsibility
- a common scheme of other allowances
- a common contributory superannuation scheme for all teachers
- a single scheme of Conciliation and Arbitration.

The following paragraphs are a précis of the recommendations of the tribunal:

1 Common Basic Scale

The tribunal recommended a scale for married men and one for women and single men as follows:

Married men: £950+£35x5+£45x5+£50x7 = £1,700
Women and single men: £750+£28x5+£36x5+£40x7 = £1,350

Teachers with two years' full-time training would enter at the minimum point of the basic scale; teachers with three years would enter at the second point;

---

3 The published document became known as the Ryan Tribunal Report.

teachers with four or more years would enter at the third point; and teachers denied promotion would receive a long-service increment at the commencement of their twenty-fifth year of service at the rate of £75 for married men and £59 for women and single men.

The tribunal recommended that the Department of Education should pay recognised secondary teachers' total emoluments and that secondary school management should have no discretion in making supplementary payments to their staff.

2 The Points System

Principals and vice-principals in all schools would be paid graded allowances based on the 'points rating' of the school. Pupils would be assigned a points weighting depending on age in accordance with the following scale:

Age of pupils	Points weighting
under 9 years	1
aged 9 years and under 13 years	2
aged 13 years and under 15 years	3
aged 15 years and under 16 years	4
aged 16 years and under 17 years	5
aged 17 years and over	6

The points rating would be determined for each school based on attendance of pupils on 1 February of the previous year.

3 Posts of Principal and Vice-Principal

Allowances paid to principals and vice-principals would be determined by the points category of the school in accordance with the following scale:

Points rating of school	Allowances to	
	Principal	Vice-Principal
	£	£
Under 75	110	–
75–149	140	–
150–299	200	100
300–449	260	150
450–599	325	200

	Allowances to	
Points rating of school	**Principal**	**Vice-Principal**
	£	£
600–749	400	250
750–899	475	300
900–1,099	550	350
1,100–1,299	625	400
1,300–1,499	700	450
1,500–1,699	775	500

4 Posts of Special Responsibility

Eight posts of responsibility with graded allowances would be created as follows:

Grade of post	**Annual allowance £**
I	100
II	125
III	150
IV	200
V	250
VI	300
VII	400
VIII	500

The number and grades of posts of responsibility would be determined by reference to the points rating of the school as follows:

Points rating	**Number of posts**	**Number of posts in each grade**							
		I	II	III	IV	V	VI	VII	VIII
less than 450	–	–	–	–	–	–	–	–	–
450–599	1	1	–	–	–	–	–	–	–
600–749	2	1	1	–	–	–	–	–	–
750–899	3	2	–	1	–	–	–	–	–

Points rating	Number of posts	Number of posts in each grade							
		I	II	III	IV	V	VI	VII	VIII
900–1,099	4	2	1	1	–	–	–	–	–
1,100–1,299	5	2	1	1	1	–	–	–	–
1,300–1,499	6	2	1	1	1	1	–	–	–
1,500–1,699	7	2	2	1	1	–	1	–	–
1,700–1,949	8	2	1	1	1	1	1	1	–
1,950–2,199	9	2	1	1	1	1	1	1	1

5 Qualification Allowances

All teachers with a pass degree would be paid a pass degree allowance.

6 Other Allowances

It was recommended that:

- current allowances – widow's allowance, children's allowances, island allowance, and the marriage gratuity – should be retained at an increased level
- the allowance for teaching in schools in Gaeltacht areas should change from a percentage of salary to a flat-rate amount
- the Department of Education should investigate the feasibility of paying an allowance to teachers in schools in which acute difficulties were being experienced in recruiting staff.

Other recommendations:

- a common contributory superannuation scheme for all teachers
- a common C&A Scheme
- the common basic salary, the points system and the new system of allowances should come into effect from 1 September 1968 for all teachers who entered the profession on or after that date, and interim measures should apply to accommodate teachers currently in the profession.

Review of the Common Basic Scale

The recommended common basic scale affected the various groups of teachers differently and to assess its effect it is necessary to refer to the salaries that were determined by the tenth wage round award in 1966.

National Teachers

National teachers would be assimilated at the point of the new common scale corresponding to the point reached by them on their old scale.

National Teachers	Married Men	Women/Single Men
Tenth round, 1966:	£822–£1,542	£659–£1,229
Common Basic Scale, 1968:	£950–£1,700	£750–£1,350

A married man would get a gross increase of £128 (15.57%) at the minimum of the scale and £158 (10.25%) at the maximum. However, as national teachers would have to pay a 5 per cent contribution to the pension scheme, the net increases would be £80 10s. (9.79%) and £73 (4.73%), respectively. The net increase for women and single men would range from 8.1 per cent at the minimum to 3.8 per cent at the maximum.

There was, however, an advantage to joining a contributory pension scheme. Henceforth, pension and lump sum would be calculated on a salary figure that had been increased by an additional 5 per cent.

Secondary Teachers

Secondary teachers would be assimilated at the point on the new common scale two increments above the point corresponding to the point reached by them on their old scale.

Secondary Teachers	Married Men	Women/Single Men
Tenth round, 1966:	£892–£1,652	£709–£1,309
Common Basic Scale, 1968:	£950–£1,700	£750–£1,350

The ASTI viewed the report with dismay as the salary proposed would result in a reduction in income for nearly all of its members who were in receipt of the 12.5 per cent negotiated with Catholic Headmasters Association in 1964.

Vocational Teachers

Vocational teachers' salary placing would be similar to that of secondary teachers.

Vocational Teachers	Married Men	Women/Single Men
Tenth round, 1966:	£942–1,662	£754–£1,324
Common Basic Scale, 1968:	£950–£1,700	£750–£1,350

The scale for married men increased by £8 at the minimum and £38 at the maximum; the scale for women/single men decreased by £4 at the minimum and increased by £26 at the maximum; graduate teachers would get a £50 pass degree allowance.

The Points System

National teachers were totally opposed to the age-related points scheme as they held that the points weighting given to younger children was totally out of proportion. This situation was further aggravated by the tribunal's recommendation that pupils aged thirteen years and over should be given a rating of one point after 1 December 1972, because by that date the Department envisaged that all pupils over twelve years of age would be in attendance in post-primary schools.

The Principal and Vice-Principal

Under the proposed scheme a principal of a national school with 300 pupils and a principal of a post-primary school with an attendance of 100 pupils would each receive an allowance of £325; a principal of a national school with 730 pupils and a principal of a post-primary school with an attendance of 245 pupils would each receive an allowance of £625.

As most secondary schools were run by religious communities, allowances for principals and vice-principals were not of concern to lay secondary teachers; they were, however, of concern to vocational teachers.

Posts of Responsibility

The proposed scheme of graded posts had little relevance for most primary schools as almost two-thirds of primary schools had three teachers or less. A national school would require 300 pupils on the roll to achieve a points rating of 450 to qualify for one Grade I post among six assistants. A post-primary school with 300 pupils would qualify for six posts, two Grade I and one each of Grades II, III, IV and V, for ten staff teachers; a similar situation would apply in vocational schools.

A Review of the Report

The establishment of the tribunal had raised expectations among all teachers. It was generally expected that a common basic salary, with a generous increase, would be introduced for all teachers and that other aspects of conditions of employment would be reviewed. This did not happen.

The principles on which the findings of the tribunal were based were generally acceptable to the teacher unions, but the recommendations did not fulfil these principles in a satisfactory manner for any of the teacher unions. The various recommendations created problems for national teachers and secondary teachers in different ways.[4]

The members of the tribunal did not seem to appreciate the nuances that applied to the employment of teachers in the different systems nor did they appear to understand the school systems in which they worked. The report exhibited the over-influence of officials from the Departments of Education and Finance. The representatives from the Department of Education did not see any valid reasons why the maximum of a common basic scale should be higher than £1,300 for unmarried teachers and £1,625 for married teachers.[5] The Department of Finance representative strongly opposed a significant pay increase for teachers and warned the tribunal not to award a high common basic scale because of the probability of consequential demands by other groups in the public sector.[6]

The Department officials appear to have been successful in having the common basic scale set at the very minimum, and the recommended scales did not show any appreciation of the salary position reached by the different groups of teachers up to that time.

While national teachers were happy with the establishment of the principle of a common basic scale, they regarded the allowances for principals and vice-principals as totally unsatisfactory. The tribunal failed to recognise that the proposal to give a senior pupil in a secondary school a points rating six times that of a pupil in a primary school would be unacceptable to national teachers. In addition, the scheme of graded posts of special responsibility had practically no relevance to national schools.

The salary offered was most unacceptable to secondary teachers, particularly when the withdrawal of payment from schools managers was taken into consideration. The post of principal or vice-principal in religiously controlled secondary schools was of no relevance to lay teachers and they did not have any posts of promotion. Charles McCarthy has commented on 'the essentially inferior and supplementary role which lay secondary teachers had in religious schools, where they were infrequently consulted, given no substantial responsibility and never involved in policy matters'.[7]

It would appear that the proposed scheme of graded posts was structured in a way that would compensate secondary teachers for being denied an opportunity for promotion. The vocational system was staffed by lay teachers who had their own system of promotion and posts.

4   Ryan Tribunal Report, p. 14
5   Ryan Tribunal Report, pp. 36–7 and p. 55
6   John Coolahan, *The ASTI and Post-Primary Education in Ireland, 1909–1984*, p. 275
7   Charles McCarthy, *A Decade of Upheaval: Irish Trade Unions in the 1960s*, p. 205

The report did not recommend qualification allowances for 'Confined Register' teachers in secondary and vocational schools. These teachers had non-graduate (non-university) qualifications to teach Home Economics, Music, Art, Physical Education and felt very aggrieved that they were not awarded an allowance equivalent to that for a pass degree and pass Higher Diploma in Education.

Any understanding of the structure and management of the three different school systems would have shown that the same scheme of promotion did not have to be proposed for the primary and post-primary systems. The organisation of the two systems was different, one was class-based, the other subject-based, and each of them catered for a different age-range. If sufficient money had been apportioned to the two systems in an equitable manner, an organisational structure for each system could have been devised.

The report, which was meant to be a move towards a unified teaching profession, resulted in four years of conflict and dispute. It was not until 1973 that the ASTI finally agreed to accept the implementation of a common salary scale and a common system of Conciliation and Arbitration.

The Reaction of the Teacher Unions

On 4 July 1968 Seán Brosnahan wrote to the Minister for Education requesting the implementation of the report. The INTO had achieved its main objective – a common basic salary scale. It took the pragmatic view of getting the salary operational first and then following up on the other recommendations.

At a Special Convention on 15 June 1968, VTA delegates rejected the recommendations by sixty-four votes to eighteen due to concerns about equivalence, qualifications and allowances. On receiving assurances on these points VTA members accepted the report in a ballot.[8]

At a meeting on 1 June 1968 the CEC of the ASTI rejected the report and threatened immediate action if the Minister adopted it. Meetings took place between the Joint Managerial Body (JMB) for secondary schools and representatives of the Department of Education on 19 June and on 1 and 8 July 1968, but the negotiations were unsuccessful. An ASTI Special Convention on 30 July 1968 decided to hold a ballot on strike action and to establish a strike fund.[9]

Further attempts to resolve the tribunal problems continued, and at a meeting on 18 October the Minister for Education presented to the representatives of the INTO, VTA, and ASTI what he declared was his final offer. The revised salary scales incorporated the tribunal common basic salary award and the first phase

---

8 John Logan (ed.), *Teachers' Union: the TUI and its Fore-Runners in Irish Education, 1899–1994*, p. 177
9 John Coolahan, *The ASTI and Post-Primary Education in Ireland, 1909–1984*, p. 278

of the eleventh wage round. In addition, a common scheme of allowances for qualifications was offered and the allowances for Honours Primary, Masters' and Doctors' degrees were each raised by £50.

The Minister also made it a condition that future salary negotiations would have to be conducted through common Conciliation and Arbitration machinery and that common superannuation arrangements should apply. The revised scales were to operate from 1 July 1968.[10] The results of a ballot by members of the three unions were as follows:

	INTO	VTA	ASTI
acceptance	7,607	1,754	424
rejection	766	488	2,392
spoiled	16	0	–
votes recorded	8,389	2,242	2,816 [11]

At an ASTI Special Convention on 19 October it was resolved that if its case was not satisfactorily heard by Arbitration by 17 January 1969 members would come out on strike on 1 February 1969.[12]

The JMB issued statements indicating that it would support the teachers' strike and close schools. The INTO and the VTA opposed the strike and insisted that they would have to be represented at any meetings to resolve the strike, and any offers made to secondary teachers would also have to be made to them.

Following a general election in December 1968, Brian Lenihan was re-appointed Minister for Education.

All efforts to resolve the difficulties failed and secondary teachers came out on strike on 1 February 1969. The JMB closed schools, declaring that they had no alternative but to suspend classes. Consultations took place between representatives of the Department of Education and the JMB to try to resolve the strike. In March a formula was devised whereby the Religious Orders offered that the money created by the points rating for principals, vice-principals and posts of responsibility in secondary schools could be pooled and divided among lay teachers as a 'Special Functions Allowance' (SFA).[13]

10 This was the proposed date for the implementation of the recommendations of the Ryan Tribunal award.
11 At this time the approximate membership of the organisations was: INTO 10,200; ASTI 3,000; VTA 2,200.
12 John Coolahan, *The ASTI and Post-Primary Education in Ireland, 1909–1984*, pp. 282, 283
13 In 1967–68 lay teachers accounted for 55 per cent of the total number of teachers employed in secondary schools.

All secondary teachers who opted to accept definable functions would be paid an allowance, ranging from £100 to £300 from the tenth point of the common basic scale upwards.

This agreement was strongly opposed by the other teacher unions. They viewed the SFAs as part of the personal salary of the teacher and a departure from the principle of the common basic salary. The INTO wrote to the religious communities advising them that as the SFA proposal was deemed partisan and prejudicial to the interests of national teachers 'the Central Executive Committee has decided, as a protest, to review the whole question of lay–religious relations and to effect a phased withdrawal of the services of lay personnel from certain schools conducted by Religious Communities in certain areas'.[14]

At a meeting with the Minister for Education on 14 February representatives of the INTO and the VTA were offered revised salary scales. The 18 October 1968 salary scales were reduced by one increment and, while each point was increased, the maximum remained unchanged. It was also proposed that pass and honours degree allowances would be increased by £25, all increases to operate from 1 July 1968. Further, the Minister agreed that in future when salary scales were increased, all allowances would be proportionately increased.

That same day (14 February 1969), at a Secondary Teachers' Conciliation Council meeting, the secondary teachers were offered the same increases and a scheme that incorporated the SFAs. ASTI members accepted the deal in a ballot by a majority of 1,717 to 538, and the strike was called off. A working party comprising two representatives each from the ASTI, the JMB, and the Department of Education worked out a schedule of duties that holders of definable functions would have to perform to qualify for the payment of the SFAs.

Relations between the ASTI, the Department of Education and the two other teacher unions became very bitter. The INTO and the VTA immediately lodged claims for increased allowances for posts similar to those conceded to secondary teachers, and for increases to the allowances for principals and vice-principals.

At a Special Conference in Liberty Hall, Dublin, on 24 May 1969, INTO delegates rejected the offer made on 14 February and resolved to come out on strike. The services of 2,700 members of the Dublin branches were withdrawn for one day on 28 May and a limited strike continued in twelve schools in Dublin city and in two schools outside the city. Ten of the schools were either convent or monastery schools. A further five schools outside the city were selected to come out on strike on 3 June. The VTA held a two-day strike on 27 and 28 May 1969.

Strikes by the three teacher unions had now taken place within a four-month period as a consequence of the recommendations of the Ryan Tribunal. The

---

14 CEC Report to Congress 1969, p. 61

situation had become so fractious that, when a resolution was finally arrived at, a residue of bitterness and betrayal remained.

Second Report by Professor Louden Ryan

On 3 June 1969 the Department invited the INTO, VTA and the ASTI to participate in discussions under the chairmanship of Professor Louden Ryan in an attempt to resolve the salary dispute. The INTO suspended its strike action and, even though the ASTI did not participate in the discussions, Professor Ryan issued his report on 13 June 1969. He stated that:

> ... the Tribunal's recommendations have been breached by the settlement made with the ASTI, and the stage is now set for a process of 'leap-frogging' ... If the process of 'leap-frogging' within the teaching profession is allowed to continue, the cost of teachers' emoluments may rise faster than taxpayers' capacity to pay, and the profession is bound to suffer loss of status by its example and loss of public sympathy. The only prospect of preventing continuous 'leap-frogging' in emoluments as between the three main groups of teachers is a common salary scale and common system of allowances for qualifications, principals and vice-principals' allowances and posts of special responsibility.[15]

Professor Ryan recommended that an *ad hoc* committee be established consisting of representatives of the Departments of Education and Finance and an equal number from the INTO, the VTA and the ASTI to sort out the issues and that the balance of the eleventh wage round and future wage rounds should be used to erode the SFAs. The ASTI rejected this second Ryan Report and refused to participate in the *ad hoc* committee.

Jack Lynch led Fianna Fáil back to government with an overall majority following the general election in June 1969. Pádraig Faulkner was appointed Minister for Education.

The *ad hoc* committee issued a number of revised recommendations and proposed the establishment of a 'Comparability Committee' that would recommend to the Minister allowances for non-graduate teachers employed in secondary and vocational schools. This committee was to comprise three representatives from the INTO, two from VTA, two from ASTI, and two from the Department of Education. The ASTI agreed to take part in the committee.

Minister for Education Salary Proposals, 16 September 1969

On 16 September 1969 Pádraig Faulkner presented new salary scales that incorporated the balance of the eleventh wage round and, in addition, the

---

15 CEC Report to Congress 1970, p. 33

maxima of the common basic scales increased by £60 from 1 April 1970, and all allowances increased by 3 per cent from 1 June 1969.[16]

He set down a procedure that would, in time, restore the principle of the common scale, but with due regard to the rights of existing secondary teachers under the agreement of March 1969. He also insisted that the proposed salary and allowances would have to be processed through a common scheme of Conciliation and Arbitration, as would all future salary revisions.

The proposals were accepted by the INTO and the VTA but rejected by the ASTI as it considered the Minister's offer a revocation of the March 1969 (SFA) agreement. In spite of various representations and meetings the situation remained unresolved.

Review of Posts of Responsibility

At a joint meeting of the INTO and VTA Conciliation Councils, on 2 and 10 October 1969, it was agreed that:

- the points rating of pupils according to age should remain unchanged
- schools with a points rating under 150 should be the first category for principals' and vice-principals' allowances
- the eight grade posts should be replaced by just two posts, Grade A and Grade B, with an allowance of £270 and £120, respectively
- the long-service increment should be at the rate of £75 from 1 July 1968 and £77 from 1 June 1969
- an allowance of £125 per annum should be paid to teachers who were widows, with effect from 1 July 1968.

The number of Grade A and Grade B posts was to be in accordance with the following pattern (the Ryan recommendations are shown for comparative purposes):

---

16 John Logan (ed.), *Teachers' Union: the TUI and its Fore-Runners in Irish Education, 1899–1994*, p. 178

	New Scheme Number of Posts			Ryan Recommendations Number of Posts in each Grade						
Points Rating	A	B	I	II	III	IV	V	VI	VII	VIII
less than 450	–	–	–	–	–	–	–	–	–	–
450–599	–	1	1	–	–	–	–	–	–	–
600–749	–	2	1	1	–	–	–	–	–	–
750–899	–	3	2	–	1	–	–	–	–	–
900–1,099	–	4	2	1	1	–	–	–	–	–
1,100–1,299	1	4	2	1	1	1	–	–	–	–
1,300–1,499	2	4	2	1	1	1	1	–	–	–
1,500–1,699	3	4	2	2	1	1	–	1	–	–
1,700–1,949	4	6	2	1	1	1	1	1	1	–
1,950–2,199	5	9	2	1	1	1	1	1	1	1
2,200–2,449	5	10	ditto							
2,450–2,699	5	11	ditto							
2,700–2,949	6	11	ditto							

In December 1969 agreed terms of a common C&A Scheme were signed by the INTO and the VTA, and Dermot McDermott, Chief Conciliation Officer of the Labour Court, was appointed as an independent chairman.

On 19 February 1970 the INTO lodged a number of claims at Conciliation Council on behalf of national teachers, but the principle one was a twelfth round salary claim. The VTA lodged a claimed that (1) vocational teachers should receive special functions allowances, similar to those paid to secondary teachers, as well as post of responsibility allowances, and that (2) all non-graduate vocational teachers should receive the £75 pass degree allowance. Because of lack of progress with these claims VTA members went on national strike from 11 to 17 February 1970.[17]

Posts of Responsibility in Capitation Schools

Prior to a Conciliation Council meeting on 12 June a CEC deputation met the provincials of the Irish Christian Brothers and agreement in principle was reached on the introduction of a promotion structure in capitation schools, similar to that which existed in classification schools. The Conciliation Council meeting on 12 June adopted the common basic salary agreement and proposed the provision of the money required.

At subsequent meetings the Provincials agreed that lay personnel in schools controlled by the Order would be eligible for all posts, exclusive of the

17 John Coolahan, *The ASTI and Post-Primary Education in Ireland, 1909–1984*, pp. 282, 291

principalship, and that, all things being equal, seniority would apply in the awarding of posts.

Because the Ryan Tribunal had not considered the special circumstances of the age of pupils in infant schools or the teacher/pupil ratio in special schools, the CEC negotiated that the points rating of a primary school could be determined by multiplying the number on rolls by 1.5 or by the Ryan scale, whichever was more beneficial, with effect from 1 July 1968.[18]

Revised Points Rating, 1975

An agreement in 1973 between the teacher unions and Department of Education officials that the points rating applicable to pupils under nine years of age and pupils aged sixteen and seventeen should be revised was not implemented until 1975, when a new schedule of points came into effect from 1 July:

	Age of Pupils 1970	Points Weighting 1975
Under 9 years	1.5	1.75
Aged 9 years and under 13 years	2	2
Aged 13 years and under 15 years	3	3
Aged 15 years and under 16 years	4	4
Aged 16 years and under 17 years	5	6
Aged 17 years and over	6	8

A school could choose to determine its points rating by either using the Ryan Scale or by multiplying the enrolment by 1.5. It was also agreed that, henceforth, the points rating of a school would be calculated on the enrolment of 30 September and come into effect the following 1 July.

Twelfth Round Salary Increases

The Conciliation Council agreed to the implementation of the terms of the twelfth round wage agreement as follows:

- with effect from 1 April 1970 the salary scales of teachers would be increased by 7 per cent, subject to a minimum increase of £78 per annum
- with effect from 1 January 1971 there would be a further increase of 10 per cent on the pre-twelfth round scales, subject to a minimum increase of £91 per annum
- allowances would attract the same percentage increases, calculated to the nearest pound

18 Conciliation Council Agreed Report, 12 June 1970

- the long-service increment would be increased to £82 and £90
- the increment to pre-1946 single teachers would increase to £59 and £65 per annum.

In May the Department issued circular M56/70 to secondary school managers advising them that from 1 June 1970 appointment to posts would be at the discretion of the manager and not on the basis of seniority.[19] Because seniority of service was a matter of principle for the ASTI, it threatened that unless the Minister withdrew the circular, it would instruct its members not to act as examiners at certificate examinations. The Minister refused and ASTI members refused to mark the examination scripts. The Minister issued new salary proposals on 3 July 1970.

During the teachers' salary dispute a number of interventions were made by representatives of the JMB and the Parent School Movement, which further increased tensions between the teacher unions. Eventually, on 22 February 1971, Maurice Cosgrove, President of the Irish Congress of Trade Unions (ICTU), successfully brokered an agreement between representatives of the three teacher unions.[20] In a ballot on 26 February the ASTI members accepted the proposals, 56.6 per cent for and 43.4 per cent against. The INTO CEC accepted them on 27 February, and some days later the VTA signified its acceptance.

The principle of the common basic salary was now established and all future claims would be processed through a common C&A Scheme. The new scheme did not become operative until 9 October 1973 and, in the interim period, ASTI representatives attended the joint INTO/VTA Conciliation Council meetings as observers.

Teacher Unions Together

Over the next number of years the difficulties that followed the Ryan Tribunal began to abate and the officers of the three teacher unions began to co-operate. The unions were now free to progress claims of particular interest to their own members and, in many instances, joint claims that affected all teachers.

This period also saw many major developments in the fields of education: enrolment in primary schools increased; secondary schools no longer charged fees; a free school-transport system operated throughout the country; and vocational schools were preparing pupils for all State examinations.

Other important developments included:

---

19 John Coolahan, *The ASTI and Post-Primary Education in Ireland, 1909–1984*, pp. 282, 292
20 Maurice P. Cosgrove, General Secretary of the Postal Workers Union of Ireland, had been a member of the Ryan Tribunal.

- In 1968 a Widows' and Orphans' Contributory Pension Scheme was introduced for public servants, including teachers.
- The concept of negotiated national wage rounds became the norm.
- In 1972 the Minister for Finance, George Colley, accepted the principle of parity of pensions with salaries earned by officers of the same rank.
- Thomond College opened in 1972 to educate graduate specialist teachers for the post-primary sector.
- In a national ballot on 10 May 1972, 83 per cent of voters agreed to Ireland's membership of the European Economic Community as from 1 January 1973.
- Students entering teacher training colleges from 1974 would complete a three-year course leading to a BEd degree.[21]
- The PAYE system of tax deduction was extended to all public servants for the tax-year 1979–80.

Salary Developments, 1972–78

Thirteenth Round and Grade Increase

The thirteenth round wage agreement had two phases:

- First phase: an increase of £104 per annum from 1 January 1972
- Second phase: an increase of 4 per cent on basic salaries and a cost-of-living supplement of up to £33 from 1 January 1973 in annual terms.

During 1971 an arbitrator had awarded Executive Officers a 5 per cent grade award and the Official Side conceded that because this had disturbed an established relationship, an increase of 5 per cent could be amalgamated with the first phase payment.[22] This created a new salary scale of fourteen points, down two.

The Official Side endeavoured to restrict the percentage increase to basic pay only and on appeal, the Employer-Labour Conference ruled that allowances were part of basic pay and should be increased. This was a very important judgement as it determined the principle that would apply to all succeeding awards.

In March 1973 a 'National Coalition' between Fine Gael and Labour came to power by a narrow margin, with a fourteen-point programme of action. Liam

---

21 Dáil Report, 23 October 1973. Carysfort College, Blackrock; St Patrick's College, Drumcondra; and Mary Immaculate College, Limerick, became constituent colleges of the National University of Ireland (NUI); the Church of Ireland Training College, Rathmines; Sion Hill College, Blackrock; and St Mary's College, Marino, became associated colleges of the University of Dublin (Trinity College). The first BEd degrees were conferred in 1977.

22 An Arbitration award of 5 per cent to Executive Officers had disturbed an established relationship between the salaries of teachers and those of civil servants.

Cosgrave became Taoiseach and Richard Burke was appointed Minister for Education.[23]

Fourteenth and Fifteenth Rounds and Equal Pay

The Commission on the Status of Women had recommended in 1971 that negotiations should commence to phase in the payment of equal pay to men and women doing the same work or work of equal value and that the first payment should be 17.5 per cent of the difference between the existing scales.

It was agreed that, in conjunction with the payment of the first phase of the fourteenth round, 17.5 per cent of the differential between each of the scale points on the respective scales should be eliminated from 1 June 1973.[24]

The second phase of the fourteenth round was due to come into effect from 1 June 1974 but it was substituted by the first phase of the fifteenth round. The second phase of the fifteenth round came into effect from 1 December 1974 and it was agreed that 50 per cent of the remaining equal pay differential should be eliminated with effect from the same date.[25] The final phase of the fifteenth round, a cost-of-living escalator round, came into effect from 1 March 1975.

The Notional Agreement

It was agreed that the second phase of the fourteenth round, which had been substituted, would be paid in four equal instalments, at six-monthly intervals, from 1 December 1974, 1 June 1975, 1 December 1975 and 1 June 1976.

Grade Award

In addition, the arbitrator, Rory O'Hanlon, awarded teachers a 5 per cent increase with effect from 1 January 1975, prompted by a grade award made to Executive Officers.

The Sixteenth Round National Wage Agreement, 1 June 1975

The sixteenth round agreement allowed for salary reviews with effect from 1 June 1975, 1 September 1975, 1 December 1975 and 1 March 1976.

---

23 A Fine Gael/Labour coalition government came to power in March 1973. It was replaced by a Fianna Fáil government in July 1977, which was replaced by a Fine Gael/Labour coalition government in July 1981. This coalition government lasted for less than a year and was replaced by a Fianna Fáil government in March 1982. This government lasted only nine months, when it was again replaced by a Fine Gael/Labour coalition government. From that date a combination of political parties have provided different Coalition governments.

24 Conciliation Council for Teachers, Agreed Report No. 4/74

25 Conciliation Council for Teachers, Agreed Report No. 7/74

The National Wage Agreement of 1977

Following an Interim Agreement for six months, a new national wage agreement commenced on 1 January 1977 with a pay pause of three months; the second phase was for a period of seven months from 1 April; the third phase was for a period of four months from 1 November. The agreement expired for teachers on 28 February 1978 and a new one commenced with effect from 1 March 1978.

Equal Pay

The Anti-Discrimination (Pay) Act of July 1974 set 31 December 1975 as the date by which equal pay would have to be fully implemented. A salary scale, common to men and women without any marital differentiation, would be payable from 1 January 1976.

In October 1975 the three teacher unions lodged individual claims for the application of the final phase of equal pay, to be paid with effect from 31 December 1975. Disagreement was recorded at Conciliation Council and a joint claim was referred to Arbitration.

Before the Arbitration Board could convene the Minister for Finance announced that he was going to apply equal pay to all public servants, i.e. married female teachers and widows would be placed on the scale for married men with effect from 1 January 1976. This was not full implementation of the principle of equal pay, even though the Minister claimed he was fulfilling his obligations under the Anti-Discrimination (Pay) Act, 1974. Single women and single men would continue to be paid at a different scale.

The Arbitration Board, meeting on 25 November and 13 December 1975, conceded the claim for full application of equal pay but failed to establish dates for its implementation. Events intervened that delayed the reconvening of the Board to complete its deliberations.

At a meeting with the Public Services Committee of the ICTU on 23 December 1975, the Minister for the Public Service requested public service unions to postpone the claim for implementation of the final phase of the equal pay provisions. The unions insisted that the provisions of the 1974 Act should be fulfilled and that any attempt by the government to introduce amending legislation would be opposed.

As the principle of equal pay had been agreed by the government in the Treaty of Rome and was enshrined in a directive from the EEC Commission, the ICTU, at the behest of the public service unions, lodged a complaint with the commission in Brussels on the government's failure to implement the equal pay provisions in full. The commission ruled that the government had to implement the equal pay provisions in full. This process of representation and the fact that the Civil Service Executive Union had supported a test case on the application of the equal pay provisions to the High Court, resulted in a delay in the consideration of the teachers' claim.

The claim was eventually considered by the Arbitration Board on 10 and 25 November, on 13 December 1976, and on 2 March and 2 May 1977.[26]

The teachers' side claimed that the government was obliged to comply with:

- the recommendations of the Commission on the Status of Women in 1971
- the terms of the Anti-Discrimination (Pay) Act, 1974
- Article 119 of the Treaty of Rome
- the EEC Commission Directive 75/117/EEC.

The Official Side submitted a statement from the Minister for the Public Services stating the government was committed to the elimination of the marriage differential as soon as circumstances permitted but that, due to economic circumstances, the government was claiming inability to pay.

The Arbitration Board issued its findings on 22 June 1977 and recommended that one-half of the remaining differentials between the scales payable to married and unmarried teachers should be eliminated with effect from 1 January 1977 and the balance from 1 June 1977. The Coalition Government decided to implement this finding.

However, following a general election in July 1977, Fianna Fáil came back to power and one of its first decisions was to grant full equal pay with effect from 1 July 1977.[27]

For the first time in history female teachers were to be paid at the same rate as men, and the situation of single male national teachers was restored to that which applied prior to 1946.

However, as the full implementation of equal pay should have been paid from 1 January 1976 and not from 1 July 1977, the unions sought the payment of arrears.

On 19 October 1978 a comprehensive agreement was reached between the Public Services Committee and George Colley, Tánaiste and Minister for the Public Service, and, as a quid pro quo, the ICTU withdrew the charges made against the government to the European Commission in Brussels. The agreement covered all of the matters arising from equalisation of pay. The main terms, as they applied to teachers, were as follows:

---

26 Richard Burke was succeeded by Peter Barry as Minister for Education in December 1976.

27 John Wilson was appointed Minister for Education from 15 July 1977. Fianna Fáil served until June 1981.

Arrears

It was agreed that the arrears due to single men and female teachers who served during any of the period from 31 December 1975 to 30 June 1977 would be paid in three annual instalments commencing on 1 July 1979.

Children's Allowances

All those holding teaching posts before 31 December 1978 would retain their entitlement to children's allowances subject to the usual conditions. In addition, married female teachers, including widows, would be entitled to allowances on the same basis as married men, with effect from 31 December 1975. Double payment of public sector children's allowances would not be permitted. Persons entering or re-entering former marriage-differentiated positions after 31 December 1978 would not have an entitlement to allowances; that date was subsequently changed to 31 December 1979.

It was also agreed that, with effect from 31 December 1975, the allowance payable to married teachers would be paid in respect of children of unmarried teachers under the conditions laid down in the Equal Pay Agreement.

Marriage Lump Sums

It was agreed that all teachers who married between 1 January 1976 and 30 June 1980, and who remained in the teaching service, would be entitled to a lump sum payment on marriage. It was possible for a couple to be entitled to two marriage lump sums.[28]

Superannuation

The superannuation benefits of those who retired in the period 31 December 1975 and 30 June 1977 were revised and upgraded; pension arrears due were paid in three annual instalments, commencing on 1 July 1979.

The Equal Pay Agreement had to be processed through the different Conciliation Councils. At a meeting on 30 October 1979 the ASTI refused to sign the agreement as it had been rejected by its members in a ballot. Furthermore, it was not prepared to agree a settlement that would apply the package to INTO and TUI members only.[29] The Minister had to implement the package by Ministerial Order and the first phase of the arrears was paid to single men and female teachers, primary, secondary and vocational, in December 1979. The payment of all the arrears due signalled the full implementation of equal pay for all teachers.

---

28 The lump sum on marriage varied from £322 to £345, less tax.

29 All parties had to be in agreement before a report, either 'agreed' or 'disagreed', could be issued by the Conciliation Council.

Salary Review, 1968–78

Over a ten-year period from 1 July 1968 to 1 March 1978, the minimum of the old scale for married men had increased by 252 per cent, from £1,000 to £3,572, and the maximum by 219 per cent, from £1,825 to £5,815; the respective increases for women and single men were 347 per cent, from £800 to £3,572, and 301 per cent, from £1,450 to £5,815. The salary scale had also been shortened by two points, from sixteen to fourteen increments

Pension Amendments[30]

Contributory Pension Scheme for National Teachers, 1968

At the time of the Ryan Tribunal there were three separate superannuation schemes; the scheme for national teachers was non-contributory and compulsory; the scheme for secondary teachers was contributory and optional; the scheme for vocational teachers was contributory and compulsory.

In most instances, the benefits provided under the separate schemes were similar to the provisions and benefits that civil servants enjoyed. National teachers had one benefit that did not apply to other teachers: a national teacher who was fifty-five years of age and had thirty-five completed years of pensionable service could retire and receive a pension and lump sum, calculated as for normal retirement.

The pension scheme for national teachers was converted to a contributory scheme with effect from 1 July 1968. The enabling Statutory Instrument to put this into effect contained a number of other amendments as follows:

- that the pension and lump sum of a teacher who retired on 30 June 1968 on grounds of age or disability would be revised as if the salary scale and allowances introduced on 1 July 1968 were operative on 30 June 1968
- that, on payment of the appropriate contribution, any absence during the strike by national teachers between 28 May 1969 and 8 June 1969 would be reckoned as pensionable service
- that certain service in the Irish Folklore Commission would reckon in full as pensionable service
- that certain service as a secondary or preparatory college teacher would reckon in full as pensionable service.[31]

---

30 Most of the amendments to the National Teachers' Pension Scheme have qualifying conditions attached. The relevant regulations should be referred to for a full understanding of the benefits.

31 National School Teachers' Superannuation (Amendment) Scheme, 1972, Statutory Instrument No. 173 of 1972

Pension Concessions, 1973

From the late 1930s the INTO had been endeavouring to process a number of claims regarding pension and added years for pension credit for certain categories of national teachers, but without success.

In 1973, during the inter-teacher disputes arising from the Ryan Tribunal, an occasion arose when a trade-off was required from the INTO to allow the Department of Education the flexibility to grant a particular concession to the ASTI. An agreement was reached whereby the INTO got concessions on three long-standing pension claims, as follows:

1 Pre-1934 Service

It was conceded that full credit for lump sum purposes would be allowed to JAMs and lay assistant teachers who retired on or after 1 July 1971, in respect of recognised pre-1934 service in convent or monastery capitation schools, (that service was already taken into account for pension). A nominal contribution of £1 was deducted in respect of each year of such service.

2 Redundancies in the 30s and 40s

Teachers who were unable to secure pensionable posts in national schools during the existence of overall redundancy in the teaching service between 1 July 1926 and 30 June 1947, or who had been employed as supernumeraries during that period, were granted credit of added years for superannuation purposes of up to a maximum of five years; the effective date of the concession was 1 July 1971. Teachers who retired after the effective date had their rates of pension and lump sum revised; teachers who had retired before the effective date had their rates of pension revised.[32]

As an extra benefit, it was subsequently confirmed that the pensions of widows and children of teachers who had died but who would have qualified for pensionable credit under the terms of this concession would be revised as appropriate.[33]

3 Marriage Ban Service

It was conceded that service given by married female teachers while the ban was in force, which in normal circumstances would have been recognised as pensionable service, would be regarded as pensionable service with effect from 1 July 1971. Teachers who retired after the effective date had their rates of

---

32 Letter from the Department of Education, 13 June 1973, CEC Report to Congress 1974, p. 41
33 Department of Education Circular, December 1973, CEC Report to Congress 1973, p. 45

pension and lump sum revised; teachers who had retired before the effective date had their rates of pension revised.[34]

A number of claims were still outstanding concerning groups of women affected by the marriage ban and the CEC continued to submit claims on their behalf, but without success.

Amendments to the National Teachers' Pension Scheme, 1974

Following the lodgement of a number of claims at Conciliation Council, the INTO was successful in achieving the following:

- Lump sum or gratuities would henceforth be calculated on the basis of three-eightieths of pensionable salary for each year, or part of a year, of pensionable service, subject to a maximum of forty years.
- Those days in excess of completed years of pensionable service would be taken into account in calculating pension and gratuity.

Amendment No. 1 would give a maximum lump sum of 120 eightieths after forty years of recognised service; it had been after forty-five years. Amendment No. 2 meant that every day of service, if required, could be counted in computing pension and lump sum. As a year's service for teachers is counted as 365 days, service on a Friday to Monday inclusive is counted as four days' service.

The expression 'retiring salary' was changed to mean the aggregate of:

- the annual rate of salary on the last day of pensionable service
- the annual rate of a principal's or vice-principal's allowance as long as it had been held for the three years preceding retirement without change of category
- the annual rate of a qualification allowance as long as it had been held for the three years preceding retirement
- the average over three years of all other allowances.

Amendments to Teacher Pension Schemes from 1 July 1976

Following discussions at meetings on 27 December 1975, 18 February 1976, 5 April and 7 July 1977, and 16 March 1978, the Teachers' Conciliation Council agreed to recommend amendments that would apply to national, secondary, comprehensive and community teachers in pensionable service on or after 30 June 1976.[35] The arrangements were as follows:

---

34 Letter from the Department of Education, 3 March 1975, CEC Report to Congress 1975, p. 20

35 Conciliation Council for Teachers, Agreed Report 10/77

Pension Service

- The minimum qualifying period of pensionable service required for the grant of a pension and lump sum was reduced from ten to five years.
- The existing prohibition on the award of a death gratuity in respect of a teacher with less than five years of pensionable service was replaced by a prohibition on the award of a death gratuity in respect of a teacher whose pensionable service, together with the additional service which he/she could have had if he/she had served to normal retirement age, was less than five years.
- The pensionable service of a teacher who retired with entitlements to a disability pension or who died in pensionable service would be augmented as follows: (a) a teacher with not less than five and not more than ten years of pensionable service would be credited with an equivalent amount of added service, (b) a teacher with more than ten but less than thirteen and one-third years of pensionable service would be credited as having twenty years of reckonable service, (c) a teacher with thirteen and one-third years of pensionable service would have six and one-sixth years of pensionable service credited as added service. The added years' provisions were subject to the condition that they did not take the teacher above the voluntary retirement conditions, i.e. a national teacher who could retire at fifty-five years of age and had thirty-five years of service. Should a person granted added years return to the service, such credit would cease to be part of his/her pensionable service; should he/she retire again any credit due could be added then.

Transferability of Superannuation Rights

It was agreed that members of the National and Secondary Teachers' Superannuation Schemes could participate in the Civil Service and the Local Government Transfer Schemes. Pension credit was now portable into any of the participating employments recognised in the transfer network scheme.[36]

Preservation of Superannuation Benefits

Under the preservation of benefits a teacher who retired voluntarily, and who did not take up employment in any of the transfer network employments, and had at least five years of recognised service, could preserve his/her superannuation benefits. At age sixty, he/she could apply for a preserved

---

36 The Superannuation and Pensions Bill, 1962 was introduced mainly 'to facilitate transfers between branches of the public service, where such transfers are desirable to promote better performance of public business, by enabling a transferee to carry into his new appointment pension credit earned in his first post'. The Minister for Finance during the second reading of the bill in the Dáil, DEPD, Vol. 202, col. 1594. A similar provision applied to public sector employees in the United Kingdom under the Superannuation (Miscellaneous Provisions) Act of 1948 (see Rhodes, 1965, p. 83); quoted in Gerard Hughes, *The Irish Civil Service Superannuation Scheme*, p. 123

pension that would be calculated as for normal or voluntary retirement and on the salary scales in operation at the time of application. Where a teacher with preserved benefits died before the age of sixty, a preserved death gratuity would be payable to his/her legal personal representative.

Refund of Marriage Gratuity

Where a woman married after 30 June 1958 and received a marriage gratuity, the limit on the period of time during which such teachers might refund the gratuity and receive pensionable credit for their service prior to marriage was abolished.

Added Days

The existing provision which allowed service after the end of the school year in which the teacher reached the age of sixty-five to be reckoned in certain circumstances for an award under the National or Secondary Teachers' Pension Schemes was discontinued.

Other Items

The Civil Service Superannuation Code, 1976

The Civil Service Superannuation Code was derived from twenty separate Superannuation Acts, which made it difficult for civil servants to view their pension terms as a whole. The Superannuation and Pensions Bill, 1976 provided for the consolidation of the statutory pension schemes to facilitate administration and simplification of the civil service superannuation code; the consolidation has not yet been completed due to the scale and complexity of the task.[37] A similar consolidation of teachers' superannuation schemes has been underway for a number of years.

Pensions and Grade A and Grade B Posts

At Conciliation Council on 13 June 1978 it was agreed, with effect from 30 June 1978, to treat the allowances for Grade A and Grade B posts in the same way as principals' and vice-principals' allowances for the purpose of calculating pensions and lump sums; they would not be averaged over three years.

Date of Commencement of School Year

From the establishment of the national school system in 1831, the date of commencement of the school year had been 1 July each year. In 1978 it was agreed between INTO, Management Associations, and the Department of

---

37 Gerard Hughes, *The Irish Civil Service Superannuation Scheme*, p. 124

Education that the date for the commencement of the school year should change to 1 September, starting from 1 September 1979. This had transitional consequences for teachers in the service with regard to the normal date of retirement and for recognised service for pension purposes. The following arrangements were agreed with the Department:

- that the appointment of new teachers would be sanctioned from 1 September and salaries would be paid from that date
- that the summer vacation would consist of the months of July and August
- that the date of retirement for all those due to retire on 30 June would become 31 August and that salary would be paid for the vacation months of July and August
- that teachers whose birthdays fell during the months of July or August could continue in recognised service until 31 August of the following school year.[38]

The INTO interpreted paragraph 4 to mean that as teachers whose birthdays fell during the months of July or August could continue in service until 31 August of the following school year, such service should be recognised for pension purposes.

In June 1982 the Department of Education rejected this interpretation, claiming that, while those teachers would be paid to the end of the school year, the months of July and August should not be recognised for pension purposes.

Eventually the problem went to Conciliation Council and the Official Side was obliged to concede the claim, but not without attaching a number of conditions:

- that no further superannuation claims arising from the change in the school year would be made
- that the concession would not be cited as justifying any proposal to increase the retiring age for any group of teachers
- that the concession would apply only to national teachers whose service commenced before 1 July 1979.[39]

These new arrangements had a number of advantages for teachers appointed before 1 September 1979:

- they would receive two months' salary instead of pension for July and August in their final year of service
- they could benefit from two extra months of service recognised for pension purposes, if it was required

---

38 Previously, if 1 July fell on a Sunday, one day's pay was deducted from salary and allowances.

39 Teachers' Conciliation Council Agreed Report 10/83

- teachers with birthdays in July and August could extend their recognised teaching service for a period of up to fourteen months.

Review of the Period 1968 to 1978

The twenty years from 1948 to 1968 had been a period of teacher unrest and teacher disunity. Separate C&A Schemes operated and each salary settlement was followed by other leapfrogging agreements. Fraternisation between the different teacher groups was non-existent, and claims and assertions about status, equivalence, parity, and qualifications were often made to emphasise differences.

The next ten years, from 1968 to 1978, proved to be a very difficult but vibrant period for every group involved in education.

Enrolments in primary schools increased at a phenomenal rate, not only at the infant level, but at different age stages in the schools. While the number of teachers employed increased from 14,091 to 17,083, the number of schools decreased by 1,390 due to the government's policy of amalgamating small schools.[40] Other changes included:

- A New Curriculum was issued to primary schools in 1971.
- School Boards of Management were established in national schools in 1976.
- The first national teachers graduated from training colleges with a university degree in 1977.

A massive expansion occurred in the post-primary sector following the abolition of school fees and the provision of free school transport by Donogh O'Malley in 1967. The concept of 'Equality of Educational Opportunity' became the byword and the fulfilment of the aspirations of parents for their children. A radical change of attitude was perceived in parents with regard to their children going on to second-level education. It was no longer a consideration for children in rural Ireland that second-level education was available only to those who could afford the fees for a boarding school.

The vocational education system distanced itself from the conditions under which it was established in 1930; the vocational school was no longer the school where students attended to learn shorthand and typing, woodwork and metalwork. The curriculum expanded to provide Department of Education certificate courses and examinations.

Minister O'Malley, in an attempt to establish a single unified teaching profession, established the Tribunal on Teachers' Salaries in 1967. The tribunal

---

40 Membership of the INTO in the Republic increased from 13,700 to 16,600 (21%), but it was noticeable that teacher numbers increased at a greater rate in some counties than others, particularly in the east and south.

started out with great promise but, in retrospect, the aspiration was too ambitious to be achieved in one attempt. This has been shown to be true as, in spite of many attempts since then, it still remains unfulfilled.

On publication of the report, most teachers and their leaders considered that they had been badly served by the tribunal and by the representatives of government departments. There followed a ten-year period, 1968 1978, of strikes and threats of strikes, of dissension among the three teacher unions and between them and officials in the Departments of Education and Finance.

The three sectors in education – primary, secondary and vocational – were distinct, separate and operating as independent units with different conditions of employment applying to teachers in each sector. An awareness of the experiences in the operation of the three different Conciliation and Arbitration Schemes over the previous eighteen years would have made this obvious. The tribunal recommendations did not appear to have any understanding of the situation in the different sectors.

It was accepted by the tribunal that to achieve the objective of the terms of reference radical changes would have to be introduced, but it was not recognised that bringing about change would cost money.

The officials from the Departments of Education and Finance, in their submissions to the tribunal, responded to the terms of reference in a very narrow way, emphasising almost exclusively the financial consequences of any awards that might be contemplated. Furthermore, it did not appear to be appreciated that radical changes were about to take place in the provision of the education service. When imagination and foresight were required, they were missing.

The proposals put forward by ministers and officials to resolve the disputes were badly thought-out; they never seemed to know when to stop digging in the trench. Over an eleven-month period the proposed salary scales were revised four times:

	1 July 1968	**1 June 1969**
Married Men	Minimum £950	Maximum £1,700
	Minimum £1,065	Maximum £1,900
Single Men/Women	Minimum £750	Maximum £1,350
	Minimum £865	Maximum £1,525
		One increment less

If, initially, half of the money that had ultimately to be provided to resolve the problems had been made available, the disputes would not have occurred. Eventually the leaders of the teacher unions managed to achieve some sense of order out of the chaos.

Notwithstanding these difficulties, the ten-year period from 1968 to 1978, following on the economic revival initiated by Seán Lemass, was marked by change and advancement in every field, including the field of education. The country's population and marriage rate increased and many who had been obliged to emigrate returned, bringing their families with them.

The period ended on a hopeful note. While the attempt in 1975 to establish An Chomhairle Mhúinteoireachta (The Teachers' Council) failed and while a single unified teaching force was not to become a reality, differences between the teacher groups began to disappear. Changes took place in the chief officerships of the teacher unions and a new era of friendship, co-operation and camaraderie developed.

In official circles a clearer understanding of the concerns and power of the different teacher groups was evident. Relations between the partners in education – teacher unions, school management, parent groups – and officials in the Departments of Education and Finance became reasonably satisfactory and conducive to working together for the betterment of the education service.

11

The Beginning of Teachers United, 1978–82

The Salary Review Body, 1980

Inter-union Co-operation

Seán Brosnahan, General Secretary INTO, and Matt Griffin, General Treasurer INTO, retired with effect from 30 June 1978, and Gerry Quigley and Michael Moroney were elected as their successors, assuming duty on 1 July 1978.[1]

During the following years changes took place in the senior permanent officerships in the other teacher unions. Kieran Mulvey was appointed General Secretary of the ASTI in April 1980 in succession to Maura MacDonagh, and Jim Dorney was appointed General Secretary of the TUI in succession to Christy Devine in 1982.

The change in officerships in the unions was marked by a period of active inter-union co-operation and a receding of the difficulties that had arisen following the Ryan Tribunal Report of 1968.

Regular meetings were held between senior officials of the respective unions, and from early in 1980, subcommittees and working parties were established to foster close inter-union co-operation between the unions in the pursuit of common objectives in the following matters:

- The Conciliation and Arbitration Scheme (C&A Scheme)
- Claims for Conciliation Council
- A Major Salary Review
- Specialist Teachers' Claim
- Qualification Equivalence
- Points Ratings
- Promotion Opportunities
- Teachers' Superannuation
- Common Facilities and Services for Members
- Policy on Parent–Teacher Meetings
- Education for the Disabled

---

1 The post of General Treasurer encompassed the post of Deputy General Secretary.

- In-service Education
- School Discipline
- An Chomhairle Mhúinteoireachta[2]
- Income Tax[3]

At an early stage the Executive Committees of the three unions decided to seek a major salary review, and to take industrial action, if necessary, in pursuit of the claim. Success in having the Salary Review Body established in 1981 and the favourable conclusion of the subsequent negotiations were attributable to the co-operation and agreement among representatives of the working group dealing with the C&A Scheme.

The National Understandings

The National Wage Agreement of 1977 expired for teachers on 28 February 1978. A new National Wage Agreement was ratified by delegates at an ICTU Conference on 22 March 1978, which provided for an increase of 8 per cent from 1 March 1978 and a further increase of 2 per cent from 1 March 1979.[4]

Clause 7 of the agreement provided that employers and trade unions might negotiate further salary improvements that would add not more than 2 per cent to the total salary bill, and that in certain circumstances they could refer claims for a higher amount to the Labour Court or to a public service Arbitration Board.

Executive Officers and Higher Executive Officers in the civil service were awarded an increase by an arbitrator under Clause 7. To maintain the recognised relativity between teachers and those in comparable positions in the public service, the teacher unions submitted a 'status' claim to Conciliation Council for an increase of 15 per cent. As the Official Side was not prepared to make any offer, disagreement was recorded and the claim was submitted to Arbitration.

The arbitrator issued his findings on 26 April 1979 and awarded the following phased increases on the common basic scale:

- an increase of 4.5 per cent backdated to 1 July 1978
- an increase of 3.3 per cent from 1 January 1979.

---

2   In September 1978 a working party of the three unions was established to devise modifications to the original An Chomhairle Mhúinteoireachta proposals that would be acceptable to all parties; the TUI had difficulty with the concept when it was announced in 1975.

3   On 22 January 1980, 700,000 PAYE employees took part in demonstrations organised by Trades Councils throughout the country to protest against the tax system, and members of the three unions played a prominent role in them. See CEC Report to Congress 1979

4   Conciliation Council Agreed Report 2/79, the application of the Second Phase National Wage Agreement 1978, 2 per cent with effect from 1 March, 1979

Combined with the 2 per cent National Wage Agreement increase from 1 March of 1979, this gave an overall increase in excess of 10 per cent of the basic scale over a twelve-month period. All allowances were increased by the same percentages.[5]

The National Understanding, 1979

Early in 1979 the unions were successful in negotiating the 'National Understanding for Social and Economic Development' agreement. The document, in addition to setting down pay proposals, contained an extensive agenda covering various aspects of national policy on social issues.

The original agreement was rejected by 319 to 118 votes at the ICTU Special Conference held on 23 May 1979; the three teacher unions cast their votes against acceptance of the package. In response to the rejection, the government immediately announced a limitation of 7 per cent on increases in public service pay over a period of six months.

On 25 July 1979, following further negotiations, a special ICTU Delegate Conference accepted revised proposals by 297 votes to 135; the INTO voted against the revised agreement as the new proposals were not considered to be substantially improved. Notwithstanding this, teachers accepted the fifteen-month agreement at a Conciliation Council meeting on 30 July 1979; it provided a pay increase in two phases:

- First Phase: an increase of 9 per cent from 1 June 1979 until March 1980[6]
- Second Phase: an increase of 7 per cent plus £2.40 per week from 1 March 1980[7]

The 1979 agreement also provided for a tax rebate of £39 million to PAYE taxpayers. This rebate was paid in the form of an extra tax-free allowance of approximately £175 for every taxpayer in the month of December 1979. Where both a husband and wife were PAYE taxpayers they were both entitled to this allowance.

In addition, the income limit for eligibility for benefit under the Health Acts was raised to £7,000 per annum and the government gave commitments on the development of the education service.

The cumulative effect of these increases on the minimum and the maximum of scales was as follows:

---

5   Conciliation Council Agreed Report 5/79 implementing the terms of Arbitration Board Report No. 7
6   Teachers' Conciliation Council Agreed Report 13/79
7   Teachers' Conciliation Council Agreed Report 16/79

	Minimum	Maximum
1 March 1978	3,572	5,815
1 March 1980	4,712	7,594
Increase	1,140 (31.9%)	1,779 (30.6%)

Limitation on Salary Claims

The National Understanding included a 'Limitation on Claims' provision that specifically placed a prohibition on the submission and processing of claims during the period of the National Understanding. This would prevent the teacher unions from pursuing their major salary review claim unless a strategy could be devised that would prevent the government from claiming that they were in breach of the agreement.

As a first step in exhausting the existing machinery, on 1 June 1979 the unions lodged an agreed composite claim for a special salary increase at the teachers' Conciliation Council which would:

- restore the 1970 purchasing power of teachers
- give teachers an equitable share of the increased national wealth
- establish a new salary level for teachers relative to the position of other groups with comparable professional qualifications and responsibilities.

It was expected that the Official Side would not make any offer on the claim and disagreement would be recorded. This would be used as a platform to demand from the government the establishment of a Review Body; it would be claimed that Arbitration would not suffice because an arbitrator could only issue a finding based on established relativities.

At a subsequent meeting of the Conciliation Council on 30 October 1979, the Official Side rejected the teachers' claims. At this point the ASTI decided to pursue its claim to Arbitration on its own.[8] This caused some difficulty with the other unions and they decided to proceed together on their own campaign.

On Saturday, 12 January 1980, the INTO and TUI issued a joint statement to the media to the effect that, if a decision was not taken by 1 February 1980 to establish a Review Body, a programme of industrial action would be initiated.

It was proposed that the first one-day strike and demonstration would be held during the third week of February; it would involve over 7,500 members of the INTO and TUI from Dublin and the surrounding areas. Subsequently there

---

8   Teachers' Conciliation Council Agreed Report 15/79 recording disagreement on an ASTI claim for a 40.3 per cent increase in salary and allowances; this claim was submitted to Arbitration

would be a series of regional stoppages covering the whole country. The ASTI Standing Committee also decided to ballot its members on strike action in furtherance of its salary claim, and it was expected that its members would join with the other teachers.

During January the Rev. John Beatty, Secretary, Catholic Primary School Managers Association; the Rev. Cornelius Sayers, Secretary, Diocesan Offices, Archbishop's House, Dublin; and Br Declan Duffy, Secretary of the Joint Managerial Body for secondary schools, wrote to the Minister supporting the teachers in their request for a Review Body.[9]

On 23 January 1980 the Minister for Education, John Wilson, invited representatives of the three teachers' organisations to meet with him and his officials for discussions. The Minister reported back to Cabinet, which, at its meeting on 29 January 1980, decided in principle to establish a Review Body on teachers' pay and conditions.

On 29 February 1980 the following terms of reference were agreed between the unions and officials of the Departments of Education and the Public Service:[10]

A:

1   to examine and report on the levels of salary and allowances of teachers on the common basic scale, taking cognisance of the circumstances of other groups with comparable professional qualifications and responsibilities

2   to have regard in the overall assessment of salary levels, allowances and promotion opportunities, to the nature and conditions of their work, including hours of work and length of school year, and the role and value of the teacher in society

3   to make an interim report by 30 September 1980

4   to submit the final report and recommendations by 31 January 1981.

B:

1   to make recommendations in regard to the procedure for the determination and review of the conditions on which persons might be appointed in various capacities for work in connection with the Certificate Examinations of the Department of Education, including the rates of payment for such work.

The Review Body on Teachers' Pay

The executives of the three unions endorsed the terms of reference and, early in April, the Minister for Education announced the membership of the Review Body as follows: Mr Justice J. P. N. Ryan, chairman; Richard N. Cooke, SC;

---

9   CEC Report to Congress 1980, pp. 15–6
10 Letter from Liam Ó Laidhin, Secretary, Department of Education, CEC Report to Congress 1980, p. 18

Professor Dermot McAleese, Trinity College; and Michael Collins and John Walsh, both members of the Labour Court.

The Review Body held its first meeting on Friday, 18 April and agreed the rules of procedure, which were similar to the ones that applied for the Ryan Tribunal of 1968. All parties involved would submit written submissions and make oral presentations; they would be entitled to attend as observers at all oral hearings. In addition, the Review Body decided to place advertisements in the national newspapers inviting submissions from any interested parties.

It was agreed that the oral hearings would commence on Friday, 27 June with the INTO presentation of its submission.[11] Its written submission, which was elaborated on in the oral presentation, dealt in detail with the following topics:

- cost of living as a factor in salary adjustments
- increase in GNP (Gross National Product), as it affects workers generally
- changes in the role of the teacher
- increases in the common basic scale
- the incremental range
- number of promoted posts
- value of promoted posts
- special position of teachers in relation to promotion
- additional allowance for school-related activities
- rent allowance
- professional allowance
- travel expenses
- backdating of awards.

The INTO submitted a number of figures in support of its claim for a considerable increase in remuneration. One table of figures showed that between 1969 and 1979 the Consumer Price Index had increased by 241.7 and another one showed that between 1970 and 1978 the GNP had increased by 32.3 per cent. It was claimed that teachers, over the previous decade, had not been compensated in full for the increase in the cost of living nor had they benefited from the increasing wealth of the nation, and to remedy this the following increases would be required:

- Basic Salary Scale Minimum   16.1%
- Basic Salary Scale Maximum   27.3%
- Long Service Increment   47.7%
- Grade A Post   50.5%

---

11 The INTO negotiating team was Micheál MacSuibhne (President), Gerry Quigley (General Secretary), Michael Moroney (General Treasurer), and Tom Gilmore (CEC).

- Grade B Post   51.4%
- Vice-Principal (1,100–1,299 pts)   50.0%
- Principal (1,100–1,299 pts)   43.4%

While the INTO claimed that an increase was justified due to the increase in the cost of living, its fundamental claim was for a major salary review and a departure from its traditional relativity with Executive Officers in the civil service. This relativity was deemed inappropriate as it was inequitable. It sought:

- a shortening of the incremental scale
- a major increase in the number of posts
- special qualifications' allowances that would follow the same pattern as allowances for posts
- that the number and grade of posts granted to a school should be determined by the number of teachers on the staff.

In all, the Review Body held twenty-seven meetings, including ten oral hearings, and it received written submissions from forty-six other parties.

The Interim Report of the Review Body

The Review Body submitted an Interim Report to the Minister for Education on 22 September and it was published on 9 October 1980. The report only covered sections A (1) and A (2) of the terms of reference in its recommendations; it was indicated that the final report would be issued by 31 January 1981, which would contain recommendations on section B of the terms of reference. The findings were arranged under the following main headings:

- Common Basic Scale
- Principals' and Vice-Principals' Allowances
- A and B Posts of Responsibility.
- Qualification Allowances and Other Allowances

Common Basic Scale

The Review Body recommended that the existing incremental span should be reduced by two points, to thirteen points, and that five special increments, payable on completion of certain phases of service, should be introduced. The recommended scale would be as follows:

- £5,050 – 5,250 – 5,450 – 5,650 – 5,850 – 6,050 – 6,250 – 6,700 – 7,000 – 7,300 – 7,600 –7,900 – 8,200
- £8,500 (on completion of three years at £8,200)

- £8,850 (on completion of five years at £8,500)
- £9,250 (on completion of five years at £8,850)
- £9,700 (on completion of five years at £9,250)
- £10,200 (on completion of five years at £9,700).[12]

Of great importance to the teacher unions, it recommended:

> We do not see the existing relativity with the Civil Service Executive Officer as an appropriate determinant of teachers' salary. We therefore recommend that this relativity cease forthwith.[13]

The old relativity was broken and, henceforth, the teacher unions would be able to use the salary movements of those with similar educational qualifications as a guide when seeking salary revisions.

Principals' and Vice-Principals' Allowances

The Review Body recommended that increased allowances should be paid to principals and vice-principals and that the points range 'ceiling' should be raised. It was not prepared to accept the principle of an open-ended points range.[14] The allowances recommended for principals and vice-principals in the new categories were as follows:

Allowances for Principals and Vice-Principals

Points Rating	Principal (£)	Vice-Principal (£)
2,950–3,199	4,290	2,724
3,200–3,449	4,390	2,794
3,450 and over	4,490	2,864

A and B Posts of Responsibility

The Review Body declared that it seemed clear to it that the system of posts of responsibility, as it was structured, did not adequately serve the needs of pupils, teachers or management, and that the situation was further complicated by the existence of Special Functions Allowances. It recommended that:

---

12 Interim Report of Review Body on Teachers' Pay, 1980, paragraphs 2.2 and 2.3

13 Interim Report of Review Body on Teachers' Pay, 1980, paragraph 2.5

14 The points range for schools for the payment of principals' and vice-principals' allowances had been capped at 1,700 points.

- the A Post system should be retained with an allowance at its present level
- in future, A Posts should be advertised within the school and have fully delineated duties and responsibilities attached to them
- the creation of B Posts should be discontinued and that posts generated by the existing system should be phased out (It considered that the recommended salary scale was adequate to cover the responsibilities that had been attached to B Posts.)
- Special Functions Allowances should be retained only until such time as they were exceeded by amounts accruing through long-phased increments
- the Department of Education should provide supplemental monies so that all posts, whether generated by the points system or retained on a personal basis, would be fully paid.

Qualification Allowances and Other Allowances

The Review Body considered that the allowances payable were reasonable and adequate and rejected the request for increases to the rates. Its opinion was that, having established what it considered to be an adequate basic rate for the job, allowances, other than those derived from increased responsibility, should be treated as distinct and supplemental.

Effective Date

It was recommended that the new scale and the new allowances should take effect on and from 1 September 1980.

Specialist Teachers

It recognised the complexity of the Specialist Teacher issue, and the conflicting positions taken by the unions and, consequently, it could see no way of resolving this issue directly which would not create as many problems as it would solve.

Reaction to the Interim Report

The establishment of the Review Body had raised teachers' expectations, but this body made the same mistakes as the Ryan Tribunal of 1968. Like the members of the tribunal, the members of the Review Body did not appreciate the conditions that applied to the employment of teachers in the different sectors. All of the recommendations fell short of what had been expected, and problems were created for national and post-primary teachers in different ways.

The Review Body recommended a scale salary that 'overtly recognised that supervision, substitution, parent contact and pastoral care are integral parts of the teaching function and essential to the proper running of a school' and that allowances for posts of responsibility should be retained at their current level and that the B Post should be discontinued. The presumption of the Board that the scale salary should pay for functions that were previously part of the posts of responsibility system, and that one avenue of promotion should be abandoned, appears to signify a lack of understanding of the system operating in schools at that time.

The recommended thirteen-point basic salary scale gave an increase of 7.17 per cent and 8.97 per cent on the respective minimum and maximum points on the 1980 scale; teachers had claimed that an increase of 16.1 per cent on the minimum point and 27.3 per cent on the maximum point were required to compensate for the rise in the Consumer Price Index.

The proposed salary did not respond to the unions' concern about the slippage in the relative value of the salaries of their members in comparison to the salaries of similarly qualified professionals.

The proposed salary scale, with its five long-phased increments, would mean that a national teacher who started to teach at age twenty, or a post-primary teacher at twenty-two, would be fifty-six years of age when he/she reached the super-maximum of £9,700.

Teachers had sought an increase of 43.4 per cent for principals; an increase varying upwards from 28.4 per cent was recommended. Teachers had sought an increase rising from 36.6 per cent to 50 per cent on the allowance for vice-principals; an increase of 28.4 per cent was recommended.

The teacher unions had sought an increase in excess of 50 per cent on the allowances attached to the A and B posts; the Review Body recommended that the A Post allowance should remain at its current rate and that B Posts should be discontinued. Although only 304 national teachers held A Posts and 1,599 held B Posts, out of a teaching force of 18,364 teachers, this recommendation was set to reduce even further national teachers' prospect of promotion to a post.

The recommendation to raise the points 'ceiling' was of no significance to primary schools; no primary school had any prospect of achieving the maximum under the old points system. Raising the points ceiling would increase allowances for principals and vice-principals in large post-primary schools and would also increase the number of post-primary teachers who would qualify for A Posts.

Negotiations with the Minister

The three Executive Committees rejected the recommendations as being 'absurd' and 'insulting', and a campaign was organised to persuade the government not to adopt it.[15] The following reasons were put forward for its rejection:

---

15 Letter from the chairman of the Review Body to the Minister for Education, dated 30
   October 1980

- the low percentage increases in the common basic scale
- the excessive length of the basic scale
- the introduction of 'long-phased increments'
- the reduction of promotional opportunities, especially for younger teachers, which would result from the elimination of B posts
- the failure to increase the value of A Posts
- the failure to increase the value of qualification allowances
- the failure to make any effort to resolve the long-standing problem of specialist teachers
- the absence of any provision for retrospection to the award.

On 10 October 1980, following discussions between the Minister for Education and representatives of the unions, a press statement was issued on the following agreed terms:

1 Negotiations on the Common Basic Scale will commence on 14 October 1980.
2 Parties to the negotiations will be those who are represented at the Conciliation Council for teachers.
3 The negotiations will be conducted under the chairmanship of the Secretary of the Department of Education, with the aim of concluding by 22 October 1980.
4 If agreement is reached the terms of the agreement will be processed through the Conciliation Council for teachers.
5 The outstanding issues already submitted by the unions to the Review Body shall be processed through the Teachers' Conciliation and Arbitration Scheme on the understanding that the Minister supports the view that these discussions shall be finalised by mid-December 1980.

Negotiations commenced with officials from the Departments of Education and Public Service on 14 October under the chairmanship of Liam Lane, Secretary of the Department of Education. Little progress was made and an urgent meeting was sought with the Minister for Education. Negotiations were resumed on 21 October under the chairmanship of the Minister and on 23 October settlement proposals were agreed.

At a special meeting that morning the CEC considered a report on the negotiations and noted that the following improvements had been achieved:

- The Review Body's salary proposals were improved at every point of the scale, with inclusive increases ranging from 12.5 per cent at the first point, 13.7 per cent at point five, 15.3 per cent at point ten, 17.3 per cent at point thirteen, and 14.6 per cent at point fifteen.
- period over which they would be paid was reduced by ten years. The proposed revised schedule was as follows:

- – £9,150 at point 18, giving an increase of 20.5 per cent
- – £9,650 at point 22, giving an increase of 27.1 per cent
- – £10,200 at point 26, giving an increase of 34.3 per cent.
- All B Posts would be retained, subject to the allowance for a B Post being subsumed in the final long-phased increment.

The unions' opinion that the Review Body had gone outside its terms of reference when recommending that duties should be attached to posts was accepted.

All attempts to secure a retrospective date for the implementation of the revised salaries and allowances failed. The decision not to grant retrospection created a problem for the unions with regard to teachers who retired between April and September 1980.

The new proposals were accepted by union members in a ballot and the agreement was subsequently endorsed at the Teachers' Conciliation Council.[16] The Official Side recorded that the increases recommended by the Review Body would have cost £34 million and that the new agreement cost £48 million, an increase of £14 million.

Resignation of the Review Body

During the controversy with the Minister the media had speculated on the operation and future role of the Review Body. On 8 January 1981 the chairman issued a press statement explaining that members of the Review Body had tendered their resignation on 30 October 1980 but that in deference to the Minister's wishes they had delayed making it public. Now, in the light of events he wished to place on record that:

- the Board had fulfilled its obligations and made recommendations as required
- the members were dissatisfied that within a few days of the publication of its report all of its work had been completely ignored and fresh negotiations entered into
- while the members had expected some criticisms of their findings, they did not expect the intemperate and irrational reaction of the teachers' representatives.

He concluded, 'it is obvious that the Pay Review Body can no longer serve any useful purpose and we tender our resignation herewith'.[17]

In response, the teachers' unions issued a joint press statement agreeing 'that the Pay Review Body can no longer serve any useful purpose' in the

---

16 Teachers' Conciliation Council Agreed Report 4/80
17 Letter from P. Noel Ryan (Chairman) to the Minister for Education, 30 October 1980,
   CEC Report to Congress 1981, p. 60

determination of teacher pay and allowances as it had failed to appreciate the implications of its proposals.[18]

Arbitration on Responsibility and Qualification Allowances

The outstanding issues were referred to the Teachers' Conciliation Council:

- qualifications allowances
- specialist teachers
- posts of responsibility
- payment in full for all posts generated by the points system.

No progress was made as the Official Side was only prepared to offer the allowance rates recommended by the Review Body. Again, the three unions requested direct intervention by the Minister 'to open up the road to genuine negotiation and conciliation'.[19] He acknowledged the request but did not respond to it.

To progress matters the unions presented an agreed claim at Conciliation Council on 6 February 1981. The Official Side responded by repeating the recommendations of the Review Body. The teachers declared disagreement on the claim and referred it to Arbitration.[20]

Teachers' Arbitration Board

The arbitrator, Conor Maguire SC, presented his report to the government in November 1981 and recommended that:

1 an increase of 25 per cent in qualification allowances should be granted with effect from 1 July 1981
2 allowances for principals, vice-principals, A and B Posts, as at 1 March 1980, should be increased by 30 per cent with effect from 1 September 1980
3 no principal should receive an allowance less than an A Post allowance, and no vice-principal should receive an allowance less than a B Post allowance, with effect from 1 September 1981
4 a teacher promoted to an A Post or a B Post should retain that position and the appropriate allowance on a personal basis provided that he/she did not voluntarily move to another school
5 sufficient monies should be made available to ensure that all posts generated by the School Points System were paid in full
6 the Comprehensive School Allowance should be continued

18 CEC Report to Congress 1981, pp. 61–2
19 Letter from Gerry Quigley, on behalf of the three unions, to the Minister for Education, 12 December 1980, CEC Report to Congress 1981, p. 58
20 Teachers' Conciliation Council Disagreed Report 2/81

7   the specialist teachers' claim clearly involved a principle governing remuneration, and as such was not open to Arbitration under the Conciliation and Arbitration Scheme for Teachers.[21]

Comment

The arbitrator's ruling was seen by teachers as a vindication of their campaign and, in addition, some very important principles had been established that would be of benefit in the future. The arbitrator had ruled on the minimum allowance for a principal's and vice-principal's post, on the permanency of a post once obtained, and on the provision of sufficient money for all posts. There was disappointment that he had not dealt with the specialist teachers' claim.

Subsuming of the B Post

One problem remained in that the arbitrator did not make any specific reference to the Review Body recommendation that the Grade B allowance should be subsumed at the maximum of the extended salary scale. The unions subsequently requested a ruling on this from the arbitrator but he recommended that the problem should be resolved between the parties.

The Department of Education implemented the recommendation of the Review Body and started to subsume the B Posts from the commencement of the school year 1980–81. In order to protect its position, the INTO advised members affected by the change to operate as if they still held the posts and to continue to perform the attached duties even though payment was withdrawn. It took the view that it was possible that, sometime in the future, payment of B Posts could be restored.

The unions submitted a claim on this problem to the Conciliation Council and, as the Official Side refused to make any offer, it was referred to Arbitration.[23] The arbitrator's report was not signed until 12 October 1984, when he ruled that, with effect from 1 September 1984, B Posts should not be subsumed. The teachers had claimed retrospection to 1 September 1980 but the arbitrator did not concede it.[23]

The failure to get retrospection created a problem for teachers who had retired in the intervening period, between 1 September 1980 and 1 September 1984; their superannuation benefits had been affected. During 1985–86, the INTO lodged a number of claims at Conciliation Council seeking redress for these teachers.

The Official Side conceded the claim for some teachers but only partially for others:

---

21 Arbitration Report No. 11
22 Teachers' Conciliation Council Agreed Report 1/83 recording disagreement on the claim of subsuming of B Posts, Arbitration Report No. 12, and the subsequent Agreed Report 4/86 on the consequential superannuation arrangements
23 Arbitration Report No. 13

- teachers who retired after 1 September 1984 would be given credit for the B Post allowance in calculating pension and lump sum
- teachers who retired before 1 September 1984 would be given credit for the B Post allowance in calculating pension with effect from 1 July 1985; there would be no retrospection and the lump sum would not be revised.[243]

Public Service Pay

The Second National Understanding

During July, August and September of 1980, while the Review Body was in session, the government, employer organisations and the social partners negotiated a new National Understanding to cover a fourteen-month period. This agreement came into effect for teachers from 1 October 1980 with the following terms:

- The First Phase would operate for a period of eight months and would be for an amount of 8 per cent of basic pay plus £1.00 per week.
- The second phase would operate for a period of six months and the basic pay of employees would be increased by 7 per cent.
- A meeting of the Employer-Labour Conference would be convened to consider an upward adjustment in the amount of the second phase in the event of the Consumer Price Index (CPI) figure for the period mid-May 1980 to mid-February 1981 exceeding 10 per cent.
- A trade union could not take any form of industrial action to force an employer to enter into an agreement at variance with the terms of the agreement.
- It provided that 'all Labour Court recommendations or Arbitration findings that had been issued by 31 July 1980, or offers [that] had already been made, or a case [that] had been referred to a Labour Court hearing, a Joint Labour Committee, an Arbitration Board or Review Body, could be processed'.

This provision was important for teachers as they had special pay increases pending as a result of negotiations with the Minister.

Even though the problems with the recommendations of the Review Body had not been resolved by this time, the unions proceeded with a claim for payment of the first phase of the National Understanding from 1 October 1980 and, shortly afterwards, for payment of the terms of the second phase from 1 June 1981.[25]

24 Conciliation Council Agreed Report 4/86
25 Teachers' Conciliation Council Agreed Report 5/80; Teachers' Conciliation Council Agreed Report 5/81

Negotiations on a New National Understanding, 1981

Prior to the expiry of the Second National Understanding the ICTU started to explore the possibility of concluding another agreement on pay with employers.

The negotiations were conducted in the context of severe economic difficulties with a high level of unemployment. It was being projected that the CPI would increase by between 20 to 25 per cent over the following fifteen months.[26]

The employer side was not prepared to reach agreement on the principle of equal treatment for workers in the public and private sectors. The ICTU would not countenance discrimination against workers in either sector.

Negotiations broke down and the Executive Council of the ICTU recommended that unions should pursue claims through their own established machinery. The three teacher unions and the public service unions submitted claims to their Conciliation Councils seeking increases in pay at a level sufficient to maintain living standards.

In an effort to avoid individual claims being processed, the Minister for Labour and the Public Service, Liam Kavanagh, initiated negotiations with the Public Services Committee of the ICTU, and a draft agreement on public service pay was reached on 17 December 1981 in full and final settlement of all cost-increasing labour claims for the period of the agreement.

Draft Agreement on Pay in the Public Service

The agreement was endorsed by the Public Services Committee on 9 February 1982. It covered a period of fifteen months and provided increases in basic pay as follows:

- The first phase increase would operate for a period of three months and would be for an amount of 2 per cent of basic pay or £4 per week, whichever was the greater.
- The second phase would operate for a period of seven months, and basic pay would be increased by 6 per cent.
- The third phase would operate for a period of five months, and basic pay would be increased by 5 per cent.[27]

It was agreed that Labour Court recommendations, Arbitration findings or Review Body recommendations issued on or before 17 December 1981 could be implemented. This was an important exception for teachers as it guaranteed

---

26 A Fine Gael/Labour coalition government was in power from 1 July 1981 to March 1982 with John Boland as Minister for Education.

27 The increases in basic pay would be paid to teachers from 1 December 1981, from 1 March 1982, and from 1 October 1982.

payment to teachers of the awards on responsibility and qualification allowances made by the arbitrator in November 1981.

INTO members accepted the agreement, with 9,664 voting for and 837 against, and it was processed through Conciliation Council.[28]

Over the four-and-a-half-year period from 1 March 1978 to 1 October 1982 the first point of the salary scale had increased by 99 per cent and the fifteenth point by 97.5 per cent.

Salaries, 1 March 1978 to 1 October 1982

Scale Point	1.3.1978 £	1.10.1982 £
1	3,572	7,110
2	3,709	7,368
3	3,843	7,626
4	3,980	7,883
5	4,114	8,205
6	4,252	8,462
7	4,396	8,719
8	4,540	8,976
9	4,688	9,363
10	4,832	9,684
11	4,977	10,070
12	5,163	10,456
13	5,348	10,841
14	5,533	11,163
15	5,815	11,484
18		12,068
22		12,723
26		13,445

Representatives of the three unions continued to meet regularly and in late 1982 the following claim was lodged with the Conciliation Council:

> Claim from the INTO, TUI and ASTI that the salary and allowances paid to teachers in Primary, Secondary, Vocational, Community and Comprehensive Schools be increased to take account of pay awards in both the civil and public service since the 1st September 1980.[29]

This claim was to have relevance for the 1985 salary dispute.

---

28 Teachers' Conciliation Council Agreed Report 2/82
29 Conciliation Claim 182/82

Council of Education Unions

Inter-union co-operation between the teachers during this period was further endorsed by the establishment of a Council of Education Unions (CEU) in November 1981. The Council was initiated to 'provide for structured liaison and exchange of information among ICTU unions engaged exclusively in the education sector and to assist the development of an overall trade union view of education'. It consisted of the five teachers' organisations affiliated to the ICTU and had a total membership of over 41,000. The organisations were: the Association of Secondary Teachers Ireland (ASTI); Irish Federation of University Teachers (IFUT); Irish National Teachers' Organisation (INTO); National Association of Teachers in Further and Higher Education (NATFHE); and the Teachers' Union of Ireland (TUI). Christy Devine, General Secretary of the TUI, was elected as the Council's first chairman, and Kieran Mulvey was elected as its secretary.

The establishment of the council meant that for the first time ever there was a structure that provided a representative forum for all sectors of education, covering first-, second- and third-level education. The following topics were identified as relevant for consideration by the council:

- Specialist Teachers' Claim
- Promotion Opportunities
- Claims with the Conciliation Council
- The Conciliation and Arbitration Scheme
- Teachers' Superannuation
- Common Facilities and Services for Members
- Policy on Parent–Teacher Meetings
- Education for the Disabled
- Working Party on In-service Education
- School Discipline.

Close liaison was maintained between the Council and teacher TDs and Senators.[30]

---

30 From 1979, representatives of the ASTI and TUI were invited to an annual function hosted by the INTO for all teacher TDs and Senators. A Fianna Fáil/Progressive Democrat Coalition government served from March 1982 until December 1982. Three Ministers for Education served during this short period: Dr Martin O'Donoghue from 9.3.82 to 6.10.82, Charles Haughey, Taoiseach, and acting Minister for Education, from 7.10.82 to 27.10.82, and Gerard Brady from 28.10.82 to 14.12.82. From December 1982 to February 1986 a Fine Gael/Labour Coalition government was in power; Garret FitzGerald was Taoiseach and Gemma Hussey was Minister for Education from 14 December 1982 to 13 February 1986. She was replaced by Paddy Cooney.

Pension Developments 1979–1982

While a considerable amount of time and effort was directed at salary issues during this period, progress was also achieved on a number of pension claims.

Signed Conciliation Council Reports

Among the reports recorded in the Conciliation Council were the following:

1   A claim seeking a revision of the averaging arrangements (for pension purposes) of all allowances payable to teachers was disagreed.[31]
2   It was conceded that a teacher returning to service after a break would not have to serve for ten years before previous service could be counted for pension purposes.
3   It was conceded that the long-phased increment should be treated as an allowance for superannuation purposes with effect from 30 June 1979.[32]
4   A purchase scheme to enable teachers to buy back past pensionable service was introduced.[33]
5   Arising out of the introduction of the long-phased increments to the scale salary, an amendment to the Teachers' Superannuation Scheme had to be negotiated to cover the situation whereby national teachers who had at least thirty-five years of pensionable service could retire voluntarily on or after reaching their fifty-fifth birthday and receive full benefit from the long-phased increments.[34]

Claims Lodged at Conciliation Council

A number of claims were submitted and discussed, but no progress was made in their resolution:

1   that service for teaching in underdeveloped countries, for which incremental credit had been granted, should be recognised for superannuation purposes
2   that a teacher who had at least five years of pensionable service could retire on or after his/her fifty-fifth birthday, and that pension and gratuity would be computed as for normal retirement
3   that every year of service given by a school principal would count as two years for pensionable service, and that pension and gratuity would be computed as for normal retirement
4   that service in secondary schools prior to registration would be recognised for pension purposes.

---

31 Disagreed Report 4/79
32 Agreed Report 7/80
33 Agreed Report 8/80
34 Agreed Report 6/81

The INTO submitted a claim to Conciliation Council that pension credit should be given for all service for which pension deductions had been made. The Official Side was not prepared to discuss the matter as this provision had implications for all public service employees. The INTO proposed that an overall body for the public service should be established to oversee the application of schemes and investigate their operation. This was not conceded, but the INTO succeeded in persuading the Public Services Committee of the ICTU to set up a working party, representative of public service unions, to investigate the matter.[35] Subsequently, a report entitled 'Pension Schemes in the Public Sector' was adopted by the Public Services Committee and distributed to all the unions in the public service with the recommendation that it should be used by the individual unions in seeking amendments to their respective superannuation schemes.

Increases in Pensions

From 1975 to 1982 the standard practice established under pension regulations was to increase public service pensions on 1 July each year by reference to changes in the rates of pay of serving officers within the previous twelve months. Normally salary revisions necessitated only one adjustment in pensions, but during years when a number of salary adjustments were made or where a salary adjustment came into effect very near the 1 July date, a delay occurred in the pension adjustment and the payment of arrears.

During the school year 1978–9, four salary adjustments were required and many complaints were received in INTO head office about delays in the payment of increases to pensioners. Representations were made to the pension section of the Department of Education and procedures for updating the payment of arrears were agreed.[36]

1980 Retirals

The decision of the Ministers for Education and Finance not to concede retrospection of the awards arising from the Review Body beyond 1 September 1980 created a problem for teachers who retired on 31 August 1980.

As the Review Body had been convened in April these teachers felt aggrieved on two counts: they had not received any arrears of salary, and their pensions and lump sums had been calculated on salaries that did not reflect the increases granted.

---

35 A letter to the Chairman of the Public Services Committee, ICTU, from Michael Moroney, General Treasurer, INTO, 29 April 1980
36 Letter from Miss R. Mee, Pension Section, Department of Education, to Michael Moroney, General Treasurer, INTO, 28 January 1980, CEC Report to Congress 1980, p. 24

Various representations made to the Department of Education seeking to secure the recalculation of the pensions and gratuities of these teachers were unsuccessful.[37]

At the request of the Retired Teachers' Association, on 22 November 1982 the CEC sought a Senior Counsel's opinion. The opinion was not favourable; he saw no prospect of success in a legal action on the issue. Representations to successive Ministers for Education were unsuccessful. The government did not concede the principle of pension parity until the 1984 budget.

The Marriage Ban and Trainee Teachers

Women who were in attendance at Preparatory Colleges, Training Colleges, or who were pupil-teachers at the time the Marriage Ban was introduced from 1 October 1934 were caught by the ban and had to retire when they married.

After the removal of the ban in 1958, many of these teachers came back into the service. The teaching service given before they were compulsorily retired on marriage could be reclaimed for pension purposes by the repayment of the marriage gratuity, and any service given from 1 July 1958 was recognised as appropriate service. However, the period of compulsory retirement deprived many of them of sufficient service to qualify for full pension, and they sought credit to enable them to claim maximum pension.[38]

A claim seeking credit for years lost due to retirement on marriage was progressed through Conciliation Council, and the Official Side was eventually prevailed upon to grant a maximum credit of five years for pension purposes in the case of a female teacher who was in pensionable service on or after 30 June 1979.[39]

As the Official Side was not prepared to improve on the offer of five years' credit and, following legal advice, the women concerned voted to accept the offer.[40]

The INTO was subsequently successful in getting the same terms extended to certain teachers trained in the UK who were also affected by the marriage ban. They had come back to Ireland and, having taken up teaching posts, had been obliged to retire on marriage.[41]

---

37 Letter to John Wilson, Minister for Education, from the three General Secretaries, 19 February 1981
38 Married female teachers, to whom the marriage ban applied, were granted pension credit for temporary service in national schools between 1934 and 1958, where such service would be regarded as pensionable service but for the operation of the marriage ban.
39 Added years had been conceded under the Redundancy Scheme of 1974. Pensionable credit, up to a maximum of five years, was granted to teachers in respect of periods of unemployment during the existence of overall redundancy in the teaching profession between 1 July 1926 and 30 June 1947.
40 Legal Opinion from Niall McCarthy SC on 5 September 1980, CEC Report to Congress 1981, pp. 88–97
41 Teachers' Conciliation Council Agreed Report 4/82

Comment

The marriage ban issue was finally resolved in 1984 when the Departments of Finance and Education agreed to concede that service given by female teachers while the marriage ban was in force could be reckoned for incremental purposes, where such period(s) of service would have been regarded as incremental service but for the operation of the marriage ban.[42]

Review, 1978–82

The period commenced with changes in the senior officerships of the teacher unions and the establishment of close personal relationships among senior union officers. Numerous subcommittees and working parties were established to consider issues of common concern and to develop plans for their achievement. The Council of Education Unions was established in 1981 'to assist the development of an overall trade union view of education'.

From the early 1980s the teacher unions became active participants in ICTU affairs; each of the unions had a member elected to the Executive Council. The teacher union block became one of the most powerful groupings in national negotiations, and it had a major influence in national understandings and agreements on pay in the public service, which had become the norm. These agreements produced order and stability in industrial relations.

In tandem with the national agreements, the teacher unions processed claims covering many different aspects of pay and conditions through the Conciliation and Arbitration Scheme. They were also successful in persuading the government to establish a Review Body on Teachers' Pay, out of which they achieved a substantial salary increase and broke the relativity with Executive Officers. Women who had been affected by the Marriage Ban got some recognition for pension purposes for service lost.

A review of Public Service Superannuation Schemes was carried out by the Public Services Committee of the ICTU and teacher unions were successful in having many claims for revisions and amendments to their schemes adopted.

The effectiveness of the teacher unions during this period established the groundwork for major advances in all fields. In 1985, the teacher unions, under the umbrella of Teachers United, became involved in a major dispute with the government over the payment of an Arbitration award and established themselves as the strongest interest group in the public service.

---

42 Teachers' Conciliation Council Agreed Report 4/84

12

Particular Developments

Introduction

This chapter examines four developments that were central to the enrichment of teachers' pension schemes:

1   Widows' and Children's Contributory Pension Scheme, 1968
2   Spouses' and Children's Contributory Pension Scheme, 1981
3   Indexation of Pensions
4   Pension Credit for Service in Capitation Schools

It also recounts the history of the specialist teachers' claim.

Widows' and Children's Contributory Pension Scheme, 1968

While the general provision of pension schemes for civil servants commenced in 1810, formal pension coverage for dependents is of relatively recent origin. Providing for the dependents of married men who died was always a problem, and deemed to be very costly.

Civil servants maintained a constant demand that their widows and children should be protected by the provision of a pension. Teachers, like all other public service employees, watched what they had achieved and followed their success.

The first major move away from pension provision in the narrow sense was achieved in 1909 when, in addition to the payment of a pension, a lump sum on retirement or death in service was introduced for male civil servants. Teachers were not offered this benefit, nor were female civil servants. The cost of this extra benefit was recouped by having the pension paid to male civil servants calculated on eightieths of retirement salary instead of sixtieths.

After the establishment of the Free State, civil servants in Ireland monitored the progress made by civil servants in England. New schemes implemented in England were, invariably, introduced in Ireland within a few years and, in some instances, the schemes developed by the Irish civil service were more sophisticated.

The Brennan Commission, in its final report in 1936, recommended that the cost of the introduction of pensions for dependants of civil servants, widows and orphans, should be actuarially investigated. There is no record of this being carried out.

From 1 January 1950, following the implementation of the Roe Committee's recommendations, male and female teachers were granted, in addition to pension, the payment of a lump sum on retirement, and the period of service that qualified for the payment of a lump sum following death in service was reduced from ten to five years.

With effect from 1 April 1951 the scheme of children's allowances payable to Executive Officers in the civil service was extended to married male teachers, widows of teachers and teacher-widows. In 1959 a claim that these allowances should be paid for all eligible children was conceded.[1]

Superannuation Act, 1956

The Superannuation Act of 1956 enabled a civil servant, on retirement, to surrender part of his pension to provide a pension for his widow or one dependent in the event of death in retirement. The amount payable was calculated as the actuarial equivalent of the amount surrendered so that in the long run the value of the pension surrendered should balance the value of the pension paid to dependents.[2] Very few civil servants availed of this scheme. It was speculated that the reason the scheme was not successful was due to the circulation of stories and rumours such as, 'a man who opted to make provision for his widow died the next day and half his pension had been lost in the transaction'.

In February 1961 the INTO sought the same concession for teachers but without success.[3]

In 1965 the CEC submitted a scheme to the Department for a managed Widows' Pension Scheme, similar to one introduced in Scotland, but no progress was made on the project.[4] It had proposed that both the State and teachers should be equally responsible for the cost; these principles were incorporated into the Widows' and Children's Scheme introduced in 1968.

Efforts in the Dáil, and elsewhere, to get the Minister for Finance to introduce a pension scheme for dependents were resisted until 1967 when a Civil Service Widows' and Children's Contributory Pension Scheme was agreed with the Department of Finance.[5]

There was no Dáil debate on the terms of the scheme, and no official account seems to have been given of the method by which the contribution rates were

---

1   Conciliation Council Report, 23 March 1959, Claim No. 30
2   Similar arrangements had been made in the UK in the Superannuation Act of 1937 (see Rhodes, *Public Sector Pensions*, 1965, p. 79)
3   CEC Report to Congress 1961
4   CEC Report to Congress 1965, p. 35
5   DEPD, Vol. 202, col. 1634

determined. It appears, however, that the contribution rates were determined on the experience of running an equivalent scheme for the British civil service. The employee periodic and non-periodic contribution rates were designed to meet half of the cost of the scheme, and the other half would be paid by the State.[6]

Widows' and Children's Contributory Pension Scheme for Teachers

The INTO and ASTI were successful in having a similar scheme introduced for teachers with effect from 23 July 1968.[7] The scheme provided for the payment of pensions to the widows and children of male teachers who died in the service or on pension.[8]

Conditions of the Scheme

The following conditions applied:

- The scheme would be optional for existing male teachers.
- It would be compulsory for all future male teachers.
- A teacher who opted out would not subsequently be allowed to join.
- A teacher who opted out would deprive his widow and/or orphans of any benefit from the scheme.
- Contributions to the scheme would be made on a periodic and a non-periodic basis.
- The periodic contribution rate would be set at 1.5 per cent of annual pensionable remuneration.[9]
- The non-periodic contribution would be 1 per cent of retiring salary for each year of reckonable service for which periodic contributions from pay had not been made.
- Participants in the scheme, widowers or single people, who did not marry would receive a refund of the contributions that had been deducted.

All male teachers in the service were sent details of the scheme; teachers who wished to be members of the scheme did not have to do anything, those who wished to opt out had to sign a declaration accepting that his dependents could not benefit from the provisions of the scheme at any future date. The INTO encouraged its members to join the scheme in order to provide a valuable

---

6 The Civil Service Widows' and Children's Contributory Pension Scheme was formalised under Statutory Instrument No. 132 of 1977.

7 Vocational teachers were members of the Local Government Superannuation Scheme.

8 Vocational teachers were covered under Local Government legislation and the VTA processed its claim through that conciliation machinery.

9 Teachers in Northern Ireland had to pay a contribution of 2 per cent for a similar scheme.

measure of security for their wives and dependent children. A small number of teachers did opt out and their dependents suffered.

Contributions were eligible for income tax relief at the marginal income tax rate, and from an actuarial and benefit point of view no policy offered by any commercial insurance company could match the scheme's total benefits. Half of the premium was either actually or notionally provided by the employer, i.e. the government.

Scheme Benefits

Widows and orphans of teachers who died after completing five years of pensionable service would benefit as follows:

- The widow would receive a pension equal to one-half of the accrued pension which the contributor would have got if he had served to age sixty-five.
- One-sixth of the widow's pension would be payable for each eligible child up to a maximum of six.
- Orphans would receive the following proportion of the pension that the widow would have received, where the number of children was:
  one: one-third of the widow's pension
  two: one-half of the widow's pension
  three: two-thirds of the widow's pension
  four: five-sixths of the widow's pension
  five: the whole of the widow's pension.
- A child was deemed to be in benefit until age sixteen or age twenty-one if still pursuing a full-time course of education.
- The widow of a teacher pensioner would receive one-half of her late husband's pension.
- A widow who remarried would have her pension suspended; no benefit would be payable for a child conceived from another union.
- There would be no abatement or suspension of the widow's pension on her re-employment in the public service.

Ex-gratia Pensions

In 1969, following requests and representations from inside and outside the Dáil, the Minister for Finance, Charles J. Haughey, introduced an *ex-gratia* scheme for the widows of public servants who retired or died prior to 23 July.[10] The pension benefits payable under the *ex-gratia* scheme were set at half the benefit that would be paid to a widow under the contributory scheme; this was deemed to be the amount due from the State's notional contribution.

---

10 The Civil Service Widows' and Children's Ex-Gratia Pension Scheme was formalised under Statutory Instrument No. 133 of 1977.

This was deemed unsatisfactory and a lobby group, 'The Pre-1968 Public Service Widows' Association', campaigned over the years for equalisation of payments to all widows and dependents. As a result of this campaign, the *ex-gratia* pension was increased to two-thirds of the contributory rate in 1977, five-sixths in 1979, eleven-twelfths in 1986, and to full parity with the contributory scheme from 1 January 1992.

Amendments to the Scheme for Teachers, 1977

A number of amendments to the Teachers' Widows' and Children's Pensions Scheme were agreed with effect from 30 June 1977:

1   Pensionable service to qualify for benefit was defined as 'pensionable service given, together with the additional service which he [the teacher] could have had if he had served to normal retirement age'.
2   On the death of a member in service, a widow would receive one month's salary at the rate her husband had at the time of his death.
3   On the death of a pensioner, a widow would receive one month's pension at the rate of pension payable to her husband at the time of his death.
4   Children's pensions were improved to one-third of the widow's pension, subject to a maximum of three.
5   The first orphaned child would receive an amount equivalent to two-thirds of the widow's pension; the second child would receive one-third.
6   A child permanently incapacitated before he/she attained the age of sixteen, or the age of twenty-one if in full-time education, would continue to receive a pension as long as he/she was incapable of maintaining himself or herself.

Spouses' and Children's Contributory Pension Scheme, 1981

In June 1979 the INTO and ASTI submitted a claim to the Conciliation Council seeking an amendment to the Widows' and Orphans' Pension Scheme that would allow women to join. There was a delay in processing the claim as some female members of other unions were processing a similar claim at the Labour Court.

At Conciliation Council in January 1981 the Official Side offered a scheme to teachers that had already been accepted by the civil service unions. The INTO objected to this procedure on a number of grounds:

1   Teachers were being offered a *fait accompli* and thereby denied the opportunity to make representations about the provisions of the scheme or the necessary premium.
2   The unions that had accepted the new scheme were predominantly male; membership of the INTO was 80 per cent female and they were obliged to pay the same premium as men.

should not have to pay the same premium as men because actuarial ...cs confirmed that women lived longer than men, and the probability of a ...im being made on the death of a woman was less likely than on the death of a man and therefore the premium should reflect this fact.[11]

4   Commercial insurance companies sought a lower premium from women for all life insurance policies.

The Official Side refused to change the scheme as the other public service unions had already accepted it, and offering an amended scheme to teachers would cause too many problems. Discussions extended over a number of meetings and, eventually, with reservations, the INTO and the ASTI accepted the scheme, which came into effect from 1 June 1981.

The scheme, which was renamed the Spouses' and Children's Pension Scheme, gave a female teacher the opportunity to ensure that her husband and children would be protected if she predeceased her husband.[12] The same conditions of membership that had applied to men in 1968 were offered to women; they were in the scheme unless they opted out. Sixty per cent of women opted out of the scheme:

Details and Option Forms Distributed

Number of forms sent out	15,168
Number of teachers who opted in	1,368
Number of teachers who opted out	9,187
Number of teachers who did not reply	4,613

The benefits, which were available to either spouse, remained unchanged, but a number of new issues required clarification, and the following information was supplied:

- There was no cover available for the children of widows or single parents unless the people concerned married during membership of the scheme. If the single parent married, the child could be adopted and brought within the ambit of the scheme.
- The entitlement to a spouse's pension existed where a legal marriage was in existence at the date of the member's death. Therefore, legal separation, non-cohabitation or the grant of a Church annulment did not affect the issue unless the

---

11 Report of the Central Statistics Office (CSO), 24 June 2004: In 1926, men had a life expectancy of 57.4 years, while women could expect to live just 0.5 years longer. Life expectancy at birth for males born in 2002 was 75.1 years, compared to 80.3 for females.
12 Teachers' Conciliation Council Agreed Report 3/81

spouse in question was co-habiting or had remarried in Church law to another individual.
- People who married after retirement were not covered by the scheme.[13]

Due to delays in clarifying these matters the option date for teachers was extended to 30 November 1981. As a consequence of the change in date a number of concessions were negotiated:

- All female teachers, in pensionable service at any stage between 1 June 1981 and 31 October 1981, were given the option of joining the scheme or contracting out.
- Teachers who had previously opted out of the scheme could now opt in.
- Membership was compulsory for all new admissions to the National Teachers' Superannuation Scheme or the Secondary Teachers' Superannuation Scheme on or after 1 November 1981.
- Re-entrants to pensionable service on or after 1 November 1981, who had not previously contracted out of the scheme, were also compulsorily included in the scheme, except those who were not in pensionable service on the last day of the option period. They were granted an option to re-enter pensionable service.

The first pension deduction was made from salary cheques issued to female teachers on 16 December 1981; the arrears due for the period 1 June to 30 November 1981 were not deducted.

The Arrears Due

Early in September 1982 female teachers in the scheme were informed by the Department that it was intended to collect the arrears by instalments from salaries, with the first deduction being made from salaries on 9 September 1982. This communication caused many women to query their position. Some who had opted out now wished to opt in, some who had opted in now wished to opt out, and others stated that it was the first they had heard of the scheme and they wished to opt out.

In response to these complaints, the INTO requested the Department of Education to grant female teachers another opportunity to exercise options. Unexpectedly, the Department agreed that teachers who had not exercised their options (4,613 in number) and who had subsequently expressed a desire to opt out would be allowed to do so. This decision was welcomed by the INTO and it was not queried that the original circular had stated that where no reply was received, a person would be deemed to have opted for membership.

Subsequently, it transpired that the restricted re-opening of the option was mainly for the benefit of nuns. When the original forms went to the convents

---

13 Letter from General Treasurer to the Secretary of the Teachers' Conciliation Council, dated 9 October 1981, CEC Report to Congress 1982

they were not replied to and, consequently, the nuns were automatically included in the scheme; they became aware of this when they were informed about the arrears due. Both they and other teachers who had not exercised their options were given another opportunity to opt out.

The arrears due were collected from the other liable female teachers.

Revised Spouses' and Children's Pension Scheme, 1984

A revised Spouses' and Children's Pension Scheme came into operation for various categories of public servants on 1 September 1984, and it was offered to teachers. The following conditions applied:

1   The opportunity to exercise options was re-opened and the following would be permitted to join the revised scheme:
   • serving teachers who had opted out of the existing scheme
   • teachers who had opted out of the existing scheme and were now retired
   • surviving spouses of retired persons who had opted out of the existing scheme
   • surviving spouses of persons who had opted out of the existing scheme and had died in service

2   Pension cover was extended to the following categories of dependents:
   • the spouse and children (including step-children) of a member who married after retirement
   • children of non-married members
   • children conceived (or adopted) by a member after retirement
   • children of a member whose spouse died before membership commenced and who did not re-marry prior to retirement.

3   The following conditions were attached to the revised scheme:
   • Serving teachers (men and women) who were members of the existing scheme could remain in the old scheme or join the revised scheme.
   • New teacher appointees (other than religious) would automatically become members of the new scheme.
   • Members of the revised scheme who had not married by retirement would not be entitled to a refund of contributions made.

The INTO and ASTI recognised that the extra benefits would be welcome as would the re-opening of the option opportunities, but the non-refund of contributions was a major obstacle preventing acceptance of the revised scheme. It was calculated that, as a general rule, about 35 per cent of the teaching profession did not marry. Under the current scheme they had their contributions refunded; teachers joining the new scheme and all new teacher-appointees would not be entitled to a refund.

As the revised scheme had been accepted by all the other public servant unions, the Official Side was not prepared to offer an amended scheme to teachers.

Following consideration by their respective executives, the ASTI and the INTO advised the Conciliation Council that the terms offered were unacceptable.[14]

At a meeting on 2 January 1991 the Department of Finance again offered the revised scheme to the INTO and ASTI. As the conditions had not changed, the CECs decided not to accept the offer.

In 1993 the ASTI/INTO/TUI lodged a claim at Conciliation Council seeking an amendment to the Spouses' and Children's Pension Scheme which would allow contributors to assign the benefits. No offer was made on this claim.[15]

Review

The original scheme introduced for male teachers in 1968 was a significant social breakthrough. It ensured that the widow and relevant dependents of a male teacher, who died in the service or in retirement, had an income; this was of particular significance to one-income households. With the introduction of the new scheme, the standard of living of the family would be retained after the teacher's death.

The extension of the scheme in 1981 allowed women in the service to ensure that their spouses and children were protected.

The Commission on Public Service Pensions, established on 13 July 1996, issued an Interim Report in August 1997 and its Final Report on 14 November 2000. It recommended that:

- the offer made to primary and secondary teachers in 1984 to join the revised scheme should be repeated
- the scheme should be modified to allow payment to a nominated financially dependent partner
- the provision requiring a spouse's pension to cease on grounds of remarriage or co-habitation should be removed.

A revised Spouses' and Orphans' Scheme for teachers came into operation from 1 September 2005. Teachers in service had the option of retaining the conditions in the original scheme or joining the new scheme.

---

14 As members of the Local Government Superannuation Scheme the TUI had accepted the revised scheme.

15 The claim to permit assignment of benefits was conceded in 2003.

Indexation of Pensions

There was an inherent problem with regard to the pensions paid to retired public servants: once the amount of the pension had been fixed, there was no procedure for any amendments to compensate for inflation and rises in the cost of living. Consequently, the longer the pensioner lived the more his/her standard of living decreased and the more precarious his/her position became.

The Pensions (Increase) Act, 1920 authorised graded increases to public servants, but teachers in Ireland did not benefit to the same extent as others. During the late 1940s, the 1950s and 1960s different governments reviewed pensions but, while it was accepted that partial compensation should be paid, direct indexation was not deemed obligatory.

For many years the INTO endeavoured to persuade successive governments to accept the principle of parity of pensions; this would mean that salaries and pensions would increase from the same date and by the same proportionate amount. The teacher unions, in conjunction with the other public service unions, submitted claims to Conciliation Councils, but without success.

The Superannuation Act, 1947

Consolidated salary scales were introduced for civil servants with effect from 1 November 1946. The Superannuation Act, 1947 provided for an adjustment to their pensions, lump sum and gratuity awards.[16]

Teacher pensioners did not get their first increase until 1 April 1949 and, even then, it applied only to those who had retired prior to 31 October 1946.[17]

In 1950 increases ranging from 30 per cent on pensions in excess of £346 3s. 1d. and 50 per cent on pensions less than that amount were granted.[18] Pensions (Increases) Acts in 1956, 1959, 1960, and 1964 provided for graduated percentage increases; those in receipt of the highest pensions got the lowest percentage increase.[19] These Acts invariably applied only to those who had retired some years before the date when the particular Act was passed, i.e. the 1956 increase applied only to those who had retired before 1 November 1952.

Opposition members of the Dáil sought the indexation of pensions to the cost of living, in line with the system operating in other European countries. They argued that similar arrangements for automatic adjustment should be made for civil servants in Ireland.

---

16 Frank Aiken, Minister for Finance, DEPD, Vol. 108, col. 195
17 See Chapter 9
18 DEPD, Vol. 118, col. 2469
19 Civil service pensions in Britain and Northern Ireland had been increased seven times between 1920 and 1959, while they had been increased only three times in the Republic. Gerard Hughes, *The Irish Civil Service Superannuation Scheme*, p. 118

The Committee to Consider Post-Retirement Pension Adjustments in Public Service Pensions, 1964

In 1964 Senator Brosnahan tabled a motion in the Seanad calling on the government to adjust pensions to the level that current employees were receiving when going out in retirement. He was supported by fifteen Senators of all shades of political opinion. The Minister for Finance, Dr Ryan, stated that he was prepared to ensure that no pension would lose its cost-of-living value but that he was not prepared to agree that those on pension were entitled to a share in the expanding national prosperity.

A short time afterwards, in September 1964, he appointed 'The Committee to Consider Post-Retirement Pension Adjustments in Public Service Pensions'. It was to inquire into the principles that should underlie post-retirement adjustments in public service pensions.[20]

The committee investigated the public service pension provisions in fourteen OECD countries, mainly European. It submitted its report to the Minister for Finance in 1965.

The committee noted that about one-third of the countries surveyed had non-contributory pension schemes, while the remainder required their civil servants to contribute from 4 to 6.5 per cent of salary.[21] It found that most countries had formal arrangements for indexing civil service pensions in line with increases in the cost of living or with increases in the current pay of civil servants.[22] Only Ireland and countries in the British Commonwealth used informal methods of adjusting pensions.

The committee rejected a parity claim as it would be too costly and would give preferential treatment to employees in the public sector relative to employees in the private sector. It argued that any improvement in public servants' superannuation schemes should be matched by payment of a contribution.[23] It recognised that it would be difficult to get public service employees to make such a contribution and, consequently, suggested that non-contributors should bear part of the cost by having their pension based on pay averaged over the last three years of service rather than on retiring pay. The averaging would result in a reduction in the amount of pension paid, which would compensate for the additional benefit conferred by indexation. Such a proposition did not find favour with the public service unions.

The committee recommended that Ireland should adopt formal methods for indexing public service pensions in line with increases in the cost of living and

---

20 CEC Report to Congress 1965, p. 19

21 Gerard Hughes, *The Irish Civil Service Superannuation Scheme*, Table A1.4, p. 119

22 *Ireland* (1965) pp. 13–17, see Gerard Hughes, *The Irish Civil Service Superannuation Scheme*, p. 9

23 Existing pension schemes for civil servants, national teachers (pre-1968) and the defence forces were non-contributory.

that adjustments should be granted only when a pay increase was granted to serving personnel in all categories.[24] Enacting another recommendation of the committee, the Pensions (Abatement) Act of 1965 provided that, where a public service pensioner was re-employed, his/her pension would not be abated unless the employment was that from which the pensioner had retired.

While formal methods of indexation were eventually adopted from 1970, the quid pro quo recommendation of calculating pension on average pay in the last three years of service was not applied.

Superannuation Act, 1964

The 1964 Superannuation Act provided that future increases in public service pensions could be authorised by statutory regulations made by the Minister for Finance and tabled before the Houses of the Oireachtas. This power was used to issue Pensions (Increase) Regulations:

1   A regulation of 1966 provided for an increase of 5 per cent in pensions from 1 October 1964, based on salaries operating before the date of the eighth-round pay increase.

2   A second regulation of 1966 provided for an increase of approximately 9 per cent in pensions from 1 August 1965, based on salaries operating between the eighth and ninth-round pay increases.

3   A regulation of 1968 provided for an increase of up to 12 per cent on pensions from 1 August 1967, based on salaries operating prior to the ninth-round pay increase.

4   A regulation of 1969 provided for an increase of up to 5 per cent on pensions from 1 August 1968.

The New Era for Pensions, 1970

In his budget speech for 1969, Charles J. Haughey, Minister for Finance, announced that he had decided in principle to adopt parity and would move towards it over the coming years. As a start, the pensions of those who retired before the general pay revision of 1 February 1964 would be brought up to the level of the pensions of their colleagues who retired with the benefit of that pay revision, with effect from 1 August 1969.[25]

Regulations in 1971 provided for an increase with effect from 1 August 1970, which was based on June 1968 rates of pay. This narrowed considerably the gap between the date on which the increase in pension was given and the latest date of retirement to which it referred.

The principle of pension parity was progressed further in succeeding budgets. The Regulations for 1972, 1973 and 1974 granted increases in pension with

24 *Ireland* (1965) p. 19
25 CEC Report to Congress 1970, p. 8

effect from October of the previous year based on rates of pay in June 1969, January 1972 and July 1973, respectively. From 1975 to 1982 the regulations increased public service pensions on 1 July each year by reference to changes in the rates of pay of serving officers within the previous twelve months.

One result of these indexation moves during the 1970s was that pensions increased at a faster rate than pay, which in turn was increasing faster than consumer prices. The financial position of all retired public servants improved dramatically.

Full Parity, 1984

In December 1981 the Public Services Committee made representations to the Coalition Government to concede the long-standing public service claim for pension parity. Liam Kavanagh, Minister for Labour and the Public Service, responded that the matter would be considered at budget time and representations would be given due regard by the government in the course of its deliberations.

In 1983, during the course of the Public Service pay negotiations, a breakthrough was achieved. The Minister for the Public Service, John Boland, agreed, as an exceptional measure and subject to the acceptance of the pay proposals, that all public service pensions, including the pensions of those who retired on 31 August 1983, would be recalculated on 1 September 1983 on the basis of the first phase increase of the Public Service Pay Agreement. Thus, in this one instance full parity was conceded.

In his budget speech Alan Dukes, Minister for Finance, announced that the government had decided that, with effect from 1 February 1984, pensions would increase at the same rate and on the same dates as pay increases in accordance with terms negotiated in general pay agreements. This concession of parity would not apply in respect of grade or special salary increases; parity in that instance would be dealt with in the context of negotiations for the next pay round and the new arrangements would be implemented in 1985.[26]

The final step was taken by the Minister for Finance in the 1986 budget when he announced that the indexing arrangements would apply in respect of grade or special salary increases granted from 1 July 1986. Henceforth, the pensions of retired public employees would be increased at the same time as the salaries of comparable employees in the service, and at the same rate.

The additional benefit conferred by indexation was taken into account when considering salary reviews in the public service. The Review Body on Higher Remuneration in the Public Sector in 1979, and a Conciliation and Arbitration Board in 1983, built in a factor of 3 to 3.5 per cent as the value of post-retirement adjustments when comparing civil service pay to private sector pay.[27]

---

26 Budget, 1984, p. 16
27 Mr Hugh Geoghegan, Chairman, Conciliation and Arbitration Board, 3 May 1983

Indexation in Great Britain

The arrangements for the indexation of civil service pensions in Ireland are, in general, more advantageous to public servants than the arrangements for indexation in the British public service. In Ireland pensions are indexed in line with increases in pay, whereas in Britain they are indexed in line with increases in the cost of living. As pay generally increases faster than prices, the indexation arrangements in the Irish scheme mean that the real value of the pension actually increases during retirement whereas in Britain it remains constant.

Review of Indexation

In a little over twenty years the situation had changed fundamentally for public service pensioners. There was now an established procedure for automatic pension review, and indexation ensured that pensioners shared in the expanding national prosperity and were assured of a stable standard of living.

Pension Credit for Service in Capitation Schools

Commissioners of National Education

The commissioners changed the method of payment for teachers with effect from 1 October 1839, from a capitation basis to the payment of a personal set salary. The conductors of schools run by religious teaching orders were given the option of retaining the original capitation method or adopting the new classification salary system. The majority of the religious communities, mainly nuns, opted to retain the old capitation system. Thus, two categories of schools were created, 'Capitation Schools' and 'Classification Schools'

The conductors of 'Capitation Schools' received grants on the basis of a per capita payment in respect of each pupil in average enrolment, and lay assistant teachers employed in these schools were paid by the conductors of the schools. This changed following the salary agreement of 1920 when the assistants were paid directly by the commissioners. However, the service given by lay assistants or by members of religious communities in capitation schools was not recognised for pension purposes.

Teachers in classification schools, lay and religious, received personal salaries and were members of the pension scheme.

Department of Education

The system of 'Capitation Schools' and 'Classification Schools' was retained by the Department of Education after independence in 1922; nearly all convent schools and less than half of the monastery schools were capitation schools.

Capitation schools could elect at any time to change to the classification system.[28]

Lay assistants and JAMs were allowed to join the pension scheme of 1934, but even then only two-thirds of the service given prior to 1934 was recognised for pension purposes.

Report on Investment in Education, 1966

In 1966 a committee under the chairmanship of Patrick Lynch, Professor of Economics UCD, published a report entitled 'Investment in Education'.[29] The committee conducted a detailed investigation into the education systems in Ireland and made a series of recommendations which influenced governments in their decisions on the long-term further expansion of the education systems.

The different types of national schools in operation were identified as follows:

Ordinary schools, teachers paid by personal salaries	4,231
Convents, paid by personal salaries	92
Convents, paid by capitation	362
Monasteries, paid by personal salaries	91
Monasteries, paid by capitation	63
Total	4,839

The majority of monastery schools were classification schools, with the staff being paid personal salaries; this position only applied to 20 per cent of convent schools.

Pilot Studies

The Lynch Committee conducted two pilot surveys; the first examined capitation schools in Counties Offaly and Carlow, the second all schools in County Kildare. It was found that the majority of trained lay teachers employed in capitation schools tended to be young and were paid at the minimum of the salary scale. It was found that 20 per cent of 'recognised' religious community teachers were untrained, and, in addition, that 17 per cent of the total teaching force was made up of supernumeraries.

The State saved money because the communities had large numbers of nuns available to be employed as supernumeraries. If they had not been available, pressure would have built up, forcing the government to reduce teacher-pupil ratios and employ more trained teachers.

28 Rules for National Schools, Department of Education, 1934

29 Figures relate to the school year ended 30 June 1962, Department of Education Annual Report 1961–62, Investment in Education: report of the survey team appointed by the Minister for Education in October 1962, Pr. 8311 (1966)

Supernumerary Teachers

The supernumerary teacher, as the name implies, was an appointment in excess of the minimum staff permitted by the regulations of the Department of Education. The Lynch Report identified that, in addition to the 14,091 recognised national teachers, some 461 supernumerary teachers were employed in capitation schools. Practically all of them were women, over 74 per cent were untrained, and the great majority were nuns.

Trained supernumerary lay assistants were, invariably, young female teachers employed in convent schools because they had been unable to get permanent recognised posts.[30] The employment situation, particularly for young women, had been exacerbated when many married women returned to work following the removal of the marriage ban on 30 June 1958. Many teachers leaving training were glad to get a supernumerary position and did not question the conditions attached to the post; they were employed by the school on a year-to-year basis, were paid a salary at the minimum of the scale for assistant teachers, and had no right to a permanent position.

Teachers who had served as supernumeraries felt particularly aggrieved because untrained teachers and JAMs had been paid on an incremental scale and all their teaching service was recognised for pension purposes. The only concession they got was that up to five years' service given before 1947 would count for pension purposes.

The Lynch report concluded that:

> … from an economic point of view, however, these supernumeraries supply a service for which the State makes no payment … Their presence plays no small part in reducing the size of classes in capitation schools to manageable proportions.

These teachers started a campaign to address the disadvantages they suffered.

Pension Claim for Capitation Service

By the early 1970s two problems were coming to prominence with regard to teaching service given in capitation schools.

Fewer young people were joining the religious communities and becoming teachers, and many of the nuns and brothers of the teaching staff were approaching retirement age with no entitlement to pensions. The economic reality of supporting an ageing community from the capitation grant was beginning to cause serious concern to the conductors of religious communities.

In addition, significant numbers of nuns and brothers, who had served as

---

30 The conditions covering the appointment of a supernumerary are set down fully in Rule 87 (30) of the code of the Commissioners of Education and Rule 105, Department of Education.

teachers in capitation schools, were leaving their communities and taking up positions as lay teachers. These teachers were discovering that their previous service as members of capitation school communities did not count for pension purposes. They also found the transition to secular life difficult because they had lived in a closed community where all of their immediate needs had been supplied; they had never received a pay cheque and had no experience of dealing with the problems of budgeting and controlling their living situation.

Conciliation Agreed Report 5/75

In 1973 the INTO submitted the following two claims to Conciliation Council:

1   that all service given by teachers who were formerly members of Religious Orders should be taken into account for pension and gratuity[31]
2   that all service given by teachers who were serving, or had served in capitation schools, should be taken into account for the purpose of pension and gratuity. (This was the supernumerary claim.)

These claims were discussed at meetings held on 11 June and 1 November 1973, 11 April 1974, 30 April and 1 July, 1975.[32] While the INTO was processing the claims on behalf of its members, any concessions achieved would be of benefit to members of the communities who were still teaching, and to some lay teachers who had moved to teach in post-primary schools.

The basis of the INTO claims was that differentiation between service given by teachers in different categories of schools was inequitable and should be corrected. The ASTI and TUI supported the claim.

The Primary School Managers' Side supported the INTO claim in respect of the lay teachers but, in addition, claimed that teaching members of religious communities should have all service given by them recognised for pension purposes. The Secondary School Managers' Side supported these arguments.

The Official Side, while claiming that capitation payments had traditionally been regarded as including an element in lieu of pensions, conceded that there was some evidence to suggest that this element did not represent the full cost of pensions and there might be a case, therefore, that the State had a certain undischarged liability in this respect.

The Official Side stated that it could not under any circumstances agree to recognise capitation service per se for pension purposes but it was prepared to make the following offer:

---

31 The INTO had been successful in the past in getting all service as a member of staff of a capitation school recognised for increments.
32 Conciliation Council for Teachers, Agreed Report 7/75

... that in the case of teachers who were serving, or had served in capitation schools, and whose pensionable service ended on or after 30 June 1974, one-half of the service given by such teachers on the minimum staff of a capitation school would be reckoned as pensionable service under the National School Teachers' Superannuation Schemes.

The Official Side was not prepared to make any offer on the claim for supernumeraries, reiterating the cardinal principle 'that service which was not directly remunerated on a personal basis was not pensionable'.

The INTO representatives were disappointed with the offer but as the Official Side was not prepared to improve on it, and recognising the economic and budgetary situation of the time, they accepted the offer and the agreement was signed on 5 December 1975.

This pension concession was a considerable breakthrough and a very important principle had been conceded: service given by individual members of a religious order on the staff of capitation schools was recognised in its own right. While the concession was of benefit, it did not totally resolve the problem and many of those teachers suffered badly when they came to retire.

This agreement encouraged conductors of capitation schools to accelerate the transfer to classification status.

End of Capitation Service

By 30 June 1978 there was only one capitation school in the system; the rest had changed over to the classification system. The realisation that all service in a classification school qualified as pensionable service had had its effect.

Numbers of Different Types of National Schools

	1962	1978
Ordinary schools, teachers paid by personal salaries	4,231	2,873
Convents paid by personal salaries	92	425
Convents paid by capitation	362	1
Monasteries paid by personal salaries	91	150
Monasteries paid by capitation	63	0
Total	4,839	3,449 [33]

The changeover of schools from capitation to classification involved a radical change in the method of funding primary education. While the Department of

---

33 This figure of 3,449 includes 104 Special Schools. The decrease in the number of schools by 1,390 was a result of the amalgamation of small schools policy; the number of teachers increased from 14,091 to 17,083.

Education no longer had to pay capitation grants, it was now responsible for the direct payment of salaries to all primary teachers and responsible for the pensions for lay and religious teachers.

Conciliation Agreed Report 2/78

Conciliation Council Agreement 5/75 had recorded that one-half of the service given by a teacher on the minimum staff of a capitation school could be reckoned as pensionable service provided that, as a minimum, the previous five years of service was pensionable service given in classification schools or as a lay teacher in a capitation school.

The implementation of the five-year rule caused considerable difficulties, and the INTO was successful in having the five-year requirement reduced to one year in 1978.[34] No progress was made on the claim that all capitation service should be allowed in full for superannuation purposes.

The INTO continued to press for pension recognition for all of this service and, finally, in 1996 it was successful in having all service given in capitation schools conceded in the restructuring provisions of the 1996 Agreement on Pay and Conditions of Service.

Review of Capitation Service

From the end of the eighteenth century, communities of nuns and brothers had provided an education for girls and boys when there was no alternative system of education. When the national school system came on stream in 1831 they became an integral part of the system. The provision of facilities and finance was never sufficient, but the religious communities kept the system going from their own resources and those provided from other sources.

When the Irish Free State was established, there was not a town or a city that did not have one or more convent or brothers' school. The situation with regard to resources did not change; while money was scarce, education was never denied to those who wished to avail of it. By 1966 convent and monastery schools, capitation and classification, accounted for 12.5 per cent of all national schools in which 39 per cent of pupils were enrolled. This was probably the apogee of this development. Vocations to the religious orders began to decrease thereafter and many left the communities.

The purpose of the claim for the recognition of service given in capitation schools was but an effort to get compensation for what was, in many instances, a service never fully valued by the State but appreciated by those who benefited from it.

---

34 Conciliation Council for Teachers, Agreed Report 2/78

Specialist Teachers

In 1971 the President of the ICTU, Maurice Cosgrove, negotiated an agreement to resolve the differences between the teachers' unions arising from the Ryan Tribunal recommendations. One of the issues central to the ongoing dispute was the restoration of specialist teachers to their pre-1968 position of parity.

As the Conciliation and Arbitration Scheme was not formally established until 1973, the hearing of a claim that a pass degree allowance, a Higher Diploma in Education allowance and three increments should be paid to the teachers involved, was delayed. It was eventually considered at Conciliation Council on 13 November and 4 December 1973, and on 24 January 1974. Disagreement was recorded as the Official Side held that to concede it would breach the newly established pay relationships among teachers in general.

The arbitrator, R. J. O'Hanlon, ruled that the claim was not arbitrable under the Conciliation and Arbitration Scheme as it sought payment of a special allowance in favour of a category which had hitherto enjoyed no such allowance. This would involve the creation of a new and important principle in relation to teachers' salaries, and principles governing the remuneration of teachers were not arbitrable. He urged that some appropriate tribunal should be given jurisdiction to assess the claim on its merits as a matter of urgency.

All efforts made by the teacher unions to find a basis to have the claim processed were unsuccessful.

A Working Party

In November 1978 an inter-union working party under the chairmanship of Tom McGrath, Industrial Officer of the ICTU, was established to resolve this long outstanding claim.[35] Within a short period of time a unanimously agreed report was submitted to the three unions. The report was adopted by the CEC and endorsed by the Special Congress on 23–24 February 1979; it was also adopted by the TUI at its Annual Easter Convention in 1979, but the ASTI Standing Committee rejected it.

While the INTO and TUI were of the view that the report of the working party allowed for the formation of a claim that did not require an amendment to the Conciliation and Arbitration Scheme, all efforts to agree a common claim by the three teacher unions for submission to Conciliation Council failed.

The Review Body of 1980 recorded that due to the complexity of the issue and the conflicting positions taken on it by the different unions, it saw no way

---

35 The members of the working party were: Pierce Purcell (ASTI), Michael Cahill (ASTI), James Dorney (TUI), Christy Devine (TUI), Tom Gilmore (INTO), Gerry Quigley (INTO), and Tom McGrath (chairman).

of resolving the issue directly which would not create as many problems as it would solve.[36]

An agreed composite claim was presented to Conciliation Council on 6 February 1981 but the Official Side was not prepared to make any offer. It was referred to Arbitration, and in his report in November 1981, the arbitrator, Conor Maguire, again ruled that the claim was not arbitrable.

In 1984, following consultations between the General Secretaries of the three teachers' unions and the chairman of the Teachers' Conciliation Council, it was decided, once again, to table the specialist teachers' claim for further consideration. The teachers presented the claim at Council, and it was turned down again.[37]

In May 1984 Gemma Hussey, Minister for Education, met representatives of the three teacher unions to investigate the claim. She subsequently responded that she held out no hope, even in a more favourable economic climate, of a favourable adjudication of the claim, given its previous history.[38]

Information supplied by the Department of Education in 1984 put into context the scale of the problem and the probable cost:

Category of School	No. of Teachers	Cost
National	12,486 (84.8%)	£5,718,588
Secondary	795 (5.4%)	£364,110
Vocational	1,140 (7.8%)	£522,120
Comprehensive and Community	293 (2.0%)	£134,194
Total	14,714	£6,739,012

The table sets out the total cost to the Exchequer for the payment of an allowance equivalent to that for a BA Degree to teachers in national, vocational, secondary, and community and comprehensive schools, who were not in receipt of such an allowance.

The claim was put forward at the Employer-Labour Conference meetings in April 1986, as one of the unresolved claims on the Conciliation Council agenda that might be used as a trade-off against the £75m 'arrears due' retrospection claim arising from the 1985–6 Arbitration dispute. The Official Side stated that the claim was not up for consideration as part of any package to resolve the Arbitration dispute.

The claim was raised with the Minister for Education, Paddy Cooney, in July 1986. He stated that it was not possible, under the provisions of government pay policy, to consider the claim until 1989 at the earliest.

36 Review Body on Teachers' Pay, 1980, Interim Report, par. 3.2

37 Conciliation Council Report 4/84 recording disagreement on the claim

38 Letter from Peter Baldwin, Private Secretary to Minister for Education, to E. G. Quigley, CEC Report to Congress 1985, pp. 3–4

The claim remained unresolved until 1996 when the question of 'Qualification Allowances' formed a major part of the negotiations of the PCW Agreement. The specialist teachers' claim was finally resolved, in conjunction with the claim for a degree allowance for non-degree national teachers.

13

The Teachers United Era, 1982–87

Introduction

During this period regular meetings were held by representatives of the three teacher unions, ASTI, INTO and TUI. A number of items were permanently on the agenda, and on other occasions meetings were held to deal with specific items. Among the matters discussed were:

- Teachers' Salary Claims
- Specialist Teachers' Claim
- Conciliation & Arbitration
- Conditions of Service
- B Posts
- Education Cuts
- ICTU
- European Trade Union Committee for Education (ETUCE)
- Joint Services and Facilities
- School Discipline
- In-service Education
- Education for the Disabled
- Curriculum and Examinations Board
- Career Breaks/Job Sharing
- Teacher Indemnity
- Public Relations

While at times difficulties arose regarding particular items, every effort was made to maintain a united front.

Economic Difficulties, 1982

Government's Public Service Pay Freeze

In a surprise announcement on 30 July 1982 the Fianna Fáil government declared that, due to serious economic difficulties and disquieting deficits in the public finances, it intended to implement a series of measures to reduce public expenditure and thereby prevent an increase in taxation. It proposed:

- to request the Public Services Committee to postpone until 1 January 1983 the payment of the third phase of the 1981 public service pay agreement[1]
- that the government would not pay, or agree to pay, any further special pay increases in 1982 or in 1983
- to continue the existing embargo on the filling of vacancies in the public service until at least March 1983[2]
- to reduce projected expenditure for government departments for 1982 by £75 million, which would result in a reduction of £7.53 million in the estimates for the Department of Education.

On 6 August 1982 the Public Services Committee rejected the proposals on public service pay and turned down an invitation to talks from the Minister for the Public Service, Gene Fitzgerald. Furthermore, it recommended that the unions should participate in a co-ordinated campaign of industrial action to defend all pay agreements reached in the public sector.

The Council of Education Unions (CEU) agreed to co-operate fully with this programme of action.

On 9 August 1982 the General Purposes Committee of the ICTU denounced the government's proposed actions and sought an urgent meeting with the Taoiseach, declaring that:

> Congress wishes to emphasise that responsibility for any industrial relations breakdowns arising from the Government's statement must lie squarely with the Government for its cynical and dictatorial abrogation of agreements entered into with Trade Unions.[3]

A meeting with the Taoiseach on 17 August was inconclusive and subsequently the Taoiseach sent a detailed memorandum on the government's position to the Executive Council. The memorandum was considered at a special meeting on 19 August 1982 and, notwithstanding this, the Executive Council called for a mass trade union demonstration in Dublin on the afternoon of Friday, 24 September, and a subsequent national stoppage to coincide with the opening of the Dáil session in October 1982, to protest against the government's proposed action.

At a further meeting between the Executive Council and the Taoiseach on 10 September, the government accepted that pay policy for 1983–84 was a matter for determination by the unions operating through the relevant internal trade union channels. It was agreed that negotiations should proceed as quickly as

---

1   The third phase, which was for a period of five months, gave an increase of 5 per cent from 1 October 1982.

2   This embargo required that two out of every three vacancies should be left vacant.

3   CEC Report to Congress 1983, p. 10

possible and that consideration would be given to economic indicators such as unemployment, prices, jobs, taxation.

Renegotiation of the 22nd Pay Round

Discussions between representatives of the Public Services Committee and the Minister for the Public Service commenced on 20 September 1982 and, following two weeks of intensive negotiations, a draft agreement for an amendment to the 1981 Public Service Pay Agreement was reached on 4 October. The outcome of the negotiations was that:

1   the payment of the 5 per cent third phase, due on 1 October 1982, would be postponed to 1 January 1983
2   the money due for the period October–December 1982 would be paid in two equal instalments, on 1 February and 1 June 1983
3   special pay awards would be implemented over a phased period
4   unions would be entitled to process claims within the appropriate negotiating machinery, but no implementation date could be set
5   the existing provisions relating to minor claims particular to an individual employment would be maintained
6   the existing provisions relating to claims arising out of a structural or significant technological change, etc., would be maintained
7   superannuation entitlements would be protected.

All public service unions held ballots of their members on the draft agreement and it was accepted by a substantial majority.[4]

Early in December 1982, in order to protect their negotiating position with regard to 'special' or 'status' pay settlements in other sections of the public service, the teacher unions submitted a holding claim to the Teachers' Conciliation Council (ref. 182/82).

On 14 December 1982 the Fianna Fáil government was replaced by a Fine Gael/Labour Coalition government, with Garret FitzGerald as Taoiseach, Alan Dukes as Minister for Finance, John Boland as Minister for the Public Service and Gemma Hussey as Minister for Education.[5]

In January 1983 the Minister for Education declared that the government intended to cut a range of educational services in each of the education sectors.

The teacher unions organised demonstrations against the cuts, and an estimated 7,000 teachers took part in a demonstration in Dublin on 26 January 1983.

---

4   Conciliation Council for Teachers, Agreed Report 6/82
5   This government remained in power until 10 March 1987.

23rd Pay Round, Public Service Pay Agreement, 1983

As the 22nd Pay Round was due to terminate in various employments by the end of December 1982 or early in 1983, the Executive Council of the ICTU issued a document providing general guidelines on the pay policy to be pursued in the next pay round.[6]

All the public service unions, including the teachers' unions, submitted cost-of-living salary claims to their respective Conciliation Councils. The claim submitted by the teachers (ref. 200/83) is not to be confused with the 'status' claim lodged in December 1982 (ref. 182/82).

From the government's perspective it was far better to have a centralised negotiated agreement, but the Public Services Committee refused to enter into negotiation until a pattern of settlements in the private sector had emerged. Eventually, following a declaration from the Minister for the Public Service that there was a basis for genuine negotiations on public service pay, discussions commenced on 21 April 1983.[7]

Following lengthy negotiations, a draft salary settlement was agreed. It would operate from the end of the 23rd Round agreement and last for a period of fifteen months. Its provisions were as follows:

- The first stage from 1 March 1983 would be for six months, during which a pay pause would apply.
- The second stage would be for five months and basic pay would be increased by 4.75 per cent.
- The third stage would be for four months and basic pay would be increased by 3.25 per cent.
- Minor claims, which were particular to an individual employment, could be negotiated by the relevant employers and trade unions.
- The existing arrangements under the 1981 and 1982 agreements for the processing of other claims would continue.

In addition, Minister John Boland agreed that, subject to the acceptance of the pay proposals, all public service pensions, including the pensions of those who retired on 31 August 1983, would be recalculated on 1 September 1983 on the

---

6   The 22nd Pay Round was due to end for teachers on 28 February 1983.

7   The Public Services Committee negotiating team was: Greg Maxwell, Chairman, Union of Professional and Technical Civil Servants (UPTCS); Doug McEvoy, Vice-Chairman, Local Government and Public Services Union (LGPSU); Dan Murphy, Secretary, Confederation of Shipbuilding and Engineering Union (CSEU); Gerry Quigley, INTO; Terry Quinlan, Post Office Workers Union (POWU); Kevin Duffy, Building Workers Trade Union (BWTU), and one representative each from Irish Transport and General Workers Union (ITGWU) and Federated Workers Union of Ireland (FWUI).

basis of the first phase salary increase. This was a significant breakthrough regarding recognition of pension parity. A claim that the retirement lump sums for those retiring on 31 August 1983 should also be recalculated was not conceded.

A majority of INTO members voted in favour of accepting the agreement and it was endorsed by the Teachers' Conciliation Council on the 29 September 1983.[8]

The Public Service Arbitrator, 1984

A new public service arbitrator was due for appointment from 1 August 1984 and, due to the perceived delay by the government in sanctioning an appointment, the Public Services Committee threatened to hold a national one-day protest stoppage of all public service unions on Wednesday, 3 October 1984. On 24 September the Minister for the Public Service announced the re-appointment of Hugh Geoghegan SC for a further one-year term.

Building on Reality, 1985–1987

The government's economic plan *Building on Reality, 1985–1987* was published in July 1984. The plan provided that special salary increases sanctioned up to then or already committed would be paid but that there would be only minimal increases in public service pay over the following three years:

> It is the government's hope that public service employees who have relatively secure jobs will accept that the national interest requires a policy of this kind if new jobs are to be created for our young people and for those at present unemployed.[9]

The INTO rejected the government's proposals on pay and stated that any attempt to set aside awards made to teachers under the agreed scheme of Arbitration would lead to industrial action and disruption of the education service.

The government's estimates for 1985 made no provision for salary increases. The teacher unions issued a joint statement claiming that an increase of approximately 15 per cent would be necessary to restore salaries to 1981 levels and that an additional increase of the order of 8 to 10 per cent would be required to compensate for projected inflation. Tables were published which showed that 38 per cent of teachers' salaries was retained by the Exchequer in taxation, contributions to pensions, PRSI (Pay-Related Social Insurance) and levies.[10]

---

8 Teachers' Conciliation Council Agreed Report 6/83. The agreement would end for teachers on 31 May 1984.

9 *Building on Reality 1985–1987*, Government Publications Office, July 1984

10 A written question was submitted by Proinsias de Rossa, TD, to the Minister for Education requesting information for the tax year 1983–84. The written response was forwarded to the teacher unions.

24th Round, Public Service Pay

The teacher unions presented their cost-of-living salary claim at Conciliation Council on 5 April 1984 and it was discussed at a number of meetings. On 25 September, as the Official Side was not prepared to make any offer, disagreement was recorded and teachers indicated that they intended to proceed to Arbitration.[11]

For tactical reasons the teacher unions decided not to proceed immediately to Arbitration as several critical public sector claims were being processed at that time and results from them would influence the teachers' case.

Although the 23rd Round Pay Agreement ended on 31 May 1984, it was not until 9 November 1984 that the Minister for the Public Service invited representatives of the Public Services Committee to a meeting to discuss proposals on pay in the public service. The committee declined his request stating that it was surprised to receive his invitation at that stage as the current round was at an advanced stage of negotiation throughout the public service; civil servants had referred a salary claim to the arbitrator. Furthermore, he had publicly stated that there was no scope for negotiations.

A request from the Minister for a meeting to discuss machinery for pay determination in the public service was also declined.

Early in December 1984, the teacher unions submitted their cost-of-living claim, seeking an increase of 14 per cent, to the Teachers' Arbitration Board. They also claimed that the phasing arrangements in place for the payment of grade claims should be revised.

Cost-of-Living Civil Service Arbitration Award, 1985

On 10 January 1985 the arbitrator recommended a nineteen-month pay agreement for civil servants as follows:

- a seven-month pay pause from 1 June 1984 to 31 December 1984
- a 3 per cent increase with effect from 1 January 1985 to 30 June 1985
- a 3 per cent increase with effect from 1 July 1985 to 31 December 1985.[12]

This finding put pressure on the Minister for the Public Service and he invited the Public Services Committee to meet him for discussions on a general increase in public service pay. The committee met the Minister on 28 January 1985 but the negotiating teams found it impossible to reach agreement.

Before the Arbitration Board could be convened to consider the teachers' claim, the government offered the terms of the civil servants' Arbitration award to all civil and public service unions. The CEC, at its meeting on 1 February

11 Teachers' Conciliation Council Report 6/84 recording disagreement
12 Arbitration Report No. 448

1985, decided to accept the offer.[13] The alternative course would have been to proceed to Arbitration where the claim would be considered by the same arbitrator and he would make the same award.

Conciliation Council Agreed Reports, 1982–85

During the period from Easter 1982 to Easter 1985, in addition to claims for increases in basic salary, the Teachers' Conciliation Council considered many other claims. Agreement was reached on a number of them, disagreement was recorded on others, and many were postponed for further consideration. Only 'minor claims' could be processed under the terms of the 1983 Public Service Pay Agreement and, even though some concessions were of major significance, the Official Side agreed to classify them as 'minor claims' so that they could be processed.

1   Agreed Report 2/84

The Official Side agreed that, with effect from the commencement of the school year 1983–84, the allowance of a principal or vice-principal, which was due to be reduced because of a fall in the points rating of the school, should be retained on a personal basis so long as he/she remained in that post in the school.

2   Agreed Report 3/84

Agreed Report 3/84 recommended that 'other allowances' should be increased by 25 per cent in line with the terms of Clause 4.2 (d) of the 1983 Public Service Pay Agreement, i.e. 40 per cent of the increase from 1 October 1983, and the balance from 1 December 1984.

3   Agreed Report 5/85

This Agreed Report allowed teachers, whether lay or members of religious communities, to get up to seven years' incremental credit for service given in overseas countries designated as being under-developed; the previous limit had been five years (Agreed Report 9/79).

4   Agreed Reports 3/85 and 3/86

From the introduction of allowances for qualifications an anomaly had existed with regard to the allowance paid to teachers for different classes of Masters' degrees.

The allowance for a Master's degree by thesis or examination was considerably less than the allowance for a Master's degree (1st or 2nd Honours) and only half the value of the allowance for Primary Degree (1st or 2nd

---

13 Teachers' Conciliation Council Agreed Report 2/85

Honours). The Review Body in 1980 had recommended that all Masters' degrees should be at the rate applicable to an Honours Master's degree. The unions submitted a claim on 12 December 1983 and, finally, in 1985 the claim was conceded for degrees awarded by universities in the Republic with effect from 1 April 1985.[14]

It was subsequently agreed that unclassified Masters' degrees awarded by Scottish/English/Welsh/Northern Ireland universities would be assessed by the Department of Education on the basis of statements from the university or educational authority concerned, and those awarded by other universities would be assessed on an individual basis by the Department of Education.

Arbitrator's Report

At a Conciliation Council meeting on 23 January 1985 the Official Side accepted the arbitrator's finding that principals in one-teacher schools should retain their allowance where the loss would occur due to circumstances outside their control, i.e. due to falling enrolments. He was not prepared to concede the same concession for the Island, Gaeltacht, Teaching through Irish, or Itinerant Domestic Science allowances.

Payment of Salary Cheques

The issue of monthly salary cheques directly to teachers was conceded in 1918, and from the mid-1950s teachers could apply to receive salary twice a month.

In 1979 and again in 1982 the INTO sought the introduction of fortnightly pay for teachers but the Department of Finance turned down the requests. Finally, with effect from December 1992, fortnightly pay was introduced for national teachers. Under the new payroll system permanent and temporary teachers would receive 26 salary cheques each year.

In July 2004, twenty years after the introduction of fortnightly pay for serving teachers, pensioners were paid their pension on a fortnightly basis.

A PayPath facility[15] was introduced for national teachers from 3 December 1984; teachers could designate a financial institution into which they could have their salary electronically lodged. Pensioners also had the PayPath facility made available to them.

Department of Education, Athlone

The decentralisation of the Primary Section to offices in Athlone caused considerable difficulties for the Department of Education. Members of staff in Dublin were given the option of moving to Athlone or being redeployed

---

14 Teachers' Conciliation Council Agreed Report 3/85
15 The electronic transfer of pay from an employer's to an employee's bank account

elsewhere in the civil service. Many members of staff, with years of experience in the Department of Education, were redeployed to other sections within the general civil service. Vacancies in the Department of Education were filled by officers from other Departments who were willing to move. When the section moved to Athlone it contained sixty new members of staff.

Notional Service Purchase Scheme (NSPS), 1983

A scheme for the purchase of notional service for pension purposes was introduced for the civil service, for employees in the public service and for those in Local Government. The notional service could be purchased by payment of periodic or lump sum contributions.

Even though the teacher unions lodged a claim in December 1979 for a similar scheme for their members, an agreement was not signed until 17 May 1982.[16] The scheme allowed a teacher to purchase any number of years of notional service as long as he/she did not have more than a total of forty years at the date of normal retirement; it was not possible to buy years to satisfy early retirement requirements.

Over the years the INTO submitted many claims seeking amendments to the early retirement provisions for teachers but they were always turned down due the prohibitive cost that would be incurred from the immediate payment of pensions and lump sums.

At a Conciliation Council meeting in March 1990, the Official Side offered an early retirement scheme that would allow teachers to retire at age fifty or over with pension and lump sum computed in accordance with actuarial tables. The teacher unions rejected it.

Arbitration Dispute, 1985–86

In December 1982 the following 'status' claim had been lodged at Conciliation Council by the teacher unions:

> That the salary and allowances paid to teachers in primary, secondary, vocational, community and comprehensive schools be increased to take account of pay awards in both the civil and public service since 1st September, 1980. (ref. 182/82)

During the following two years the claim was debated with the Official Side on a number of occasions but other matters intervened to prevent it being resolved:

- government's proposed pay freeze in 1982
- change of government on 14 December 1982

---

16 Teachers' Conciliation Council Agreed Report 10/81

- negotiations on the 23rd Round Public Service Agreement
- the publication of the economic plan *Building on Reality, 1985–1987* in 1984
- negotiations on the 24th Round Public Service Agreement.

Eventually, in December 1984, disagreement was recorded on the claim and the teacher unions referred it to Arbitration.[17]

The Arbitration Board convened on 27 June 1985 to determine the claim.

The Arbitrator's Findings, 7 August 1985

On 7 August 1985, in accordance with established procedure, the arbitrator sent a confidential copy of his preliminary report to the parties. He recommended that the salary and allowances of all teachers should be increased by 10 per cent, 5 per cent with effect from 1 September 1985, and the balance with effect from 1 March 1986.

However, in a departure from the practice that had applied with all previous Arbitration reports, the terms of this draft report were leaked to the media.[18] The teacher unions were convinced that the report was leaked by a government source in order to provide another opportunity for government Ministers to continue their attack on the public service and, on this occasion, on teachers in particular.[19]

Statements issued by Ministers seemed to lend credence to this view, and in another instance on 12 August *The Cork Examiner* attributed a government spokesman as saying, 'there will be no backing down on the government's decision not to concede the special 10 per cent teachers' award'.

It was estimated that the increase would cost £10 million in 1985, £55 million in 1986, and £60 million in each subsequent year. These increases would cause problems for the government due to the economic difficulties in the country and adverse public finances.

In its submission the Official Side had requested the arbitrator to reject the claim irrespective of its merits because of the serious plight of the public finances. The arbitrator stated that he had taken full regard of the economic circumstances of the State but that he had considered the claim on its merits, as not to do so 'would constitute a quite unjustified discrimination against teachers as distinct from all other professional grades in the public service'.[20]

On 14 August 1985 the government proposed that there should be no pay increases in the Public Service for at least twelve months from the expiry dates of the 24th Round Public Service Agreement.

---

17 Teachers' Conciliation Council Report 1/84 recording disagreement on the claim
18 The provisions of the Conciliation and Arbitration Scheme state 'the proceedings of the Board will be confidential and no statement concerning them will be issued other than the Chairman's report'.
19 CEC Report to Congress 1986, p. 2
20 Arbitration Board Report No. 14

This announcement drew an immediate angry response from trade unions, and Donal Nevin, General Secretary ICTU, issued a statement the following day:

> If the Minister's statement is a first indication of a threat to dismantle the Conciliation and Arbitration Scheme in the public services, then it is embarking on a path that out-Thatchers anything that has been done by the present British Government.[21]

On 19 August the Minister for Education, Gemma Hussey, in a statement to a Fine Gael meeting in Bray that clearly referred to the teachers' Arbitration award, stated, *inter alia*:

> It is vital that all those organisations that publicly clamour for increases should address themselves to the morality of what they are about: are they so bound up in self-justification and media attention that they can't stand back for the sake of the country? ... I find it difficult to imagine that teachers would calmly watch some of the weak sections of the economy penalised, or see education services directly cut back, in order to improve their position ... It is only sanity for Ireland to say to itself that a paroxysm of industrial unrest at this juncture would undo all the advances of the last few years. Equally, an increase in pay at this juncture would achieve the same sorry result.[22]

On RTÉ radio on 20 August Minister Hussey stated that payment of the teachers' award would mean that the government's public service pay policy would be 'seriously breached' and that 'the award simply can't be paid'.

The attack by the Minister for Education on teachers and their unions was regarded as 'a singularly inept and offensive attack on public service unions in general and teachers' unions in particular'; and her advice 'that those organisations who publicly clamour for increases should address themselves to the morality of what they are about' was seen as arrogant.

The quotation about the 'morality' of the unions seeking payment of the arbitrator's findings was to prove to be of enormous advantage to the teacher union leaders in the subsequent campaign. It was quoted very often to the disadvantage of the Minister.[23]

The Teacher Unions' Plan of Action

Representatives of the three teacher unions met on 26 August to draw up proposals to initiate a campaign to secure payment of the Arbitration award. Later that week a 'Plan of Action', containing the following resolutions, was approved:

---

21 CEC Report to Congress 1986, p. 6
22 Ibid., p. 2
23 CEC Report to Congress 1986, p. 5

1 In the event of the government refusing to honour a public service Arbitration Award, the three teacher unions, ASTI, INTO and TUI, will initiate a programme of industrial action which will include the withdrawal of teaching staff. This action will at various stages affect every primary and post-primary school in the country.

2 Mass meetings will be held in each area to coincide with the industrial action. The meetings will be addressed by officers of the unions concerned.

3 Public representatives will be lobbied concerning their attitude to the implementation of the award.

4 A national one-day strike will be held in December 1985.

5 A common bulletin will be prepared by the three teacher unions for distribution to their respective membership.

6 The unions will not participate in any negotiations to amend the award in any respect.

In September a National Co-ordinating Committee, with three representatives from each union, was established to manage the 'Teachers United' Arbitration campaign.[24] The committee met regularly to develop strategy, implement the overall plans of the campaign, and oversee the issue of 'Teachers United Bulletins' and other documentation to members. Press matters were dealt with on a daily basis by each of the unions in turn. A campaign action fund was established and each union contributed to expenses incurred in proportion to their membership.

County campaign co-ordinators were appointed in every county on the following basis – one representative from each union per county and four representatives from each union for Dublin. They were responsible for the co-ordination of joint activities in their areas, such as organising and supervising strikes, maintaining local media contact, lobbying public representatives, and maintaining close links with their head offices.[25] Briefing sessions were arranged for the county co-ordinators and documentation was circulated to them on a regular basis to keep them informed about issues as they arose.

Special Branch meetings were held during September and October to brief members on the campaign.

The Teachers United group held meetings with political parties. Three political parties declared that they were in favour of retention of the Conciliation and Arbitration machinery and the honouring of the Arbitration awards; Fine

---

24 The National Co-ordinating Committee became known colloquially as 'the Nine Apostles'.

25 The first general meeting of the co-ordinators was held in Dublin on 28 September 1985 and an information pack was distributed. The pack contained a newsletter, statistics on the claim, lists of public representatives, guidelines and advice on issuing letters to the papers and on dealing with local media.

Gael representatives expressed support for the Conciliation and Arbitration system but would not commit themselves to honouring the award in full.

The ICTU and the Public Services Committee

On 4 September the Public Services Committee recommended that affiliated unions should stage a one-day strike by all workers in the public service on 15 October 1985 to protest against the government's proposed public service pay freeze and its failure to re-appoint a public service arbitrator. The Dublin Teacher Union Co-ordinators organised the participation of teachers in the one-day strike.

The Taoiseach, Garret FitzGerald, wrote to the Executive Council of the ICTU on 7 October 1985 inviting it to meet with him to discuss, among other things, an appropriate process that would enable the government to avert the strikes.

The Executive Council replied, stating that it could not accept the invitation as there was an established mechanism to discuss public service pay, the Public Services Committee.[26]

Subsequently, on 9 October 1985, the Minister for the Public Service, John Boland, invited the Public Services Committee to meet him to try to find a solution to the public service pay problems. The committee met the Minister on 11 October but it proved abortive as the Minister would not agree to the committee's conditions on the pay freeze, Arbitration/Labour Court awards, and the appointment of an arbitrator.

The one-day stoppage by public service unions took place on 15 October and was supported by upwards of 6,000 teachers.

Following the one-day strike the Public Services Committee declined another request for a meeting as there was no indication of a change in the government's position and it did not wish to become a forum for central discussions with the government on pay in the public service.

This decision was influenced by the teacher unions who held the view that it would be inappropriate for any other union, or group of unions, to discuss the teachers' special award.

Throughout December and January 1986 reports of discussions held by the Minister for the Public Service with individual civil service and other public service unions were leaked regularly to the media. It was clear that the government was doing everything possible to try to subvert the negotiating position of the teacher unions.

The Teachers United Campaign

Teachers United decided that a national one-day stoppage would take place on 5 December 1985 but that this would be preceded by a series of one-day

---

26 CEC Report to Congress 1986, pp. 3–4

regional strikes. The country was divided into eleven regions and, in conjunction with the strikes, general meetings attended by members of the three unions were held in central venues in each area. Each rally was addressed by three members of the Teachers United Committee, one from each union.

National One-Day Teachers' Strike

Croke Park, Dublin, the national stadium of the Gaelic Athletic Association (GAA), was secured as the venue for the national one-day strike rally on 5 December 1985.[27] Over 22,000 teachers, about 50 per cent of the total teaching force in the country, travelled by special trains, coaches and cars to Croke Park.

In addition to Irish trade union leaders, representatives of teachers' international bodies, the World Confederation of Organisations of the Teaching Profession (WCOTP) and the International Federation of Free Teacher Unions (IFFTU), addressed the rally.

The teachers paraded through Dublin city and congregated at Molesworth Street, opposite the gates of Dáil Éireann in Kildare Street; the rally finished with some more speeches, and a letter addressed to the Taoiseach was delivered to the Dáil.[28]

Conciliation Council

Following exchanges of correspondence between the three unions and the Conciliation Council, a meeting of the Conciliation Council was held on 16 December 1985. The Official Side stated that it was prepared to make an offer on the 25th Pay Round subject to two essential conditions:

1 that agreement would have to be arrived at between the two sides on the phasing of outstanding Arbitration findings and the processing of any further claims for special increases
2 that meaningful discussions, as a matter of urgency, would have to take place about the machinery for pay determination.

The 25th Round pay offer made to teachers consisted of three phases, was for a period of twenty-four months, and contained an overall increase of 5 per cent.

---

27 Cumann na mBunscoil is a national organisation of primary school teachers whose principal objective is to organise and support the playing of the GAA's national games in primary schools. Liam Mulvihill, Director General GAA, had trained as a national school teacher and also served for a number of years as a schools inspector of the Department of Education. His predecessor as Director General, Seán Ó Siocháin, also trained as a national teacher and had been involved in the 1946 teachers' strike. Many teachers have been Presidents of the GAA, the majority of these were national teachers.

28 A video was made of the proceedings on that day and copies were made available from the union head offices. A special souvenir issue of the 'Teachers United' bulletin was also produced.

The teachers' representatives rejected the offer and responded:

- that the government was in breach of the Conciliation and Arbitration Scheme by failing to appoint an arbitrator
- that the unions had been prepared to discuss the machinery for pay determination over the last two years but the Official Side had not; the teachers were still prepared to enter into discussions
- that the implementation of an Arbitration award could not be discussed in the Conciliation Council as the matter had already been determined.

The teachers' representatives demanded a direct meeting with the Ministers, and the Official Side undertook to arrange this meeting.

Direct Discussions with Ministers

Meetings between the teachers' representatives and the Ministers for Education and the Public Service were held on 2, 10, 13 and 15 January 1986. At the meeting on 15 January the Minister for the Public Service tabled a revised 25th Round offer; it was an improvement on the offer made on 16 December 1985 as it offered an overall increase of 7 per cent. This new offer also contained proposals for the long-phasing of Arbitration awards, commencing on 1 December 1986; this was to the disadvantage of teachers as the arbitrator had granted them a first phase increase from 1 September 1985.

The Minister stated that as these terms had been accepted by the other unions, they would not be improved on and that there was no question of any back-money being paid.

The acceptance by the civil service unions of the phasing-in of Arbitration awards was a set-back for teachers. While it could be claimed that the phasing applied only to civil service awards, the government could claim that it should apply to all awards paid from Central Funds.

The teachers' representatives rejected the proposals as they were being presented as a *fait accompli* without any input from the teacher unions. They stated that they could not be bound by the result of negotiations conducted by other trade unions; only the teacher unions were entitled to negotiate on behalf of teachers.

On 21 January 1986 the teachers' unions again wrote to the Ministers for Education and the Public Service to formally demand the appointment of an arbitrator. The three General Secretaries wrote to the Taoiseach on 24 January 1986 requesting him to intervene personally in the dispute. No response was received from the Taoiseach.

On 30 January 1986 a reply was received from the Minister for Education to the letter sent on 21 January, which stated:

If it were possible for your unions to give me a commitment that you would take away for decision by your members the draft 'Proposals for a Pay Agreement' settled in negotiations with other public service unions (copy attached) I would, for my part, be prepared to recommend that the Government appoint an arbitrator in the immediate future. In saying this I have taken into account the commitment you have already given to enter into meaningful discussions (to be completed by 1 August, 1986) about changes in the C&A Scheme. I would of course, be only too pleased to meet with you should you wish to have clarification on any of these matters.

The main points of the draft 'Proposals for a Pay Agreement' were as follows:

1   The 25th Pay Round would be for a period of eighteen months as follows:
    • four-month pay pause from 1 January 1986
    • 3 per cent increase from 1 May 1986, the phase to last for eight months
    • 2 per cent from 1 January 1987, the phase to last for four months
    • 2 per cent from 1 May 1987, the phase to last for a period of two months.

2   The Arbitration award would be paid in the following way:
    • one-third of the relevant increase from 1 December 1986
    • one-third of the relevant increase from 1 December 1987
    • the outstanding balance to be paid from 1 July 1988.

The teachers replied stating that no clarification of the government's position was required.

With no sign of the teachers' campaign coming to an end, the government announced that it intended to introduce a motion in Dáil Éireann to set aside the arbitrator's award and to substitute alternative proposals. This procedure was permitted under the provisions of the Conciliation and Arbitration Scheme, but it had never been invoked.

The Teachers United group immediately set in train a major campaign to counter the government's intentions. Meetings were held with the various political parties over the period 28–31 January 1986. County co-ordinators organised a canvas by local teachers of all TDs in their own constituencies. Some 200,000 postcards were printed and distributed to all union members for posting to local TDs asking them to support the payment in full of the Arbitration award.

Statement by the ICTU Executive Council, 4 February 1986

On 4 February 1986 the ICTU Executive Council issued a second statement condemning the government for its continued failure to reappoint an arbitrator. It advised that as, in its opinion, the Irish Government was in breach of its obligations under the International Labour Organisation's conventions by virtue of its non-appointment of an arbitrator and in the manner in which it set aside an award made to teachers under the Conciliation and Arbitration Scheme, it proposed to have the matter raised at the forthcoming International Labour Conference in Geneva, as indicated by Norman Goble, Secretary General of WCOTP at the rally in Croke Park.

The Executive Council stated that it was reluctant to take this step and arraign the government before this international forum for a breach of an international convention, but unless the government appointed the arbitrator without further delay it would have no option.

This action of the Executive Council was viewed by the teachers as a major victory as they considered that the government, and in particular, the Taoiseach, Garret FitzGerald, would be concerned about its reputation at a major international forum.

The Dáil Vote, 6 February 1986

On Thursday, 6 February 1986 the Minister for Education, Gemma Hussey, proposed a motion in Dáil Éireann on behalf of the government to set aside the arbitrator's award and to substitute a proposal to pay the 10 per cent award in three phases, one-third from 1 December 1986, one-third from 1 December 1987, and one-third from 1 July 1988.

After a four-hour debate the motion was adopted in the Dáil. The government parties, with the support of the Progressive Democrats, had a majority of twelve votes in the division. The Fianna Fáil amendment to the motion, calling for further talks regarding the implementation of the award, was defeated.

The teacher unions condemned the government on this unprecedented action and at Special Delegate Conferences an 8 February motions were adopted instructing the respective executives to ballot members on strike action.

The Minister for Education criticised the union leadership on this action and questioned teachers' constitutional and legal rights to withdraw their services. This statement further inflamed the situation. The teachers responded, claiming that not only did they have a legal and constitutional right to withdraw service, but that they were entitled to engage in industrial action under the provisions of the C&A Scheme.

Strike ballots were conducted at specially convened meetings and the overall results were as follows:

Union Total	Valid Poll	In Favour
ASTI	7,564	6,017 (80%)
INTO	15,698	13,366 (85.14%)
TUI	75% of membership	81% of votes cast

The Teachers United Committee decided that strike action should take place during the period prior to Easter.

Teachers United Opinion Polls

During the campaign Irish Marketing Surveys conducted a number of polls on behalf of Teachers United. The purpose of the polls was to ascertain public reaction to the teachers' campaign, and also to gauge public opinion on the manner in which the government was dealing with the teachers. Teachers United used the information to determine its strategy on future actions.

A poll conducted between 11 and 22 January 1986, and published on 7 February, indicated that the government appeared to be out of touch with the views of the general public, and with parents in particular, on the payment of the teachers' Arbitration award. It also showed that the Minister for Education had dropped three places to fifth in the public's rating of the performance of individual Ministers.[29]

Political analysts concluded that the Minister's fall in the public's rating was directly related to her handling of the teachers' Arbitration dispute. On 13 February the Taoiseach announced a Cabinet reshuffle; Patrick Cooney was appointed Minister for Education and Gemma Hussey Minister for Social Welfare.[30]

The Strike

The executives of the teacher unions organised a programme of regional strikes that would take place on three days in three consecutive weeks in March.

The strikes in the three regions took place and all teachers participated. The Arbitration dispute was the main item of concern at the annual conferences during Easter 1986. Delegates were given a report on the campaign and resolutions were adopted congratulating Teachers United and instructing the CECs to take whatever action it deemed necessary to secure full implementation of the Arbitration award.[31]

After the Conferences

Following the conferences the ASTI and TUI conducted a ballot of their members on industrial action and a ban on certificate examinations. The

---

29 In August 1985 Irish Marketing Surveys had conducted an opinion poll for *The Sunday Independent* on the public's rating of the performance of individual Ministers. Gemma Hussey was ranked second among members of the cabinet.

30 At this time also, government plans to cease funding Carysfort College of Education were leaked to the president of the college.

31 The INTO Congress was held in Tralee from 30 March to 4 April 1986. A full account of the actions taken by Teachers United in organising the campaign was printed in the CEC Report to Congress 1987, p. 1

Minister condemned this proposed action and announced that he intended to recruit inexperienced and untrained personnel to mark and assess certificate examination papers. On 13 April 1986 the Teachers United Committee placed a large advertisement in all of the national Sunday newspapers questioning the Minister's intentions and asking parents to use their influence with local TDs to bring the dispute to an end.[32]

The Minister for Social Welfare, Gemma Hussey, made another public statement about the dispute, and the teachers responded, suggesting that the most useful contribution that Mrs Hussey could make would be to stop meddling in a matter that was the direct responsibility of another Minister.[33]

During this time there was considerable speculation in the public arena about various interests attempting to bring the government and the teachers together. However, these hopes were dashed when, on 10 April 1986, the Minister for Education, Patrick Cooney, made an apparently intransigent statement on the government's position.

A second wave of strike action by the teachers was scheduled to begin on Monday, 5 May 1986 and was to run for at least four weeks, on the same three-days-a-week basis as the action taken during the previous term.

In the meantime, the following motion was listed by Fianna Fáil for debate and vote in the Dáil on Wednesday, 16 April 1986:

> Dáil Éireann, in view of the deep and wide-spread anxiety of parents and pupils in regard to the holding of school examinations this year, calls on the government to arrange for the immediate appointment of an independent arbitrator in their dispute with the teachers.

While, on the face of it, the motion called for the appointment of a mediator, it was, in fact, a motion of no confidence in the government. The government faced the prospect of a critical division in the Dáil.

On the evening of Tuesday, 15 April 1986 the Taoiseach presented the government's case to the public on RTÉ television and appealed to teachers not to disrupt the examinations. He claimed that the teachers had caused a national crisis by their repudiation of the vote in the Dáil. He reiterated earlier statements by the Minister for Education that there was no role for a mediator in the dispute.

In the *Today Tonight* programme immediately following the Taoiseach's broadcast, Gerry Quigley responded to the Taoiseach pointing out that his broadcast had been made in the middle of a two-day parliamentary debate on the Fianna Fáil motion, and it probably had a great deal more to do with the Taoiseach's political difficulties than any imagined constitutional problem with

32 CEC Report to Congress 1987, p. 4
33 A Teachers United Committee press statement issued on 8 April 1986

the teachers. He challenged the Taoiseach on his refusal to mediate even though all responsible bodies supported it – Church and school authorities, teachers, management bodies, parents and pupils. He indicated that the government still had a chance to stand back and not allow the dispute to continue.

On the following evening, Wednesday, 16 April 1986, during the course of his address to the Dáil and prior to the vote on the Fianna Fáil motion, the Minister for Education indicated that the government had changed its position and that it was now prepared to accept third-party intervention by a body such as the Employer-Labour Conference.

At the end of the debate a government amendment to the Fianna Fáil motion was carried by 79 votes to 69. The acceptance by the Minister of third-party intervention was the key factor in ensuring support for the government.

On the following day the unions sent a letter to the Minister stating that they were prepared to participate in discussions without preconditions on either side and that they had asked the ICTU to contact the chairman of the Employer-Labour Conference on the matter.[34]

At this time protests and demonstrations were being organised by parents and student groups expressing anxiety regarding the possible effects of the dispute on the certificate examinations.

The ICTU published a statement, signed by all members of the Executive Council, in support of the teachers in a large advertisement in the national newspapers on Sunday, 20 April.

The Fianna Fáil Position

When interviewed on RTÉ radio in April 1986, Charles J. Haughey declared that in his view the government had lost all sense of proportion on the teachers' pay issue, that Fianna Fáil would settle with the teachers by getting them to give the maximum possible time for payment, and that the amount of money required to settle the dispute was minimal, especially when compared to the large sums of money which the government had spent on Dublin Gas, The Insurance Corporation of Ireland (ICI), Private Motorists Protection Association (PMPA), and Irish Shipping.[35]

---

34 The Employer-Labour Conference was established in 1970 as a national forum for the discussion and review of developments and problems in industrial relations, pay determination and related matters. The employer side of the Conference is comprised of representatives of the employer organisations, including the State and state-sponsored bodies as employers. The labour side consists of members of the Executive Council of the ICTU and officials of Congress. The Steering Committee of the conference, which meets monthly, and more frequently if required, is available to assist with the agreement of the bodies directly concerned in the resolution of industrial disputes.

35 All of these companies were experiencing severe financial difficulties and the government had made provisions to rescue them.

Haughey believed that when the long-term negative impact of the dispute was taken into account, the price of Arbitration was low compared to the damage being done to the economy and to the education system.

Talks at the Employer-Labour Conference

Talks commenced in the Employer-Labour Conference on Tuesday, 22 April 1986, and continued for ten days and nights.

The process of mediation in the Employer-Labour Conference is such that direct negotiations do not take place between the parties in dispute. Conference officers consult with each party separately and convey the position of one party to the other.

On the tenth day of the talks the Official Side offered, as a final settlement among other proposals, that £35m would be provided for the payment of *ex-gratia* payments to teachers in lieu of retrospection. The teachers' side requested more time to draw up alternative proposals to the government's offer but the Official Side was not prepared to agree to this and withdrew the offer. The talks broke down on Friday, 2 May 1986.

On the same day, Tomás Breathnach, chairman of the Teachers' Conciliation Council, sent a letter to the unions offering *ex-gratia* payments totalling £35m over four years as follows: £15m would be paid in 1986 and a further £20m would be spread over the following three years.[36]

The CEC confirmed its decision that the terms offered in the letter were unacceptable.

Negotiations with the Ministers

With the breakdown of talks and the threat to boycott the certificate examinations, public and political pressure on the parties to seek a settlement to the dispute intensified. Direct negotiations were eventually reopened between the unions and the Ministers for Education and the Public Service on 5 May 1986.

On Thursday, 6 May, the Minister for Education stated that the government would not make any further cash available but that it was prepared to discuss a formula in the context of the last offer made at the Employer-Labour Conference. This was accepted by the unions as a basis for the continuation of negotiations.

The talks continued for several days and a draft set of proposals was agreed. The union negotiators submitted the proposals to their respective Executive Committees and the executives decided to ballot their members on the proposals.

---

36 CEC Report to Congress 1987, p. 11

The Agreement Proposals

The terms of the 25th Pay Round and the proposed method of payment of the Arbitration award were the same as those offered by the Minister on 30 January 1986.

It was agreed that the increases in the 25th Round and the proportionate percentage increases arising from the phasing of the arbitrator's award would also apply to responsibility and qualification allowances.

The £35m *ex-gratia* payments would be made as follows:

- 1 July 1986   £15m
- 1 June 1987   £10m
- 1 January 1988   £5m
- 1 January 1989   £5m[37]

The amounts of individual payments would be pro rata to a teacher's gross salary and allowances; £225,000 was held in reserve to allow for *ex-gratia* payments to be made to teachers not on the June 1986 payroll but who had given some service in the period 1 September 1985 to 30 June 1986.[38]

It was agreed that defined minor claims could continue to be negotiated and that discussions on outstanding matters that had previously been raised by the teachers or the Official Side would be concluded by 31 December 1986.

Pensions

The pensions of retired teachers would be revised by the same percentages as teachers' salaries. Lump sum entitlements would be calculated by reference to amounts and effective dates of Arbitration awards. The *ex-gratia* payments were not deemed to be salary and therefore would not be incorporated into calculations for pension or lump sum.

The government agreed to reappoint Hugh Geoghegan SC as chairman of the Teachers' Arbitration Board for the period up to 31 December 1986. While the teacher unions considered his term of office (seven months) as too short, they decided to accept Geoghegan's reappointment under protest and advised the government accordingly.

Ballot of Members

The unions put the agreement out to ballot, and the proposals were accepted by a large majority in each of the unions. The percentage of voters in favour of

37 Letter from Bernard Cúc, dated 13 June 1986, Department of Public Service, CEC Report to Congress 1987, pp. 18–19
38 Formulae were negotiated for the payment of the *ex-gratia* payments.

acceptance was: INTO: 72 per cent, ASTI: 79 per cent, TUI: 78 per cent. The Teachers' Conciliation Council was convened to record acceptance of the 25th Pay Round terms on 18 June 1986.[39] As the other financial provisions arose out of the arbitrator's report, implementation of these was a matter of administrative arrangements agreed between the teachers and the Departments of Education and Public Service.

Salaries

Teachers' salaries were revised with effect from 1 May 1986, 1 December 1986, 1 January 1987, 1 May 1987, 1 December 1987, and 1 July 1988. Over the fifty-eight month period from 1 September 1983 to 1 July 1988, salaries increased on average by approximately 30 per cent.

Superannuation

Pensions were revised from the same dates and by the same percentage increases as salaries. Lump sum entitlements were calculated by reference to the amounts and the effective dates recommended in the arbitrator's findings. This meant that the calculations were made as if the arbitrator's findings had been implemented in full:

- The lump sums of teachers who retired between 1 September 1985 and 28 February 1986 were based on salaries increased by 5 per cent.
- The lump sums of teachers who retired after 1 March 1986 were based on salaries increased by 10 per cent.

Review of the Campaign

The dispute commenced on 7 August 1985 when the arbitrator sent a confidential copy of his report to the parties involved and statements appeared in the media to the effect that the government could not and would not pay the award. Teachers United was formed and an intensive nationwide industrial dispute began between the government and the teacher unions. As happens in all such disputes, a compromise was eventually negotiated and a settlement reached. However, this did not happen until May 1986.

The 25th Round

Prior to the teachers' dispute the government was not inclined to commence negotiations on a pay round with any union. In August 1985 it announced that there would be a public service pay freeze, that Arbitration or Labour Court

---

39 Teachers' Conciliation Council Agreed Report 1/86

findings would not be implemented, and that recruitment to the public service would be severely restricted. This announcement caused an impasse between the government and all the unions affiliated to the Public Services Committee.

During the dispute the government tried to undermine the teachers' position by initiating negotiations with individual unions or groups of unions in the public service. By early December it thought it had negotiated a 25th Pay Round with some public service unions but when this was turned down by teachers on 16 December 1985 it had to offer revised terms to get a settlement. It is unlikely that the terms of the 25th Round would have been as high but for the rejection by the teachers of the original terms, and the government's ongoing dispute with them.

The Arbitrator's Award

The teachers eventually got a 10 per cent increase but it was phased in over a nineteen-month period, commencing fifteen months later than the date originally recommended by the arbitrator. The government had been successful in delaying the payment of the award by a considerable period of time and had saved a reported £110m.

Mention of this sum by the Minister for Education in the Dáil on 6 February 1986 alerted teachers to the amount they were losing in retrospective payments. They used this information to negotiate the payment of an *ex-gratia* sum of £35m. However, it could be claimed as a victory for the government because it had saved £75m and, as the *ex-gratia* payment was not part of pensionable salary, pension benefits applied only from the revised dates for the implementation of the award.

Teachers tried to make the shortfall of £75m an issue in the general election in March 1987 but it was obvious that it was not going to be paid. Its non-payment was used in the statement of claim at the Arbitration hearings in 1990.

The Government

When the government received the arbitrator's confidential report on 7 August 1985, it could have invited the teacher unions to discuss the state of the public finances and its difficulty in honouring the report. It might have been possible to reach an agreement to delay or stage the payments. This opportunity was not availed of and, instead, the Minister for Education and other government spokespersons publicised their intention not to pay the award. Teachers' response was to establish Teachers United.

Gemma Hussey made inflammatory statements which did not help the situation. Her 'morality' speech, in particular, raised teachers' hackles and was widely quoted to her disadvantage throughout the campaign. Even as Minister for Social Welfare, Gemma Hussey continued to make ill-advised statements about the dispute.

Efforts to encourage mediation were rebuffed. There is no doubt that the Taoiseach faced a serious dilemma as the overall economic situation was not good. However, a less confrontational policy might have yielded better results. His declaration of a 'National Crisis' over the national airwaves seemed, at best, an overreaction to a pay dispute with teachers. It certainly heightened public awareness of the dispute and enhanced the prestige and standing of the leadership of teacher unions.[40]

In the end, negotiations took place, a compromise was agreed, and an accommodation arrived at. Comments made by the Fianna Fáil leader, Charles Haughey, in a radio interview seem to encapsulate the strategy that the government should have adopted. He stated that good government was a matter of taking a sensible, mature and responsible approach and not about confrontation; that it was a matter of trying to involve the parties in consultation, negotiation and persuasion; and that he had never found the trade union movement recalcitrant in this regard. He believed that there were sensible people in the Irish trade union movement and that when the long-term negative impact of disputes was taken into account, the price of Arbitration was a mild one compared with the damage done to the economy and to the education system.[41]

Recognition of Strike Period

After the settlement of the dispute in May 1986 the teacher unions lodged a claim at Conciliation Council seeking that days lost by teachers due to industrial action in 1985 and 1986 should be recognised in full for incremental purposes. The Official Side conceded the claim as a gesture of conciliation and as an exceptional matter, with one proviso: the day of the General Public Service strike, 15 October 1985, would be excluded from the scope of the concession.

The signing of this Agreed Report signified the end of the Arbitration award dispute.

The following table shows the progression of salaries over the ten-year period from 1978 to 1988:

Point	1.3.1978	1.10.1982	1.7.1985	1.7.1988	% Increase
1	3,572	7,110	8,159	9,875	176.5%
15	5,815	11,484	13,177	15,906	173.5%
26	5,815	13,445	15,427	17,615	202.9%

40 ICTU Delegate Conference, July 1986
41 CEC Report to Congress 1987, p. 10

During this period a number of major developments occurred with regard to pensions:

1   Agreement was reached on the updating of procedures for the processing of pensions.
2   The Scheme for the Purchase of Notional Service was introduced in 1983.
3   A breakthrough on the question of the indexation of pensions was achieved during negotiations on the Public Service pay agreement of 1983.

Teachers United

Because of the high profile of the Teachers United group, and the general recognition of the effectiveness of its campaign, teachers were recognised as the strongest campaigning force in the trade union movement. All of the achievements were secured through limited industrial action – six days.

The campaign was a concrete expression of teacher unity, and it was considered the golden era of the teacher movement. A greater trade union consciousness developed among teachers; joint meetings of the respective Executive Committees were held; and there was unanimous participation by members in the campaign. Co-operation and fraternisation by teachers in all spheres of the education system was at its height.

However, the Teachers United Campaign turned out to be the apogee of the Teachers United movement.

Frequent joint meetings continued to be held and progress made on a number of outstanding issues. However, at the end of the salary campaign some of the euphoria for teacher unity dissipated. Further development was bedevilled by the three 'Ps' of policies, politics and personalities.

14

National Social Programmes, 1987–95

Programme for National Recovery (PNR), 1987–1991

The ICTU Executive Council endorsed the Programme for National Recovery (PNR) on 9 October 1987 and recommended it to affiliated unions.[1] The agreement applied for the period 1 July 1987 to 31 December 1990 and encompassed a wide range of social and economic areas:

- General Pay Agreement
- Pay Agreement in the Public Service
- Industrial Relations
- Redundancy
- Tax Reform
- Tax Evasion, Collection and Enforcement
- Greater Social Equity
- Social Welfare
- Education
- Labour Legislation
- Employment Equality
- Review and Monitoring Committee

Clause 2 of the agreement provided for a pay pause for the first six months and then an increase, with effect from 1 January 1988, 1 January 1989 and 1 January 1990, of 3 per cent on the first £120 of basic weekly pay and 2 per cent on any amount over £120, subject to a minimum of £4 per week, with effect from 1 January 1988, 1 January 1989 and 1 January 1990.

Nearly all public service unions balloted their members on the agreement. While the ballots were in progress the ICTU felt obliged to issue statements requesting Gemma Hussey of Fine Gael and Máirín Quill of the PDs to stop issuing statements suggesting that public servants, and teachers in particular, should forego their increases to offset cuts being made in the estimates and 'to

---

1 The ICTU negotiators were led by Gerry Quigley, General Secretary INTO, Vice-President ICTU, and Peter Cassells, Assistant General Secretary ICTU.

stop masquerading as defenders of school children while supporting massive cuts in expenditure on primary education'.[2]

The ICTU Special Delegate Conference on 19 November 1987 adopted the agreement by 181 votes to 114; 66.7 per cent of INTO members had voted in favour of it. In January 1988 the Teachers' Conciliation Council agreed that the 3 per cent increase would apply on the first £6,262 of salary and 2 per cent on the balance; it was also agreed that an increase of 2 per cent would apply to allowances.[3]

Over a three-year period, teachers received the following payments:

1 January 1988	1st Phase, 26th Round
1 January 1988	3rd Phase, £5m *ex-gratia* payment
1 July 1988	3rd and final phase, arbitrator's 10 per cent award
1 January 1989	2nd Phase, 26th Round
1 January 1989	final £5m *ex-gratia* payment
1 January 1990	3rd Phase, 26th Round

Over a twelve-year period, 1978 to 1990, salary points one, fifteen and twenty-six increased as follows:

Scale Point	1.3.1978 £	1.10.1982 £	1.5.1986 £	1.1.1990 £	% Increase
1	3,572	7,110	8,405	10,400	191%
15	5,815	11,484	14,572	16,675	187%
26	5,815 [4]	13,445	15,890	19,491	235%

Over the same period the Consumer Price Index increased by 180.9, which meant that teachers had the benefit of an actual increase in income.

The Cutbacks Campaign, 1987–88

The 1988 Book of Estimates was published on 13 October 1987 and shortly afterwards the Department of Education issued Circular 20/87 proposing increased pupil/teacher ratios and a 50 per cent reduction in expenditure on primary school buildings. The INTO organised local and national campaigns demanding the recall of circular 20/87. The government suffered a serious

2 Peter Cassells, Assistant General Secretary ICTU, quoted in CEC Report to Congress 1988, p. 6. Peter Cassells was appointed General Secretary ICTU in January 1988 when Donal Nevin retired from the post.
3 Teachers' Conciliation Council \ 1/88
4 Up to 1980 the salary scale had fifteen points extending over fifteen years; from 1980 the salary scale had eighteen points extending over twenty-six years.

setback when its amendment to a Fine Gael Private Member's Motion, decrying the effects of the circular, was defeated in a Dáil vote on 24 November 1987. The following morning, in response to the defeat, it proposed to initiate a full review of primary education.

The Minister for Education also established a Primary Quota Review Committee to examine the best possible arrangement for the deployment of teachers within the limits of expenditure laid down in the Book of Estimates. The INTO instructed its members not to co-operate with the committee; the National Parents Council (NPC) and the Catholic Primary School Managers Association (CPSMA) also declined to participate.

Primary Education Review Body (PERB)

The PERB was officially launched at a reception in the Shelbourne Hotel, Dublin, on 18 February 1988. Professor Tom Murphy, President UCD, was appointed chairman, and the following were represented on it: INTO, ASTI, TUI, NPC, CPSMA, Primary Curriculum Review Committee, Department of Education, Colleges of Education, and Minister for Education nominees.[5] Sean Ó Duinneacha, a primary school inspector, was appointed secretary to the committee.[6]

It was expected that the PERB would complete its work by the end of 1990 and that the final report would make recommendations, taking demographic trends into consideration, on the structure of primary education, demographic trends, the quality of primary education, and school organisation.[7]

In order not inhibit the PERB, the Minister for Education withdrew Circular 20/87 and agreed the following improvements for primary schools in disadvantaged areas from the beginning of the 1990 school year: ninety-five additional teaching posts, thirty additional remedial posts, and an increase from £0.5m to £1.5m in the fund for disadvantaged schools.

Teachers' Special Salary Claim

Clause 3.4 of the Public Service Pay Agreement permitted unions to submit special salary claims but specified that any award made would have to be paid in phases as follows: (a) 40 per cent with effect from 1 May 1991, (b) 30 per cent with effect from 1 March 1992, (c) 30 per cent with effect from 1 September 1992.

---

5 The INTO nominees were: Tom Gilmore, President, John White, Vice-President, Gerry Quigley, General Secretary, Michael Moroney, General Treasurer, and CEC member Joe O'Toole.

6 Sean Ó Duinneacha subsequently became Secretary General, Department of Education and Science.

7 The Report of the Primary Education Review Body was formally presented by Dr T. Murphy, chairperson, to both the Taoiseach and the Minister for Education on 7 December 1990.

In October 1989 the teacher unions presented a special salary claim at Conciliation Council seeking increases comprising the following elements:

- an element based on analogues for the period since the teachers' Arbitration award in 1985 and other relevant comparisons
- an element to provide for a reduction in the number of years required to reach the maximum of the scale
- an element to take account of the increase in the responsibility of teachers at all levels arising from significant changes within the education system, including curricular developments.

Disagreement was recorded at a meeting in June 1990 as the Official Side was not prepared to make any offer.[8] The claim was submitted to Arbitration in July 1990 and was heard by the Arbitration Board on 14 December 1990.

Arbitration Findings

In accordance with established procedure, the arbitrator sent a confidential report of the preliminary findings to the parties on 21 December 1990.[9] He recommended as follows:

1   Increases in the Common Basic Scale:

Incremental Point	Increase
1–4 inclusive	8%
5–14 inclusive	9%
15	10%
1st long-phased incremental point (after three years on point 15)	10%
2nd long-phased incremental point (after four years on the first long-phased point)	11%
3rd long-phased incremental point (after four years on the second long-phased point)	12%

2   An increase of 10 per cent in qualification, responsibility and other allowances

3   All increases to be paid in three phases as laid down in the PNR.

As in 1985, and contrary to established practice, the terms of the draft report were leaked to the media. However, in this instance the government accepted the findings and agreed to pay the award. Memory of the major Arbitration dispute in 1985–86 was still fresh in everybody's mind.

---

8   Teachers' Conciliation Council Agreed Report 2/90 (ref. 239/89)
9   Arbitration Report No. 17. CEC Report to Congress 1992, pp. 5–6

Programme for Economic and Social Progress (PESP), 1991–1993

In January 1991 the social partners agreed the Programme for Economic and Social Progress (PESP) in succession to the PNR; it was adopted by 229 votes to 109 at an ICTU Special Delegate Conference on 21 February 1991. The PESP had a number of sections that were of particular relevance to primary teachers and for primary education:

- Pay proposals
- Taxation
- Staffing of primary schools, including ancillary staff
- Financing of primary education
- Areas of disadvantage
- Ancillary services in primary schools.

The Education Provisions

The PESP confirmed the importance of the education system for the future well-being of the country as well as its role in the country's economic development. The following provisions were detailed:

- Efforts would be intensified to address the needs of those with educational difficulties and under-achievers, in particular during the compulsory cycle.
- Particular attention would be paid to children suffering educational or social disadvantage through early identification and the provision of remedial teaching, guidance and counselling and the development of home-school links.
- At primary level, the overall pupil/teacher ratio would be reduced to 25:1 by September 1992, to be reviewed at the end of 1993.
- An additional £0.5m in 1992 and £1m in 1993 and subsequent years would be allocated to in-service education for teachers
- An allocation of £1m in 1991, £2m in 1992 and £3m in 1993 would be made to assist in various areas of disadvantage at all levels of the education system.
- Commencing in 1992, a programme would be implemented to replace all substandard buildings at primary and second level, and at VEC third-level colleges by the year 1997.
- A phased programme, to commence in 1992, would be introduced to expand the provision for caretaking and clerical services to all national schools with 100 pupils upwards and second-level schools with 200 pupils upwards.
- A Green Paper, framed as a strategy paper on education, would be issued by summer 1991; a White Paper would be issued in early 1992 and this would be followed by an Education Act.

Taxation

The government gave undertakings to reduce the standard income tax rate of 30 per cent to 25 per cent by 1993, and to make further movement towards a single higher rate.

Pay Proposals

The following pay increases were agreed:

- Year one: 4 per cent of basic pay with a minimum increase of £5 per week
- Year two: 3 per cent with a minimum increase of £4.25 per week
- Year three: 3.75 per cent with a minimum increase of £5.75 per week.

The PESP pay agreement had a provision that was to prove very important in reaching the In-school Agreement of 1996.[10] Clause 3 provided that, as an exceptional matter, employers and trade unions would be entitled to negotiate further changes in rates of pay and/or conditions of employment for an amount up to but not exceeding 3 per cent of the salary bill.[11] The manner of application of this clause in the public service was set down in a separate Memorandum of Understanding. Discussions could commence not later than 1 July 1993, and any pay increases agreed would have to be implemented on a phased basis commencing not earlier than the second year of the agreement.

Teachers' Pay and Conditions under the PESP

Teachers accepted the full terms of the PESP and agreement was recorded.[12]
Over a three-year period teachers would be entitled to increases as follows:

PESP		1990 Arbitration Award	
1 January, 1991	4%	1 May 1991	40% of award
1 January, 1992	3%	1 March 1992	30% of award
		1 September 1992	30% of award
1 January, 1993	3.75%		

---

10 The 1996 agreement fundamentally changed the in-school management of schools in every sector.

11 This became known as the 'local bargaining' clause.

12 Teachers' Conciliation Council Agreed Report 2/91

PESP and the Public Service

During the month of July 1991 a number of Ministers made statements claiming that the Exchequer's financial position had deteriorated since the 1991 budget due to:

- a fall in revenue arising from a slowdown in economic activity
- a significant increase in unemployment payments because of a sharp increase in the number of people unemployed
- an increase in the cost of the Health Services.

In August the Minister for Finance made comments to the effect that the government would be unable to pay the salary increases due to public servants. On 26 September the Public Services Committee issued a statement declaring that it was opposed to any renegotiation of the PNR or the pay terms of the PESP. The ICTU also made it clear that it was opposed to any renegotiation of the PESP, including any proposal to reschedule public service pay increases. At a meeting of the Central Review Committee of the PESP on 8 October the Taoiseach emphasised his commitment to the PESP but declared that solutions would have to be found on an equitable basis.

The ICTU responded by suggesting that an effective method of enforcement and collection of taxes would solve the Exchequer's short-term financial problems and that the creation of more jobs would generate more tax revenue for the government and at the same time reduce expenditure on social welfare.

On 19 November the Minister for Finance invited the ICTU to an urgent meeting to explore the impact of various spending options on public service staff. While reiterating that it was not prepared to renegotiate the terms of the PESP agreement, the ICTU met with the Minister on 22 November.

The Minister reviewed the Exchequer position and indicated that the government would be taking steps to reduce the spending budgets of the different Departments, and that the public service pay-bill of £340m, an increase of 10 per cent over the 1991 levels, could not be met.

On 10 December 1991, at the request of the teachers' unions, the following organisations met to co-ordinate resistance to any attempts by the government to renege on the PESP Agreement: ASTI, INTO, TUI, Association of Garda Sergeants and Inspectors (AGSI), Association of Higher Civil Servants (AHCS), Garda Representative Association (GRA), Irish Nurses' Organisation (INO), and Prison Officers' Association (POA).

Government's Proposals on the PESP

At a meeting on 13 December an ICTU delegation was informed by Ministers that the government intended to amend the public service pay agreement as follows:

1   The 3 per cent second phase increase of the PESP Pay Agreement would be paid to all public service workers with effect from the due date but subject to a ceiling of £5 a week.

2   The balance of the special pay increases, which were due to be paid in instalments during 1991 and 1992, would be paid in total from 1 January 1993 with full retrospection.[13]

3   The 3.75 per cent final phase of the PESP would be paid, subject to a ceiling of £6.50 a week.

4   Clause 3 of the PESP, the local bargaining clause, would continue to operate.

The ICTU declared that the government's proposals were unacceptable and that it would support action by public service workers to achieve payment of the agreement in full.

Public Services Committee Plan of Campaign

The Public Services Committee met on 18 December and decided to initiate and co-ordinate a concerted programme of public service action. It decided to hold a one-day stoppage on 28 January 1992 with regional rallies in Dublin, Limerick, Galway, Waterford and Sligo.

The three teacher unions met on a number of occasions during the months of December and January to co-ordinate a campaign of opposition to the government's proposals. Teachers were balloted on a maximum of three days' strike action prior to Easter 1992; over 90 per cent of INTO members voted in favour of strike action.

All government party members of the Oireachtas were lobbied, as were Ministers prior to their cabinet meeting on 18 January.

Revised Proposals on Pay from Government

In response to the threat from the unions the Minister for Finance met the Public Services Committee on 17 January and presented revised pay proposals.

In the case of the pay element of the PESP:

- with effect from 1 January 1992 the general increase of 3 per cent would be paid, subject to a minimum of £4.25 per week and a maximum of £5 per week
- with effect from 1 December 1992 all pay rates would be adjusted by removing the ceiling of £5 per week
- people retiring between 1 January 1992 and 1 December 1992 would have their retirement lump sums calculated as if the full increase due under the PESP from 1 January applied

---

13 The postponement of payment of the special pay increases would create problems in 1993 by adding about £210 million to the public sector pay and pensions bill.

- with effect from 1 January 1993, the general increase of 3.75 per cent would be paid, subject to a minimum of £5.75 per week and a maximum of £6.50 per week
- with effect from 1 December 1993, all pay rates would be adjusted by removing the ceiling of £6.50 per week
- people retiring between 1 January 1993 and 1 December 1993 would have their retirement lump sums calculated as if the full increase due under the PESP for 1 January applied.

In the case of Arbitration awards:

- all pay rates would be adjusted by paying the two phases due, with effect from 1 December 1992
- full retrospection would be paid to the dates due from 1 January 1993
- people retiring between 1 March 1992 and 1 December 1992 would have their retirement lump sums calculated as if the two phases had been paid.

In the case of retrospection, further discussions would be held with the ICTU in 1993 with a view to agreeing a specific timetable for recoupment of the losses arising from the application of the ceilings of £5 per week and £6.50 per week. Recoupment would be paid not later than January 1994.

The Public Services Committee decided to defer the one-day stoppage planned for 28 January to allow time for affiliated unions to consult their members.

The General Secretaries of the three teacher unions informed the Minister for Finance that teachers would not be prepared to remove the threat of industrial action unless the government addressed the educational non-pay elements of the PESP Agreement. The Minister agreed to meet the teacher unions to clarify the government's response to the teachers' demands.

On 24 January, at a meeting with the Minister for Education, the following non-pay proposals were agreed for implementation prior to the end of the PESP:

- a new staffing schedule designed to reduce the pupil/teacher ratio from 25.8:1 to 25.2:1 in primary schools
- an additional £0.25m for in-service education for teachers over and above the normal budgetary allocation
- an allocation of £0.5m for the initiation of caretaker and clerk-typist schemes in schools
- an additional £0.25m to be added to the existing £1.5m allocated to the Programme of Special Measures for Schools in Disadvantaged Areas
- no additional funding would be made available for school buildings in 1992 over and above normal budgetary allocation.

The CEC, while regretting the government's decision not to implement in full the terms of the PESP, decided to postpone the campaign of action in order to monitor the implementation of the latest proposals. On 3 February 1992 a revised staffing schedule for the school year 1992–93 was issued.

Second Revised Proposals on Pay from Government

At a Conciliation Council meeting on 22 December 1992 the Official Side stated that the government had decided to meet its pay commitments under the PESP:

- negotiations would be conducted with the ICTU to agree a schedule for the payment of arrears due arising from the non-payment of the full PESP
- the arrears due would be included in the salary cheques of 31 December 1992
- meaningful dialogue would take place in the near future on pay determination machinery
- no offer would be made on any claim previously presented.

The government and the ICTU reached final agreement on 4 June 1993 on outstanding aspects of the PESP, as follows:

- the arrears due under the PESP would be paid in full in January 1994[14]
- discussions on the question of public service pay determination machinery would be brought to an early conclusion with a view to having machinery in place not later than 31 March 1994
- a Public Service Arbitrator would be appointed until March 1994.

Pensions

Teachers retiring during these periods had their retirement lump sums calculated as if the appropriate increases had been paid from the dates due. As pensions were indexed, they were revised from the dates that salaries were revised.

Programme for Competitiveness and Work (PCW), 1994–1997

Initiative of the Minister for Finance, 1993

In a general election in January 1993 the Labour Party won a record thirty-three seats, and on 12 January a Fianna Fáil/Labour Coalition government took office,

---

14 In direct negotiations with the Department of Education, the INTO was successful in having the arrears owed to teachers in respect of the first period paid on 23 December 1993 and the arrears for the second period paid on 26 January 1994.

with Albert Reynolds as Taoiseach and Dick Spring as Tánaiste.[15] Niamh Bhreathnach was appointed Minister for Education and Bertie Ahern as Minister for Finance.

In his 1993 budget speech Bertie Ahern announced three initiatives that would have consequences for public sector pay:

- the imposition of a 1 per cent income levy
- the introduction of a new method for pay determination
- the payment by public servants of full-rate PRSI.

He proposed to commence collection of the income levy from all salaries through the PAYE system from 6 April 1993.[16] The trade union movement strongly objected to the imposition of the levy.

Bertie Ahern stated that the government was totally committed to changing the method of pay determination in the public service to produce a new system that would be more transparent and operate on assessment criteria which, while being fair to staff, would be responsive to the interests of the government and tax-payers.[17] He also said that the government was committed to putting public servants on the same footing as other employees for PRSI, and he intended to include it on the agenda for proposed discussions with the ICTU.[18]

The PCW Agreement

An ICTU Special Delegate Conference, on 30 September 1993, authorised the Executive Committee to enter into discussions with government and employers on a post-PESP programme as long as the government agreed to remove the 1 per cent income levy, reverse all social welfare cuts and complete the programme within an agreed time span.

Despite intensive representations throughout the months of October, November and December the government failed to respond to the ICTU's demands.[19]

Following indications from the Minister for Finance that the question of the 1 per cent levy would be dealt with in the budget, representatives of the ICTU entered into formal negotiations with the government on 10 January 1994. At

15 The government only lasted for two years but it helped to ensure Fianna Fáil dominance of Irish politics by showing that the party would enter into coalition with any group if the numbers were right.
16 Section 7 of the Finance Act, 1993. Abolition of the 1 per cent levy was announced in the 1994 budget.
17 This was ultimately to lead to the Benchmarking process introduced in 2002. In hindsight, the question may be asked 'Has Benchmarking been more effective than the Conciliation and Arbitration process?'.
18 Financial Statement of the Minister for Finance, 24 February 1993
19 CEC Report to Congress 1994, pp. 28–9

the end of ten days of negotiations an agreement on pay was reached with the private sector on a total payment of 8 per cent over three years as follows:

- no pay freeze
- 2 per cent increase in 1994
- 2.5 per cent in 1995
- 2.5 per cent for the first six months of 1996 and 1 per cent for the second six months.

Talks on a public sector pay deal concluded on 25 January with terms slightly different to those for the private sector. The public sector pay deal was for a period of three-and-a-half-years, commencing with a five-month pay pause (the government had sought twelve months) and providing an increase in salary and allowances of 8 per cent over the rest of the period. Its terms were as follows:

1 January 1994 to 31 May 1994:	a five-month pay pause
1 June 1994 to 31 May 1995:	an increase of 2 per cent
1 June 1995 to 31 May 1996:	an increase of 2 per cent
1 June 1996 to 30 September 1996:	an increase of 1.5 per cent
1 October 1996 to 31 December 1996:	an increase of 1.5 per cent
1 January 1997 to 30 June 1997:	an increase of 1 per cent

It was agreed that no automatic additional increases could be sought through local bargaining but that outstanding claims under the PESP could be pursued.[20] Strikes or any other form of industrial action by trade unions, employees or employers in respect of any matter covered by the agreement were precluded.

In his budget speech on 26 January 1994 the Minister announced increases in income tax personal allowances and in the standard rate tax bands and the removal of the income levy.

The PCW also contained the following provisions:

- The government agreed to continue the process of tax reform.
- The Central Review Committee would continue to monitor the achievement of the targets and objectives of the new programme.
- New public service pay determination machinery would be in place not later than 31 March 1994.
- A new programme to provide 40,000 jobs would be in place by the end of 1994.
- The pupil/teacher ratio at primary level would be reduced annually.
- Additional schools would be included in schemes for the disadvantaged.
- Provision would be made for the expansion of remedial and guidance services.

---

20 Teachers' Conciliation Council Agreed Report 1/94

- Provision would be made for the phased development of a full psychological service in primary and post-primary schools.
- Provision would be made for the phased appointment of caretaking and clerical staff in primary and post-primary schools.
- Provision would be made for a planned programme to replace or refurbish substandard schools at primary and post-primary level.
- Provision would be made to tackle problems in Special Education.
- Provision would be made for undertaking a major expansion in in-service training at all levels for teachers.
- Capitation grants would be increased at primary and post-primary level.
- Proposals would be brought forward for the establishment of a welfare service for teachers.
- The scheme of assistance towards the provision of school books for necessitous pupils would be extended.
- Arrangements for improving access to third-level education for those from disadvantaged areas, including mature students, would be developed.
- A designated senior official in the Department of Education would be assigned responsibility for the promotion and implementation of gender equality policy in all areas of the education system.

The agreement was accepted in a ballot by INTO members and the teacher unions submitted claims to Conciliation Council seeking:

- the application of the basic pay provisions of the PCW
- the 3 per cent available under Clause 2 (iv) of Annex 1 of the PESP
- an advance payment of 1 per cent permitted under Clause 2 (iv) of Annex 1 of the PESP.

Discussions were held at the Teachers' Conciliation Council on 24 March, 19 April, 4 May and 10 May 1994. Agreement was recorded only on the application of the basic pay provisions of the PCW.

Draft Proposals for a New Scheme of Conciliation and Arbitration for Teachers

Teachers had two problems with the existing C&A Scheme: superannuation claims were not arbitrable, and conditions of service were not conciliable or arbitrable.

At a Conciliation Council meeting on 22 December 1992 it was agreed, in accordance with the PESP, that discussions on new public service pay machinery would be progressed with a view to having machinery in place not later than 31 March 1994. Following representations from public service unions, Eoghan Fitzsimons SC replaced Hugh Geoghegan as Public Service Arbitrator.[21]

In 1993 Bertie Ahern made reference in his budget speech to the government's desire to have changes introduced into the method of pay determination for the public service. In February the Official Side presented a document at Conciliation Council proposing revisions to the Teachers' C&A Scheme. The Official Side stated that it was the government's objective that the various C&A Schemes in the public sector should follow a common layout, format and terminology to the greatest extent possible, and any variations in language and terminology should reflect real differences.

The new draft proposed that:

1   the scope of the scheme should be broadened to include other types of teachers at first and second level; the groups or classes of teachers would be determined in discussions
2   grades of teachers could seek a review of their pay and conditions of employment at intervals of not less than four years
3   conditions of service should be brought within the scheme; the subjects appropriate for conciliation would be determined in discussions
4   all Managerial Bodies should be allowed representation in the Conciliation and Arbitration process
5   the Official Side should be broadened to encompass representatives of managerial authorities as well as persons nominated by the Ministers, and provision should be made for consultation and co-operation between the Department and management
6   representation at Conciliation Council and Arbitration hearings should be organised on a panel basis
7   operational procedures in Conciliation should be revised to include the use of subcommittees, and representation of the Departments and of management on the subcommittee should reflect the sector being dealt with
8   representation on the Conciliation Council and the number of advocates in Arbitration should reflect the tripartite nature of the scheme and should provide adequate representation for the Departments and for the management side while recognising the common interests of the Ministers and of the managerial bodies
9   a Facilitator should be introduced to assist at Conciliation
10 the current Arbitration Board should be replaced by a combination of a three-person Arbitration Board and a single Adjudicator, with separate provision for advocacy and witnesses
11 parties to the scheme would, by agreement, jointly refer factual data assembled by them in respect of any claim to an independent unit within the Labour Relations Commission

---

21 Mr Hugh Geoghegan had been the Public Service Arbitrator from 1984.

12 the right of the Minister to refer an Arbitration finding to the Dáil should be retained

13 the scheme should contain a more explicit statement on the prohibition of industrial action.

Many aspects of the proposals were unacceptable to the teachers. The main objections were:

1 The proposal that the right to partake in the councils would be subject to a decision by the Minister for Education was considered an intrusion into union rights and an attempt to reduce the right to direct representation.

2 It was considered that too many intermediate steps were being introduced into the negotiation process.

3 Although salary, superannuation, and conditions of service claims could be considered at Conciliation Council, claims on conditions of service and superannuation would remain non-arbitrable.

As it was a fundamental principle sought by the teachers' side that all claims that were conciliable should also be arbitrable, the draft proposals were rejected by the executives of the three unions. The INTO Congress of 1993 adopted a resolution instructing the CEC to vigorously oppose any attempt to dismantle the C&A Scheme.

Review of Conciliation and Arbitration Proposals

The schedule to complete the talks by 31 March 1994 was not maintained, and other events intervened, such as the introduction of full PRSI for all new employees in the public service and the lengthy negotiations to finalise the PCW In-School Agreement.

The 1997 Partnership 2000 pay agreement committed the parties to complete negotiations within six months on revised C&A Schemes. The CEC submitted proposals for consideration under the Partnership 2000 review.

Council of Teachers' Unions (CTU), 1990–93

As a result of the Teachers United campaign in the 1985–86 Arbitration dispute, the possibility of full unity of primary and post-primary teachers in a single organisation surfaced and gained momentum.

In May 1989 Donal Nevin was invited by the unions to assist in facilitating teacher unity. A working group, chaired by Nevin and consisting of five representatives from each of the three unions, prepared a document entitled 'Proposals for a Council of Teachers' Unions'. In March 1990 the executives of the three unions approved the document.

The plan proposed the establishment of a Council in which the three unions would be represented, more or less in proportion to their membership numbers. It would not be a decision-making body; it could formulate proposals by consensus but the decision on these proposals would be made by the respective executives. The executives would have to refer them to their conferences and ultimately to the members who would vote on them by secret ballot.

It was obvious, however, from the long interventionist method proposed for decision-making that restrictions were being placed on the role and function of the Council – the Irish syndrome of the 'three Ps' (policies, politics and personalities) was in operation.

The quest for teacher unity received a further setback with changes in the officerships of the unions. Gerry Quigley, General Secretary INTO, took early retirement in 1991, and Kieran Mulvey retired as General Secretary of the ASTI after being appointed as the first Chief Executive of the Labour Relations Commission.[22]

Nevertheless, an administrative structure was put in place with the appointment of an Executive Officer who was responsible for the operation of the Council and for managing affairs between meetings. The first meeting of the Council took place in the Burlington Hotel on 4 December 1990 and it met regularly thereafter.[23] In addition to regular discussions, three subcommittees were established in 1991 to examine specific projects:

1   review the schedule of qualifications' allowances paid to teachers
2   advise on early retirement options for teachers
3   investigate equity in promotional opportunities for teachers in the different sectors.

CTU and Qualifications' Allowances

The qualifications' subcommittee submitted a report to the Council, which was adopted and referred to the respective Executive Committees. Based on recommendations in the report the unions lodged a claim at Conciliation Council:

1   that the allowances on the schedule of academic qualifications should be reviewed
2   that the schedule of academic qualifications that qualified for the payment of an allowance should be amended by the addition of other agreed academic qualifications

---

22 Senator O'Toole took up duty as General Secretary-Designate INTO from 1 September 1990. Charlie Lennon was appointed as General Secretary ASTI in succession to Kieran Mulvey.

23 The INTO representatives on the CTU generally comprised the President, Vice-President, General Secretary, General Treasurer, Northern Secretary and up to seven members of the Central Executive Committee.

3   that each certificate or diploma held should qualify for payment of an allowance
4   that allowances for all certificates and diplomas could be held together with one of the degree allowances
5   that recognised teachers in service who did not have a degree qualification allowance should be paid an allowance equivalent to that for a primary degree.

No progress was made in processing these claims and, in addition to a claim regarding specialist teachers, they were not resolved until the Pay and Conditions Agreement of 1996.

CTU and the Voluntary Early Retirement Scheme, 1987

The ASTI and the TUI submitted a claim to Conciliation Council in 1986 seeking that their members should have the provision of retirement at fifty-five years of age with thirty-five years' service, similar to that available to national teachers. It was discussed at a number of meetings but the Official Side was not prepared to make any offer; this refusal was not received favourably by the post-primary unions.

In 1987, as part of its efforts to overcome economic difficulties and reduce the public service pay-bill, the government offered public service employees a Voluntary Early Retirement Scheme. Its provisions were offered to teachers with the purpose of allowing a minimum of 1,300 teachers to leave the service.

Although the National Parents Council (Primary) and the teacher unions objected to the scheme, the Department of Education sent information and application forms to teachers, 4,189 of whom applied for it: (2,300 primary, 939 secondary and 950 vocational). Only 570 were granted redundancy under the scheme (374 primary, 138 secondary and 58 vocational).

In 1989 the three teacher unions lodged the following claim seeking a revision of the teachers' pension scheme:

That (a) the number of years' service required for a full pension be reduced to thirty years and that (b) after twenty years of service a teacher who retires be entitled to an immediate pension based on the number of years' service. (Claim 241/89)

On the 29 March 1990 the Official Side offered an early retirement scheme to teachers which permitted retirement from age fifty but the lump sum and pension paid would be computed in accordance with an actuarial table as follows:

Early Retirement Scheme, Actuarial Table, 1990

Age at which payment of benefit commences	Factor to be used in calculating		
	(a) lump sum	(b) pension	
		Male	Female
59	0.98	0.93	0.94
58	0.95	0.87	0.89
57	0.93	0.81	0.84
56	0.91	0.76	0.80
55	0.89	0.72	0.76
54	0.87	0.67	0.72
53	0.85	0.63	0.68
52	0.83	0.60	0.65
51	0.81	0.57	0.62
50	0.79	0.54	0.59

A male teacher retiring at age 55 would receive only 89 per cent of the lump sum and 72 per cent of pension. The unions rejected the scheme and demanded the establishment of an independent review to determine teachers' pensions.

On 3 April 1990 the unions published a document on early retirement and wrote to the Minister for Education seeking a formal review of pension schemes for all teachers. Teachers based their case on a range of international studies indicating that stress was a major occupational problem among teachers.[24] They claimed that studies had indicated that, in comparison to other professions, school teachers suffered one of the highest levels of occupational stress.

The teacher unions provided statistics from the optional contributory Salary Protection Insurance Schemes, which they had arranged for their members. Members of these schemes were able to avail of early disability retirement and get a guaranteed income of 75 per cent of their teacher's salary. The statistics showed that the number of claimants was increasing every year and, in nearly all cases, the reason for early retirement was stress-related:

---

24 The Nordic Council's 'Nord-stress project', Council of Europe, 1982; The International Labour Organisation (1981), ILO Information 1990; Gorton Poll, 1982, USA; Research in Britain and Northern Ireland

Basis for Claims under the Schemes, 1976–90

	Depressions/ Anxiety	Mental Illness	Other Psychological	Cardio- Vascular	Total
ASTI	46	4	15	31	96
	47.9%	4.2%	15.6%	32.3%	
INTO	121	10	38	46	215
	56.3%	4.7%	17.7%	21.3%	
TUI	20	5	31	17	73
	27.4%	6.8%	42.5%	23.3%	

On 20 July 1990 the Minister for Education indicated to an INTO deputation that while she was prepared to consider proposals for early retirement, the prospect of modifications to the existing scheme of voluntary early retirement was remote, and she subsequently referred the unions to the actuarial-based scheme offered at Conciliation.[25]

Teacher Unions Stress Survey, 1991

In November 1990 the CTU commissioned the Work Research Centre to undertake comprehensive research on the levels of stress among teachers. A survey was conducted to identify:

- the principal sources of stress amongst teachers
- recommendations for possible remedies.

The authors of the report listed eight main conclusions and made twelve recommendations. The recommendations referred to:

- class size
- curriculum development
- a code of behaviour
- resources
- role of teacher
- career development
- in-service training

25 Mary O'Rourke, Minister for Education, 13 March 1987 to 13 November 1991

- stress management training
- welfare service
- forum for discussion of views and social support
- monitoring and evaluation of stress management measures.

In 1992 the CTU asked KPMG, Pension and Actuarial Services, to provide costings on early retirement options for a notional primary and a notional post-primary teacher taking early retirement at different ages and with different numbers of enhanced years. Based on the results of this study and on CTU recommendations, the following claim was presented at Conciliation, autumn 1992: 'Claim by ASTI/INTO/TUI that teachers be entitled to retire from the teaching service on a pension from fifty years of age on the basis of accrued pension entitlement with ten years' enhancement.'

The Minister for Education indicated in her speech at the INTO Congress and the ASTI and TUI conferences in 1993 that she was prepared to examine proposals for early retirement with all the interested parties.[26]

The Minister's statements were received with acclamation and applause. However, in a statement to the Dáil Select Committee on Social Affairs on 15 December 1993, the Minister qualified her statement.[27] Nothing more was done on the subject until considerable changes were included in the Pay and Conditions Agreement of 1996.

Preserved Benefits

The Pensions Act of 1990 brought in the concept of preserved benefits for contributions made after 1 January 1991. Employees with at least five years' service became entitled to a preserved benefit on their post-1991 contributions if they left their employment before normal retirement age. The preserved benefit at retirement would be based on the salaries applying at that time.

A subsequent Pensions (Amendment) Act in 1993 provided preserved benefits after two years' service and removed the embargo on the recognition of pre-1991 service. On taking up a new employment a person could retain the preserved benefits or transfer pension credits to a new employment scheme.

CTU and Promotional Opportunities for all Teachers

In 1968 the Ryan Tribunal introduced a graded points system, based on age of pupils, for determining the system of promotion available to teachers in different schools. The disparity between the number and type of posts in

---

26 Niamh Bhreathnach, Minister for Education, at the INTO Congress in Waterford at Easter 1993
27 Report of the Dáil Select Committee on Social Affairs, 15 December 1993, p. 809

primary and post-primary schools was the cause of dissatisfaction among national teachers.

Each union had its own policy on the promotional opportunities that should be available in their respective schools. Different claims were lodged at Conciliation but progress was not possible as no claim could be processed through the C&A Scheme unless there was unanimous agreement among the three teacher unions.

In an effort to overcome the different operational and philosophical problems associated with the points system, a CTU subcommittee was mandated:

- to investigate promotional opportunities for all teachers
- to investigate equity of promotional opportunities for teachers in the different sectors of the education system
- to draft an agreed claim or claims to be lodged with the Conciliation Council to improve promotional opportunities for teachers in all sectors.

Following protracted discussions, at a meeting on 2 March 1993 the subcommittee agreed a report and framed a claim for submission to Conciliation Council. The claim was to be achieved as follows:

(i) a general increase in the points rating for pupils
(ii) a specific increase in the points rating for pupils in the lowest categories
(iii) the provision of an additional vice-principal in schools of 2,450 points and over
(iv) the creation of a new category for pupils of eighteen years of age and older.

The CEC, with reservations, adopted the subcommittee's report but the executives of the other two unions rejected it.

The report was considered by the delegates at Congress 1993 and, as they did not like the disparity in the number of posts available to the different sectors and the imbalance in the distribution of the available pool of money, they, contrary to the wishes of the platform, debated a motion demanding that the CEC:

(a) seek a review of the points system with the Department of Education to bring about a uniform points rating for all pupils irrespective of age or school category
(b) seek the support of other teacher unions towards achieving this aim
(c) convey to the other teacher unions that the INTO would withdraw from further discussions on teacher unity until it received their support in gaining an equal points system for posts of responsibility.

Although delegates were told that the proposed motion would jeopardise inter-union relations, it was passed. Following Congress the resolution was brought to the attention of the other two unions.

In its response the ASTI stated that:

- it was not prepared to accept the major change to the points system proposed in the resolution
- it recognised the deterioration in the number of posts in the primary sector by supporting the joint claim for improvements in the points system
- it would be prepared to consider alternatives to the points system for the calculation of allowances and allocation of posts in schools
- it regretted that the future of teacher unity should be placed in jeopardy by the INTO Congress resolution.

The TUI acknowledged the correspondence but then circulated a detailed document regarding the promotion problem to its School Representatives and Branch Secretaries. The document recorded a history of events since the Ryan Tribunal in 1968 and continued by stating that the TUI regretted to report that:

- after some three years of discussion on teacher unity, with both the ASTI and INTO, a serious setback had been encountered in the unity discussions
- the setback had been caused by the INTO passing a resolution at its Annual Congress on the revision of the points system
- at the behest of the INTO in the recent past, protracted discussions had taken place between the three unions with a view to getting a common position on a new points arrangement, but no agreement was reached
- the Ryan Tribunal had recommended a system of posts of responsibility, which had been advocated by the ASTI and TUI, and opposed by the INTO
- post-primary schools were more complex to run and manage than primary schools and the posts of responsibility system should and must reflect this
- a points system that did not take students' age into account would result in a massive re-allocation of resources from post-primary to primary schools
- a unilateral position adopted by one union seeking a uniform arrangement for posts of responsibility was not just or equitable
- no issue should be the subject of an ultimatum in the context of teacher unity
- the TUI Executive was of the view that making any one policy matter a precondition to discussing teacher unity was a false position.

When the CEC became aware of the TUI document it circulated a statement to INTO members responding to the issues raised:

- it rejected the statement that post-primary schools were more complex to run and manage than primary schools
- it would never be the INTO's wish that improvement at primary level should take place at the expense of the also underfunded post-primary sector

- the INTO had proposed to the Ryan Tribunal that posts should be determined in proportion to the number of teachers on the school staff
- the INTO sought 'equity of promotional opportunities' and it proposed that primary teachers' promotional opportunities be improved to the extent available at post-primary level
- the position adopted by the ASTI Standing Committee about being prepared to consider alternatives was welcomed.

A rift had been created and the final CTU Council meeting was held on 14 June 1993. All formal activities of the CTU, other than the administration and financing of the Health and Safety training courses, ceased to operate from 31 August 1993.

With the demise of the CTU, the TUI invited the ASTI to enter into bilateral talks with a view to establishing a single union to subsume the existing ASTI and TUI. The Standing Committee of the ASTI and the Executive Committee of TUI held a joint meeting, and a working party was established to draft proposals for submission to the executives of the unions within three to four months.

The CEC convened a Branch Secretaries Conference on 17 September 1993 to consider the matter and initiated a comprehensive internal debate with a view to determining the organisation's position on the question of teacher unity. A Special Congress on 19 February 1994 adopted six composite motions which were presented to Congress. The final motion mandated the CEC to negotiate progress with the ASTI and TUI towards teacher unity on the basis of the federal and divisional structure agreed at Congress 1993.

No further developments on teacher unity occurred during the following eighteen months. At a meeting on January 1996 the CEC and the ASTI Executive reached agreement on the following:

- that a working party on benefits should be established
- that a joint approach regarding balloting should be agreed
- that similar voting schedules should be adopted
- that a committee should be established to investigate the feasibility of establishing a forum or National Federation to provide a united voice on specific issues and joint activities
- that the possibility of holding joint executive meetings should be investigated.

In spite of various attempts very little progress was made in fulfilling these objectives.

The discussions, claims and reports that had been a major part of the CTU's activities while it had been in operation were to become very relevant during the negotiations on the Pay and Conditions Agreement of 1996. Many of the recommendations made in reports were ultimately implemented in the final agreement of 1996, and the points system was discarded.

Promotion in National Schools

The Congress resolution of 1993 had instructed the CEC to seek a review of the points system with the Department of Education so that a uniform points rating for all pupils, irrespective of age or school category, could be implemented. The General Treasurer was mandated to draw up a report that would establish the organisation's policy to achieve that end.

The report proposed that the Ryan Tribunal of 1968 had been in error when suggesting a similar management and promotion structure for primary and post-primary schools; schools in the primary sector and in the post-primary sector were structured, organised and managed differently, namely:

- The primary sector consisted of approximately 3,400 schools, rural and urban, and over two-thirds of them had less than seven teachers on their staffs.
- There were approximately 850 post-primary schools, all in urban areas, and these varied from large to very large in size.

The pool of money available for promotion posts was not apportioned in accordance with the number of teachers in the different sectors.

	% of teachers	% of money	% promoted
National	50.3	42.0	39.9
Secondary	29.0	35.7	54.8
Vocational	14.5	15.8	51.8
Comprehensive	6.2	6.5	49.1

The CEC adopted the proposal that the INTO should seek:

- a significant increase in the pool of money available
- an equal division of the pool of money for promotion posts between the primary and post-primary sector
- a different in-school management and promotion structure for primary and post-primary schools
- a significant increase in the number of teachers in promotion posts
- a retention of the concept of seniority for entitlement to posts of responsibility
- the establishment of an additional category of posts with specific responsibilities attached to them.

Again, this report was to have a major influence in the 1996 agreement.

Conciliation Council Claims, 1987–96

The PNR, PESP and PCW had clauses that provided for the settlement of exceptional claims or claims deemed to be minor claims, and teachers were successful with a number of claims at Conciliation Council under these headings.

1 In December 1987 it was conceded that the averaging arrangements that applied to allowances for principals, vice-principals and other posts of responsibility for pension would now apply to qualifications and other allowances.

2 It was agreed that the expression 'retiring salary' as defined in paragraph 3(iii) of Agreed Report 14/75 should be amended to read 'the sum of the annual rate of scale salary on the last day of pensionable service and the annual rate of any allowance payable on the last day of service'.[28]

3 The INTO was successful in getting agreement for the payment of a B Post Allowance to Visiting Teachers of Travellers with effect from 1 May, 1990.[29]

4 In May 1991 the INTO was successful in a claim to have eligible part-time specialist teachers in Special Schools declared entitled to pro-rata incremental, superannuation and holiday and sick leave credit.[30]

5 The unions were successful with a claim that, with effect from 1 January 1991, a Grade A or Grade B Post Allowance would be paid to a teacher who carried out the duties of such post while the post-holder was absent on sick leave or maternity leave.[31]

6 Subsequently, it was agreed that the terms of the agreement would apply to teachers who carried out the duties of a post-holder absent under Rule 116 (Absence of Teachers at University Courses).

7 The Official Side conceded that a period on Career Break, in addition to being recognised for incremental credit, seniority, and permanency of post, should also be recognised for superannuation purposes, with effect from 1 September 1991. Arrangements were negotiated for teachers to pay appropriate pension contributions.

8 Agreement was reached whereby vice-principals and holders of posts of responsibility allowances, who were redeployed because of declining enrolments, would continue to receive their allowances as long as they remained in the schools to which they were redeployed.

---

28 Other allowances included Gaeltacht Grant, Teaching through Irish Allowance, Island Allowance, Rural Science Honorarium, Allowance for Itinerant Domestic Science Teachers, and a special allowance payable to teachers in Comprehensive Schools. Teachers' Conciliation Agreed Report 4/87

29 Teachers' Conciliation Council Agreed Report 1/91

30 Letter from the Department of Education to Michael Moroney, General Treasurer INTO, May 1991, CEC Report to Congress 1992, p. 29

31 Teachers' Conciliation Council Agreed Report 3/91

Substitute Teachers

Substitute teachers were not included within the scope of the C&A Scheme, and discussions on their conditions of service took place outside Conciliation but had subsequently to be confirmed by Conciliation Council agreements. The INTO was successful in a claim that all service given as a substitute should be recognised for incremental credit. This was a major breakthrough as it meant, in effect, that incremental credit was being allowed twice for the same term of service; the teacher who was absent would get incremental credit and the teacher working as a substitute would also get credit.[32]

On 13 February 1993 the INTO successfully completed negotiations on a scheme to have service given as a substitute teacher recognised for superannuation purposes.

Retired Teachers as Temporary Teachers

When a retired teacher returns to work as a temporary teacher, salary and pension are treated in one of two ways:

- When a retired teacher enters into short-term temporary work, the Department recoups from the gross salary a sum equal to the gross amount of the pension to which the retired teacher is entitled.
- When a retired teacher enters into a long-term contract, i.e. for an indefinite period, the Department ceases payment of the pension and the temporary teacher is paid at the increment point he or she had attained at the date of retirement.

PRSI in the Public Service

The Old Age Pension Act of 1908, introduced by Lloyd George, established a scheme whereby weekly cash payments, subject to a means test, were made to qualified persons who were seventy years of age or more. Many retired teachers qualified for the Old Age Pension as their pensions were so low. The first compulsory Social Insurance Scheme in Great Britain and Ireland was given effect by the National Insurance Act, 1911, again introduced by Lloyd George. The scheme provided protection to some of the poorest sections of the community against the hazards of ill health and unemployment. Insurance was made compulsory for almost all those aged over sixteen years who were either manual workers employed under a contract of service regardless of income rate, or non-manual workers whose remuneration did not exceed a specified limit. Teachers, who were not members of the teachers' pension scheme, came under

---

32 Teachers' Conciliation Council Agreed Report 4/91

the provisions of the Act. Managers were recouped by the Treasury for the insurance contributions that they were obliged to make.

Major reviews of the Social Welfare Insurance Scheme were carried out in 1934, 1947,[33] 1952, 1961,[34] 1974, 1979, 1994 and 1995. The last fundamental change was carried out in 1995 when the Minister for Finance declared that all new employees in the public service after 1 April 1995 would be compulsorily insured at the full PRSI rate.

Social Welfare Act, 1952

Under the Social Welfare Act of 1952 everybody in employment was issued with a social welfare insurance card and assigned a personal number. The employer retained the card and affixed an insurance stamp to it for every week that the person was employed.[35] When people changed employment they took their card with them and gave it to their new employers. The expression 'he was given his cards' came to mean that after being sacked the social welfare card was returned to the employee.

There were two types of stamps:

1   Class A, called a full stamp, was used by those in private employment; it guaranteed access to the full range of social welfare benefits.
2   Class D, the restricted stamp, was used by those in the public service; it only gave entitlement to a Widows' and Orphans' Contributory Social Welfare Pension and some benefits under the Health Acts.

The Class A stamp was a lot more expensive than a Class D stamp. The differentiation between public and private employees arose because public servants did not require the full range of social welfare benefits because of their conditions of employment. Male employees did, however, require protection for their dependents should they die in office and that was provided by a Social Welfare Widows' and Orphans' Pension.

A woman who worked outside the home and whose husband died was entitled to a Social Welfare Widow's Contributory Pension based on her own insurance contribution record, regardless of her age and any income, whether from employment or other source.

Registration under the scheme was compulsory and contributions were income-related; the first income limit was fixed at £600 per annum. On reaching

---

33 The Department of Social Service was established in 1947 to co-ordinate and administer more efficiently the various Social Welfare schemes already in operation.
34 The qualifying age for the Old Age Contributory Pension was seventy; it was reduced in 1973, 1974, 1975 and 1977, when it became sixty-six years.
35 Stamps were available for purchase in post offices.

the income limit, compulsory contributions ceased as did eligibility to benefit, but continued eligibility could be retained by becoming a Voluntary Contributor.

Voluntary Contributor

Voluntary contributors applied for their own personal insurance card, retained their original number, and affixed a social welfare stamp to the card every week. The INTO advised married male teachers to become voluntary contributors to ensure cover for their dependents and avail of Health Act benefits.

Due to increases in salaries the Minister for Finance raised the income limit for compulsory insurance cover every couple of years. This meant that a person could move from being compulsorily insured to being a voluntary contributor and back again. Unless voluntary contributions were paid during the intervening periods the social welfare contribution record would be broken and eligibility to benefit could be lost. By 1966 the income limit for compulsory contributors had reached £1,200 per annum.

Social Welfare Record of Teacher Pensioners

Teachers who retired either voluntarily or on a disability pension before the compulsory retirement age of sixty-five were advised to maintain a social welfare record in order to ensure continued entitlement to benefits. A social welfare record could be maintained:

- if either the husband or wife was in employment and paying a PRSI contribution
- by signing on for credits at the Local Employment Exchange, or
- by submitting a doctor's certificate regularly as required.

At first, pensioners wishing to retain a record were required to attend at local social welfare offices, generally once a month, or less, depending on local practice. With effect from 1 July 1993 the Pre-Retirement Credits Scheme (PRECS) came into effect. Pensioners were no longer obliged to attend at local offices but were simply required to complete a yearly declaration to the effect that they continued to satisfy the retirement condition.

Social Welfare Act, 1974

From 1 April 1974 the income limit was fixed at £2,250 per annum; women were included as compulsorily insured persons; and Deserted Wife's Benefit and Occupational Injuries Benefit were added.[36] The social welfare contribution was fixed at 15p per week, and the contribution on behalf of female teachers

---

36 All lay teachers serving in a pensionable capacity in national schools were in this category.

was paid by the Department of Education; it was increased to 26p from 6 January 1975.[37]

Benefits from 1968

With the introduction of the teachers' Widows' and Children's Contributory Scheme in 1968, the eligibility of a widow for benefits increased considerably, and this still applies:

1   A woman who works in the home, and whose teacher-husband dies, will receive a pension under the Teachers' Contributory Scheme and a Social Welfare Widows' Contributory pension.

2   A woman who works outside the home, and whose teacher-husband dies, will receive her salary, a pension under the Teachers' Contributory Scheme, and a Social Welfare Widows' Contributory pension.

3   A woman entitled to one or both of the pensions is entitled to allowances for any eligible children in accordance with the rules and regulations of the schemes.

4   The Spouses' and Children's Pension Scheme of 1981 extended cover to the husband of a female teacher in the scheme who dies in service or, having been in the scheme, dies while on pension.

The Pay-Related Social Insurance (PRSI) System, 1979

In the 1979 budget the Minister for Finance abolished the Social Insurance stamps and cards system and introduced the PRSI contribution system. With effect from 6 April 1979 Social Welfare and Health Act flat-rate contributions were changed into a percentage of pay to be collected by the Revenue Commissioners through the PAYE income-tax system. The differentiation between contributions and benefits for those in the private sector and public servants remained unchanged. As equal pay now applied, men and women had to pay the same contribution rate except for women in receipt of Widow's Pension, Unmarried Mother's Allowance, Deserted Wife's Benefit or Allowance, who were exempt from paying social welfare contributions.[38]

Tax relief on the pensions' portion of the social welfare contribution was abolished. The contribution income limit was fixed at £5,500 per annum.

Survivor's Pension under the Social Welfare Scheme

In 1991 the INTO sought equality of treatment for all widowed persons under the social welfare code.[39]

---

37 CEC Report to Congress 1975
38 CEC Report to Congress 1979
39 CEC Report to Congress 1992

A contributory widow's pension was payable to a widow, regardless of age, if the contribution conditions were satisfied on either her late husband's or her own insurance record at the date of her husband's death. Men who became widowers did not qualify for a social welfare pension or orphans' allowances even though they had a contribution record or even if the late wife had been contributing.

The anomaly was brought to the attention of the Minister for Social Welfare, and the Minister for Equality and Law Reform was requested to press for a change in the social welfare code to obtain equality of benefit for all contributors.

The unions adopted a CTU recommendation to initiate a High Court action on behalf of three named plaintiffs, one from each union, to seek equality of treatment.

The statement of case claimed that certain provisions of the Social Welfare Acts were unconstitutional as they were discriminatory in their application as between widows and widowers. The alleged list of discriminations was as follows:

1   A man makes PRSI contributions from which only the surviving widow can benefit.
2   A woman makes contributions from which only she can benefit; if she dies the widower does not benefit.
3   Where both the husband and wife are contributors, only the widow can benefit.
4   Surviving dependent children can benefit only if the father dies; they cannot benefit if the contributing mother dies.

Shortly before the budget for 1994 was due, an application was made to the High Court for a date to hear the case and the defendants were informed. In his budget speech, the Minister for Finance, Bertie Ahern, announced that from October 1994 the Widows' (Contributory) Pension would be called the Survivors' (Contributory) Pension and 'the proposed new PRSI scheme will provide for pensions for widowed men and women on an equal basis without any earnings restrictions'.

The 'Survivors' Pension was paid with effect from 28 October 1994 and no reference was made regarding its introduction at that time.

PRSI for Public Servants, 1995

The proposal to require public service employees to pay the same PRSI contribution as private sector employees had been a matter of discussion over a long period of time. It is difficult to assess whether this proposition was a matter of equity or the fulfilment of a philosophical desire. From a philosophical perspective the concept that all employees should have the same liabilities and be entitled to the same benefits seems to be associated with particular political beliefs. From an equity point of view, there is no doubt that there was resentment against what was perceived as 'the preferential treatment of public employees'. They were deemed to have the best conditions of service – safe, secure, pensionable jobs – and in the eyes of industrial employees they did not have to pay 'the same penal social welfare contributions'.

From a financial point of view, the receipt of social insurance contributions from public servants must have seemed like an un-mined gold vein to the government; having a cash flow of 7.75 per cent of the payroll instead of 3.15 per cent would have been of great benefit to the Exchequer. Furthermore, as all the new employees would be young the cash benefit to central funds would be greater in the early years and only diminish as the years went by when benefits would have to be paid.

Another consideration for the government was that public service occupational superannuation schemes were very expensive to maintain and a heavy drain on Exchequer finances. Experts were forecasting that the 'pension time-bomb' was ticking and that the problem was worsening. By transferring part of the pension liability to social welfare and getting increased income from revised PRSI contributions, a part resolution to that problem would be found.

In 1982 the Joint Programme for Government, published by the Coalition Parties, stated that 'there would be negotiations with Public Service Unions to extend full social insurance cover to public service employees under the PRSI system'.[40] There were also indications that the government might raise or abolish the ceiling for PRSI contributions. The Public Services Committee opposed any such move.[41]

In December 1982 the Executive Council of the Irish Conference of Professional and Service Associations (ICPSA) established a special subcommittee to prepare a report on the effects of such action and wrote to the Minister opposing it.[42] The Coalition Government did not proceed with the proposal.

The question of PRSI in the public service next surfaced in the budget speech on 25 January 1989 when Bertie Ahern announced that the government had decided in principle to extend full social insurance cover to all public sector workers currently on the modified rate of PRSI. He stated that the government

---

40 Fine Gael/Labour Coalition Government December 1982 to March 1987: Garret FitzGerald was Taoiseach, Dick Spring was Tánaiste, Alan Dukes was Minister for Finance, and Gemma Hussey was Minister for Education.

41 Letter to Daniel Murphy, Secretary, Public Services Committee from Alan Dukes, Minister for Finance, 24 January 1983, CEC Report to Congress 1983, pp. 51–8

42 The ICPSA represented 60,000 employees in twelve organisations in both public and private sectors.

intended to raise its proposals with the ICTU, with a view to implementing the new system on an agreed basis from April 1990. On 12 July 1989 a new Coalition (FF/PDs) government came to power. No substantial discussions took place between the government and the ICTU on the matter.

However, the subject had not gone away. In his budget speech on 24 February 1993, the Minister for Finance, Bertie Ahern, stated that the government was committed to working towards putting public servants on the same footing as other employees and that he intended to include it on the agenda for proposed discussions with the ICTU.

A short time after the budget a joint Government/ICTU Working Party was established to consider the application of full social welfare insurance to public servants. A report with four main sections was compiled:

1   Factual background material
2   Respective views of the government and the ICTU
3   Issues in relation to the co-ordination of occupational superannuation schemes and the social insurance system
4   The application of full PRSI only to new entrants into currently modified employments.

In his budget speech on 26 January 1994 the Minister for Finance announced that the government was satisfied that there was a convincing case for phasing out modified PRSI classes in the public sector and that they would no longer apply to public sector employees recruited on or after 6 April 1995.

The new contribution scheme would apply only to new employees as people in employment up to that date had contracts of employment and could not be forced to join the new scheme.[43] Employees were given the option of joining the new scheme or remaining in the old one; as it was the general consensus that the old scheme was better than the new one, nobody opted to join the new scheme.

The INTO General Secretary denounced the proposal as being 'invidious, divisive and discriminatory against new entrants into the Public Service and would hurt the youngest in the job'.[44] Ministers and all members of the Oireachtas were lobbied but without success. A legal opinion was sought but it did not provide any support, stating that 'there is no realistic prospect of being able to mount a legal challenge to the change in government policy concerning future recruits to the public service'.[45]

In his reply to a letter of protest from the General Secretary of the ICTU, the Minister stated:

---

43 The 1829 'No Detriment Rule' was being applied
44 Press statement by Senator Joe O'Toole, General Secretary INTO, 2 February 1994, CEC Report to Congress 1994, p. 14
45 CEC Report to Congress 1995, p. 35

It was partly as a result of this comprehensive examination (by the joint Government/Irish Congress of Trade Unions Working Party) that ... I am convinced that the present arrangements whereby entire categories of employments within the public sector are excluded from full social insurance cover cannot be allowed to continue indefinitely. I am satisfied, therefore, that the decision to introduce full PRSI for post 5-April 1995 recruits represents the best way of moving towards a situation in which employees in currently modified public sector employments are ultimately put on the same footing as other employees in both the public and private sector.[46]

The INTO, in conjunction with all the other public service unions, failed in its efforts to prevent the new system coming into operation from 6 April 1995. The teacher unions failed to have the salaries of new teachers adjusted to compensate for the increased PRSI deductions from their salaries.

The Department of Education issued explanatory leaflets to all new teachers to explain the mechanisms in respect of sick leave, maternity leave, and the longer-term implications with regard to pension entitlement. On retirement, the lump sum would be paid as heretofore and the pension would be paid from two sources, the Department of Education and the Department of Social Welfare. Henceforth, in a complete change from previous practice, queries on conditions of service from teachers in Class A had to be directed to the Department of Social Welfare; the Department of Education saw no role for itself in providing information to teachers on any of these benefits.

Review 1987–95

Both the government and teachers had high and low points during this period. The government agreed to the PNR with effect from 1 July 1987, but by the end of the year it was introducing a range of cutbacks, and the INTO organised local and national campaigns objecting to them.

The PERB presented its report to the Minister for Education on 7 December 1990 and its comments on demographic trends and recommendations on the structure and organisation of primary schools influenced government policy on the provision of primary education in future years.

An arbitrator awarded teachers a salary increase in December 1990 and the government, to the surprise of the teachers, agreed to implement it.

The government entered into the PESP, another three-year national programme with effect from 1 January 1991, but within twelve months it was claiming inability to pay. By the end of this difficult period things were beginning to look better and the PESP was followed by the PCW.

Teachers were successful in having a system of fortnightly pay introduced, but the parties failed to agree on new pay determination machinery.

---

46 CEC Report to Congress 1996, p. 24

In spite of the best efforts of those involved, the Council of Teachers' Unions did not survive. This affected inter-union relations, and while co-operation was achieved during most of the PCW negotiations, there were strains and cracks beneath the surface.

The introduction of full PRSI for all new appointments to the public service from 6 April 1995 was a severe blow to teachers. There would now be two classes of teachers, and new entrants would not have the same conditions of service as existing teachers. The range of benefits under the social welfare scheme was not as extensive as the conditions of service that had been negotiated for teachers down through the years.

The pay elements of the PESP were paid, and a procedure to process the outstanding local bargaining 3 per cent claim was agreed. The Celtic Tiger was beginning to purr loudly. The PCW national agreement was negotiated, and after three years the PCW Agreement on Pay and Conditions of Service of Teachers was accepted in a ballot by INTO members in March 1996 and by ASTI and TUI members in February 1997.

15

Into a New Era, 1994–2000

The 3 per cent Local Bargaining Clause of the PESP

Under the PESP, discussions on the 3 per cent local bargaining clause were supposed to commence not later than 1 July 1993, but by the end of the agreement on 31 December 1993, no public service union had succeeded in securing the additional money.

The Official Side initiated discussions on arrangements for dealing with claims under this clause at the Teachers' Conciliation Council on 29 May 1991. The 3 per cent could be used as:

Option 1   payment for all cost-arising claims for improvements in pay and conditions of service under consideration, or

Option 2   payment of one cost-increasing claim in respect of any grade of staff.

The Official Side had a preference for Option 1 as this would dispose of every claim submitted by teachers to any section of the Department of Education. It presented to each union a list of outstanding claims that had been identified. The list had three sections: joint union claims, single union claims and conditions of service claims.

The unions objected to this procedure and declared that conditions of service issues were not appropriate for consideration under the C&A Scheme and should not be resolved from the money available under Clause 3. They formally submitted a single cost-increasing claim for a general increase in salaries and allowance.[1]

By the time PCW negotiations were completed in January 1994 no progress had been made as the Official Side had not been in a position to make offers due to the Exchequer's financial position.

The PCW Agreement

As part of the PCW negotiations, ICTU representatives insisted that the new agreement would have to contain a mechanism to allow for progress on the

---

1   Clause 3 of the PESP provided that, as an exceptional matter, employers and trade unions would be entitled to negotiate further changes in rates of pay and/or conditions of employment for an amount up to but not exceeding 3 per cent of the salary bill.

outstanding claims under the PESP. This was agreed and Clause 2 (iv) of Annex 1 of the PCW clarified the two options and set down how they were to operate and how the money would be phased.[2] The following phases for payment of the 3 per cent were agreed:

1 April 1994	1.0%
1 June 1995	0.75%
1 June 1996	0.75%
1 June 1997	0.5%

Option A

Discussions commenced at Conciliation Council on 24 March 1994, where the Official Side expressed its preference for restructuring as envisaged under Option A. It wished to deal with all claims that had been submitted by teachers and to negotiate 'on the basis that real changes involving savings and improvements in efficiency and effectiveness will be achieved'.[3]

The teacher unions, while reserving their position, agreed to enter into negotiations under the terms of Option A but they made it a condition that if all claims, conciliation and conditions of service were being dealt with, negotiations need not, and could not, be restricted to a limit of 3 per cent.

At the Conciliation Council meeting on 10 May, the teacher unions reached agreement with the Official Side that the following claims would be considered:

1   superannuation/early retirement opportunities
2   posts of responsibility and promotion issues
3   qualification issues, including specialist teachers' claim
4   shortening of the incremental scale
5   recognition of the input of experienced, un-promoted teachers who chose not to opt for early retirement.

The unions claimed that, as a first step in the negotiations and as permitted under Clause 2 (iv), teachers should be paid a 1 per cent increase in salaries and allowances, with the balance being offset against the outcome of further negotiations. The Official Side agreed to this with effect from 1 April 1994.

It was agreed among the parties that the claims for early retirement and promotions would be processed first. The unions put forward a joint claim seeking that teachers should be entitled to retire from teaching service on a pension from fifty years of age with accrued pension of ten years' enhancement. (Army officers, Gardaí, prison and fire officers could retire on full pension with thirty years' service.)

---

2   The PCW was adopted at an ICTU delegate conference on 22 March 1994.
3   Programme for Competitiveness and Work, pp. 80–81

The Official Side responded by stating that it was prepared to negotiate changes to teachers' superannuation schemes, subject to certain conditions, which would allow for early retirement provisions in the following instances:

(a)   in the case of those teachers who no longer found themselves able to function at an acceptable level of professional performance

(b)   in situations where there were teachers who were surplus to requirements but who could not readily be transferred elsewhere.[4]

Working groups of the Conciliation Council were established to process claims on voluntary early retirement and changes in the teachers' superannuation schemes. Primary and post-primary sub-groups were established to consider problems particular to their sectors.

Media Coverage of the Early Retirement Scheme

Following the Conciliation Council meeting on 10 May, *The Sunday Business Post*, *The Evening Press*, and *The Sunday Independent* published articles that commented adversely on teachers' early retirement claims. The unions considered these criticisms and comments unbalanced and offensive and sought a right of reply, but without success.[5]

Teachers' Voluntary Early Retirement Scheme

In June the unions submitted a comprehensive document entitled 'Voluntary Early Retirement Scheme' in which the question of teachers who were no longer able to function at an acceptable level was considered.

Differences of opinion regarding the presentation of some claims became apparent between the TUI and the other two unions and it withdrew from the joint claim and as co-author of the document. The INTO and ASTI requested the Department of Education to consider the document to have been submitted by them alone.

Following a meeting in September 1994 the unions came to an agreement on new composite proposals for submission.[6] However, in spite of representations from the teachers, no meeting of the Conciliation Council was convened. A

---

4   The changes sought by the Official Side were: Cross-diocesan boundary redeployment, cross-panel transfers, embargo on permanent appointments from March to August inclusive, increased radius for compulsory redeployment, teachers on panel to do substitute work, drop the last-in/first-out arrangement.

5   The INTO issued a strongly worded statement in July 1994 warning that attempts to dismiss, sack or force teachers to retire through a compulsory early retirement scheme would put management and the Department of Education in breach of the Unfair Dismissals Act.

6   CEC Report to Congress 1995, pp. 21–2

further difficulty was created for teachers by the non-appointment of a new Public Service Arbitrator.

A New Government

A new Coalition Government (Fine Gael/Labour/Democratic Left) was formed on 15 November 1994, and there was renewed optimism that progress could be made at Conciliation Council.[7]

However, because no Conciliation Council meeting had been held since June, the unions believed that stalling tactics were being employed. The Chairperson of the Conciliation Council was informed on 24 January 1995 that unless a meeting was held within the next fourteen days and the official side had made an offer on early retirement and re-opened negotiations on the other issues, the Executive Committees would initiate procedures for the implementation of a programme of industrial action. While the official side claimed that the problem was caused by the non-availability of a new pay determination system, the threat achieved its purpose and arrangements for a meeting of the Conciliation Council in early February were agreed.

Offer from the Minister for Education, 1995

On 7 February the Minister for Education got Cabinet approval to make an offer to the teacher unions. When it became clear to the INTO that the offer was merely a proposal to equalise 55/35[8] arrangements with post-primary teachers, it advised the Minister that an unbalanced proposal was unacceptable and that primary teachers expected an improvement in their existing arrangements.

In spite of INTO representations, an offer on 55/35 was tabled at Conciliation Council on 10 February. The Official Side tried to balance the offer for all teachers by stating that it was prepared to discuss the position of teachers who found themselves unable to function at acceptable levels and those who became surplus to requirement.

The INTO delegation withdrew from Conciliation Council claiming that it had been misled and the CEC decided to embark on a campaign of industrial action.[9]

Officials in the Department of Education initiated negotiations during the week 13–17 February in an attempt to establish structures that would facilitate the reopening of talks on all aspects of the teachers' claims. No significant

---

7   John Bruton was Taoiseach, and Niamh Bhreathnach was Minister for Education from December 1994 to 1997.

8   A teacher's right to retire at age fifty-five as long as he/she had thirty-five years' recognised service.

9   The INTO delegation consisted of the President, General Secretary and General Treasurer.

progress was made and an emergency meeting of the CEC on 18 February decided on a framework for a campaign of industrial action. Further discussions took place with the Official Side and the possibility of appointing a facilitator to progress all of the issues contained under Option A was put forward.

On 20 February the INTO agreed to resume negotiations on condition that the outcome of any conciliation process would include improvements applicable to primary teachers and that the Minister was prepared to recommend the facilitator's report to government.

Appointment of a Facilitator

In early March, Seán Healy, Director of the Labour Relations Commission Advisory Service, was appointed as an agreed facilitator. His role was to facilitate discussions with a view to identifying proposals relating to early retirement and other outstanding claims. When the INTO secured an understanding that the outcome of discussions could include improvements in the offer to primary teachers, it resumed negotiations.[10]

The facilitation discussions commenced on 8 March and continued until 12 April. During the six-week period the teacher unions modified their opening claim and offered to increase teachers' superannuation contributions from 6.5 per cent to 6.75 per cent. The Official Side put forward a number of proposals for discussion and outlined its general requirements for flexibility and change, but it made no proposals on early retirement. The unions responded with a political lobby of government members to convince them of the case for special retirement arrangements for all teachers.

On 17 April the facilitator informed the unions in writing that the government was not 'disposed to agree to the improvements sought by the teachers' unions' but that 'it was prepared to agree to a detailed study of the teacher unions' claims by an independent and competent team of experts, including actuarial consultants', the study to be completed within a four-month time frame.[11]

The government refused to give any prior commitments in relation to the findings of the report and before the teacher unions had an opportunity to discuss the government's proposals, the Department of Education issued a public statement indicating that talks with the teacher unions had broken down.

The Minister for Education at 1995 Congress

In her speech to Congress delegates the Minister for Education stated 'that anything I might say at this time would not be useful or productive'. In response to the Minister's speech the INTO President presented her with a copy of a report that had been completed by KPMG, Pension and Actuarial Consultants,

10 CEC Report to Congress 1996, p. 11
11 Ibid., p. 12

which demonstrated that, not only would teachers' proposals have no immediate cost to the Exchequer, but that only marginal costs would accrue to the State after a ten-year period.

Teacher Unions' Campaign of Action

The CEC conducted a ballot of all members during May to take part in industrial action for up to six days, the first day of action being scheduled for 23 May.[12]

The post-primary unions decided to ballot their members for a series of one-day strikes, but the TUI Executive postponed its ballot until the autumn. Notwithstanding this the INTO and ASTI proceeded with their proposed industrial action.

In an attempt to re-open negotiations the teacher unions proposed to the government that all pension-projected costs, based upon agreed assumptions, should be submitted to an independent professional review. They also accepted that the claim should be resolved within the financial terms of the PCW.

The Actuarially Projected Costs

At a number of sidebar meetings government officials claimed that their actuarial reports did not sustain teachers' claims, but they declined to take up the unions' challenge and submit the reports to independent professional review.

After meeting with representatives of the INTO and ASTI, school management authorities sent a letter to the Taoiseach appealing to him 'to ensure a speedy and satisfactory resolution of the present dispute between the teacher unions and the Departments of Education and Finance'.[13]

The INTO also met representatives of the National Parents' Council (Primary) who, while reluctant to endorse industrial action, pledged support for the teachers in their claim for early retirement provision.

An estimated 15,000 INTO and ASTI members, from counties Dublin, Louth, Meath, Kildare and Wicklow, attended the march and rally at Leinster House on Tuesday, 23 May; TUI officers did not participate in the demonstration. A one-day stoppage and demonstrations were also staged by teachers in Munster and South Leinster; teachers in Connaught, Ulster and North Leinster were to take action at a later date.

Senator O'Toole, General Secretary INTO, had a motion on early retirement tabled for the adjournment debate in the Seanad on 24 May. The government initiated a public relations offensive to coincide with the Seanad debate. It released a document to the media entitled 'Briefing on Teachers' Early

---

12 On 16 May 1995 the INTO issued a press statement indicating that 85 per cent of the members, voting at branches, had supported industrial action. INTO Rules required a two-thirds majority in favour of strike action.

13 CEC Report to Congress 1996, pp. 9–23

Retirement Claims'. The government claimed that the actuarial cost of the teacher unions' claim would be as high as £30 million per year and that the extra 0.25 per cent contribution, which would yield £2.5 million a year, would not be sufficient to cover the cost of a new scheme. The actuarial report prepared for teachers calculated that allowing 150 teachers to take early retirement each year for fifteen years would cost £24 million.

Teachers claimed that the government's use of life-time actuarial tables as the basis for calculating its position was invalid and misleading and a cash-flow method should have been used, as had been used by their actuaries.

The government claimed that an early retirement concession to teachers would have implications for the wider public service which could cost as much as £100 million per year. Teachers argued that their claim was 'ring-fenced' on the grounds that the proposals did not apply to other groups in the public service who already had special pension entitlements, and that the Superannuation Act of 1956 already allowed enhanced arrangements of up to ten years for professionals in the civil or public services.

Memorandum of Understanding

In an effort to resume substantive talks the Minister for Education convened round-table talks in June; the talks involved the ICTU, the three teacher unions, and government Ministers. On 13 July a joint government/ICTU statement was issued announcing that a basis had been found for the resumption of negotiations. The agreement to resume talks was formalised in a Memorandum of Understanding which included provisions for early retirement arrangements with enhancement of between two and five years. It was proposed that negotiations would recommence in September and be completed by the end of October. The three Executive Committees accepted the Memorandum and suspended the programme of non-cooperation and industrial action.

Time in School Circular

A major problem arose before negotiations could recommence when the Minister for Education issued Circular 11/95, *Time in School*, on 11 August. This circular set down terms regarding the school year, the length of the school day, provisions for exceptional closures, suggestions for good management and the provision of information for parents. The issuance of the circular was criticised by the teacher unions as it was considered an attempt by the Department to determine what should constitute the school year and the school day before negotiations had commenced.

It was viewed as provocative and insensitive and a grave error of judgment on the part of the Minister. On 22 August the Department was obliged to send a letter of clarification to all Boards of Management and to principal teachers seeking to explain that it was not an attempt to pre-empt the outcome of future negotiations in those areas.[14]

Proposals for the Agreement on Pay and Conditions of Service of Teachers

Resumption of Negotiations

Negotiations recommenced on 14 September and, while initially focused on the early retirement issue, discussions on other outstanding issues continued on the basis that 'nothing is agreed until everything is agreed'.

In spite of the commitment to conclude negotiations by 31 October, by December not much progress had been made; the Official Side negotiators had been unable to signify agreement on anything because of a lack of political clearance. In January 1996 the CEC, claiming that 'the government's breach of faith has led us to the precipice once again', threatened industrial action.[15]

Following this threat, negotiations resumed and progressed rapidly. On 23 February the Official Side presented a document to the unions and management setting down detailed proposals on:

- retirement and pension provisions
- early retirement provisions
- incremental salary scale offers
- payments in respect of qualifications
- in-school management restructuring
- flexibility and change required under the PCW.

The INTO prepared a document, based on the presented proposals, and circulated it to every member recommending it as a positive package for the long-term betterment of teachers, pupils, parents, management, and the education service.[16]

Pension Provisions

Equalisation of Pension Provisions

A pension would be payable to all teachers on the Common Basic Scale who retired at fifty-five and had not less than thirty-five years' pensionable service.

---

14 CEC Report to Congress 1996
15 INTO Press statement, CEC Report to Congress 1996, p. 23
16 INTO Document: Proposals for Agreement on Pay and Conditions of Service of Teachers under Clause 2 (iii) of Annex 1 of the Programme for Competitiveness and Work, February 1996

A scheme was proposed for the provision of added years for the computation of pension benefits for teachers who retired on disability or to the estate of teachers who died in the service.

Special Purchase Scheme for Secondary Teachers

A special purchase scheme would be established whereby secondary teachers could gain superannuation credit for incremental service not previously recognised. The Secondary Teachers' Superannuation Scheme would become compulsory for all new teachers.

Pension for Temporary and Part-Time Teachers

Superannuation arrangements would be established for part-time teachers in post-primary schools and for temporary teachers in community/comprehensive schools.

Pensions for Service in Capitation Schools

All service given as a teacher or as a supernumerary in a capitation school would be recognised in full for pension purposes.

Income Tax Relief on Pension Contributions

Tax relief would be allowable on employee contributions up to a limit of 15 per cent of salary in the year in question.

Early Retirement Scheme for Primary and Post-Primary Teachers

Strand One

Strand One would be for teachers who were consistently unable to achieve an acceptable level of professional performance.

Strand Two

Strand Two would be for teachers aged fifty years or over who had served for a minimum of twenty years and found that they could no longer function at the level of commitment associated with educational reform.

Strand Three

Strand Three would be for teachers who were in posts surplus to requirements and who could not readily be redeployed.

General Provisions of the Early Retirement Scheme

- The number of retirements permitted under the scheme would be limited to a quota of 300 per annum.
- A teacher accepting early retirement would not be eligible for future employment in any capacity as a teacher or lecturer in any school or college recognised and funded directly or indirectly by the Department of Education.
- If a teacher accepted early retirement under this scheme and was subsequently employed in any area of the public sector, payment of pension to that person under the scheme would be adjusted.
- Applications under Strands One and Two would be submitted for initial processing to an Early Retirement Advisory Committee (ERAC).
- An Early Retirement Consultative Council (ERCC) would review the policy guidelines of the ERAC and the operation of the early retirement procedures and propose changes where they were deemed necessary.
- The effective date for the Early Retirement Scheme was set at 31 July 1996.

Payment in Respect of Qualifications

In response to teachers' claim for a degree allowance for specialist teachers and national teachers who trained prior to 1977, the Official Side proposed that a Pass Degree Allowance would be paid to all recognised primary and post-primary teachers who did not hold a degree qualification. In addition it was proposed that the payment of an Honours Degree Allowance would be paid to holders of all degrees conferred and designated as honours degrees by appropriate awarding authorities, that agreed procedures would be established for dealing with appeals for the payment of allowances in respect of qualifications, and that a budget of £100,000 per annum would be allocated for the payment to teachers of course and examination fees incurred by them in the successful completion of in-career training courses approved by the Department and school management which did not count towards a qualification in respect of which an allowance was payable.

Incremental Salary Scale

The Official Side proposed a reduction in the length of the Common Basic Scale for teachers by deleting the eighth point on the incremental scale. The shortened scale would be implemented in two equal phases with effect from 1 June 1996 and 1 September 1997, respectively.[17]

---

17 The eighth point was removed as a means of providing a benefit to younger teachers going up the salary scale. It was estimated that it would be of benefit to 28,000 of the 40,000 teachers. The early retirement proposals were of benefit to older teachers.

Allowance for Teachers with Thirty-five Years' Service

Teachers with thirty-five years' or more incremental service, who did not have any post of promotion and who had been on the maximum of the Common Basic Scale for at least ten years, would be paid an annual allowance of £1,000.

In-School Management Proposals

These proposals were organised into five categories, the main features of which were as follows:

1   New Structure for Posts of Promotion

Revised schedules for the allocation of posts to schools would be based on the numbers of approved teachers employed in schools, and separate revised schedules for allowances and posts of responsibility would be established for primary and post-primary schools. A current vice-principal would be classified as Deputy Principal, an A Post holder as Assistant Principal, and a B Post holder as a Special Duties Teacher.

2   Rate of Allowances

Allowances held by Principals, Deputy Principals, Vice-Principals, 'A' Posts and 'B' Posts would be increased by an average of 28 per cent, if the conditions attached to the upgraded posts were accepted.

3   Effective Dates

The increased allowances would be implemented as follows:
Principals and Deputy Principals:

- one-third of the increase with effect from 1 September 1996
- one-third with effect from 1 September 1997
- full increase with effect from 1 September 1998.

Assistant Principals and Special Duties Teachers:

- one-third of the increase with effect from 1 January 1997
- one-third with effect from 1 September 1997
- full increase with effect from 1 September 1998.

4   Appointments to all Posts

All appointments to new posts would be filled by way of competition in accordance with formal selection procedures agreed between representatives of the teachers, managers and the Department. The responsibilities and duties attached to all posts were defined as follows:

- The Principal, Deputy Principal and holders of posts would form the in-school management team.
- The Principal would have overall responsibility, under the authority of the Board of Management/VEC, for the day-to-day management of the school.
- Before taking up an appointment, post-holders would have to enter into a contract to undertake the duties of the grade to which they were being appointed.
- Following a consultative process, duties would be assigned by the Principal to ensure that the necessary tasks, duties and responsibilities to meet the pastoral, curricular and administrative needs of the school were undertaken.

5   Monitoring of In-School Management

The Department of Education proposed that monitoring of the revised in-school management would be carried out. It also proposed that certification would be sought periodically from the school authorities signifying that they were satisfied that the duties attached to posts were being carried out.

Flexibility and Change

As their contribution to flexibility and change, primary teachers would be expected to adopt the following conditions:

- The school year would be standardised, with common commencement dates, vacation periods and core mid-term breaks.
- Primary teachers would have to supervise for the first day of a colleague's absence (post-primary teachers for two class periods per week for absent colleagues).
- Teachers would have to submit an agreed formal school statement making provision for participation in fifteen hours per year of professional non-teaching activities outside of normal school time, and give a commitment to participate in parent–teacher liaison.

The Department of Education would issue an agreed circular, *Time in School*, which would set down the arrangements for both primary and post-primary teachers.

Reaction of the Teacher Unions

In March the INTO received the following clarification on outstanding issues:

- all post-holders would be eligible for new allowances

- all existing post-holders, including holders of posts in a personal capacity, would be offered new contracts on the basis of the duties defined for these posts
- every A post-holder would be offered a post as Assistant Principal
- every B post-holder would be offered a post as a Special Duties Teacher
- on accepting the new post the allowance appropriate for these posts would be paid
- the holder of a personal allowance, on accepting the new post, would lose the privilege of retention of an allowance on a personal capacity
- all Privileged Assistants would receive a 28 per cent increase in their allowances as long as defined duties were fulfilled in the school
- where a post-holder was unsuccessful in securing a revised post or where a post-holder did not opt to change, there would be no increase to that allowance other than the regular pay round increases.

The three teacher unions conducted a ballot of their members on the package; INTO members accepted it, 67.1 per cent for, 32.9 percent against, while members of the two post-primary unions rejected it.

The Department's circular, *Time in School*, had caused considerable resentment among many post-primary teachers who found many aspects of the flexibility and change sought by the Department unacceptable. Reservations were also expressed about aspects of the in-school management proposals and about the language and conditions relating to early retirement provisions.

The General Secretary and General Treasurer of the INTO met representatives of the Retired Teachers' Association on 19 March 1996 and confirmed the CEC's determination to ensure that retired teachers would benefit in full from the deal. In response to INTO representations, the Minister for Education indicated her intention to honour the claim that the full 3 per cent of the deal would be applied to retired teachers.

On 29 March the Minister issued a press statement noting the decisions of the teacher unions but declaring that this set-back should not negate the progress that had been achieved. Officials of the Departments of Education and Finance later communicated the Minister's proposal to appoint a facilitator to try to resolve the problems that had arisen between the parties.

Congress delegates adopted a CEC motion which declared that the Minister's proposal to appoint an independent facilitator was a genuine attempt to resolve the current difficulties, and would allow further consideration of particular areas of the package, and the implications of certain aspects which had not been contemplated during the negotiations.

The ASTI and the TUI Executive Committees also referred the proposal to their Easter Conferences for decision. The ASTI delegates decided to participate in the facilitation process. TUI delegates voted against participation in the facilitation process and demanded that the deal should be renegotiated; they adopted a comprehensive motion detailing their demands.

As it was recognised by all that implementation in full was not possible without the agreement of all parties involved, efforts were immediately put in train to try to resume negotiations.

Revised Proposals for the Agreement

After the Teachers' Conferences, 1996

In an effort to break the impasse, on 23 April the Minister for Education appointed Seán Healy as facilitator; he had acted in a similar role in February 1985. The TUI objected to the manner in which he had been appointed, rejected an invitation to meet him and sought direct talks with the Minister. Following further talks the TUI agreed to participate in the process.

At a special meeting on 11 May, the CEC decided against participation in any new national pay agreement unless the government was prepared to implement the deal at primary level.[18]

The Facilitator and Revised Proposals

Protracted negotiations were conducted from May to December 1996 under the chairmanship of Seán Healy. The original document was examined paragraph by paragraph; the language was revised, inflections deemed objectionable were removed, interpretations were provided, and amendments agreed. Finally, on 13 December 1996 a document was presented to the three teacher unions for agreement. The key amendments to the original proposals are set out below.[19]

A   Superannuation

1   Equalisation of Pension Provisions

The equalisation of primary and post-primary teachers' pension provisions was to be achieved as follows:

- Pre-service training periods for qualification as a teacher would be reckoned for the purposes of achieving the thirty-five year threshold for retirement on the basis of two years for four years' training and one year for three years' training.
- Actual teaching service purchased for pension purposes would be reckoned for the purpose of achieving the thirty-five year threshold for retirement.

---

18 The PCW Public Service Pay Agreement was due to expire on 30 June 1997.
19 The amendments should be read in conjunction with the original agreement.

2   *Early Retirement Scheme for Primary and Post Primary Teachers*

The voluntary early retirement scheme, with the three strands, remained but the language used to define which teachers were eligible to apply under the strands was amended.

3   *General Provisions of the Early Retirement Scheme*

The limit of 300 retirements permitted under the scheme was increased to 400. Priority would be given to retirements under Strands One and Three and retirements under Strand Two could not be more than 250 per annum. The quota arrangements would be subject to review.

4   *Capitation Service*

It was agreed that the 5 per cent superannuation contribution would not be required for any recognised service given prior to 1 July 1968.

B   Qualification Allowances

Qualifications were clarified and defined, but no substantial amendments were made.

C   Incremental Salary Scale

Allowance for Teachers with 35 Years' Service

It was proposed that the £1,000 annual allowance would be increased to £1,015 with effect from 1 October 1996 and would attract future pay increases.

D   In-School Management

It was proposed that the seniority proposals in 'In-school Management' would be addressed separately in the different sectors. At primary level seniority would have a significant weighting in all promotion posts except for that of principal.

E   Flexibility and Change required under the PCW

The proposals on flexibility and change were radically reviewed. The following specific provisions were proposed:

- Arrangements for meetings: arrangements would be agreed between management and staff.
- Staff meetings and student review meetings: schools could make provision to allocate from normal school time a period equivalent to the time given outside school.

It would be the responsibility of the principal teacher, the Chairperson of the Board of Management and the CEO to ensure and certify that the necessary duties were performed.[20]

Phased Implementation of the Deal

Immediate Problems

While negotiations were ongoing with the facilitator, the unions met frequently to establish agreed negotiating positions. Talks also took place between the INTO and the Catholic Primary School Managers' Association (CPSMA) to identify problems that might arise in the implementation of the in-school management provisions.

By the end of August 1996, however, it had become clear to the INTO that the post-primary unions would not be in a position to conclude a revised agreement for a number of months. This created a problem as there were particular proposals, of relevance only to primary teachers, which were in danger of not being implemented. The immediate problems were:

1   The pension entitlements of teachers retiring compulsorily on age grounds at the end of the school year, 31 August 1996, would be seriously affected.
2   Some teachers would be denied the opportunity to avail of the early retirement proposals under the three strands in 1996.
3   Two thousand additional promotion posts were to be created in primary schools from 1 January 1997.

While it was recognised that implementation in full was not possible without the agreement of all the other parties involved, the INTO initiated a campaign to seek the implementation of aspects of the deal relating to the primary sector only and to set aside the other elements pending an agreement with the post-primary unions.

Ad-Hoc ERAC (The Early Retirement Advisory Committee)

The government agreed to facilitate the implementation of the early retirement options at primary level prior to 31 December 1996.

The ASTI was prepared to allow the primary teachers' quota to retire but the TUI was not. It objected to the implementation of any superannuation element of the package on the grounds that all such matters required a Conciliation Council agreed report. It held that the signing of such an agreement would bind the TUI into agreement terms rejected by its members in a ballot. This action

---

20 INTO Publication, *Eolas*, No. 26, 12 June 1996

was not appreciated by the INTO as 7,000 TUI members were perceived to be preventing 35,000 INTO and ASTI members from reaching an agreement.[21]

In order to overcome the TUI objections, the Minister agreed to convene an Ad-Hoc ERAC to consider applications from INTO members.[22]

The TUI became aware of this and wrote to the Minister for Education seeking clarification of the government's position regarding the unilateral implementation of one aspect of the deal.

Eventually, arising from meetings between the General Secretaries, agreement was reached on the text of an INTO resolution to be placed before the respective Executive Committees of the three unions.[23]

The proposal was accepted by the Standing Committee of the ASTI. The TUI Executive, while endorsing the wording of the proposal, 'in order to allow the gathering of information about those National Teachers who wished to retire in 1996', continued to hold the view that the implementation of the early retirement element of the deal was a matter for Conciliation Council.

The process commenced and national teachers who wished to retire before the 20 December were invited to submit completed application forms to the Department by 13 November. The first batch of applications was processed by the Ad-Hoc ERAC on 3 December and recommendations were made to the Minister for Education. Seven out of the ten applicants under Strand One and eighteen out of twenty-seven under Strand Two were successful; but the Department was not prepared to process the Strand Three applications as the procedures for its implementation had not been finalised.

Following representations to the Minister the Ad-Hoc ERAC was reconvened on 18 December and it was agreed to establish criteria and procedures for resolving problems, including the difficulties that had arisen in relation to the interpretation of applications from teachers. Further meetings of the Ad-Hoc ERAC took place on 20 February and 14 April 1997.

During this period parallel meetings continued to take place between the unions and various government Departments with a view to reaching an agreement on the other outstanding aspects of the package.[24]

---

21 CEC Report to Congress 1997, p. 20

22 The following were nominated as the respective members of the committee: Seán Healy, Chairman, Patrick Curtin, Department of Education, Michael Moroney, INTO, Sister Eileen Randles, CPSMA.

23 CEC Report to Congress 1997, p. 21

24 The General Treasurer, Michael Moroney, had announced at the 1996 Congress in Belfast that Congress 1997 would be the last Congress he would address as General Treasurer as he intended taking early retirement on 31 May 1997. John Carr was elected as General Treasurer-Designate and took up the position on 1 October 1996.

The Schedule for Promotion Posts

Discussions commenced on 15 November 1996 between the INTO and education officials to agree a mechanism for the distribution of the 2,000 posts which were due to be introduced with effect from 1 January 1997.

A schedule, based on the actual number of schools in the system and their eligibility to posts under the points system, gave the following positions:

Principals	3,316
Vice-Principals	1,523
A Posts	306
B Posts	1,711
Total	6,856

However, the Department records showed that the actual number of allowances paid in February 1996 was as follows:

Principals	3,640
Vice-Principals	1,964
A Posts	306
B Posts	1,711
Total	7,621

This meant that 765 allowances were held in a personal capacity as follows:[25]

Personal Principals' Allowances	324
Personal Vice-Principals' Allowances	441

It was agreed that a new schedule of promotion posts would have to include both these and the additional posts on offer.

The offer was as follows:

1 January 1997	2,000 Special Duties Teachers (B Posts)
1 September 1998	600 Special Duties Teachers (B Posts)
1 September 1998	390 Assistant Principals (A Posts)
Total	2,990

The Schedule would have to provide for actual posts (6,856), personal posts (765) and new posts (2,990), an overall total of 10,611 posts. The INTO also

---

25 Personal allowances were held by teachers, called privileged assistants, who had been involved in amalgamations, school reorganisations or a reduction in enrolment due to demographic trends.

proposed that some extra posts would have to be provided for teachers who were being paid 'Acting-up Allowances' in the absence of the post-holder on paid or unpaid leave. The Department agreed that flexibility in the creation of a small number of posts would be recognised.

The INTO negotiators sought that any agreed schedule of promotion posts should contain the following elements:

- that a Deputy Principal would be appointed in all three-teacher schools
- that a Special Duties Teacher would be appointed in all four-teacher schools
- that nine-teacher schools would be entitled to an additional Special Duties Teacher
- that approximately 50 per cent of primary teachers would be in promotion posts
- that special schools should receive particular consideration to ensure that no school would be adversely affected as a result of the distribution of the additional posts.

In order to accommodate these objectives a formula was agreed whereby some of the posts in the offered schedule could be converted into posts that were required.

Because of the likelihood that the promotion posts' package would not be concluded for implementation on 1 January 1997, the CEC informed the Department on 19 December that it would reject the Partnership 2000 National Agreement if a deal was not implemented. The CEC received an immediate response from the government stating:

We are favourably disposed to implementing the proposals in relation to the 2,000 'B' posts as soon as possible. We are prepared to enter immediate discussions with the INTO and the relevant Management Bodies on the new schedules and arrangements for filling the new posts. Contact with other unions will continue.[26]

On 3 January 1997 the INTO negotiators presented a schedule to the Department which they believed was a fair and equitable distribution of promotion posts across the various categories of schools.

The Schedule from 1 January 1997 showed the position as follows:

Principals	3,316
Deputy Principals	2,469
Assistant Principals	306
Special Duties Teachers	3,778
Grand Total of Promoted Teachers	9,869

---

26 CEC Report to Congress 1997, p. 23

The completed draft Schedule, from 1 September 1998, showed the position as follows:

Principals	3,316
Deputy Principals	2,469
Assistant Principals	531
Special Duties Teachers	4,876
Grand Total of Promoted Teachers	11,192
Percentage of Teachers Promoted	54%

The Implementation of the Schedule for Posts of Responsibility

The schedules were agreed and the decision was confirmed by letter on 24 January 1997. It was agreed that Special Duties Teacher posts would be retrospective to 1 January and that special schools would receive particular consideration to ensure that no school would be adversely affected as a result of the distribution of the additional posts.

Partnership 2000 was endorsed by a majority of the delegates at the ICTU Conference on 30 January. Both ASTI and TUI members accepted the re-negotiated package in their respective ballots.

Circular 6/97, setting down the revised in-school management structures in primary schools, was not issued until June 1997 but the posts due for 1 January were filled.

The Reduction in the Length of the Scale

The Department issued Circular 31/97, which set down the revised salary scale and allowances. The first phase of the elimination of the eighth point together with arrears, retrospective to 1 June 1996, was paid on 26 June 1997. The second phase was implemented from 1 September. A total of £3.4m was paid to 10,417 teachers, providing an average payment of £328.

Long-Service Allowance

The agreed annual allowance of £1,000 was indexed to salary increases as follows: £1,000 with effect from 1 August 1996; £1,015 with effect from 1 October 1996; £1,025 with effect from 1 January 1997.

A total of 1,720 teachers had their salaries adjusted and £1.3m was paid in retrospective payments on 26 June. Thereafter the allowance was applied automatically to eligible teachers' salaries on completion of ten years on the maximum of the scale.

Qualification Allowances

A phased payment of the qualification allowance to non-graduate and specialist teachers commenced on 26 June 1997. A total of 4,926 teachers received payments of qualification allowances amounting to (including arrears) £5.8m, representing an average payment of £1,181 for each teacher.

Promotion Post Allowances

Payment of the promotion post allowances was delayed because of the need to negotiate a number of issues arising from the application of new in-school management arrangements. Following satisfactory negotiations all revised allowances, with arrears, were paid.

Between March and June 1997 the INTO conducted a series of meetings with the CPSMA to establish a 'Management Procedure for Appointments to Posts of Responsibility in National Schools' and also to establish procedures to operate the early retirement provisions.[27]

In-school Management

During the summer and autumn of 1997 the INTO, management and the Department of Education and Science (DES) completed negotiations on a number of outstanding items, including the transition period for many schools from a points rating system to a teacher posts system, the establishment of an agreed mechanism for conducting appeals, and the establishment of procedures for the appointment of persons to 'acting' positions.

Pension Credit for Service in Capitation Schools

The INTO had endeavoured to process the following two claims for most of the twentieth century:

1 that capitation service should be recognised in full for superannuation purposes[28]
2 that supernumerary service in capitation schools should be recognised in full for superannuation purposes.[29]

---

27 The Management Procedure for Appointments to Posts of Responsibility in National Schools included a schedule of duties, a mechanism for the review of duties assigned, appointment procedures, and an appeals procedure on non-appointments.

28 'Capitation service' was service given by teachers as members of religious orders on the minimum staff of capitation schools, primary or post-primary.

29 A concession had been granted with effect from 1971 whereby up to five years would be granted for pension purposes for supernumerary service given up to 30 June 1947.

Concessions had been achieved in 1921, 1934, 1971, 1975 and 1978. From 1978, however, the Official Side had not been prepared to make an offer on any contingent claims on the Conciliation Council agenda and the INTO resubmitted them for consideration under the restructuring package allowed under the terms of Clause 2 (iv) of Annex 1.

The Offer

The Official Side made the following offer, with effect from 1 February 1996:

1   All capitation service would be recognised as pensionable service under the relevant superannuation scheme, subject to payment of contributions where appropriate.
2   All supernumerary service given by members, or former members, of religious orders or by lay persons in capitation schools would be recognised as pensionable service under the relevant superannuation scheme subject to a deduction from retirement lump sum of a superannuation contribution equal to 2.5 per cent of reckonable remuneration in respect of each year of supernumerary service.

It was agreed that the implementation of the concessions would be carried out in the context of phasing arrangements for a PCW restructuring package, and the DES promised to process them at the earliest opportunity.

The package, which resolved this long-standing problem, was of benefit to teachers serving in primary schools, and some who had transferred to post-primary schools.

Cost of the Capitation Package

The offer was costed on the basis of projected retirements of teachers with capitation and/or supernumerary service. A summary of the projected costs was as follows:

'Capitation Service' Costs:

	No. of Teachers	Average Annual Cost (Gross)	Average Annual Cost (Net)
Primary	650	£469,492	£365,160
Secondary, Community and Comprehensive	225	£104,096	£80,963
Total	875	£573,588	£446,123

Supernumerary Costs:

	No. of Teachers	Average Annual Cost (Gross)	Average Annual Cost (Net)
Primary	455	£158,193	£140,618
Secondary, C&C	52	£ 6,513	£ 5,790
Total	507	£164,706	£146,408
Grand Total		£ 738,294	£592,531

Recognition of all Capitation Service

The difference between the payment of members of religious communities in capitation schools and in classification schools had been created in 1839. This difference had been continued with the introduction of the Teachers' Superannuation Act of 1879. By the end of the 1970s all capitation schools had converted to classification schools and all teachers were paid personal salaries.

Supernumerary service had never been recognised for salary payment or for incremental purposes; some small concessions had been achieved with regard to recognition for pension purposes. In 1996 all service given as teaching members of religious communities was declared eligible for recognition for superannuation purposes. This capitation package was a belated recognition for a group of teachers who had given valuable teaching service to the State.

Superannuation Implications of PCW Agreement

Following acceptance of the deal, negotiations took place to agree how the different elements would be applied in the calculation of superannuation benefits. The following arrangements were agreed:

1   Teachers in Service

For teachers in the service and who retired during the phasing of salary and allowances, the lump sum and pension would be assessed on the salary and allowances as at the date of retirement. Where a teacher retired during the operation of the phasing, the pension would be revised as the phases came on stream.

If a post-holder remained in the same post category and accepted the duties attached to the revised post, averaging would not apply. If a post-holder changed category within three years, averaging would apply.

On or after 31 July 1996, up to six and two-third years of added service could be credited, subject to such added service not exceeding the additional pensionable service that would have accrued had the teacher continued in service up to age sixty.

2   Retired Teachers and Pension Parity

Initially the Department refused to revise the pensions of retired teachers as their pensions had been assessed on the situation that applied at the time of their retirement. As restructuring had occurred post-retirement the revised allowances could not apply.

The unions regarded this as a departure from the practice of indexing pensions. The Retired Teachers' Association mounted a campaign to secure indexation for its members. The CEC recognised that this was a problem that applied to all retired public pensioners whose unions had successfully negotiated the local bargaining 3 per cent.

Indexation of pensions was easy to apply when salary and allowances were increased by standard amounts, but, for the first time in the public service, increases varied considerably, not only between each grade or group, but also within grades and groups.

On the one hand, the application of traditional indexation in the education sector would have resulted in retired, un-promoted teachers receiving no benefit from the deal. On the other, the application of the percentage increases to all pensioners would result in promoted people not getting the full benefit of the increase in their allowances

It was decided to pursue the question on a broad trade union front. The CEC proposed the following:

1   that pensioned teachers should receive a pro-rata increase in their pensions reflecting the same allowance increase enjoyed by teachers in the service at the same promoted level

2   that pensioned teachers who had not been in a promotion post should receive a minimum increase of 3 per cent.

The net effect of this proposal would be that the concept of traditional parity would be maintained; all retired teachers would receive an increase of not less than 3 per cent and other pensioners would get recognition for having been in promoted posts.

This proposal was endorsed by the Retired Teachers' Association and adopted by the Public Services Committee. It was presented to the Minister for Finance in July 1997 but he declared that he was not in favour of giving pensioners the productivity increases granted to employees.[30] During the months of October and November several representations were made to Ministers but without success. The CEC and the Retired Teachers' Association held a demonstration outside Leinster House on 12 November. The Minister for Finance finally

---

30 Charlie McCreevy, Minister for Finance

conceded the claim; over 70,000 public service pensioners received increases at a cost of £23m, i.e. 4.6 per cent of the public service pension bill.

In conceding the claim, the Minister for Finance stated that the 'policy in relation to all future restructuring deals will be determined in the light of the recommendations in the final report of the Commission on Public Service Pensions' and this matter was referred to the commission for consideration.[31]

Early Retirement Arrangements

Early Retirement Advisory Committee (ERAC), 1997

During 1997 ERAC met on six occasions and made the following recommendations to the Minister:

Strand	Primary		Post-Primary		Totals
	Allow	**Disallow**	**Allow**	**Disallow**	
I	18	2	35	5	60
II	29	4	57	3	93
Totals	47	6	92	8	153

A total of 153 teachers applied for early retirement under Strands One and Two and 139 were successful; nine primary teachers were granted early retirement under Strand Three.

Early Retirement Consultative Council (ERCC), 1997

The function of ERCC was to agree criteria and review the policy guidelines of ERAC and to propose changes where such were deemed necessary. A number of difficulties occurred in the operation of ERAC and the first meeting of ERCC took place on 30 June 1997.[32]

Clarification was sought by ERCC from the Department on the following issues:

1 the necessity for inspectors' reports in support of early retirement applications in the light of the practical situation that such reports would not always be available at second-level

---

31 CEC Report to Congress 1998. The Commission on Public Service Pensions was established by the government in February 1996. It was projected that the cost of public service pensions would double within twenty-five years. The Commission issued an Interim Report in August 1997; it presented its Final Report on 14 November 2000.

32 Membership of the committee for the school year 1997–98 were: Seán Healy, Independent Chairperson; John Carr (INTO), representing the teacher unions; Sr Eileen Randles (CPSMA), representing the managerial authorities; and a representative from the Departments of Education and Finance.

2   the eligibility of teachers on career breaks to apply for early retirement

3   the situation with regard to late applications.

The DES replied as follows:

- It was acknowledged that inspectors' reports might not always be available and that the absence of an inspector's report should not prevent ERAC considering an application on its merits.
- It ruled that only teachers on career breaks who were due to return within one year might, as an exceptional measure, apply for early retirement under Strand I.
- It ruled that ERAC could apply discretion to the consideration of applications received after the closing date, but subject to the quota not being exceeded.

John Carr objected to the ruling about teachers on career break and the unions made representations to the DES that teachers on career break should be eligible to seek early retirement under all Strands. Following negotiations, arrangements were agreed to facilitate some teachers who wished to take early retirement while on career break.

The scheme continues to operate and items of concern are considered from time to time by ERCC.

Review of the Agreement

The PESP applied to all employees in the public service with effect from 1 January 1991. The 3 per cent local bargaining increase was supposed to be implemented from 1 January 1992, but by the time the PESP ended on 31 December 1993 no progress had been made; the government had run into financial difficulties and the Official Side had made no offers.

The next national agreement, the PCW, came into effect on 1 January 1994 and the unions ensured that it contained a provision that would enable negotiations on the outstanding 3 per cent to be completed.

The teacher unions commenced discussions on 24 March 1994 but final agreement was not reached with all parties until March 1997. During the intervening period there were strikes, threatened strikes, glitches and delays. Eventually, with the assistance of a facilitator, a comprehensive agreement on teachers' pay, conditions of service and revised in-school management procedures was signed.

The main results of this agreement were: a radical change in the system of promotion to posts of responsibility and the promise of a change to the operating practices of teachers. The question of moving away from the Common Basic Scale did not surface; the incremental salary scale was reduced; and teachers who would never get a post of responsibility were rewarded for their contribution to the education service.

The most important concession from national teachers' point of view was the abandonment of the points system; the pool of money for promotion posts was considerably increased and primary and post-primary schools each got new promotion structures.

Allowances for qualifications were increased, and non-graduate and specialist teachers' claims were resolved.

Some of the retirement and pension provisions were common and others were particular to the different sectors: all capitation service was recognised for pension purposes and an early retirement scheme was introduced.

The Official Side and school managements got new structures for administration within schools, and teachers gave commitments regarding flexibility and changes in the operation of their conditions of service. The following points were negotiated separately by the unions with management and officials of the DES:

- appointment procedures for new promotion posts
- standardisation of the school year
- parent–teacher meetings outside school hours.

Total Cost of the PCW Package

The resolution of the outstanding problems cost more than the originally proposed 3 per cent local bargaining increase. This point had been made by the teachers at the beginning of the negotiations when it was stated that the 3 per cent limit could not be retained if conditions of service were made part of the deal. The total cost came to 5.6 per cent of the wage bill and it was apportioned as follows:

Total Cost of the PCW Package

	millions
1% April 1994	£12.00
Early Retirement/Superannuation Provisions	£7.70
Post-35 years £1,000	£3.60
Reduction in Scale	£11.40
New A and B Posts, Post-primary	£2.91
New A and B Posts, Primary	£5.53
Total	**£43.14**
	64.7%

	millions
Specialist Teachers	£8.8
Revised Principal's Allowance	£6.48
Revised Vice-Principal's Allowance	£2.68
Revised A and B Post Allowances	£5.57
	£23.53
	35.3%
Overall Total	**£66.67m**

The negotiations extended over a period of three years, and because each union endeavoured to get the best benefits for its members, relations between the teacher unions became strained at times. For instance, the first set of proposals was accepted by the INTO but rejected by the ASTI and the TUI, and when the INTO sought the implementation of benefits that were of particular concern to primary teachers alone, it was vigorously opposed by the TUI.

Problems were overcome and trade-offs and compromises were made, but when the final proposals had been agreed and had become fully operational, the experience of the exercise resulted in a lessening of the fraternisation and co-operation that had previously existed between the unions.

Partnership 2000

At a Conciliation Council meeting on 25 June 1997 agreement was reached regarding general pay increases (under Clause 2 of the Annex to Partnership 2000) to teachers on the Common Basic Scale. In addition, Clause 4 of the Annex to Partnership 2000 permitted a local bargaining adjustment of 2 per cent to scale salary and allowances, to be paid with effect from 1 July 1999.

All parties to Partnership 2000 committed themselves to an extensive programme of 'Action for Greater Inclusion'. The importance of agreeing specific action programmes for the delivery of the education service in primary and second level schools was acknowledged. It was agreed that discussions on revisions to Conciliation and Arbitration Schemes in the public service would be finalised within six months.

16

Overview and Concluding Comments

Introduction

The purpose of this book was to trace the origin, evolution and development of the remuneration and superannuation schemes for national teachers in Ireland during the period 1831 to 2000. This has been done with a comparative reference to developments in the civil service; it is an accepted premise that the civil service has been the pathfinder regarding pay and pensions of employees in every sector of the public service.

Civil Servants

By the end of the eighteenth century the civil service had been organised into a number of independent departments answerable to parliament and controlled by a Secretary of State. Salaries were not standardised and pension provision was haphazard and ad hoc. The pension position was not rationalised until 1859 and the salary problem was not resolved until the recommendations of the Playfair Commission were implemented in 1875 when civil servants in different departments were regraded and each grade paid a similar salary. These revised conditions of employment established the format by which salaries and conditions in other public service areas of employment would be determined.

The Superannuation Act of 1810, which was unsuccessful in establishing a comprehensive pension scheme, was followed in 1834 by the first Act to deal exclusively with pensions. The principles that pensions would be based on retirement salary and related to age and service were laid down; the compulsory age of retirement was fixed at sixty-five and the maximum pension possible was fixed at two-thirds of average final salary.

Over the years the constant concern of parliament about the expansion of the public service was manifested by the establishment of a series of commissions; the objective in all instances being to curb expenditure. As a result of battles fought a number of benchmarks were established. The need for the service was recognised, as was the requirement that to retain a competent and contented staff a reasonable salary and pension would have to be paid.

However, in spite of numerous attempts, the question of whether the pension scheme should be contributory or non-contributory was not resolved until 1859 when civil servants were successful in establishing their pension scheme as non-contributory. The Civil Service Superannuation Act of 1859 is still the legislation on which their scheme is based. A similar scheme became the aspiration of every other public service group but, for many, a comparable scheme was not to become a reality until well into the twentieth century.

A major revision of pension schemes occurred in 1909 when male civil servants were successful in getting payment of gratuities on retirement or death in service as part of their scheme. In order to balance out the payment position they accepted that their maximum pension entitlements would be reduced from two-thirds of salary to one half. This revised benefit was not offered to anyone else, not even female civil servants.

Teachers Pre-1831

In the eighteenth and early part of the nineteenth centuries Catholics responded to the Penal Laws by supporting a haphazard nationwide system of unofficial 'pay-schools'. Protestant Education Societies established schools with the fundamental aim of educating Irish schoolchildren to be English-speaking and Protestant. Commencing in 1775, members of Catholic teaching orders provided schools in the cities and large towns throughout Ireland for the education of boys and girls of the poor.

A survey carried out in 1824 identified 11,823 schools in Ireland and these were staffed by 12,530 teachers with 585,641 pupils. Hedge schools numbered 9,352 and they catered for 403,774 scholars; these were mainly one-teacher stand-alone schools provided by individuals, unrecognised and not subject to any supervision. Teachers were dependent on fees paid by pupils for their remuneration and, in some cases, payment in kind. Religious-run schools relied on donations, subscriptions and some fees from pupils for their income. Teachers in Protestant schools were paid discretionary annual gratuities based on annual reports by inspectors.[1]

There was no training facility for Catholic teachers, nor was there any national recognition of qualifications. As a general practice, a person aspiring to be a teacher apprenticed himself to an experienced teacher and served for a number of years as his assistant. Having absorbed as much experience and knowledge as was deemed appropriate, the apprentice moved on to an area where a vacancy existed and established a school of his own. The schoolmaster, being one of the few 'educated' persons in the community, tended to be held in high esteem.

---

1   The Second Report of the Commissioners of Irish Education Inquiry, 1825–27, HC 1926–27 (12) XII

The Commissioners of National Education

A new centrally controlled national school system, under the control of the Commissioners of National Education, was established in Ireland in 1831, forty years before a national scheme was introduced in Great Britain. School managers who wished to have new or pre-1831 schools in their areas recognised had to apply to the commissioners. The system developed slowly and twenty years elapsed before the number of recognised schools exceeded 5,000. The aspirations of the commissioners were restrained by the amount of money made available each year by the Treasury.[2]

The number of trained teachers provided each year was never sufficient to meet the demands of an expanding service and, consequently, most of the teachers appointed were untrained.

Initially, males outnumbered females in the ratio of two-to-one. The first training facility provided by the commissioners catered for men only; a training facility for women was opened in the grounds of Tyrone House in 1842. The ratio of men to women being trained remained heavily in favour of men until after 1853. Although the training situation improved with the recognition of denominational training colleges in 1883, only half of the teachers employed were trained at the end of the nineteenth century.

The commissioners' rules and regulations ordered a teacher's life, work, and behaviour both inside and outside the school, and school inspectors ensured that they were fully complied with.[3] Teachers were constantly reminded that their main function was to provide elementary education for the children of the common poor and that they ought not to have ideas above their station.

Salaries for Teachers

The commissioners always recognised that the remuneration situation for teachers was not satisfactory, but although they appealed to the Treasury nearly every year for more money, there is no evidence that they staged any great battle to remedy the problem.

For the first sixty years the Treasury insisted that the gratuity paid to teachers should be subvented by funds from local sources and sought on a number of occasions to secure a local contribution as part payment of teachers' income. This attitude was unsustainable due to the poverty of the general population; many parents either could not or would not provide contributions. Eventually, in 1892 the Treasury had to abandon its consistent ideology and assume total responsibility for teachers' salaries. The Treasury at all times used the control of teachers' salaries and restriction of conditions of service as its main method of controlling costs in education.

---

2 The number of recognised schools in 1853–54 was 5,023.

3 Appendix A in all of the annual reports of the Commissioners of National Education

Teachers who depended totally on the small gratuity received from the commissioners existed at subsistence level. Some who endeavoured to earn money from other sources did so by acting as scribes, surveying land and tilling small plots; women did knitting and sewing.

In 1835 the annual gratuity paid to men for every 100 pupils enrolled was increased to £10 for men and £8 for women.[4] Inspectors' reports on the precarious position of teachers prompted the commissioners to revise the system of payment to teachers. In 1839–40 all recognised teachers were brought together at local centres to sit for examinations conducted by the inspectors and, based on these examinations and inspectors' assessments, teachers were divided into four classes for the payment of a fixed salary. This was an acceptance for the first time that the money made available for the payment of teachers constituted a 'salary'. Conductors of monastery and convent schools retained the capitation system of payment, and lay teachers employed in these schools were paid directly by the conductors.[5]

The massive increase in the cost of living that accompanied the Famine exacerbated teachers' remuneration position and the commissioners were obliged to review the situation. In 1847–48 male teachers were brought together again by the inspectors for another round of written and oral examinations and divided into fourteen different divisions and classes for salary purposes; similar examinations were conducted for women the following year. The subdivision of teachers into so many categories was a ploy to keep costs to a minimum; the majority of teachers were categorised in the lower grades with the smaller increases, and fairly substantial increases were given to the few in the higher grades.

While salaries were amended a number of times between 1848 and 1860, the increases granted did not keep pace with rises in the cost of living. No salary increases were awarded between 1860 and 1872.

During this period two events occurred that had repercussions for the teaching profession:

- emigration became the norm after the Famine, and
- from 1855 entrance to the civil service was by open public examinations conducted by Civil Service Commissioners.

Men, who formerly would have entered the teaching profession, left to bestow their talents on other countries or entered the civil service. With the increasing number of vacancies in the school system and the number of men entering the profession decreasing, the number of female teachers increased; this could be

---

4   £10 in the year 1835 had equivalent value to £587 in the year 2000.

5   By the end of the nineteenth century, convent schools numbered nearly 400, about three-quarters of which were managed by orders founded by Irish people.

said to be the beginning of the feminisation of the national school teaching profession.

The INTO

The first anecdotal record of teachers coming together occurred after the salary placement arrangement of 1839. This salary arrangement allowed a teacher to gain promotion to a higher grade by successfully completing an annual examination. This method of promotion led to the practice of teachers coming together to help each other to pass the examinations. The 1848 salary placement scheme provided further encouragement for the continuation of this practice.

Coming together in this manner must have been very difficult; teachers were dispersed throughout the country, mostly in one-teacher rural schools and means of communication and transport were very underdeveloped, but this congregating of teachers was to lead to the establishment of the Irish National Teachers' Organisation in 1868.

The meetings developed into occasions when papers dealing with some aspect of school work were discussed and, inevitably, conditions of service were considered. Such groupings began to adopt titles, such as Education Associations and Improvement Societies. The commissioners became aware of these meetings and viewed them with disquiet. They issued a circular in November 1848 admonishing teachers against any activity deemed to be contrary to the rules and regulations and warned them against making comments that reflected on officers or officials of the Education Office. The teachers persisted and news items about associations of teachers began to appear in local newspapers. It is on record that inspectors frequently chased teachers out of schools in which they had gathered for meetings.[6] In 1850 an attempt was made to bring these separate associations together as a 'Teachers' Redress Committee'. The commissioners issued a second circular warning teachers of dire penalties if they should partake in such meetings.

During the following years groups of teachers were successful in persuading politicians to make representations to the government on their behalf regarding salaries and conditions of service, but no benefit followed. Even though teachers' dissatisfaction and discontent continued, all efforts to establish a national organisation for national teachers were unsuccessful.

A number of activists in the Dublin Central Teachers' Association set their minds to establishing a national association representative of teachers. They realised that if it was to have a chance of being successful, its leader would have to be someone who was outside the profession and who would not be answerable to the commissioners. Vere Henry Louis Foster was identified as

6   T. J. O'Connell, *A Hundred Years of Progress*, p. 2

such a person; Vere Foster, Jeremiah Henly and Robert Chamney had established *The Irish Teachers' Journal* in 1867. Using the establishment of the Powis Commission (1868) as a springboard, the activists were successful in bringing representatives of a number of associations together and the Irish National Teachers' Organisation was formed. Vere Foster became its first President and James Kavanagh, secretary of the Dublin Central Teachers' Association, was appointed secretary.

This was a major event for teachers as they now had an effective central voice to promote their concerns. From the very beginning the Central Executive Committee (CEC) evolved strategies that became increasingly sophisticated over the years. Lines of communication were opened at central level with officials in the Education Office, the Resident Commissioner, the Commissioners of National Education, the Chief Secretary, and the Lord Lieutenant.

The INTO was fortunate in the appointment of Patrick Keenan, a Catholic, as Resident Commissioner in 1871; he was the first commissioner open to receive deputations from the teachers and he listened with sympathy to their problems and difficulties.[7] However, at a very early stage leaders in the INTO recognised that the Commissioners of National Education had no real power and that the central power of the Lords of the Treasury over the national school system and over the remuneration of teachers was, to all intents and purposes, almost absolute.

The 'payment-by-results' scheme, introduced in 1872, did not resolve teachers' income problems. It was consistently opposed by the INTO and was finally abandoned in 1900.

From early on it was clear to INTO leaders that the only possibility of getting concessions was through political activity. Relations with Irish MPs were established, and they were canvassed extensively and lobbied by teachers in their constituencies. To assist this process, it became a practice of the INTO to appoint one of the members of the Irish Party as its 'parliamentary secretary' or co-ordinator of activities.[8] In addition, delegations from the CEC went to London to lobby members of the government. Contacts and relations were established with organised teachers in England and Scotland.

In 1892 the Treasury finally recognised that all efforts to make the provision of education a charge on local contributions or rates had failed and it had to assume responsibility for the total remuneration of teachers.

The Irish Education Act of 1892 was the first piece of legislation to deal specifically with the remuneration of teachers and its passing marked a major achievement by the INTO. The Act marked the final step in the process of removing national schoolteachers from dependence on local sources for the

---

7   T. J. O'Connell, *A Hundred Years of Progress*, p. 485
8   Charles H. Mellon, MP for Kildare, was one such appointee, and he held this position during the 1870s and 1880s.

payment of any portion of their salaries. While the annual estimate for teachers' remuneration increased by about 25 per cent, the overall position still remained unsatisfactory; teachers in Ireland continued to lag considerably behind their colleagues in Great Britain in the matter of remuneration.

During the last two decades of the century workers generally became better organised and trade unions became more effective and powerful in seeking improved conditions of employment for their members. The INTO was to the fore in this development, becoming increasingly militant and an active force in the political scene; it emerged as an organisation of power and influence.

The INTO mounted sophisticated campaigns to bring its grievances to the attention of the public and to put pressure on politicians. These became the template for all campaigns, variations of which have been practised over the years up to the present time. The effectiveness of the campaigns can be attributed to the way the association was organised and the involvement of members in every aspect of the political arena. It succeeded in raising the status of the teacher in society.

In spite of its successes and its campaigns for the recruitment of new members, at the beginning of the twentieth century, less than half of the approximately 12,000 teachers in the service were members of the INTO. One of the main reasons put forward for this situation was that many members of the Catholic hierarchy were philosophically opposed to trade unions, and a number of them were particularly opposed to teachers in their schools being members of the INTO.

Female Teachers

Initially, male teachers outnumbered female teachers in a ratio of two-to-one, and women were paid at a lower rate than men and were also systematically denied opportunities for promotion. This situation applied up to 1855 when, in response to the establishment of public examinations for entrance to the civil service, the number of females joining the teaching service increased considerably; in 1873 there were 4,998 males and 4,548 females in receipt of class salaries from the commissioners. By the end of the century the ratio of men to women had changed to 45:55. However, the promotion stakes did not show much difference: 76 per cent of male teachers were principals, compared to 50 per cent of female teachers.

In line with historical social trends, it was only gradually that women emerged from a marginal role in the INTO to occupy officer positions and achieve the position of president. When the INTO was formed in 1868 the CEC was composed of male principals only and it remained as such until the 1890s when two male assistants were appointed. Women were allowed to attend the Annual Congress from 1883 after the adoption of the resolution 'that this

Congress recommends the attendance of lady members for the future of our meetings'. It was not until the first decade of the century that a group of strong-willed women played a very active role in the INTO. They had a 'Women's Section' in the INTO journal, in which they espoused the concerns of female teachers. The first two women were appointed to the CEC in 1907, and in 1908 Catherine Mahon led the campaign to have the Birrell Grant distributed as an equal pay award to men and women at the same grade, a fore-runner of the principle of equal pay for equal work.[9]

Catherine Mahon was elected as the first woman president of the INTO in 1912 and again in 1913. This was a major achievement as presidents rarely served a second term. She is recognised as being one of the most powerful holders of the office. In 1919 the INTO Rules and Constitution were amended to provide equality for all members, men and women, principals and assistants.

As a result of Catherine Mahon's recruiting efforts, membership rose from 5,681 in 1905 to 8,010 in 1908, and of that number women's membership rose from 2,422 to 4,070.[10] Membership continued to rise in subsequent years. Today, close to 100 per cent of national teachers are members of the INTO, and this has been a major factor in the strength of the organisation's negotiating power over recent decades.

The Twentieth Century

The twentieth century commenced with the implementation of the recommendations of the Belmore Commission by a new Resident Commissioner, Dr Starkie. The twenty years of his autocratic and dictatorial rule became known as the 'Starkie Regime' – not a good time for many teachers.

New rules and regulations were issued in 1900 and every aspect of a teacher's life in the classroom was affected. The 'payment-by-results' scheme was abandoned, the system of inspection was changed, a new curriculum was issued for every class and, of particular relevance to teachers, the method for the computation of remuneration and the system of promotion were changed.

Many teachers suffered in the fallout that occurred when the Education Office tried to implement the new salary placement provisions. The new promotion system was regarded as a numbers' game rather than a system based on ability. The implementation of the new curriculum was very difficult as little in-service training was provided, and very little new equipment and aids were provided.

All of these difficulties caused serious dissatisfaction among teachers and resulted in a long period of discontent and acrimony. The INTO became involved in disputes with the Education Office, the Resident Commissioner, the Commissioners of National Education and the Treasury, and relations were

---

9 Equal pay for doing work of equal value was not introduced until 1973.
10 Síle Ní Chuinneagáin, *Catherine Mahon, First Woman President of the INTO*, p. 60

strained between teachers, inspectors and the Education Office.

Starkie claimed that the money he had been promised to implement the new system was never made available. The Treasury, which controlled the purse strings, continued to determine the conditions of employment of teachers in national schools.

The Great War and After

On the commencement of the Great War the government imposed Standstill Orders with restrictions on increases in salaries and pensions; the salary increases that had been agreed immediately before the start of the war were not implemented.[11] While some bonuses were paid during the war, teachers did not fare well.

When the war ended it was apparent that a major review was required in the conditions and remuneration of all employees paid from the public purse. Civil servants got a salary increase and a method for determining salary reviews at six-monthly intervals, and teachers in Great Britain got considerable salary adjustments under Burnham.

In 1916 the first full-time General Secretary of the INTO was appointed. Teachers achieved a significant increase in salary in 1920, and women emerged as an important force in the ranks of the INTO.

In Ireland the Killanin Committee recommended considerable salary increases and a completely revised pension scheme for all national teachers. However, implementation of these recommendations was bedevilled by the political, religious, and economic circumstances that prevailed at the time. The MacPherson Education Bill of 1919 triggered bitter controversy between politicians, management and teachers; the INTO was in favour of the bill, the Catholic Hierarchy was adamantly opposed to it and, ultimately, it was not processed through parliament.

Eventually, national teachers were granted increased basic salaries with effect from 1 April 1920; they were offered the civil service bonus system for salary reviews but, instead, opted for consolidated salary scales. This proved to be a mistake; teachers would have fared better had they maintained an established relationship with the civil servants.

Teachers did not get their revised pension scheme, and the position of the Pension Fund continued to deteriorate until, in 1934, drastic changes had to be introduced to resolve the problem.

Pension Scheme

While primary teachers in Ireland were fortunate and noted as the first group of employees outside of the civil service to get a pension scheme, their scheme was

---

11 With the outbreak of war the Liberal Party formed a coalition with the Conservatives in 1915.

contributory and experienced considerable difficulties. All of the actuarial valuations, except for the first one in 1885, found the fund to be in deficit, and by 1896 the deficit had reached £1,200,000. It was estimated that £250,000 of the deficit was due to inadequate contributions from teachers, and the balance to the non-contribution of its share by the Treasury. In order to forestall the collapse of the fund, a new scheme was introduced that required increased contributions from teachers and reduced the range of benefits with effect from 1 January 1898.

Male civil servants got an amended scheme with the payment of gratuities in 1909, but teachers did not get similar scheme until 1951. Teachers were granted a revised scheme with effect from 1 October 1914. It was not as generous as the one enjoyed by civil servants and the date of its implementation was subsequently used by the Treasury to the disadvantage of teachers when pension increases were granted in 1920.[12] Again in 1920 teachers thought they were going to get a scheme similar to civil servants but historical events intervened.

William Starkie died in 1920 and he had not been replaced by the time the Provisional Government assumed responsibility for education affairs on 1 February 1922.

The Period 1922 to 1948

The Political Scene

National teachers had suffered very badly under the British regime and expected that under a national government things would be different. This was not to be so. The period from 1922 to 1948 was probably the most traumatic and upsetting period endured by them since the foundation of the national school system in 1831. It did not appear to matter which party was in government, Cumann na nGaedheal from 1922 to 1932 or Fianna Fáil from 1932 to 1948. Teachers experienced cutbacks and an obvious lack of sympathy under governments led by both parties.[13]

It is hard to understand how this antipathy arose when one considers that many national teachers had been active participants and, in many cases, leaders in the fight for independence. They were represented in all the political parties in the Dáil; a number of them held high-profile positions in the different political party organisations; and they were very active in their localities and held in high esteem.

The War of Independence followed by the Civil War resulted in severe damage to the economy through loss of production, destruction of property and

---

12 The Great War had commenced on 4 August 1914.

13 An examination of the antipathy between the governments in power and national teachers would be worthy of a study on its own: 'The INTO and the governments from 1922 and 1948'.

increased security costs. A truly democratic system of 'government and opposition' did not operate in Ireland until after the general election of June 1927, when the Fianna Fáil deputies took their seats in the Dáil for the first time. Even then, the political situation was very unstable and the general elections that took place were very fractious.

During this period the government had serious problems as the public finances were not in a healthy state and the economic fabric of the country was shattered. The problem of securing resources for the huge task of reconstruction was compounded by a zealous desire by the government to live within its means. At this time the idea of budgetary deficits or raising debt were not accepted practices and the government maintained its balanced budget philosophy through stringent controls in State expenditure and cutbacks.

It would appear, however, that teachers as a group were obliged to assume a disproportionate share of the effort required to remedy the national financial problems.

INTO

From its foundation in 1868, the INTO had been involved in a continuous campaign to improve the status and salaries of teachers, and its objectives were to be no different under the new regime. These ongoing battles became more intense during the first decades of the new State.

On independence in 1922, teachers came under the control of the Department of Education, which, in its turn, was answerable to the Department of Finance; remuneration obligations and pension schemes that had been established under English legislation were adopted by Dáil Éireann. Bureaucrats in the Treasury were replaced by bureaucrats in the Department of Finance, and the manner of operation did not seem to differ from one jurisdiction to the other.

Under the new regime, the INTO continued to operate and maintain its dual role: in the industrial relations field to improve its members' conditions of service, and in seeking improvements in the education field. It convened the First National Programme Conference in 1921, and instigated the convening of the Second National Programme Conference in 1925. It opposed the establishment of the Preparatory Colleges, negotiated revised procedures for the inspection system, conducted a survey on the teaching of Irish in infant classes in 1941, and published *The Plan for Education* in 1947.

Progress, however, was slow as the inherited civil service bureaucracy brought with it the imperial civil service structures and procedures. This meant a continuation, practically without any change, of practices and precedents of the previous regime. The inspection system, with teacher rating and its associated controversy, did not change. The merit mark system, which made proficiency in teaching Irish the determining factor for the award of grades, became one of the greatest sources of grievance for INTO members. A rating could affect not only a teacher's income, prospects of promotion and eventual pension, but his/her prestige and personal self-esteem. The retention of the rating system adversely affected relations between teachers, the inspectorate and the administration.

Under the leadership of T. J. O'Connell the INTO affiliated with the Trades Union Council (TUC) and the Labour Party in 1917 and formally registered as a trade union in 1918. O'Connell served as a member of the National Executive of the TUC in the 1920s and became its President in 1930. He was elected as a TD for the Labour Party on a number of occasions and became leader of the party in 1927.[14] He served for a number of sessions as a member of the Seanad. The INTO disaffiliated from the Labour Party in 1946.

While comments were made by some that O'Connell's political affiliations and party activities were not helpful to the INTO with the different governments, it could also be said that involvement in the political process helped to ameliorate the vicissitudes experienced by teachers.

Since the foundation of the State, INTO members have been active in politics and a considerable number of its members have been elected as members of the Dáil and Seanad. In 1934, three members of the INTO, including its President, were members of Fianna Fáil and voted for cuts in teachers' salaries. As a general rule, INTO members in the Oireachtas are very conscious of their organisation and have been of considerable assistance on numerous occasions.

The 1923 Cuts

The Saorstát government continued the bonus system of remuneration for civil servants and technical teachers. As a result of their pay formula civil servants were awarded substantial cost-of-living bonuses during 1920, 1921 and 1922.

In 1923, in response to severe financial difficulties, the government applied a 10 per cent reduction to the salaries of all public servants. However, the reduction was not applied equally: only the bonuses of serving civil servants were affected while the salary scales for new entrants to the service and the salaries of all serving teachers were reduced. In the autumn of 1926 a revised contract of employment was introduced for future entrants into certain grades of the civil service; the starting salary for single men was reduced by 25 per cent and women were obliged to retire on marriage. In all other instances increased benefits were to apply.

The cost-of-living index, having peaked at 165 on 1 March 1921, declined almost continuously to an index of 60 in 1936 and, as a result, the cost-of-living

---

14 T. J. O'Connell, General Secretary INTO, 1916–48. He served as a TD from June 1922 to 1932, having been successful in the elections in 1922, 1923, and in June and October 1927; he was elected as Senator in 1941, 1943, 1948 and 1954.

bonus paid at each six-month review date to serving civil servants was reduced. Conversely, when the index increased so did the bonus. For teachers, however, the situation was not so good; between the years 1923 and 1934 teachers' salaries were reduced by approximately 27 per cent.

The 1934 Salary and Pension Revisions

During the Great Depression from 1929 to 1933, following the Stock Market Crash of 1929, the national finances were in a precarious state; a collapse in the volume of exports of agricultural products caused serious trade deficits.

On 30 March 1933 the government passed the Economies Bill in the Dáil which imposed temporary cuts in the salaries of civil servants, the army, and national teachers. National teachers were the most harshly treated group under the bill.

At the end of the financial year all public servants, except national teachers, were restored to the salary position they had prior to 1 April 1933. In conjunction with a revised non-contributory pension scheme, a further 5 per cent cut in salary was imposed on national teachers with effect from 1 April 1934.

A new pension scheme had advantages and disadvantages for both the government and teachers. The obligation on the government to make good the deficit in the Teachers' Pension Fund was removed and the teachers' pay-bill was reduced by 9 per cent, a 5 per cent salary cut and a 4 per cent pension contribution. Teachers got a pension scheme that was almost similar to the scheme enjoyed by civil servants, except that it did not provide for the award of a lump sum on retirement. Lay assistants and Junior Assistant Mistresses (JAMs) were declared eligible members of the pension scheme with effect from 1 April 1934. The reciprocal pension recognition arrangements with Northern Ireland that had been available from 1922 were removed.

In an era of salary cuts and a rising cost of living pensioners suffered very badly. On retirement their pensions were based on reduced salaries, and as there was no mechanism for reviewing pensions, when the cost of living increased they had to exist on their reduced pensions. Their standard of living deteriorated, and the longer a retiree lived the more precarious his/her position became. During the reign of Fianna Fáil governments from 1932 to 1948, no pension increases were awarded to pensioners.

In addition, new rules were introduced that obliged female teachers appointed from 1 October 1934 to retire on marriage. A marriage ban was not a new concept as it had been introduced in the civil service in 1926, and Memo V7 of 1930 had provisions that applied to the employment of married women in vocational schools. The ban did not apply to secondary teachers as it was considered that their conditions of employment were a matter between themselves and the managements of private secondary schools.

Paradoxically, the imposition of these cuts and changes coincided with a strengthening of the INTO. It had branches in every town and strong connections with all political parties; it had been involved in major national events and had strong international connections; and teachers were held in high esteem by the general public. Yet, of all groups paid from the public purse, national teachers appear to have fared particularly badly: their salaries were reduced and pension entitlements amended, and female teachers were obliged to retire on marriage.

The INTO was further disadvantaged in that previous access to senior officials and ministers was curtailed; during the period from 1932 to 1948, the INTO experienced great difficulty in arranging meetings with Ministers for Education or the Taoiseach.

By 1937 it was generally recognised that the severe repercussions on the Irish economy of the bitter 'Economic War' between Ireland and Great Britain were abating and that there were increasing signs of prosperity in the country. As the cost-of-living index had increased by twenty-two points between 1934 and 1938, government ministers' salaries were increased by 70 per cent, from £1,000 to £1,700; civil servants got an increase in excess of 10 per cent; and teachers were given a 5 per cent increase with effect from 1 April 1938. A principal teacher (Highly Efficient) was now in receipt of £357 (no pension deduction); in 1920 he had received £370 (subject to a 4 per cent deduction for pension).

In a further development, new rules were introduced that obliged all female national teachers to retire on reaching the age of sixty. Many female teachers could not fulfil the requirement of forty years' service to qualify for maximum pension.

The Second World War

The Second World War commenced on 1 September 1939 and while civil servants, public servants and other sections of the community were awarded a number of bonuses between 1 January 1940 and 1 January 1943 to meet the rising cost of living, national teachers did not receive any. At this time nearly 50 per cent of teachers had a total income of less than £4 per week; over 3,000 had less than £3 per week. Requests to meet the Ministers for Education and/or the Taoiseach regarding this problem were turned down.

Eventually, with effect from 1 January 1943, an Emergency Bonus was granted to teachers. News of the bonus was promulgated by the Department of Education in a large advertisement in the national daily newspapers on the morning of 19 December 1942. No other group in the public service was treated in this manner.

In November 1944, 26,000 civil and local authority servants received increases in their ordinary cost-of-living bonus, ranging from seven shillings and nine pence to £1 3s. per week, with an additional emergency bonus of one shilling per week. Teachers were awarded one shilling per week, but nothing more.

Pensioners did not receive any award; at this time, 70 per cent of them were receiving a pension of less than £3 per week.

In December 1944 the Cabinet rejected a teachers' claim with a vague promise that the remuneration of teachers, with other classes of public servants, would be open to reconsideration when the Emergency ended. The severe financial position endured by teachers was so well-known and of concern that the Catholic Hierarchy sent a resolution to the government recommending an increase in pay; this was supported by the Catholic Clerical Managers Association, the Church of Ireland bishops and the General Synod of the Presbyterian Church.

A memorandum submitted by the Minister for Education indicates that the Taoiseach was fully aware that teachers' salary position was very bad.

With effect from 1 January 1945, civil servants got increases varying from £22 to £77 per annum, and Gardaí got increases ranging from 10 per cent to 12 per cent. The Cabinet rejected a claim by the teachers for a salary increase.

The Road to Redemption, 1948–78

The 1946 Strike

At Congress 1945, a group of teachers, mainly from the Dublin Branch, was successful in having a 'Propaganda Committee' elected to organise and pursue a vigorous campaign to achieve a salary increase. De Valera met a deputation from the CEC on 18 April 1945 and claimed that his hands were tied by the Standstill Order and justified the substantial increases to the civil servants and Gardaí 'as righting a wrong caused by a promise made to them before the enactment of the Standstill Order'.[15]

Salary proposals presented to the INTO by the Minister on 8 December 1945 were declared to be totally unacceptable and the Dublin teachers came out on strike on Wednesday, 20 March 1946. They were supported in their action by Dr McQuaid, Archbishop of Dublin, which was a great boost and endorsement for teachers. It was resented by the government, and it has been claimed that it created a difference between Dr McQuaid and de Valera that was never reconciled.

De Valera and the government set their minds steadfastly against making any concessions to teachers. Offers of mediation were turned down and, eventually, after seven-and-a-half months of a bitter strike, circumstances obliged the teachers to call off the strike and return to their schools. Salary scales, which had

---

15 Confidential Report of Meeting on 18 April 1945, SPO, S10236/B

been proposed by the Minister in December 1945, were applied by the government with effect from 31 October 1946.

Teachers' perception that they were being discriminated against by the government was reinforced when civil servants were placed on consolidated scale salaries from 1 November 1946; the old cost-of-living bonus system was abandoned. A Conciliation and Arbitration Scheme was introduced for civil servants in 1947.

The repercussions of the 1946 strike were to last for many years; it had ended badly for teachers and, together with events that had occurred and things that had been said, it left a residue of bitterness, resentment and frustration. It has been readily conceded by most authorities that the teachers' strike had a profound affect on the outcome of the 1948 general election. The teachers realised that they could not expect any relief from a Fianna Fáil government and INTO activists became very involved in the election, particularly with Clann na Poblachta, which won ten seats and became a major partner in the Inter-Party Government.

The Aftermath of the Strike

T. J. O'Connell retired as General Secretary in 1948 and was succeeded by Dave Kelleher; Seán Brosnahan was elected as President. Kelleher and Brosnahan had been leaders of the strike movement. The INTO was now recognised as a major force in industrial relations and in the political field and this did much to restore professional morale among teachers.

The new coalition government took steps to ameliorate teachers' position: the regulation requiring women to retire at sixty was withdrawn; the 'highly efficient' rating was removed; for the first time in eighteen years pensioners were granted increases; and the period that teachers had been on strike was recognised for incremental and pension purposes.

The recommendations of the Roe Committee in 1949 resulted in teachers receiving revised salary scales and major pension concessions; the most important one being a tax-free lump sum on retirement.

During these negotiations, women came to the fore as a powerful interest group: they were placed on the same scale salary as single men; the maxima of their scales were increased by the largest amount; and they fought strenuously for and achieved the same pension provisions as men, something that female civil servants did not get until 1954. At the end of the day they fared best from the recommendations.

Single men did least well, and a discontented group persisted in the service until 1968, in spite of efforts to achieve compensation for them during the 1950s and 60s.

Primary and secondary teachers got separate Conciliation and Arbitration (C&A) Schemes with effect from 1 March 1951; a scheme for teachers in vocational schools was not signed until 3 January 1957. The introduction of these new schemes was a watershed in the area of industrial relations between the government and teachers; for the next two decades teachers had a mechanism for processing salary and pension claims.

However, having different schemes did have serious disadvantages in that it engendered lack of trust and co-operation. It led to each group watching the progress of the other two groups and also to a cycle of leapfrogging claims, with each claim been processed separately under the different C&A Schemes.

The Inter-Party Government was replaced by a Fianna Fáil government in 1951 and relations with Government reverted to what they had been. Representations seeking the re-establishment of a permanent C&A Scheme received no response; negotiations on the appointment of an arbitrator were procrastinated; and claims for salary reviews and pension improvements were delayed.

Fianna Fáil was replaced by the second Inter-Party Government in 1954. The coming to power of this new government was marked by almost instant progress: the terms of a new C&A Scheme were signed on 11 December 1954; the McEnaney judgement of 1939 was implemented in 1955, with increments withheld since 1930 finally being paid; and numerous claims were processed through the respective C&A Schemes.

The main objective of the INTO at this time was to achieve parity of salary, but the ASTI, and the TUI to a lesser extent, opposed this. Particular Arbitration reports caused severe inter-union problems as it appears that arbitrators did not consider the effect their findings would have on relations between the three teacher groups.

The general election in March 1957 initiated a sixteen-year period of Fianna Fáil governments. The appointment of Jack Lynch as Minister for Education marked a radical change in policy; there was now a clear perception and desire to develop a more orderly and rational way of dealing with teachers and schools. His most notable act was to revoke the 1934 Marriage Ban with effect from 1 July 1958; it was to take many years of processing claims through the Teachers' Conciliation Council and other fora before the problems resulting from the ban were reasonably resolved.

In an effort to resolve the question of parity, Lynch established a committee in March 1958 to report on the principles that should govern the remuneration of teachers in the different sectors. The *modus operandi* of the committee was not satisfactory to the INTO and its subsequent report in 1960 was viewed with dismay. It did nothing to resolve the differences between the teachers, and the three C&A Schemes continued to operate separately, with individual Arbitration reports resulting in strikes and the threat of strikes.

Seán Lemass came to power as Taoiseach in 1959. He epitomised the new Ireland, and people responded to the challenges of the *First Programme for*

Economic Expansion. The despair and gloom of the 1950s were lifted and optimism for the future was balanced with a demand for changes in every aspect of life.

A salary dispute in 1964 nearly precipitated another controversy similar to the 1946 strike but politicians' memory of that conflict, and its results, meant that every effort was made to resolve the problem, which the Taoiseach did in direct negotiations. The INTO had truly come to power: it had direct access to officials, to Ministers, and to the Taoiseach, if necessary.

However, other problems were being created elsewhere. The differences between the teachers' unions were exacerbated by a secret agreement between the ASTI and the Catholic Headmasters' Association which granted secondary teachers an additional non-pensionable 12.5 per cent of the married standard scale as part of the basic salary. When this became public, it was resented by the other unions and it caused difficulties for the Official Side.

One of the greatest innovative changes introduced into the education system occurred in September 1966 when Donogh O'Malley, Minister for Education, announced free post-primary education and a free transport system to enable maximum participation by the children of the State in secondary education. The country and its people continue to benefit from these decisions.

The Ryan Tribunal

The twenty years from 1948 to 1968 marked a period of teacher disunity, with claims and assertions about status, equivalence, parity, and qualifications often being used to emphasise differences.

With a view to solving the teacher remuneration problem and establishing a single unified teaching force with access to common C&A, Donogh O'Malley appointed a Tribunal on Teachers' Salaries on 15 December 1967.

The establishment of the Ryan Tribunal raised teachers' expectations, but they were to be disappointed. While it conducted a full review of the conditions of service of all teachers, the tribunal's recommendations failed to satisfy any of the three groups. Aspirations may have been too ambitious, and differences over the very important areas of status and pay became more pronounced.

Most teachers and their leaders considered that they were badly served by the members of the tribunal and by the officials in the Departments of Education and Finance. The tribunal's recommendations exhibited a lack of understanding of the school systems and of the circumstances that applied to the employment of teachers in the different sectors. Reading the submissions made, it is obvious that the tribunal was very influenced by the officials.

The officials did not appear to appreciate the provisions needed to accommodate the major changes that would be required in the provision of education in Ireland, such as 'free' post-primary education and the expansion in third level. They responded in a very narrow, parsimonious manner to the prevalent problems, and the amount of money made available was not sufficient to achieve the objective of a single unified teaching force, a common basic salary, and a common scheme of Conciliation and Arbitration. When imagination, foresight or perception was required, it was not forthcoming, and four years of conflict and dispute ensued. It is highly probable that if half the extra money that had to be subsequently provided had been made available initially, the subsequent disputes would not have arisen.

The period from 1968 to 1978 was a very difficult but vibrant time for every group involved in education. A massive expansion took place in the post-primary sector and the concept of 'Equality of Educational Opportunity' became a byword and the fulfilment of parents' aspirations for their children. A New Curriculum was issued to primary schools in 1971; Ireland joined the European Economic Community on 1 January 1973; Thomond College opened in 1972 to educate graduate specialist teachers for the post-primary sector; and all students entering training colleges for national teachers in autumn 1974 embarked on a three-year course leading to a BEd degree.

Other developments had ramifications for the conditions of service of teachers:

- The national teachers' pension scheme was converted to a contributory scheme with effect from 1 July 1968.
- The Widows' and Orphans' Contributory Pension Scheme was introduced.
- The concept of negotiated national wage rounds became the norm.
- The principle of indexing pensions with salaries was accepted.
- Equal pay for work of equal value was introduced in 1973.
- A common C&A Scheme for all teachers was introduced from October 1973.
- The PAYE system of tax deduction became fully operational for public service employees from the commencement of the tax-year 1979–80.

The decade ended on a more hopeful note. Relations between the partners in education, teacher unions, school managements and the officials in the Departments of Education and Finance became reasonably satisfactory and conducive to working together for the betterment of the education service. However, the memory of the Ryan Tribunal dispute hung over inter-teacher relations and some of the outstanding problems were not resolved until 1996.

Teachers United, 1978–1991

In the four years from 1978 to 1982 changes took place in the senior permanent officerships of the INTO, ASTI and TUI, and the difficulties that had arisen because of the Ryan Tribunal began to lose significance. Personal relationships were established and regular inter-union meetings were held to promote co-operation on matters of mutual concern. National and sectional claims were processed through C&A and there was full participation in Public Service and National Wage Agreements. Pension developments also moved apace, with many revisions and amendments to regulations.

The unions' officers participated in numerous subcommittees, and working parties, lectures, courses and seminars on educational topics were co-sponsored. The teacher unions became one of the most powerful groupings in the negotiations for national agreements. On the international front, the union delegations co-operated with each other to effect the maximum impact and to secure officerships in the federations.

The Review Body on Teachers' Pay

This close inter-union co-operation proved to be decisive in enabling the unions to achieve their main objective – the restructuring of teachers' salary scale. A joint campaign was orchestrated to break the historical relationship with the salaries of Executive Officers and to establish a new benchmark with comparable graduate groups in the public service and private industry.

In 1980 the government was prevailed upon to establish 'The Review Body on Teachers' Pay'. It recommended the end of the relativity with Executive Officers and the introduction of the concept of long-service increments, but its general remuneration recommendations incensed all three groups of teachers. The Review Body, like its predecessor in 1968, showed no understanding of the conditions of service of teachers in the different sectors.

The Minister for Education had to become involved in direct negotiations to conclude a deal. Teachers' salaries increased in the range from 20 to 34 per cent.

Arbitration Dispute

After the 1946 strike, teachers' next serious dispute with the government was the Arbitration dispute of 1985–6. A major controversy ensued when the government claimed it would not or could not pay a 10 per cent salary increase awarded by an arbitrator. The Teachers United campaign lasted for ten months and involved meetings, protests, strikes, a Dáil vote, and a confrontation on national TV.

In the end negotiations took place and compromises were agreed. The government was successful in delaying the payment of the award by a considerable period of time but the teachers eventually got the 10 per cent increase. There is no doubt that the economic situation at the time was not good, but a less confrontational policy might have avoided an unnecessary dispute.

The Teachers United campaign established the teacher group as the strongest campaigning force in the trade union movement; this reputation had ongoing benefits for teacher leadership in future negotiations.

A strong trade union consciousness developed among teachers, and co-operation and fraternisation of teachers in all spheres of the education system was at its highest. However, in spite of the successes in the Teachers United campaign, it did not develop into a single teacher union movement, which many teachers in all unions had hoped for.

During this period, in addition to the Review Body and Arbitration increases, teachers' conditions of service improved in many other ways:

- National wage agreements
- Teachers' pension scheme improvements
- The introduction of indexation of pensions
- The introduction of the Spouses' and Children's Contributory Pension Scheme
- The introduction of a Purchase of Notional Service scheme.

The unions initiated and orchestrated joint campaigns for:

- Promotion Opportunities for Teachers
- An Early Retirement Scheme
- Specialist Teachers and Graduate Qualifications
- Recognition for Capitation Service.

While immediate success was not achieved with these claims, the ground work was done and they were all subsequently brought to resolution in 1996.

National Social Programmes, 1987–2000

The first National Social Programme was adopted in 1987, but almost immediately the government claimed inability to pay and introduced cutbacks in education, health and social welfare. Notwithstanding that, successive programmes were negotiated and, as they invariably ran for three or more years, they introduced order and stability into the field of industrials relations. Referred to by the acronyms PNR, PESP, PCW, the programmes set down salary increases and covered a wide range of social and economic areas.

The major events in the field of education were the cutbacks in education, the publication of the report of the Primary Education Review Body, changes in the principal officerships of some of the unions and, in spite of best efforts, the failure of the Council of Teachers' Unions to survive.

The Celtic Tiger was beginning to purr by the middle of the 1990s and by the end of the century he was roaring loudly.

A particular difficulty was caused by the introduction of full PRSI to all public sector employees recruited on or after 6 April 1995. The full ramifications of this decision will not become apparent for many years, but for the next forty years teachers will be divided into two categories with regard to conditions of service. The new entrants will be covered under the Social Welfare related range of benefits and the teachers appointed prior to 6 April 1995 will continue to enjoy the more extensive conditions which were negotiated down through the years.

Agreement on Pay and Conditions of Teachers, 1996

The 1994 PCW Agreement included a clause that facilitated the implementation of the 3 per cent local bargaining increase agreed under PESP, and following almost three years of negotiations an agreement on the pay and conditions of service of teachers was reached in 1996. This agreement radically changed the in-school management of schools in the primary and post-primary sectors, and also amended the manner in which teachers would be remunerated. When the negotiations ended, the only items remaining common to teachers in both sectors were the basic salary scale and qualification allowances.

The payment of qualification allowances to non-graduate teachers, specialist teachers and national teachers was resolved; the points system for calculating posts of responsibility in schools was abandoned; all capitation service was recognised for pension; and it was recognised that primary and post-primary sectors should be organised, administered and managed differently.

Retirement and pension provisions were standardised for all teachers, and an early retirement scheme was agreed. While a limit was imposed on the numbers that could avail of early retirement, a facility was now available whereby teachers who wished to retire early could do so. This was of benefit to the teachers concerned and, invariably, to the education system.

A comprehensive administrative structure involving parents, teachers and government departments became operational in the different sectors. For their part, teachers had to agree to flexibility and change in the management structures of the education service; some of the proposals were common to the three groups and others were particular to the different sectors. New procedures were agreed for the filling of posts of responsibility, and the historical protective mechanism of 'seniority' was abandoned. Arrangements were made for parent–teacher meetings at mutually agreeable times, but the standardisation of the school year was not achieved until 2003.

The objective of the agreement was to improve the quality of the education service. Teachers sought and got compensation for accepting extra obligations. The original PESP agreement had allowed up to 3 per cent of the salary bill for this purpose but at the end the total bill came to £66.67m, closer to 6 per cent.

The extra money was required because the changes agreed were above and beyond those that were normally comprehended under Conciliation Council claims.

While inter-union co-operation was maintained during most of the PCW negotiations, there were strains and cracks beneath the surface. Problems were overcome and trade-offs and compromises were made, but when agreement was reached and the proposals became fully operational, the experience of the exercise resulted in a lessening of the fraternisation and co-operation that had previously existed between the unions.

Revision of the Conciliation and Arbitration Scheme

Taoiseach Garret FitzGerald and Minister Gemma Hussey had sought a review of the C&A Scheme in 1985 and, while reference was made to it in the following years, no progress was made. In 1997 all parties to Partnership 2000 agreed that discussions on revisions to C&A Schemes in the public service would be finalised within six months.

Several meetings of the Teachers' Conciliation Council took place during 1997–98 in an effort to agree a new scheme. A number of areas caused difficulties:

- the impartiality of the Conciliation Council
- the independent status of a chairperson
- the role of the Labour Relations Agency
- the establishment of an agreed mechanism for processing and resolving individual claims or grievances
- the role of the government in authorising or implementing the findings of an Arbitration report
- the possible prohibitions on industrial action
- concern that one group within the Conciliation Council should have the power of veto.

Final agreement on all outstanding issues was recorded at Conciliation Council on 19 November 1998 and it was adopted at INTO Branch meetings in January 1999. The first meeting under the revised scheme was held on 18 January 2000.

Review of National Teachers' Pensions

The teachers' pension scheme, introduced in 1879, was fundamentally changed in 1934 when it was converted to a non-contributory scheme. This was reversed in 1968 when it was converted back to a contributory scheme.

Superannuation Acts of 1963, 1964, and 1976 granted powers to amend or change pension arrangements for public employees by means of Statutory Instruments. This power has been used for the following purposes: to amend the different public service schemes; to designate organisations for transfer of pension entitlements; to increase pensions to compensate for inflation. An important consequence of this has been that public service pensions are rarely discussed in the Dáil, apart from the annual debate on the Superannuation Votes, whereas previously they were a subject of frequent debate.

By the mid-1990s a serious problem in the funding of future State pensions had been identified in all European countries; the ratio of people at work to pensioners was decreasing and, with rising life expectancies, the cost of providing pensions was increasing. Countries began to take remedial steps: the earnings-related state scheme in Britain was effectively abandoned during the 1980s; Germany increased the contribution for earnings-related state pensions from 14 per cent of gross salary to 19.1 per cent; Italy gave incentives to workers to stay on after the normal retirement age; and in the US the retirement age was increased from 65 to 67.

The situation in Ireland was not as serious because the average age of its population was relatively low, and its ratio of people at work to pensioners was five-to-one. While calculations indicated that its non-funded pension system was sustainable, for the present, it was projected, however, that by mid-century Ireland's demographics would come into line with other countries.[16]

The percentage increase in public service pensions over the period from 1998 to 2003 was estimated as follows:

Service	Increase
Civil Service	60%
Health	204%
Education	64%
Social Security	53%
Other State Bodies	73%

Successive Finance Ministers have taken steps to meet this pending situation. From 1 April 1995 all new entrants to the public service are insured under full PRSI, thereby transferring part of future superannuation obligations from pension funds to Social Welfare.

The government established the Commission on Public Service Pensions on 11 February 1996 and launched the National Pensions Policy Initiative which led to the Pensions Board's 1998 report *Securing Retirement Income*.[17]

---

16 CSO statistics published on 8 September 2004 recorded that the population of the Republic had reached 4.04 million, the highest recorded population since 1871. The figures were based on the population and migration estimates for April 2004, and the increase was divided nearly equally between natural growth and immigration. Some 62,000 babies were born in the year ended April 2004, the number of births in 2000 was approximately 47,000. The next full census took place in 2006.

17 The 'Rainbow Coalition' Government, 1994–97

A working group published the *Report of the Budget Strategy for Ageing Group* in 1998, which concluded that if the government did not begin to make provision then, in the year 2056 an additional 7 per cent of GDP would be required to fund social welfare, public service pensions and health costs.

To overcome this pension time-bomb and provide for future public service pensions, the Minister for Finance, Charlie McCreevy, introduced legislation in the Oireachtas in 1999 which established the National Pensions Reserve Fund (NPRF) to specifically meet the government's liability for social welfare and public sector pensions from the year 2025 forward.[18] The legislation stipulated that an allocation, currently fixed at 1 per cent of the Gross National Product (GNP), was to be added to the fund every year for the twenty-five years of the fund's life. It also stipulated that access to the fund cannot be obtained except through amending legislation passed by the Dáil. In other words, the fund is 'ring-fenced' and cannot be raided by a subsequent government at some future date; it must be used for the purposes specified in the Act.

The fund began in April 2001 with the lodgement to its credit of the £6.5 billion received by the government for the sale of Eircom and since then it appreciates by income from investments and the appropriate contribution from Central Funds every quarter.[19]

A commission appointed by the government oversees the operation of the National Pensions Reserve Fund and its management has been assigned to the National Treasury Management Agency. The investment of the funds is carried out by chosen Pension Fund Managers who are invariably subsidiaries of international banks.

The New Century

The twenty-first century began with a revised C&A Scheme and the publication of the reports *The Commission on Public Service Pensions* and *The Public Service Benchmarking Body*.

The government approved the Pensions Commission report in principle in September 2001 and, as Charlie McCreevy announced, 'I expect the vast majority of the commission's recommendations will be implemented. This is a major achievement and the resulting reformed public service pension system will help ensure budgetary sustainability in the long run while simultaneously providing acceptable income in retirement to all public servants'.[20]

---

18 The Commission has estimated that even after twenty-five years of operation the fund will only be in a position to meet 30 per cent of this liability. *The Irish Times*, 31 July 2001, p. 16

19 The Commission's Annual Report for 2001 showed that the value of the fund as at 31 December 2001 was 7.7 billion. The quarterly allocation of the one per cent amounted to 258 million, approximately.

20 Press Statement issued by the Minister for Finance on 14 September 2004

The Benchmarking Board was established on 19 July 2000, and its report was published in June 2002 and adopted by the government. All links with previous pay deals were severed and new benchmarks were laid down for determining the salary of the different categories. The awards made may not, under any circumstances, provide a basis for any follow-on claims from employees within either the public service or the private sector. The public service unions won a major concession in the Benchmarking Report: all recommendations were pension-proofed, and relativity with the remuneration of serving public servants was guaranteed.

It is now clearly established that, in the future, remuneration and pensions will be determined by the recommendations of the Pensions Commission and the Benchmarking Board, and that decisions will apply contemporaneously to all groups. Conciliation Councils will continue to operate, but only in a peripheral manner; they will be used to record national salary and pension agreements, to provide an opportunity to have interpretations resolved, and to have minor claims discussed. Conditions of service claims will also be considered, and the availability of a Facilitator should lead to the resolution of claims that, heretofore, could not be processed. The terms of reference and recommendations of the Benchmarking Board have made the position of Public Service Arbitrator redundant for the consideration of any major salary claim. The availability of the Adjudicator will mean that unresolved claims can now be processed to an independent final determination.

Concluding Reflections

This book sets out to examine the evolution and development of pay and pension schemes for national teachers in Ireland during the period 1831–2000. The study was conducted against the backdrop of the socio-economic, educational and political circumstances pertaining at various points of time.

The historical data analysed provides significant insights into the evolution and implementation of policies, coupled with the tenor of the debate and negotiations that attended the various initiatives and reforms. It also sheds light on the strategies and priorities of the various participants negotiating these changes and improvements. In particular, it highlights the proactive approach of the Irish National Teachers' Organisation in its role as the dominant player in negotiating and agreeing changes and developments on behalf of teachers at national level.

The record shows that the INTO consistently followed a twin-track strategy in pursuit of its objectives: one strand focusing on professional educational matters, the other encapsulating a highly sophisticated template for campaigns to achieve improved conditions of employment.

Even before the INTO was formally established in 1868, teachers, although widely dispersed throughout the country, were coming together regularly in local associations or networks to discuss curricular and education issues and so enhance their teaching skills and knowledge. This coming together for discussion and debate gave them a strong professional and vocational identity and thereby facilitated their recognition in the community as being caring and concerned, and worthy of recognition as leaders.

Since its foundation, the INTO, as a representative body and a key participant in the education process, has initiated many educational developments in its own right and has consistently commented on any educational initiatives originated by others. The campaigning template used by the organisation to progress its industrial objectives was also used to promote its educational mission.

In the nineteenth century, when it opposed the 'Payment by Results' scheme and recognised that decisive power rested in London and not with the Commissioners of Education, it organised a consistent lobbying campaign of MPs in their constituencies and in parliament. The campaign was successful; the results scheme was abandoned and a new curriculum and revised education system were introduced in 1900.

After national independence the INTO convened the First National Programme Conference in 1921 to draft a revised curriculum for national schools, and it instigated the convening of the Second National Programme Conference in 1925. It carried out a major survey in 1941 that raised serious questions about the teaching of Irish in national schools and the government's policy on the revival of the Irish language. It produced the Plan for Education in 1947, which had a major influence on the content and structure of the 'New Curriculum', introduced in 1971. Its Education Committee, which was established in 1968, produced a steady stream of publications and analytical reports and surveys on issues such as the curriculum, the conditions pertaining to the education system, teaching as a career, and a teachers' council. INTO members have participated in review bodies, curriculum committees, commissions and other expert fora that have sought to raise standards and so improve the education provided for young children in Irish schools.

This evident concern for the type of education provided for school children was to the benefit of teachers when the INTO conducted campaigns to improve members' conditions of service or to ensure protection against victimisation.

The governance system of the INTO, through its structure of Annual Congress, Central Executive Committee, National Office, regional and local branches, and school staff representatives, has always been regarded as an efficient institutional communications structure for dealing with policy and practice issues. The organisation has commanded the disciplined support of its membership in approved industrial action or on policy positions taken on issues and is widely recognised by the other partners in education as capable of delivering negotiated compromises or settlements following disputes.

Public recognition of the significant role played by teachers in the education and formation of generations of young people has not always resulted in improved conditions of employment. This book charts a succession of 'false dawns' for improved pay and conditions, always attributed to a variety of reasons. Invariably all the reasons boiled down to one – it cost too much to make provision for a large number of teachers.

During the first decades of independence, teachers were urged to endure the strictures of austerity for the good of the nation; salary cuts and the withholding of pay increases obliged them to bear more than their fair share. This resulted in a seismic event in primary education – a seven-and-a-half month teachers' strike in 1946; political commentators have attributed the defeat of Fianna Fáil in the 1948 election, following 16 years in power, to this event. It had other results that have lasted almost to the present day; it established the INTO as a serious force in the field of industrial relations and an able opponent in the political arena.

Uniquely among professional groups, teachers have always been significantly active members in all the main political parties. Moreover, following every electoral contest, they have been among the vocational groups most highly represented in the Houses of the Oireachtas.

On the international front, the INTO has always seen a strategic value in taking an active role in international organisations and groupings. Among the groups with INTO representation at officer or delegate level are the World Federation of Education Associations, the World Confederation of the Teaching Professions, the International Labour Organisation, the Trade Union Advisory Committee to the Organisation for Economic Cooperation and Development, British and Irish Group, and Education International.

There followed from the mid-1960s, a succession of improvements, derived from a more prosperous environment and latent memories of the 1946 dispute, a more active INTO participation in the wider trade union movement. National wage agreements became the norm and by the mid-1980s these had expanded into an ever-widening social agenda. There were economic downturns in the Irish economy, and a few serious teacher disputes, but, nevertheless, an era of consensus building, partnership and social progress was successfully put in train. The context of, and systems for, mediating the interaction between the official side and employees' interests had altered and were now pointing to a more policy-driven agenda. A more business-like social partnership relationship developed which focused key stakeholders' attention on pivotal educational, social and economic issues. The INTO continued to play a leadership role in all of these developments, through its active involvement in sectoral negotiations and as a member of the Public Services Committee, the Irish Congress of Trade Unions and national negotiation teams.

In overall terms, it can justifiably be claimed that primary education and primary teachers in particular have enjoyed significant esteem among Irish people for almost two centuries; this is due in part to their involvement in the field of education and in part to their continued contribution to Irish society in general. This high esteem is now reflected in the status achieved by teachers as a result of the relatively improved pay and conditions enjoyed by them.

The story of how this status – of one of the oldest public service careers – was achieved can be gleaned from the pages of this book. It aims to tell us where we've come from and where we are at. It seeks to fill a gap in our knowledge in this particular area of public sector debate and interaction; and, hopefully, it provides insights against which future policies, actions and developments can be compared.

References

Acts, Bills, Orders, Statutory Instruments

20 & 21 Vic. c. 27, 17 August 1857

22 Vic. c. 26, 19 April 1859

Act of 25 Geo. 3. c. 19

Bill to Amend the Law Concerning Superannuating and Other Allowances to Persons having held Civil Offices in The Public Service, HC 1859 (2nd sess. 1) II. Amended in committee (33rd sess. 1) II

Bill to Make Further Provision with Respect to Education in Ireland and for other purposes connected therewith, HC 1919 (214) I (known as The MacPherson Bill)

British Pensions Increases Act, 1920

Civil Service Regulation Act, 1924

Civil Service Superannuation Act, 1859

Constitution of the Irish Free State (Saorstát Éireann) Act, 1922

Education (England) Act, 1902, known as the Balfour Education Act

Education (Ireland) Bill, 1919

Education (Scotland) Superannuation Act, 1919

Elementary School Teachers (Superannuation) Act, 1898

Emergency Order No. 83, (known as the Wages Standstill Order) May 1941

Finance Act, 1993

Intermediate Education (Ireland) Act, 1878

Ireland Education Act, 1892

Irish Church Act, 1869

Irish Councils Bill, 1907

Irish Education Act, 1892

Local Government Act (England), 1888

Local Taxation (Custom and Excise) Act, 1890

Ministers and Secretaries Act, 1924

National Education Commissioners (Transfer of Functions) Order, 1935

National Insurance Act, 1911

National School Teachers (Ireland) Act, 1875, the 'Permissive Bill'

National School Teachers (Ireland) Act, 1879

National School Teachers' Pension Fund (Winding-Up), 1934, Statutory Rules and Orders, 1934, No. 43

National Teachers' Superannuation Act, 1879

Old Age Pension Act, 1908

Pensions (Abatement) Act, 1965

Pensions (Abatement) Bill, 1965

Pensions (Amendment) Act, 1993

Pensions (Increase) Act, 1920, 1950, 1956, 1959, 1960, 1964

Probate Duties (Scotland and Ireland) Act, 1888

Public Services (Temporary Economies) Act, 1933

Representation of the People Act, 1918

School Teachers (Superannuation) Act, 1918, 8 & 9 Geo. V, c. 5

Social Welfare Act, 1952

Social Welfare Act, 1974

Statutory Instrument No. 132, 1977; formalised the Civil Service Widows' and Children's Contributory Pension Scheme

Statutory Instrument No. 133, 1977; formalised the Civil Service Widows' and Children's Ex-Gratia Pension Scheme

Statutory Instrument No. 156, 1964

Statutory Instrument No. 173, 1972, National School Teachers' Superannuation (Amendment) Scheme

Statutory Instrument No. 173, of 1972, formalised the National School Teachers' Superannuation (Amendment) Scheme, 1972

Statutory Instrument No. 180, 1950: The National School Teachers' Superannuation (Amendment) Scheme, 1950

Statutory Instrument No. 255, 1953

Statutory Instrument No. 330, 1948

Statutory Instrument No. 423, 1949; amended the National School Teachers' Superannuation Scheme

Statutory Instrument No. 45, 1967

Statutory Instrument, No. 247, 1959

Statutory Rules and Orders, 1916, No. 939, Treasury Chambers, 27 December 1916

Superannuation Act of 1834

Superannuation Act, 1810

Superannuation Act, 1908

Superannuation Act, 1929

Superannuation Act, 1936

Superannuation Act, 1942

Superannuation Act, 1947

Superannuation Act, 1954

Superannuation Act, 1956

Superannuation Act, 1963

Superannuation Act, 1964

Superannuation Act, 1976

Superannuation and Pensions Act, 1962
Superannuation Bill, 1922
Teachers (Superannuation) Act, 1925
Trades Dispute Act, 1916
Warrant 50 & 51 Vic. c. 71

British Government Documentation

Appendix V, HC 1857 (Sess. 2), Vol. 24

Circular, Office of National Education, November 1912, Hansard, Vol. 42, No. 112

First Report of the Commissioners of Irish Education Inquiry, 1825, HC 1825 (400), XII

Forty-second Report of the Commissioners of National Education for the year ended 31 December 1875, HC 1876, XXIV

Hansard, 5th Ser., Vol. 115, 5 April 1919

Hansard, 5th Ser., Vol. 123

Hansard, A Bill to Make Further Provision with Respect to Education in Ireland and for other purposes connected therewith, HC 1919 HC 1862, XLI, November 1919

Hansard, Vol. LXI, July 1898

HC 1867–68, XXV, Minutes of the Council, 1867–8, viii

HC 1870, XXII, Minutes of the Council, lxxxii

HC 1884–85 (105) LXI

HC 344/1872, Question 711

Letter from the Chief Secretary of Ireland to the Duke of Leinster, on the formation of a Board of Commissioners for Education in Ireland, HC 1834 (70) XL, 55, published in the Dublin Gazette, 8 December, 1831. It was reprinted in HC 1842, IX, 585

Newman Commission, HC 1861, XXI, Part 1

Patrick Keenan's Memorandum in Parliamentary Papers, HC, 1870, XXVIII, Part III

Pension Rules and Regulations, 1914

Report of Commission of Inquiry into Primary Education (Ireland), 1868–1870, (The Powis Commission), HC 1870 (c. 6) XXVIII, Vol. 1, Part 1

Report of F. H. Dale on Primary Education in Ireland, 1904, HC 1904 (Cd 1981), XX (Copy in State Paper Office, CSORP: 1914/1839)

Report of the Departmental Committee of the Superannuation of School Teachers, HC Cmd. 1962, 1923, par. 4

Report of the Departmental Committee of the Superannuation of School Teachers, HC 1923, par. 17

Report of the First Quinquennial Valuation of the National Teachers

Report of the Royal Commission on the Poor Law, 1909

Report of the Select Committee appointed to inquire on foundation schools and education in Ireland, HC 1837–38 (701), VII, 1

Report of the Vice-Regal Committee of Inquiry into Primary Education', HC 1919 (Cmd 60) XXI ; Vol. 11, Summaries of Evidence, Memoranda and Returns, HC 1919 (Cmd 178) XXI, 789 (The Killanin Report)

Report of the Vice-Regal Committee on the Conditions of Service and Remuneration of Teachers in Intermediate Schools, and on the Distribution of Grants from Public Funds for Intermediate Education, 1919 (The Molony Report)

Return of the average income from all sources of male national school teachers in Ireland, and of certified masters in England and Wales, and in Scotland, HC 1884–85 (105) LXI

Returns of Retirement Gratuities for National Teachers, 1873–79, HC 1881 (259) LXXIII

Ridley Commission, First Report, HC 1887 (c. 5226) XIX. 1; Second Report, HC 1888 [c. 5545] XVII; Third Report, HC 1889 (c. 5749) XXI

Royal Commission of Inquiry into Primary Education (Ireland), 1870, HC 1870 (c. 6), XXVIII

Second Report of the Commissioners of Irish Education Inquiry, 1825–27, HC 1926–27 (12) XII

Select Committee to consider the existing regulations respecting the grant of superannuation allowances to persons who have held civil office in Her Majesty's Service, HC 1856, Vol. 9

Statutory Rules and Orders, 1916, No. 939, Treasury Chambers, 27 December 1916

Treasury Circular, August 1897

Treasury Letters, 5562, 5/4/1880; 7514, 1/5/1880; 8/7/1897

Trevelyan and Northcote Report, 'The Organization of the Permanent Civil Service', HC 1854–1855, Vol. 30

Vice-Regal Committee of Inquiry into Primary Education (Ireland), 1913 (Dill Committee), Final Report HC 1914 (Cd 7235) XXVIII

Commissioners of National Education Documentation

Annual Report of the Commissioners of National Education, 1902, HC 1903, XXI

Eighty-Fifth Report of the Commissioners of National Education, 1918–19

Eighty-Fourth Report of Commissioners for 1917–18, HC 1919, XXI

Eighty-Second Report of the Commissioners of National Education, 1915–16

Fifteenth Report for the year ended 31 December 1848, HC 1848, XXII

First Report of the Commissioners of Irish Education Inquiry, 1825, HC 1825 (400), XII

Forty-second Report of the Commissioners of National Education for the year ended 31 December 1875, HC 1876, XXIV

MCNEI 16 February 1897

MCNEI 19 November 1907

MCNEI 1908

MCNEI 28 February 1871

Second Report of the Commissioners of Irish Education Inquiry, 1825–27, HC
    1826–1827 (12), XII, Appendix No. 22

Second Report of the Commissioners of National Education, 1834–35, HC, 1835 (300)
    XXXV

Seventh Report of the Commissioners for the year 1840, HC 1842 (353) XXIII, 217, 4

Sixteenth Report for the year ended 31 December 1848–49, HC 1850, XXV

Sixty-second Report of the Commissioners of National Education, 1895

Tenth Report of the Commissioners of National Education, HC 1844 (569) XXX

Thirteenth Report of the Commissioners of National Education, 1846, HC 1847 (832)
    XVII

INTO Documentation

CEC Reports to Congress 1909, 1912, 1922, 1932, 1937, 1938, 1941, 1950, 1952,
    1954, 1959, 1961, 1962, 1963, 1964, 1965, 1966, 1969, 1970, 1973, 1974, 1975,
    1979, 1980, 1981, 1982, 1983, 1985, 1986, 1987, 1988, 1992, 1994, 1995, 1996,
    1997, 1998

Eighty Years of Progress, 1948

Eolas, No. 26, 12 June 1996

Letter from Bernard Cúc, Department of Public Service, 13 June 1986

Letter from General Treasurer to the Secretary of the Teachers' Conciliation Council, 9
    October 1981

Letter from Gerry Quigley, on behalf of the three unions, to the Minister for Education,
    12 December 1980

Letter from John Ferguson, President INTO, published in *Irish Teachers' Journal*, 18
    May 1878

Letter from Miss R. Mee, Pension Section, Department of Education, to Michael
    Moroney, General Treasurer, INTO, 28 January 1980

Letter from Peter Baldwin, Private Secretary to Minister for Education, to E. G.
    Quigley

Letter from Sister M. Ita O'Connor, President CCPS, to D. J. Kelleher, 9 June 1959

Letter from the Department of Education to Michael Moroney, General Treasurer
    INTO, May 1991

Letter from the Department of Education, 13 June 1973

Letter from the Department of Education, 3 March 1975

Letter to D. J. Kelleher from T. Ó Raifeartaigh, Secretary, Department of Education, 20
    March 1959

Letter to John Wilson, Minister for Education, from the three General Secretaries, 19
    February 1981

Letter to the Chairman of the Public Services Committee, ICTU, from Michael
    Moroney, General Treasurer, INTO, 29 April 1980

Memorandum of Irish Teachers' Pensions, 1920

Memorandum: Objections to Proposed Regulations Compelling Women Teachers to Retire on Marriage, 4 June 1932

Pamphlet: The Case for Increase in Remuneration of National Teachers 1945, SPO 310236B

Plan for Education, 1947

Teachers' Pension Fund: Report of the Actuarial Investigation, 1926, Dublin: Educational Company of Ireland, 1929

Vere Foster Report, 1869

Irish Government Documentation

Arbitration Reports Nos. 11, 12, 13, 17, 448

Budget, 1984

Building on Reality 1985–198, (1984) Government Publications Office

Cabinet Minutes, 19 December 1944, Item 1, GC 4/39, SPO, S10236B

Circular M44/66, Department of Education

Circular to Managers and Teachers of National Schools, Office of National Education, Dublin, June 1909

Circular to Managers, Teachers and Inspectors on Teaching through the Medium of Irish, Department of Education, July 1931

Circulars 24/24, 44/24, 1/40, 6/40, 12/40, 13/40, Department of Finance

Confidential Report of Meeting with INTO CEC on 18 April 1945, SPO, S10236/B

CSORP, 1904 10032, State Paper Office, Dublin Castle

Dáil Debates, 24 February 1926

Dáil Debates, Vol. 2, November 1923

Dáil Debates, Vol. 66, 1 April 1937

Dáil Debates, Vol. 97, 2 May 1945

Dáil Report, 15 March 1932

Dáil Report, 23 October 1973

Dáil Report, 31 March 1933

Dáil Report, May/June 1933

Department of Education Circular, December 1973

Department of Education Rules and Regulations, 1932

DEPD, Vol. 108, col. 195

DEPD, Vol. 118, col. 2469

DEPD, Vol. 202, col. 1594

DEPD, Vol. 202, col. 1634

DEPD, Vol. 63, col. 1134

Interim Report, Review Body on Teachers' Pay, 1980

Investment in Education: report of the survey team appointed by the Minister for Education in October 1962, Department of Education Annual Report 1961–62

Ireland (1934) Department of Finance – Commission of Inquiry into the Civil Service: Interim Report presented to the Minister for Finance, 5 February 1934 (The Brennan Commission), Dublin: Stationery Office

Ireland (1965) Department of Finance – Report of the Committee on Post-retirement Adjustments in Public Service Pensions, Dublin: Stationery Office, Prl. 8237

Ireland (1977) Department of Finance – Working Party on Local Authority Superannuation: Interim Report, Dublin: Stationery Office, Prl. 6415

Letter from Dr John Charles McQuaid to the Minister for Education, 14 March 1946, SPO 10236B

Letter from Most Rev. Dr Staunton, Joint Secretary to the Hierarchy, to Ó Deirg, 17 October 1944, SPO, S10236/B

Letter from P. Noel Ryan (Chairman of the Review Body) to the Minister for Education, 30 October 1980

Letter from the chairman of the Review Body to the Minister for Education, dated 30 October 1980

Letter from the Secretary of the Department of Education to the Secretary of the Taoiseach, 27 March 1945, SPO, 10236B

Letter to Daniel Murphy, Secretary, Public Services Committee from Alan Dukes, Minister for Finance, 24 January 1983

Memorandum for Information of Taoiseach from Secretary of the Department of Education to the Secretary of the Taoiseach, 23 May 1946

Memorandum from Minister for Education to Government Regarding Teachers' Claim for Increased Remuneration, 8 August 1942, SPO, 10236/A

Memorandum from the Secretary of the Department of Education to the Secretary of the Taoiseach, 23 May 1946, SPO, S10236/C

Memorandum to the press from the Department of Finance, 30 March 1933

National Programme of Primary Instruction, 1922

National School Teachers' (Ireland) Fund, Statement of Accounts for 1927

National School Teachers' Pension Fund (Winding-Up), 1934, Statutory Rules and Orders, 1934, No. 43

National School Teachers' Superannuation (Amendment) Scheme, 1972, Statutory Instrument No. 173 of 1972

National School Teachers' Superannuation Scheme, 1934

National School Teachers' Superannuation Scheme, 1934

New Scheme of Payments to Teachers and of Examination and Organisation of National Schools, issued by the Office of National Education, Dublin, March 1900

Notice to Managers and Teachers of National Schools, Office of National Education, Dublin, June 1908

Proposals for Agreement on Pay and Conditions of Service of Teachers under Clause 2 (iii) of Annex 1 of the Programme for Competitiveness and Work, February 1996

Public Notice No. 4, Ministry of Education, 1 February 1922

Report of the Committee on Inspection in Primary Schools, 1927
Report of the Dáil Select Committee on Social Affairs, 15 December 1993
Rules for National Schools, Department of Education, 1934
Rules for National Schools, Department of Education, August 1932
Rules for the Administration of the Teachers' Pension Fund, 22 November 1897,
    Dublin: Alex Thom & Co. for HMSO, 1897
Saorstát Éireann: Statutory Rules and Orders, National Education Commissioners
    (Transfer of Functions) Order, No. 264, 2 August 1935
Tribunal Report on Teachers' Salaries, 1968 (the Ryan Tribunal)

Manuscript Material

Archives of the Irish National Teachers' Organisation, 35 Parnell Sq., Dublin 1
Marsh's Library, St Patrick's Close, Dublin 8
National Archives of Ireland, Bishop Street, Dublin 8, for Records of the
    Commissioners of National Education, Chief Secretary's Official Registered Papers
    (CSORP), Census Returns
Public Record Office of Ireland and the State Paper Office
Records of the Department of Education and Science, Marlborough St, Dublin 1
Records of the Department of Finance, Upper Merrion St, Dublin 2
The National Library of Ireland (NLI), Kildare Street, Dublin 2, for Parliamentary
    Papers, Annual Reports of the Commissioners of National Education and the
    Minutes of their Meetings

Newspapers and Journals

The Evening Telegraph
The Freeman's Journal
The Irish Independent
The Irish Press
The Irish School Weekly
The Irish Teachers' Journal
The Irish Times
The Schoolmaster
The Sunday Tribune

Secondary Sources

Akenson, Donal Harman (1970) *The Irish Education Experiment: the National System
    of Education in the Nineteenth Century*, London: Routledge & Keegan Paul
Akenson, Donal Harman (1975) *A Mirror to Kathleen's Face*, Quebec: McGill,
    Queen's University Press
Booth, Charles (1969) *Life and Labour of People in London (1891–1903)*, London:
    Hutchinson

Bruce, Maurice (1961) *The Coming of the Welfare State*, London: B. T. Batsford

Coolahan, John (1979) *The Education Bill of 1919, Problems of Educational Reform*, Dublin: Proceedings of The Irish Educational Studies Association of Ireland, University College Dublin

Coolahan, John (1981) *Irish Education: History and Structure*, Dublin: Institute of Public Administration

Coolahan, John (1984) *The ASTI and Post-primary Education in Ireland, 1909–1984*, Dublin: Elo Press for the Association of Secondary Teachers Ireland

Dowling, Patrick J. (1968) *The Hedge Schools of Ireland*, (revised edition), Cork: Mercier Press

Fanning, Ronan (1983) *Independent Ireland*, Dublin: Helicon

Fenton, Séamus (1948) *It All Happened, Reminiscences*, Dublin: M. H. Gill

Halévy, E. (1961) *History of the English People in the Nineteenth Century*, trans. from the French by E. I. Watkin and D. A. Barker, London: Benn

HMSO, (1895) *History of the Vote for Public (Primary) Education, Ireland, 1 January 1831–1*, Dublin: Alex. Thom & Co.

Hughes, Gerard (1988) *The Irish Civil Service Superannuation Scheme*, Dublin: The Economic and Social Research Institute

Keogh, Dermot (1994) *Twentieth-Century Ireland: Nation and State*, Dublin: Gill & Macmillan

Logan, John (ed.) (1999) *Teachers' Union: the TUI and its Fore-Runners in Irish Education, 1899–1994*, Dublin: A. & A. Farmer

Longford, Lord and T. P. O'Neill (1970) *Eamon De Valera*, London: Hutchinson

Lowe, Robert (1862) *The Revised Code of the Regulations of the Committee of the Privy Council on Education*, London: Ridgeway

Lyons, F. S. L. (1971) *Ireland Since the Famine*, London: Weidenfeld and Nicholson

McCarthy, Charles (1973) *A Decade of Upheaval: Irish Trade Unions in the 1960s*, Dublin: Institute of Public Administration

McCormick, Eugene P. (1996) *The INTO and the 1946 Teachers' Strike*, Dublin, INTO

McNeill, Mary (1971) *Vere Foster, 1819–1900*, Newton Abbot: David & Charles

Meenan, James (1966) *The Irish Economy Since 1922*, Routledge & Keegan Paul

Miller, David W. (1973) *Church, State and Nation in Ireland, 1898–1921*, Dublin: Gill & Macmillan

Moody, T. W. and W. E. Vaughan (eds.) (1986) *A New History of Ireland*, Vols. 4, 9, Oxford: Clarendon Press

Murphy, John A. (1975) *Ireland in the Twentieth Century*, Dublin: Gill & Macmillan (reprinted in 1989)

Ní Chuinneagáin, Síle (1998) *Catherine Mahon, First Woman President of the INTO*, Dublin: INTO

Ó Buachalla, Séamus (1988) *Education Policy in Twentieth Century Ireland*, Dublin: Wolfhound Press

Ó Síochfradha, S. (1956) *The Educational History of Ireland*, Dublin: The Educational Company of Ireland

O'Connell, T. J. (1968) *A Hundred Years of Progress*, Dublin: INTO

Pakenham, Thomas (1982) *The Boer War*, London: Futura Publications

Rhodes, Gerald (1965) *Public Sector Pensions*, London: Unwin Brothers Ltd

Robins, Joseph (2001) *Champagne and Silver Buckles*, Dublin: The Lilliput Press

Sweeney, Garry (1990) *In Public Service: a History of the Public Service Executive Union, 1890–1990*, Dublin: Institute of Public Administration

Titley, E. Brian (1983) *Church, State, and the Control of Schooling in Ireland, 1900–44*, Dublin: Gill & Macmillan

Tropp, Asher (1957) *The School Teacher: The Growth of the Teaching Profession in England and Wales from 1800 to Present Day*, London: William Heinemann

Unpublished Theses

Bracken, William J. (1981) 'A Study of the Contribution of the Christian Brothers to the Development of Irish Education', MEd Thesis, TCD

Bradley, William J. (1947) 'Sir Thomas Wyse – Irish pioneer in education reform', PhD Thesis, TCD

Clayton, Helen (1981) 'Societies to educate the poor in Ireland in the late 18th and early 19th centuries', MLitt Thesis, TCD

Collins, Henry P. (1980) 'Organised Teachers', MEd Thesis (314), TCD

Coolahan, John M. (1975) 'Payment by Results', MEd Thesis, TCD

Feingold, William Leo (1974) 'The Irish Boards of Poor Law Guardians, 1872–86', PhD Dissertation, University of Chicago

Griffin, Sean (1992) 'Archbishop Daniel Murray of Dublin and his Contribution to Elementary Education in Ireland, 1823–1841', MEd Thesis, TCD

Hislop, Harold J. (1990) 'The Kildare Place Society 1811–1831: An Irish experiment in popular education', PhD Thesis, TCD

Hyland, Áine (1982) 'An Analysis of Administration and Financing National and Secondary Education', PhD Thesis (651), TCD

McCarthy, Charles (1976) 'The Evolution of Trade Union Organisations in Ireland', PhD Thesis, TCD

Moroney, Michael (2001) 'The Remuneration of National Teachers, 1831–1900', MLitt Thesis, TCD

Moroney, Michael (2004) 'An Analysis of the Development of Salaries and Pensions of National Teachers and of the Role of the Irish National Teachers' Organisation in their Progression, 1831 to 2000', PhD Thesis, NUI Maynooth

Murphy, Michael (1972) 'Consolidation of Primary Schools'. MLitt Thesis, TCD

Musson, John W. (1955) 'The Training of Teachers in Ireland from 1811 to the Present Day', PhD Thesis, Queen's University, Belfast

Parkes, Susan M. (1970) 'Teacher-training in Ireland, 1811–1870', MLitt Thesis, TCD

Revington, Carol E. F. (1983) 'The Kildare Place Society: its principles and policy', MEd Thesis, TCD

Rudd, A. (1989) 'Payment by Results Comparative England/Ireland 1850–1879', MEd Thesis (2158), TCD

Index

n following a page number indicates a footnote.